THE RECORD SOCIETY OF LANCASHIRE AND CHESHIRE

FOUNDED TO TRANSCRIBE AND PUBLISH ORIGINAL DOCUMENTS RELATING TO THE TWO COUNTIES

VOLUME CXIII

INDEX TO

WILLS AND ADMINISTRATIONS

FORMERLY PRESERVED IN THE

PROBATE REGISTRY, CHESTER

1826 – 1830

Edited by

ROBERT DICKINSON, B.Sc., Ph.D.

Published for

THE RECORD SOCIETY
OF LANCASHIRE AND CHESHIRE

PHILLIMORE

London and Chichester
1972

COUNCIL AND OFFICERS FOR THE YEAR 1971/2

President

Professor A.R. Myers, M.A., Ph.D., F.S.A., F.R.Hist.S.

Hon. Secretary

B.C. Redwood, M.A., c/o Cheshire Record Office, The Castle, Chester.

Hon. Treasurer

B.W. Quintrell, Ph.D., c/o School of History, Liverpool University,
8, Abercromby Square, Liverpool 7.

Other Members of Council

Very Reverend G.W.O. Addleshaw, B.D., M.A., F.S.A., F.R.Hist.S.
J.J. Bagley, M.A., F.R.Hist.S.
C.N.L. Brooke, M.A., F.R.Hist.S.
G.A. Carter, F.L.A.
W.H. Chaloner, M.A., Ph.D.
R. Dickinson, Ph. D., F.R.I.C.
R. Sharpe France, M.A.
J.D. Marshall, B.Sc.(Econ.), Ph.D.
D. Palliser, M.A.
J.S. Roskell, M.A., D.Phil.

SBN 900592 68 0

Printed by Eyre & Spottiswoode Ltd.,
Her Majesty's Printers
at Grosvenor Press, Portsmouth.

PREFACE

THIS IS the 17th volume in the series of indexes of Chester Wills published by the Record Society. It covers the period 1826 to 1830 inclusive.

In general, the editor has continued the method adopted for Volume 107 in that the words 'parish of' have been omitted, the date of probate restricted to year and month only and codicils are not recorded. All documents, unless otherwise designated, are wills or administrations with a will attached. 'Infra' wills (i.e. those proved in a lower court and filed separately) are indicated by an asterisk at the end of the entry.

The present list has been prepared from the Diocesan Index now at the Lancashire Record Office and the entries arranged under three headings, namely Lancashire, Cheshire and Welsh wills. The originals, which have only been consulted in exceptional circumstances, are preserved in the County Record Offices at Preston and Chester, and in the National Library of Wales. Ten of the Cheshire wills cannot now be found and are listed here in italics.

In the five years 1826 to 1830 there are 9,745 items, an increase of some 13 per cent on the previous five years. A point of interest, perhaps, is the nuncupative will of Elizabeth Cooper of Liverpool.

As with the previous volume, indexes of places and of trades or professions have been added. The second index may prove useful in demonstrating the difference between the essentially agricultural Cheshire and the industrial and maritime Lancashire, although the period covered is rather short for statistical purposes.

The editor is indebted to the National Library of Wales for confirming the list of wills in their custody, and to the staffs of the Record Offices at Preston and Chester for their assistance which was freely available at all times.

This list of probate records is published with the assent of the President of the Probate, Divorce and Admiralty Division of the High Court of Justice.

ABBREVIATIONS

A	Administration Bond
Tuon	Tuition Bond
co.	County of
esq.	esquire
gent.	gentleman
*	An asterisk at the end of an entry indicates an 'Infra' will

Italicised entries refer to missing documents

ADDENDA

Seven wills and four cross-references listed below were unfortunately omitted when the list was prepared and located too late for insertion in their proper places.

p. 32	Dawson, Dorothy, Liverpool, widow. Oct. 1830 (2nd grant 1844)
p. 38	Fairbrother, Betty, Warrington, spinster. June 1828
p. 44	Gittins, Mary wife of Thomas Gittins, Manchester, woollen draper. Dec. 1829
p. 47	Griffiths, Sarah, Liverpool, widow. A May 1829
p. 73	Kilshaw, Esther *see* Biss
p. 82	McCawley, Peter *see* Carrley
p. 84	Martin, Mary *see* Ball
p.109	Rymer, William, Manchester, gent. Feb. 1828
p.127	Veary, Betty *see* Cawson
p.131	Whatmough, Ann, Leavengreave Banks, Rochdale, spinster. Oct. 1828
p.173	Pownall, William, Northen Etchells, farmer. Nov. 1829 (1st grant 1824, then wrongly entered as Brownell)

LANCASHIRE WILLS

ABBATT, Benjamin, Blackburn, druggist & surgeon. Nov. 1830
Abbot, John, Prescot, publican. A Feb. 1828
Nathan, Liverpool, victualler. May 1829
Thomas, Ulnes Walton, bachelor. Nov. 1830
Abbott, Hugh, Rainhill, innkeeper. Jan. 1830 (2nd grant 1860)
James, Haydock, farmer. April 1826
Thomas, Haydock, shopkeeper. A Nov. 1830
Ablett, Isaac, Manchester, merchant. A April 1829
Abraham, Robert, Liverpool, labourer. Dec. 1827
Abram, Henry, Burscough, innkeeper. May 1826
Peter, Liverpool, victualler. April 1827
Robert, Rufford, farmer. March 1829
William, Liverpool, gent. Sept. 1826
Ackers, John, Rainhill, yeoman. Oct. 1826
Thomas, Chorley, wheelwright. July 1826
Acton, Peter, Manchester. May 1830
William, Manchester, joiner & builder, July 1826
Adams, Alexander, Kirkaldy, co. Fife, ship carpenter. A Dec. 1830*
Mary, Liverpool, widow. March 1828
Adamson, William, Heaton Norris, publican. July 1828
Adcock, James, Much Woolton, schoolmaster. Dec. 1828
Aindow, Thomas, Birkdale, yeoman. Aug. 1829
Ainscough, Jane, Mawdesley, widow. May 1826
Ainscow, Alice, Within Trees, Walton-le-Dale, widow. May 1829
James, Chorley, plumber & glazier. Nov. 1826
Ainsworth, Betty, Silver St., Bury, spinster. A Aug. 1826*
Elizabeth, Salford, widow. A Sept. 1828
George, Heightside, Padiham, weaver. March 1826
Helen, Blackburn, widow. Nov. 1830
James, Anderton, farmer. March 1826
Jane, Blackburn, widow. Aug. 1829
John, Manchester, cabinet maker. May 1830
Mary, Rivington, widow. Nov. 1826
Peter, Wensleyfold, yeoman. Dec. 1829*
Peter, Bolton-le-Moors, grocer. A Oct. 1830
Thomas, Prescot, watchmaker. April 1828
Thomas, Manchester, gent. Nov. 1828
William, Bury, butcher. March 1828
Alcock, Elizabeth, Liverpool. Aug. 1826
Aldersley, John, Liverpool, overseer of the poor. Feb. 1826
William, Great Bolton, yeoman. Sept. 1828
Alderson, Jane, Newmarket in Manchester, widow. March 1827

Aldred, James, Manchester, butcher. A Sept. 1830
Thomas, Urmston, shopkeeper. A Sept. 1829
Alexander, William, Manchester, farmer. A Aug. 1829
Alington, Marmaduke, Lincolns Inn, Middlesex, esq. Oct. 1828 (Former grants 1820 and 1825)
Alker, John, Adlington, mercer. A Jan. 1827*
Nicholas, Aspull, yeoman. Oct. 1826
Alland, Catharine, Liverpool, spinster. A Aug. 1830*
Allcock, Nathan, Chorlton Row, cotton spinner. A June 1829
Allen, George, Liverpool, gent. April 1827
George, Chapefield, Pilkington, weaver. April 1829
James, Hale, innkeeper. A Aug. 1828
James, Trusty Hillock, Radcliffe, weaver. A Dec. 1828
John, Ormskirk, innkeeper. May 1826
Peter, Radcliffe, whitster. Jan. 1828*
Sarah, Taunton. A April 1828
Sarah, Potters Row, Radcliffe, widow. A April 1829
Thomas, Parsons Fold, Radcliffe, weaver. A Dec. 1830
William, Warrington, innkeeper. July 1828 (1st grant 1776)
Allerton, John, Ormskirk, yeoman. Jan. 1826
Allin, John, Aughton, yeoman. Sept. 1827
John, Oldham, wheelwright. A July 1830
Allum, Henry, Denton, Manchester, shopkeeper. May 1829
Almond, James, Liverpool, yeoman. March 1827 (Former grants 1785 and 1815)
John, Manchester, brassfounder. June 1829
Ralph, Higher Tonsharp, weaver. May 1828
Alred, Elizabeth, Wigan, widow. June 1827
Alsop, Alice, Latchford Hall, Blakeley, widow. Dec. 1826
Mary Ann, Chapel-en-le-Frith, co. Derby, spinster. Sept. 1828
Altham, Millicent, Dunnyshop, Accrington, widow. A Dec. 1829
Richard, Altham Hall, yeoman. Dec. 1830
Alty, Richard, Lydiate, husbandman. March 1826
Richard, Much Hoole, farmer. Jan. 1830 (2nd grant 1845)
Amaright, William, Bedford, weaver. July 1828
Ambler, Bridget, Wigan, widow. Dec. 1829
Mary, Wigan, spinster. A May 1826; 2nd grant Sept. 1829
Ambrose, William, Liverpool, cartowner. Jan. 1830
Amery, John, Liverpool, mariner. A Jan. 1830*
Thomas, Liverpool, mariner. A Jan. 1830
Anderson, Henry, Liverpool, carpenter. Oct. 1826*
Horner, Manchester, linen merchant. A Oct. 1829
John, Liverpool, mariner. Aug. 1826 (1st grant 1815)
John, Liverpool, mariner. Jan. 1827*
Robert, Liverpool, joiner. Nov. 1829
William Jamieson, Liverpool, master mariner. A Nov. 1828
Anderton, Ralph, Hoghton, farmer. Nov. 1830 (1st grant 1824)
Robert, Wrightington, yeoman. April 1826
Roger, Mawdesley, farmer. Aug. 1830
Thomas, Billinge, yeoman. Sept. 1830
Andrew, George, Oldham. A Nov. 1828
John, Round Thorn, cotton weaver. A June 1828
John, Oldham, gent. Aug. 1829
John, Foulreaks, co. York, gent. A June 1830

Andrew, John, Broughton, Manchester. July 1830
Maria, Harpurhey, spinster. Oct. 1826
Martha, Clayton. May 1829
Mary, Middleton. Oct. 1827
Samuel, Alt Hill, farmer. A Feb. 1828
Samuel, Knot Lanes, Ashton-under-Lyne, farmer. Dec. 1829 (2nd grant 1855)
William Pownall, Eccles, brickmaker. Oct. 1826*
Andrews, David, Liverpool, mariner. A Aug. 1829
Joseph, St. Georges Road, Manchester, shopkeeper. Dec. 1826
Angus, Alexander, Liverpool, insurance broker. A Nov. 1828 (1st grant 1810)
Ankers, Sarah, Liverpool, widow. Sept. 1826
Ansdell, Elizabeth, Liverpool, widow. A Jan. 1828
Spurston George, Liverpool, master mariner. A March 1828
Antrobus, Mary, Manchester, spinster. May 1828
Appleton, Henry, Liverpool, schoolmaster. A Oct. 1827*
James, Liverpool, hairdresser. May 1829
Mary *see* Boardman
Peter, Ardwick, cotton spinner. June 1826
Samuel, Bury, joiner. May 1826
William, Bury, innkeeper. April 1828
Archet, John, Liverpool, mariner. April 1827*
Arkwright, James, Liverpool, victualler. Jan. 1827*
Margaret, Liverpool, widow. July 1826
Armistead, Thomas, Liverpool. Nov. 1830
Armitage, Matthew, Hull, co. York, mariner. A Dec. 1830
Armstrong, Mary, Liverpool, widow. May 1829
Arnold, John, Liverpool, cabinet maker. Feb. 1826
Arrandale, James, Audenshaw. June 1828
Arrive, Betsey, Manchester, spinster. A Nov. 1830*
Betsey, Manchester, spinster. A Nov. 1830*
Mary Ann, Manchester, spinster. A Nov. 1830*
Nancy, Manchester, feme covert. July 1829
Nancy, St. Peters Port, Island of Guernsey, spinster. A Nov. 1830*
Thomas, Manchester, bachelor. A Nov. 1830*
Arrowsmith, Alice, Astley, widow. A May 1829
James, Darcey Lever, last of Little Bolton, counterpane manufacturer. Aug. 1829
John, Astley, cotton manufacturer. Sept. 1826
Arstall, John, Hollingreen. June 1828
Mary, Rixton with Glazebrook, singlewoman. March 1829
William, Sutton, scale beam maker. A Jan. 1826
Arter, Benjamin, Salford, overlooker. May 1827
Ascroft, Robert, Bretherton, yeoman. Dec. 1826
Thomas, Wigan, stonemason. March 1830
Ashburner, John, Coniston, machine maker. A Dec. 1830
Ashcroft, Ann Maria, Salford, spinster. A Jan. 1829
Betty, Skelmersdale, widow. A April 1826
Edward, Walton-on-the-Hill, yeoman. April 1827
Elizabeth, Mew, spinster. Aug. 1828
Grace, Aughton, widow. A July 1826*
James, Warrington, victualler. A March 1829
Martha, Tarleton, widow. A March 1830
Mary, Liverpool, widow. Sept. 1827
Peter, Liverpool, land waiter. Nov. 1826 (1st grant 1825)

Ashcroft, Robert, Liverpool, flour dealer. A Jan. 1827
Sarah, Much Hoole, farmer. Oct. 1827
William, Kirkby, victualler. July 1826
Ashhurst, Robert, Liverpool, gent. July 1830
Ashley, John, Liverpool. Jan. 1830*
Richard, Shaws Brow, Liverpool victualler. July 1830
Ashort, William, Liverpool, file cutter. July 1829
Ashton, Abigail, Widnes, singlewoman. June 1827
Elizabeth, Salford, widow. June 1830
Esther, Burton, Chorlton Row, widow. Nov. 1827
George, Mosley, Ashton-under-Lyne, labourer. Feb. 1828*; Aug. 1829
George, Prescot, appraiser. July 1830
George, Lincoln, draper. Dec. 1830
James, Liverpool, pilot. March 1829
John, White Gate Bridge, Chadderton, innkeeper. A Aug. 1827
John, Burtonwood. A March 1828
John, Denton Lane, Prestwich. June 1830
Jonathan, Denton, Prestwich, husbandman. Dec. 1826
Ralph, Island of Dominica, last of Liverpool, merchant. Dec. 1829
Richard, Warrington, chapman. A Aug. 1827
Richard, Rochdale, gardener. April 1829
Robert, Farther Heights, tallow chandler. May 1830
Samuel, Heaton Norris, yeoman. Jan. 1826*
Thomas, Liverpool, landing waiter. A May 1827
Thomas, Hollinwood, weaver. Feb. 1828
Thomas, Gooden Lane, Bury, esq. June 1830
William, Manchester, livery stable keeper. July 1829
Ashworth, Abraham, Smallbridge, shopkeeper. March 1830 (2nd grant 1846)
Benjamin, Hollinwood, weaver. Oct. 1827
Charles, Salford, publican. Aug. 1826
Elizabeth, Leigh, last of Liverpool, widow. Feb. 1827
George, Greens Brandwood, Rochdale. Sept. 1827
George, Heskin, gent. A Oct. 1829
George, Bacup, coal miner. A July 1830*
Giles, Edgeworth, calico printer. Nov. 1828
Henry, Deardengate, Haslingden, yeoman. Feb. 1827
James, Boothfold, Rossendale, shopkeeper & butcher. Jan. 1828 (1st grant 1804)
Jane, Bury. A March 1827*
John, Boothfold, Rossendale, innkeeper. May 1826
John, Top of Lee, Bury, weaver. A Aug. 1826
John, Tunicliffe, Spotland, farmer. Oct. 1826
John, Bridge End, Rossendale, yeoman. May 1827*; Sept. 1827*
John, New Church, Rossendale, cotton manufacturer. Nov. 1827
John, Liverpool, innkeeper. June 1829
John, Gambleside, farmer. Sept. 1829
Lawrence, Rautensall Forrest, Rossendale, weaver. Dec. 1827*
Lawrence, Brickfield, innkeeper. March 1830
Peggy, New Hall Hey, Rossendale, spinster. Nov. 1829
Richard, Goodshaw, shopkeeper. Feb. 1828
Richard, Scout, yeoman. July 1829
Richard, Hall Car, Rossendale, clothier. A Nov. 1829
Richard Johnson Daventry, Strawberry Hill, Pendleton, esq. Feb. 1829
Robert, Rochdale, innkeeper. A Oct. 1828

Ashworth, Robert, Radcliffe, yeoman. Sept. 1829 (2nd grant 1833)
Robert, Barrowford, weaver. A Jan. 1830
Thomas, Lancaster, labourer. A Oct. 1826
Thomas, Pikelow, Haslingden, weaver. April 1827
Thomas, Henheeds, Rossendale, farmer. Feb. 1829
Thomas, Newton Heath, silk manufacturer. A Feb. 1830
William, Brownbank, Butterworth, farmer. Jan. 1829
William, Bacup, cotton weaver. A June 1830*
Aspinall, Ann, Manchester, spinster. A June 1829
Clayton, Manchester, cotton spinner. Sept. 1826
Francis Edward, Liverpool. A Feb. 1826
John, Clayton-ley-fold, yeoman. Nov. 1826
John Bridge, Bath, esq. June 1830
Mary, Manchester, spinster. A May 1829
Thomas, Liverpool, victualler. June 1830
Thomas, Liverpool, esq. Sept. 1830 (1st grant 1813)
William, Liverpool, gent. July 1828
William, Manchester, plumber. A May 1829
Aspinwall, Edward, Aughton, yeoman. July 1826
George, Lathom, yeoman. Jan. 1827
James, Bickerstaffe, blacksmith. March 1829
Richard, Simonswood, yeoman. July, 1826
Astles, William, Oldham Road, yeoman. Feb. 1828
Astley, Alice, Charnock Richard. March 1830
Peter, Whitfield, weaver. Nov. 1827
Ralph, Whitfield, warper. Dec. 1826
Aston, William, Manchester, gunsmith. March 1827
Asworth, John, Newchurch, ironmonger. A May 1826
Atherton, Ann, Great James St., Bedford Row, Middlesex. April 1826
Ann, Wigan, widow. June 1830
Athern, Pemberton, yeoman. May 1829; July 1829
James, Cadishead, joiner. May 1826
James, Winstanley, labourer. A April 1827
John, Atherton's Quay, potmaker. A Sept. 1828
John, Wigan, yeoman. March 1829
Matthew, Warrington, cooper. Jan. 1827
Roger, Wigan, ironmonger. A Feb. 1829
Sarah, Wigan. June 1826
Thomas, Salford, tobacconist. A Jan. 1827
Thomas, Longton, yeoman. Aug. 1827
Thomas, Kirkby, yeoman. Sept. 1830
William, Orrell, gent. July 1826
William, Wigan, hardware maker. A April 1829
William, Liverpool, joiner. A Feb. 1830
Atkin, John, Liverpool, porter. A Feb. 1827
Atkins, Catherine, Wavertree, spinster. Dec. 1828
William, Liverpool, mariner. A June 1827*
Atkinson, Adam, Madras, East Indies, soldier. A Feb. 1826*
Anne, Blackburn. A Sept. 1828
Elizabeth, Ardwick, spinster. July 1826
Ellen, Preston, spinster. Dec. 1828
George, Conway Place, Liverpool, labourer. A Jan. 1830
John, Liverpool, gent. March 1826

Atkinson, John, Birchenley Lane, weaver. A March 1828
Mary, Ardwick, spinster. June 1829
Peter, Wigan, innkeeper. March 1826
Samuel, Manchester, butcher. Aug. 1830
William. Liverpool, gent. June 1826
Atkyn, Phoebe, Manchester, widow. Jan. 1826*
Austin, William, Liverpool, shopkeeper. A Jan. 1827
Auston, Charles, Liverpool, mariner. Feb. 1830*
Axon, Mary, Salford, widow. A March 1829
Ayrton, Thomas, Colne, gent. Nov. 1830*

BABBINGTON, Elizabeth, Manchester, widow. A & Tuon May 1828
Backhouse, Thomas, Liverpool, liquor merchant. April 1829
Backman, Isaac, Liverpool, mariner. May 1828
Badger, Philip, Manchester, calico printer. May 1828
Richard, Clitheroe, innkeeper. A Sept. 1830
Bagley, Samuel, Manchester, fustian cutter. A Feb. 1826*
Bagshaw, Eleanor, Chorlton Row, widow. Aug. 1827
Baguley, George, Chorlton Row, wheelwright. Sept 1828
Samuel, Manchester, silk throwster. Feb. 1826
Bailey, Elizabeth, Lytham, widow. July 1828
James, Witton, manufacturer. May 1827
John, Hoggarth End, last of Spen, Goldshaw Booth, yeoman. April 1827*
Samuel, Liverpool, bricklayer. July 1828 (2nd grant 1832)
Baines, James, Salford, yeoman. July 1830
Sarah, Liverpool, widow. A July 1829
William, Liverpool, schoolmaster. July 1829
Baird, Thomas, Liverpool, surgeon. A April 1826 (1st grant 1817)
Baitson, Sarah, Wavertree, spinster. June 1829
Thomas, Harrington, Liverpool, boat builder. July 1826
Baker, Abraham, Manchester, filer. Nov. 1830
Adam, Whiston, chapman. June 1827
Henry, Penwortham, yeoman. May 1829
James, Leyland. Dec. 1829
Joseph, Hulme, cooper. Sept. 1828
Mary, Winwick, widow. Dec. 1826
Richard, Liverpool, master mariner. A Feb. 1828
Sarah, Lowton, widow. A Nov. 1826
Sarah, Liverpool, spinster. Oct. 1829
Bakewell, James, Ringley, glue manufacturer. A Sept. 1826
Baldwin, James, Lathom, shoemaker. A Dec. 1829
John, Clitheroe, draper. March 1826
Margaret, Lancaster, spinster. May 1829
Thomas, Liverpool, plumber & glazier. A June 1829
Wilkinson, Clitheroe, ironmonger. Jan. 1830
Ball, Edward, North Meols, gardener. Aug. 1827*
George, Wardleworth, gent. A Sept. 1826
Henry, Hesketh with Becconsall, farmer. July 1827
Isaac, Rochdale. A June 1829 (2nd grant 1841)
James, Manchester, publican. A Oct. 1827
James, Ainsworth, weaver. Sept. 1829
Jane, Ormskirk, widow. June 1828
John, South Hawes, North Meols, yeoman. Jan. 1827*

Ball, Joseph, Little Woolton, farmer. A Feb. 1826
(heretofore Martin), Mary, Everton. A April 1830
Rachel, Billinge Higher End, widow. July 1827
Richard, North Meols, innkeeper. Aug., 1827*; July 1828
Richard, Formby, yeoman. Dec. 1829
Robert, Harrington, Liverpool, warehousekeeper. A Oct. 1830
Samuel, Roby, yeoman. March 1829
Thomas, Chorlton, yeoman. Oct. 1826
Thomas, North Meols, farmer. A Feb. 1826*
William, Southport, yeoman. May 1827
Ballard, Sarah, Liverpool, widow. June 1829
Balmer, Sarah, Aigburth, widow. April 1830
Thomas, Aigburth, farmer. Oct. 1829
Balshaw, William, Rainford. Nov. 1830
Bamber, Sarah, Manchester, widow. A April 1829
Thomas, Blackrod, yeoman. April 1826
Thomas, Manchester, cabinet maker. Sept. 1828
Bamford, Anna, St. George, Westminster. Feb. 1826
Ashton, Fort St. George, Bombay. A Dec. 1827 (2nd grant 1836)
Benjamin, Little Green, Middleton, labourer. Oct. 1828 (2nd grant 1835)
George, Bretherton. March 1828
Martha, Middleton, spinster. Jan. 1829
Bancks, Henry, Wigan, cotton spinner. Nov. 1826*
Bancroft, James, Stretford, yeoman. April 1827
William, Liverpool, gent. June 1830 (1st grant 1781)
Banister, Catherine, Toxteth Park, spinster. A Jan. 1830 (2nd grant 1842)
Henry, Bretherton, husbandman. March 1826*
Robert, Liverpool, clerk. Aug. 1829
Thomas, Liverpool, painter. June 1828
William, Bacup, innkeeper. June 1826
Bankes, Henry, Lowton, shopkeeper. Nov. 1827
Meyrick, Winstanley Hall, esq. April 1827; July 1827
Richard, Shevington, shopkeeper. Oct. 1828
Banks, Edward, Burscough, yeoman. April 1829
Edward, Lathom, yeoman. Oct. 1830
Henry James, Liverpool, bookeeper. A Dec. 1828
James, Sollom. May 1827
John, Liverpool, gent. Feb. 1828
John, Culcheth, yeoman. A July 1829
John, Downholland, husbandman. A Aug. 1829
John, Wigan, cotton spinner. A Aug. 1829
John, Downholland, husbandman. A Oct. 1829
Joseph, Liverpool, butcher. Jan. 1828
Joseph, Lowton,Common, farmer. June 1829
Robert, Standish, farmer. April 1829
Thomas, Rainford, husbandman. Feb. 1826
William, Walton-le-Dale, yeoman. Jan. 1826
William, Manchester, gent. March 1827
William, Scarisbrick, farmer. A Sept. 1829
Bannatyne, James, Rothery in Scotland, mariner. A May 1828
Banner, Hannah, Liverpool. April 1826
Bannerman, Alexander, Walton, Liverpool, nursery & seedsman. Oct. 1827
David, Manchester, merchant. Jan. 1830

Banning, Joseph, Mellor, grocer. July 1829
Barber, James, Pendleton, Manchester, joiner. Aug. 1830 (2nd grant 1835)
Samuel, Salford, grocer. A May 1829
Thomas, Hulme, yeoman. June 1830
Barcroft, Thomas the elder, Nuttall Farm, yeoman. Dec. 1826
Bardsea, James, Blackburn, cordwainer. Jan. 1826*
Bardsley, Daniel, Ashton-under-Lyne, innkeeper. A March 1829
John, Sett, Oldham, cotton spinner. A April 1828; July 1830
Bardswell, Charles, Liverpool, attorney-at-law. July 1829
Barker, Ann or Nancy, Leyland, widow. Oct. 1830
Charles, Liverpool, flour dealer. A Feb. 1829 (2nd grant 1836)
Ellen, Liverpool, widow. A Sept. 1827*
Hugh, Liverpool, joiner. Jan. 1826*
James, Manchester, smallware manufacturer. Dec. 1829
Josiah Banks, Strangeways, labourer. July 1829
Mary, Whikstown, North America, widow. June 1829
Robert, Great Marsden, farmer. Sept. 1828
Thomas, Tarbock, blacksmith. Aug. 1828
Barkly, Francis, Liverpool, coachman. A Feb. 1827
Barlow, Ellen, Flixton, widow. A Nov. 1830
Henry, Rhodes House, Oldham, gent. May 1827
James, Reddish, gent. April 1826
James, Manchester, shopkeeper. Aug. 1828
John, Bury St., Salford, shopkeeper & smallware weaver. June 1826
John, Entwhistle, gent. May 1828
John, Salford, turnkey. Feb. 1829 (2nd grant 1832)
Mary, Wigan. A Jan. 1827*
Mary, Culcheth, widow. A Sept. 1830
Mary, Eccles, widow. Nov. 1830
Peter, Whitefield, warper. Jan. 1830
Richard, Hindley, gent. Dec. 1829
Richard, Patricroft, miller. Dec. 1830
Samuel, Stockport, gent., formerly Collyhurst, victualler. April 1829
Samuel, Reddish, hatter. May 1829
Thomas, Moss Lane, Prestwich, gent. Nov. 1826 (2nd grant 1838)
Thomas, Salford, publican. March 1829
Barnes, Benjamin, Manchester. May 1829
Deborah Hunter, Liverpool, spinster. Jan. 1828
Edward, Bretherton, yeoman. May 1830
James, Samlesbury, clerk. A March 1829
John, Eccleston, seedsman. Jan. 1827
John, Greenoughs Row, Wigan. overlooker. A June 1828
John, Blackley, weaver. A Dec. 1828
Ralph, North Moor, Oldham, yeoman. Jan. 1827
Richard, Mellor, grocer & farmer. March 1829
Barns, John, Oldham, weaver. July 1826*
John, Pilkington, printer. June 1830
Barnett, Robert, Liverpool, mariner. A Feb. 1829*
Barnish, John, Rochdale, clockmaker. June 1829
Barnsdall, Robert, Liverpool, painter. A Nov. 1830
Baron, Ann, Blackburn, spinster. Aug. 1827
Charles, Whitfield House, Roby, gent. Aug. 1830
Elizabeth, Chorlton Row, widow. Aug. 1829

Baron, John Wigan, chapman. March 1829
John, Millend, weaver. July 1829
Thomas, Rochdale, weaver. Sept. 1830
Barrett, Adam, Heaton Norris, corn dealer. A Jan. 1830
Edward, Upholland, clerk. Jan. 1830
George, Blackburn, farmer. March 1827
James, Bolton-le-Moors, shopkeeper. A Feb. 1829
Martha, Pendleton, widow. A July 1830
Samuel, Buille Hill, Eccles, bleacher. June 1828
Sarah, Salford, last of Hulme, widow. June 1826
Thomas, Salford, manufacturer. A Oct. 1830 (1st grant 1809)
Barrington, Hannah, Liverpool, widow. Jan. 1830
Barritt, Daniel, Pendlebury, weaver. April 1828
Hannah, Prestwich, widow. Jan. 1830
James, Hinds within Bury, bleacher. June 1826
John, Bury, saddler. Nov. 1830
Samuel, Manchester, shopkeeper. A Nov. 1830
Barrow, Ann, Ratcliffe Bridge, widow. A April 1828
Benjamin, Manchester, shopkeeper. Feb. 1830*
David, Prescot, gold hand maker. Dec. 1827
Edward, Manchester, solicitor. A & Tuon Oct. 1828; Aug. 1830 (1st grant 1825, 4th grant 1838)
James, Bolton, bookkeeper. Sept. 1828
James, Pendleton, gent. Nov. 1830
John, Billinge, yeoman. Nov. 1829
Joseph, Liverpool, livery stable keeper. March 1828
Robert, Liverpool, labourer. A Sept. 1829
Samuel, Edge Hill. April 1827
Sarah, Manchester, widow. A Sept. 1828
William, Lathom, boatman. A Feb. 1830
Barsley, William, Green Hurst, joiner. A Jan. 1826
Barton, Elizabeth, Wigan, widow. Oct. 1827
Ellen, Liverpool. March 1828 (2nd grant 1834)
Hannah, Manchester, spinster. Feb. 1830
Henry, Everton, clerk. March 1827
James, Farnworth, shopkeeper. Sept. 1827
James, Upholland. Feb. 1828
James, Billinge, yeoman. Feb. 1829
John, Bury, tailor. A May 1826
John, Everton, gent. Feb. 1828
John, Manchester, trunk maker. A May 1829
John, Liverpool, bricklayer. Jan. 1830
Mary, Liverpool, widow. A Feb. 1830
Richard, Liverpool, boatbuilder. A June 1829
Robert, Ormskirk, gent. March 1828
Roger, Huyton, plumber & glazier. July 1826
Thomas, Liverpool, gent. June 1830
Thomas, Pemberton, esq. Dec. 1830
Sir William, Liverpool, knight. April 1826
William, Blackburn, porter. Tuon Sept. 1829
Bate, Sarah, Burtonwood. A Feb. 1826*
Bateman, Ann, Liverpool, widow. Jan. 1829 (2nd grant 1837)
Martha, Chorley, spinster. May 1830.

Batho, Hugh, Douglas Green, Pendleton, manager. April 1829
Battersby, Alice, Warrington, A & Tuon. Dec. 1828
Henry, Walton, yeoman. Oct. 1828
James, Hindley, shopkeeper. Nov. 1827
John, Aspull, shopkeeper. A Jan. 1830
John, Bedford, miller. Nov. 1830
Ralph, Bedford, fustian manufacturer. May 1830
Battye, Joseph, Hulme, butcher. April 1828
Bawdwen, Mary, Clitheroe, gent [*sic*]. May 1829
Baxendale, James, Lathom, yeoman. June 1830
John, Lathom, farmer. May 1830
William, Burscough, yeoman. June 1830
Baxendell, Joseph, Manchester, corndealer. Feb. 1827
Baxter, James, Cockshill, Ashton-under-Lyne. Jan. 1826*
John, Manchester, merchant. June 1826
Thomas, Hulme, plaisterer. Sept. 1830*
Baybutt, Fairhurst, Burscough, husbandman. Aug. 1828
Bayley, James, Fitton Hill, Ashton-under-Lyne, farmer. Nov. 1830
Thomas, Oldham, hat finisher. July 1827
Bealey, Richard, Radcliffe, whitster. Dec. 1826 (1st grant 1818)
Beamont, John, Warrington, last of Chester, gent. Nov. 1829*
Beard, James, Burnage, weaver. Dec. 1828
John, Gorton, tailor. April 1830
John Samuel, Liverpool, brassfounder. Aug. 1828
Thomas, Manchester, saddler. Nov. 1828*
Beardsworth, Margery, Penwortham, widow. Oct. 1826
Thomas, Whittle-le-Woods, farmer. March 1826
Beaumont, Ben, Austerlands, Saddleworth, cotton spinner. Sept. 1826
Bebbington, John, Wardle, coal merchant. March 1830
Beck, Alice, Chorlton Row. A Oct. 1830
Joanna, Manchester, widow. Sept. 1829
Thomas, Ormskirk, yeoman. March 1830
Beckett, John, Gate & Pickup Bank, farmer. Jan. 1828
John, Manchester, manufacturer. Sept. 1830
Samuel, Manchester, joiner. May 1826
William, Manchester, warehouseman. A Nov. 1826
Bedford, Thomas, Liverpool, surgeon. A Nov. 1829 (2nd grant 1854)
Bee, Richard, Eccleston, tailor. Oct. 1829
Beech, Esther, Harrington, Liverpool, widow. Aug. 1826
William, Bolton-le-Moors, publican. A June 1826
Beekman, Ellen, Liverpool, widow. May 1829 (2nd grant 1868)
Beesley, Barton, Chorley, land agent. A Sept. 1829
Elizabeth wife of Henry Beesley, Preston, cotton manufacturer. May 1827
Michael, Penwortham, husbandman. A Nov. 1829 (2nd grant 1842)
William, Fallowfield, shopkeeper. A Nov. 1826
Beeston, Jane, Manchester. A Feb. 1828
Mary, Manchester, widow. A Dec. 1826*
Beethom, Thomas, Liverpool, gent. A July 1828
Beket, James, Chorlton-cum-Hardy, husbandman. A Feb. 1826
Bell, James, Stretford, innkeeper. Dec. 1830
John, Gosforth, Cumberland, mariner. A March 1829
William, Manchester, gent. A Jan. 1826
William, Liverpool, mariner. April 1827*

Bellin, Catherine, Liverpool, widow. March 1826
Ralph, Liverpool, mariner. A Dec. 1829
Bellion, Alice, Warrington, shopkeeper. A Jan. 1827
Bellot, Abraham, Oldham, surgeon. Nov. 1829
Thomas, Manchester, surgeon. A March 1826
Belsham, James, Harrington, Liverpool. Nov. 1830
Benison, Mary, Heaton Norris, widow. A Sept. 1828
Bennet, George, Preesall with Hackinsall, gent. Feb. 1830
Bennett, Charles, Manchester, gent. Aug. 1827*
Edward, Liverpool, merchant. May. 1829 (2nd grant 1837)
George, Douglas, Isle of Man, gent. July 1829
James, Liverpool, waiter in HM Customs. A March 1828
John, Liverpool, stonemason. Aug. 1826
Sarah, Bamford, widow. Oct. 1828
Thomas, Liverpool, mariner. April 1827*
Thomas, Runcorn, formerly Manchester, gent. June 1827
Thomas, Liverpool, schoolmaster. July 1830
Benson, Sarah, Toxteth Park, widow. Dec. 1827
Thomas the elder, Lathom, pavior. June 1830
Bent, James, Moorside, Flixton, weaver. May 1826*
Bentley, Benjamin, Butcher Lane, Bury, calico printer. Nov. 1826
Benjamin, Brookhouse, Bury, yeoman. Feb. 1830*
Garside, Manchester, gent. A Sept. 1830
Henry, Litherland. Sept. 1828
James, Broughton, gent. Aug. 1829
John, Buersille Bridge, Rochdale, blacksmith. A March 1826
John, Rochdale. May 1827
John, Stretford, shopkeeper. A May 1827
John, Turton, farmer. Feb. 1828
Mary, Haughton, widow. A Sept. 1826
Mary, Brookhouse, spinster. Feb. 1830
Michael, Bentley Hall, Bury, farmer. Nov. 1829
Thomas, Bury, woollen weaver. A Sept. 1826
Berry, Christopher, Pilkington, cotton manufacturer. April 1829; Oct. 1829
Elizabeth, Ribchester, feme covert. Dec. 1829
George, Manchester, gent. A June 1827
Isaac, Haslingden, yeoman. Dec. 1828
James, Blackmoss, Pendle, farmer. July 1830
John, Billinge, delfman. Dec. 1829
Joseph, Manchester, gent. A June 1827
Joseph, Manchester, whip-maker. A June 1827
Mary, Cheetham, widow. A Feb. 1826
Peter, Manchester, auctioneer. A May 1827
Philip, Tonge, Prestwich, farmer. Dec. 1827
Samuel, Poole Lane, Failsworth, weaver. July 1828*
Sarah, Row Green, Eccles, widow. A Dec. 1826
Sarah, *see* Pearson
Susannah, Middleton. A July 1828
William, Liverpool, mariner. A Nov. 1827*
Bertenshaw, George, Little Moss, Ashton-under-Lyne, feltmaker. A May 1827
Joseph, Ashton-under-Lyne. Feb 1829
Sarah, Droylsden, wid. July 1829
Bertles, Peter, Rochdale, yeoman. June 1830 (2nd grant 1832)

Bertwistle, John, Accrington, yeoman. A Oct. 1826
Bestall, Thomas, Salford, publican. Oct. 1827 (1st grant 1825)
Beswick, Alice, Bolton, widow. June 1828
Isaac, Flixton, gent. April 1827
Jacob, Levenshulme, tailor. A Sept. 1827*
James, Waterhead Mill, gent. Aug. 1830
John, Houghton, schoolmaster. A May 1830
John, Halliwell, yeoman. Sept. 1830 (1st grant 1811; 3rd grant 1847)
Samuel, Warrington, shopkeeper. April 1830
Bethell, Margaret, Liverpool, singlewoman. Sept. 1826
Bevan, James, Lowton, esq. Sept. 1829
Bevington, Margaret, Hale, widow. A May 1830
Thomas, Liverpool, innkeeper. Aug. 1828
Bewley, Abraham, Manchester, slater. Aug. 1829
Bibby, Alice, Wigan, widow. A April 1826*
Betty, Blackburn. A March 1827*
Charles, Heaton Norris, shopkeeper. A Dec. 1828
John, Penketh. A Sept. 1827
John, Lamberhead Green, Orrell, labourer. Oct. 1827
Mary, Liverpool, victualler. A Nov. 1828
Thomas, Liverpool, victualler. A Dec. 1828*
Bigham, Samuel, Wigan, calico manufacturer. A Aug. 1830
Bigland, Alice, Liverpool, widow. June 1828
Billinge, Mary, Manchester, widow. A April 1829
Bindloss, Backhouse James, Salford, silk merchant. July 1828
Binns, Thomas, Near Nar Side Chapelry, Colne, farmer. A Nov. 1830
Birbeck, Mary Ann, Liverpool, uxor. May 1828
Birch, John, Manchester, cabinet maker. Oct. 1826
John, Chatburn, innkeeper. A Aug. 1827
John, Kearsley, weaver. A June 1828
John, Grange, gent. Sept. 1828
Thomas, Didsbury, cordwainer. May 1827
Thomas, Woolston with Martinscroft, yeoman. Oct. 1830
Birchall, Edward, Prescot, earthenware manufacturer. June 1828 (2nd grant 1838)
George, Warrington, gent. Sept. 1828
Henry, Liverpool, druggist. A Jan. 1828
Henry, Winstanley, bachelor. A May 1828
John, Whiston. July 1829
John, Manchester, warehouseman. Aug. 1829
John, Liverpool, cooper. A Sept. 1829
formerly Kilshaw, Martha, Prescot. A Oct. 1827*
Mary, Warrington, widow. June 1827
Samuel, Prescot, butcher. A Aug. 1829
Thomas, Whiston, blacksmith. A Feb. 1829
Thomas Wainwright, Liverpool, bookkeeper. A Oct. 1826
William, Manchester, flymaker. A Oct. 1830*
Bird, Joseph, Manchester, victualler. A March 1829
Joseph, Liverpool. A Nov. 1830
William, Liverpool, mariner. Aug. 1826*
Birkinhead, Sarah, Manchester, widow. Feb. 1827
Birtles, James, Edge Hill, bookkeeper. Sept. 1830*
Birtwell, Ann, Accrington, widow. July 1828
Bishop, Henry, the schooner Salisbury of Liverpool, mariner. A Nov. 1826

Biss, formerly Kilshaw, Esther, Preston, widow. A Oct. 1827*
Blabey, Daniel, Liverpool, publican. April 1829
Black, John, Liverpool, gent. A Feb. 1828 (2nd grant 1839)
  Robert Wilson (or Peter), Liverpool, mariner. A Oct. 1827*
Blackburn, Dorothy, Preston, widow. A Jan. 1827
  Elizabeth, Liverpool, widow. A Oct. 1827
  Joseph, Liverpool, gunsmith. A Aug. 1827
  Margaret, Lowton, victualler. Jan. 1829
  Margaret, Liverpool, widow. A March 1830
  Richard, Delph, innkeeper. April 1829
  William, Horwich, yeoman. Aug. 1827
  William, Rainford, farmer. Sept. 1827
Blackledge, Hugh, Withnell, cotton weaver. May 1826
  Jane, Hoghton, farmer & widow. A Dec. 1829
  Miles, Ryley Green, weaver. June 1827*
Blacklock, Joseph, Salford, gent. July 1828
Blackly, Catherine, Liverpool, widow. A & Tuon. Aug. 1826
Blackstock, Edward, Liverpool, gent. Oct. 1830 (2nd grant 1860)
Blair, George, Mill Hill, Little Bolton, whitster. March 1827
  John, The Polygon, Ardwick, merchant. May 1828 (2nd grant 1869)
Blakeley, John, Hulme, bookbinder. Jan. 1829
  John, Manchester, schoolmaster. A Jan. 1830*
  Thomas, Rooden Lane, schoolmaster. A Jan. 1829
Blakemore, Margaret, Liverpool, widow. Feb. 1830
  Robert, Liverpool, confectioner. Dec. 1827
Blakey, Richard, Burnley, gardener. Feb. 1830
  Thomas, Liverpool, master mariner. A June. 1828
Blakley, Robert, Liverpool, bricklayer. A Aug. 1830
Blaley, John, Radcliffe, gent. Oct. 1829
Blantern, Hannah, Wellington, co. Salop, widow. May 1827
  Joseph, an artillery driver in HM Service. A May 1827
Bleakley, Thomas, Rugley, weaver. Jan. 1828
Blease, John, Chowbent, innkeeper. May 1828
  William, Manchester, yeoman. June 1826
Blinkhorn, Thomas, Shude Hill, Manchester, wire worker. A June 1830
Blomiley, John, Chorlton Row, grocer. A Feb. 1830
Bludwick, John, Warrington, yeoman. May 1826
Blundell, Ann, Aughton, widow. A June 1828
  Charles, Ormskirk, yeoman. March 1828
  James, Liverpool, merchant. March 1828
  Jenny, Ormskirk, spinster. Dec. 1829
  Jonathan, Liverpool, merchant. A Aug. 1829 (1st grant 1800)
  Matilda, Liverpool, spinster. A Aug. 1829
  Nicholas Walmsley, Liverpool. Dec. 1829
  Richard, Liverpool, flour dealer. A Dec. 1826
  William, Banks, yeoman. Oct. 1829*
Blundstone, George, Manchester, gent. Dec. 1828
Blythe, James, Big Rigg, Egremont. Oct. 1829
Boam, Frank, Ardwick, agent. July 1827
Boardman, Ann, Newton, Manchester, widow. Jan. 1828
  Charles, Liverpool, livery stable keeper. April 1826
  Frederick, Manchester, attorney. A Dec. 1827 (2nd grant 1852)
  George, Wilpshire, farmer. A June 1827*

Boardman, George, Manchester, spirit merchant. Oct. 1830
James, Wigan, last of Over Hulton, yeoman. Nov. 1826
Jonathan, Lower Hulton, weaver. A May 1829
Joseph, Manchester, glazier. A Dec. 1828
formerly Appleton, Mary, Liverpool. A Oct. 1827*
Peter, Leigh. Jan., 1826. March 1826
Robert, Bolton-le-Moors, innkeeper. July 1828
Robert, Bedford, yeoman. March 1829
Thomas, Leyland Lane, Leyland, yeoman. May 1826
William, Radcliffe, cotton manufacturer. A March 1827
William, Manchester, a private in the 15th Regiment of Foot. Oct. 1830*
William Henry Fenton, Manchester, surgeon. Nov. 1827
Boiles, Ann, Stand Lane, Pilkington, widow. July. 1826
Bold, Peter, Parr, bricklayer. Feb. 1829
Bolton, James, Hindley, gent. Nov., 1826
James, Blackburn, yeoman. A June 1829
John, Ramsgrove, Blackburn, farmer. A Sept. 1827
John, Padiham, weaver. A May 1829
Richard, Blackburn, bookkeeper. July 1826
Sarah, Lower Shore, spinster. A Dec. 1829
Thomas, London, last of Liverpool, gent. March 1827
Thomas, Liverpool, mariner. A Sept. 1830*
William, Blackburn, cordwainer. Sept. 1829
William, Manchester. A Nov. 1830
Bond, Betty, Manchester, last of Bury. Nov. 1828
James, Formby, yeoman. May 1829
John, Manchester, grocer. June 1826
John, Manchester, calico printer. Oct. 1826
Margaret, Liverpool, widow. A June 1829
Nicholas, Scarisbrick, yeoman. Dec. 1828
William, Liverpool, victualler. April 1830
Bonney, Robert, Alexandria, merchant. A Sept. 1827
Boond, Richard, Preston. Feb. 1828*
Booth, Betty, Manchester, spinster. A Oct. 1826
Edward senior, Salford, butcher. A Nov. 1828
George, Brinscall, Leyland, calico printer. A June 1826
George, Heaton Norris, coal merchant. Nov. 1829
George, Oldham, coal merchant. A Nov. 1829
George, Lodge Lane, Liverpool, corn merchant. A May 1830
George, Greenacres, Oldham, coal miner. A Aug. 1830*
James, Manchester, cab maker. Feb. 1826*
James, Failsworth, farmer. A April 1827
James, Droylesden, shopkeeper. Jan. 1829
James, Woolfold, Bury, bleacher. A Sept. 1829
James, Coppull, collier. A Aug. 1830
John, Green Acres, Oldham, yeoman. A June 1826 (1st grant 1813)
John, Bury, yeoman. Aug. 1828
John, Duxbury, farmer. A Sept. 1829
John, Audenshaw, victualler. Oct. 1829
John, Ashes, Saddleworth, yeoman. May 1830
John Holme, Ashton-under-Lyne, bookkeeper. A Dec. 1829
Manasseh, Salford, yeoman. July 1830
Martha, Liverpool, widow. A May 1830

Booth, Mary, Cowhill, Prestwich, widow. Aug. 1827 (2nd grant 1837)
Richard, Bottom of Greenacres Moor, Oldham, butcher. Aug. 1826
Richard, Buckley Wells, Bury, yeoman. June 1827
Richard, Redvales, Bury, yeoman. March 1830
Robert, Constable Bridge, Rossendale, worsted spinner. A Nov. 1829*
Samuel, Gemspit, Bury, yeoman, Nov. 1826
Samuel, Middleton, butcher. May 1828
Samuel, Standish, painter. Aug. 1829
Thomas, Manchester, worsted spinner. A Nov. 1829*
Thomas, Breightmet, yeoman. Sept. 1830
William, Burscough Hall, near Chorley. A June 1826
William, Waterhead Mill, Oldham, butcher. A June 1826
Boothman, Jonathan, Blackburn. Sept. 1830
Lawrence, Billington, yeoman. April 1830
Borron, James, Withington, esq. Oct. 1826
Borrowdale, Catherine, Warrington, widow. A Dec. 1829
Borrows, John, Manchester, calenderer. Feb. 1829
Bostock, John, Blackbrook, Manchester, gent. March 1830
Robert, Bootle, merchant. A May 1826
Bottomley, George, Salford, gent. A May 1827
James, Delph, Saddleworth. Aug. 1826
James, Thurstones, clothier. A April 1828
James, Green Acres Moor, Oldham. May 1829
James, Diggle Edge, Saddleworth, clothier. Nov. 1829
John, Diggles, clothier. Feb. 1829
Sarah, Dobcross, spinster. A Feb. 1829
Boulton, John, Liverpool, mariner. A July 1830
Bourne, Ann, Liverpool, widow. July 1828
Joseph, Salford, gent. Aug. 1830
Boustead, Joseph, Liverpool, clerk & bookkeeper. Feb. 1830
Bowcock, John, Rose Hill, saddler. A June 1828
Bowden, James, Salford, farrier. A Sept. 1826
Wright, Middle Hulton. Dec. 1828
Bowe, Ann, Salford, spinster. Jan. 1830
Bower, Jeremiah, Manchester, haberdasher. Dec. 1829
Martha, Lancaster, widow. Feb. 1830
Mary, Lancaster, spinster. Feb. 1830
Samuel, Lancaster, esq. Oct. 1827
Samuel, Lancaster, gent. A Dec. 1828
William, Liverpool, cotton broker. June 1828
Bowers, Robert, Cheetham, warehouseman. Dec. 1830
Thomas, Hindley, innkeeper. A June 1826
Thomas, Ashton-under-Lyne, stonemason. Feb. 1830*
Bowker, Edmund, Colnfield, weaver. A July 1829
Margaret, Clitheroe. A Dec. 1827
Margaret, Manchester, widow. Dec. 1827
Richard, Liverpool, tobacconist. Oct. 1829
Thomas, Salford, moulder. A May 1828
Bowler, Peter, Salford, spindle maker. A June 1828
Boyd, James, Liverpool, mariner. A Dec. 1826*
Robert, Liverpool, stonemason. A Jan. 1829 (1st grant 1804)
Robert, Liverpool. Feb. 1830
Boydell, James, Martinscroft, husbandman. A Jan. 1827

Boydell, William, Winwick, weaver. Nov. 1826*
Boyers, George, Liverpool, seaman. A Oct. 1829
Boyle, Catherine, Liverpool, spinster. Sept. 1826*
Boys, John , Kirkby, wheelwright. March 1826 (2nd grant 1836)
Brabin, Thomas, Bolton-le-Moors, publican. Jan. 1828
Bracewell, Richard, Southfield, Colne, shopkeeper. A March 1827
Bradbury, Eli, New Delph, woolstapler. June 1828
James, Boarshurst, Saddleworth, woollen manufacturer. A Sept. 1826*
John, Manchester, widower. A Feb. 1830
Robert, Delph, woolstapler. July 1827
William, Manchester, publican. A Dec. 1828
Braddock, Ellen, Ainsworth, spinster. Feb. 1827
Brade, James, Everton, esq. Feb. 1829 (1st grant 1811)
Bradley, Betty, Blackburn, spinster. A Oct. 1827
James, Liverpool, painter and glazier. A Nov. 1826*
James, Northgate, Blackburn, smallware dealer. A Feb. 1830
John, Manchester, farrier. March 1827; Dec. 1828 (1st grant 1819; 3rd grant 1835)
John, Church, cutler, April 1827
John William, Salford, gent. A July 1828
Joseph, Oldham, corn dealer. June 1828
Bradshaw, Edmund, Hulme, yeoman. Sept. 1828
Edmund, Liverpool. May 1829
James, Prescot, chapman, May 1826
James, Manchester, weaver. Feb. 1827
John, Stretford, yeoman. June 1829
Johnson, Cromberry Lodge, surgeon. Dec. 1828
Lawrence, Liverpool, merchant. Jan. 1829 (2nd grant 1836)
Mary, Quarlton,spinster. May 1830
Robert, Maghull, yeoman. A Feb. 1830
Bradshay, John, Toxteth Park, yeoman. Jan. 1829
Braithwaite, Mary, Upholland, spinster. Dec. 1826
Brakell, Nanny, Penwortham, spinster. Sept. 1826
Bramhall, John, Sandy Lane End, Roby. July 1830
Bramley, William, Blackburn, innkeeper. Aug. 1830
Brandeth, Mary, Liverpool, widow. May 1829
Brandreth, Catherine, Liverpool, widow. May 1827
James, Manchester, labourer. July 1830
Joseph, Liverpool, surgeon. July 1826
William, Burscough, gent. Aug. 1828
Brandwood, James, Westhoughton. Aug. 1826
John, Holehouse, Tottington Lower End, Bury, calico printer. A May 1827
Mary, Haslingen, widow. July 1830
Branwood, Richard, Abram, farmer. April 1826
Brassey, Benjamin, Liverpool, gent. A March 1830*
Brassie, Robert, Rough Hill, gent. Nov. 1828
Brassington, Martha, Pool Hall, Muccleton, co. Salop, feme covert. April 1829
Brearey, George, Wirksworth, co. Derby, mercer and draper. Jan. 1826
Brearley, Hannah, Shawforth, Rochdale. A Feb. 1826
John, Rochdale, innkeeper. Jan. 1829
Breeze, Sarah, Liverpool, widow. Sept. 1829
Brent, John Leigh, Warrington, farmer. Dec. 1828
Bretherton, Thomas, Bretherton, innkeeper. A Dec. 1826
Brew, George, Liverpool, painter, April 1828

Briden, Daniel, Winstanley, gent. June 1829
Brideoak, Thomas, Waterhead Mill, cotton spinner. March 1826
Bridge, Edward, Cranberry Lodge, gent. A July 1828
 Elizabeth, Bury St. Edmunds, spinster. A Jan. 1830
 Hannah, Leavengreave, Rochdale, widow. A June 1826*
 James, Top of Heath, Bury, farmer. A Nov. 1828
 Joseph, Little Bolton, shopkeeper. April 1827
 Richard, Pilkington, farmer. Aug. 1830
Bridgeford, John, Cheetwood, co. Lancs., nurseryman. A Feb. 1826
Bridgens, Zachariah, Newport, co. Staffs., gent. April 1827
Bridson, Mary, Prescot, spinster. A May 1829
 William, Horwich, bookkeeper, A Dec. 1829
Brierley, Mary, Brown Lodge, Rochdale, widow. A and Tuon Sept. 1830; Dec. 1830
 Samuel, Salford, gent. May 1829 ; April 1830; Dec. 1830
 Sarah, Knottlanes, Ashton, widow. April 1830
Brierly, James, Slackcote, clothier, Oct. 1828
 Joseph, Heap, farmer. Sept. 1828 (lst grant 1799)
Briggs, Abraham, School Lane, Rochdale, butcher. A April 1827
 Ann, Great Bolton, widow. A April 1830
 Betty, Unsworth. A Jan. 1829*
 Grace, Samlesbury, widow. Dec. 1826
 Hannah, Barton Close, Prestwich, widow. A Dec. 1826
 James, Manchester, gent. May 1830
 John, Chatburn, yeoman. Nov. 1830
 Thomas, Accrington, labourer. A Sept. 1827
 Thomas, Salford, warehouseman. April 1828
Brimelow, James, Newton in Makerfield, yeoman. May 1829
 Joshua, Martinscroft Green, Warrington. Sept. 1829
 Mary, Newton le Willows, spinster. March 1830
 Peter, Pemberton, yeoman. May 1827
Brindle, Adam, Westhoughton, butcher. Sept. 1826
 George, Salford, roller coverer. A Feb. 1827
 James, Westhoughton. Dec. 1829
 Thomas, Brindle, yeoman. March 1826
 Thomas, Walton -le-Dale, yeoman. April 1829
Briscoe, John, Liverpool, mariner. A Aug. 1826*
 John, Newton Heath, cotton spinner. April 1830
 Thomas Downham, Heaton Norris, bookkeeper. Aug. 1828
Briton, Charles, Liverpool, livery stable keeper. A Jan. 1827
Britton, Rebecca, Liverpool, spinster. A Oct. 1827
Broach, Robert, Manchester, pawnbroker. June 1830
Broadbent, Dorothy, Bolton-le-Moors, widow. May 1828
 George, Harrop Cote, co. York, yeoman. Jan. 1830
 John, Scholes, Wigan, spinner. A March 1829
 William, Mytham, Saddleworth, clothier. A Sept. 1826*
 William, Chorlton Row, pawnbroker. A Oct. 1829
Broadhurst, Francis, Culcheth, farmer. A June 1829
 Hannah, Manchester, widow. A Oct. 1828
 John, Swinton, merchant. May 1827
 John, Ardwick, gent. A May 1829
 Thomas, Warrington, yeoman. Oct. 1829
Brock, John, Liverpool, mariner. June 1829
Brocklehurst, Elizabeth, Fletcher Fold, Bury, spinster. Aug. 1829

Brogden, Jeffrey, Hedge End, Great Harwood. June 1827
Bromeley, William, Reddish, hatter. May 1829
Bromiley, James, Breightmet, clogger. A Nov. 1830*
John, Mortfield, Bolton-le-Moors, bleacher. A Nov. 1830*
Joseph, Lostock, yeoman. Feb. 1829
Samuel, Harwood, yeoman. Feb. 1826
Bromilow, Alice, Lostock. March 1829
John, St. Helens, victualler. A March 1826
Thomas, Tyldesley, yeoman. March 1829
Bromley, George, Whaley, carrier. July 1829
James, Reddish, hatter. Aug. 1826
James, Liverpool, sailmaker. Dec. 1828
Nicholas, Haughton, Manchester, weaver. A Jan. 1827
Brookes, Jane, Manchester. A March 1826
Brookfield, Thomas, Cresden, North Meols. Aug. 1829
Brooks, Benjamin, Rochdale, shopkeeper. Sept. 1828
Daniel, Liverpool, woollen draper. A Feb. 1828
Jane, Everton, widow. April 1829
Samuel, Bury, grocer. Nov. 1830
Thomas, Manchester, grocer. May 1828
Thomas, Burnley, victualler. March 1830
William, Irlam, farmer, Feb. 1829
Broome, Matthew, Chorlton Row, gent. Sept. 1829
William, Manchester, yeoman. Oct. 1829 (2nd grant 1847)
Brotherton, Ann, Manchester, widow. Oct. 1830
Henry, Liverpool, tea dealer. A June 1826
James, Chapel House, weaver. March 1828
Thomas, Ince in Makerfield, gent. June 1826
Brough, Charles, Liverpool, victualler. Nov. 1830
Broun, James, Irlam, yeoman. June 1827*
Brown, Ann, Standish, last of Bolton, widow. Feb. 1827
Charles, Liverpool, carpenter. April 1828
Charles, Liverpool, bachelor. A Nov. 1830
Edward, Liverpool, mariner. A July 1828
Elizabeth, Formby, widow. Jan. 1829
George, Prestwich, labourer. Jan. 1828
George, Liverpool, mariner. A Aug. 1829
Helen, Little Crosby, spinster. March 1828
Henry, Blackburn, weaver. A June 1830*
Henry, Great Harwood, last of Arkholme, Rossendale, husbandman. Nov. 1830
James, Manchester, carpenter. Jan 1826
James, Liverpool, master mariner. A Oct. 1826
James, Atherton, weaver. Nov. 1828
James Smith, Liverpool, bachelor. A Nov. 1830
Jane, Warrington. A Feb. 1828
John, Middleton, labourer. A April 1826
John, Hulme, butcher. June 1826
John, Liverpool, flour dealer. July 1827
John, Longton. May 1828
John, Low Hill, Liverpool, gent. A Dec. 1828
Joseph, Manchester, grocer. Feb. 1826
Mary, Manchester, spinster. A April 1826
Mary, Liverpool, widow. April 1830

Brown, Nathan, Warrington, glazier. Dec. 1828
Peter, Liverpool, gent. Sept. 1827
Richard, Formby, farmer. July 1830
Robert, Manchester, druggist. Sept. 1829
Robert, Leigh, Scotland and Lima Leone, Africa, master mariner. A Dec. 1830
Sarah, Southport, widow. Oct. 1829
Sarah, Liverpool, spinster. A Nov. 1830
Thomas, Liverpool, gent. Nov. 1826
Thomas, Bahia Brazils, S. America, ship chandler. A Sept. 1828 (2nd grant 1831)
William, Cadishead, weaver. Feb. 1829
Brownbill, Dulcibella, Rainford, spinster. A Jan. 1829
Henry, Roby, farmer, Aug. 1827
James, Liverpool, watchmaker. A April 1826
Martha, Edge Hill, widow. A May 1830*
Thomas, Eccleston, last of Prescot Hall, yeoman. May 1826
Browne, Browne Holt, Hey Houses, Tottington, gent. Nov. 1829
Ezekiel, Liverpool, linen draper. Aug. 1827
Brownell, Eleanor, Brook, Walton-on-the-Hull, spinster. July 1826
Brownlow, Gwyther, Hale co. Lanc. widow *[sic]*. July 1826
Brownsword, James, Liverpool, joiner. Dec. 1830
Jane, Ormskirk, spinster. Jan. 1826
Broxup, Thomas, Manchester, packer. June 1826
Bruce, Richard, Liverpool, chemist. A July 1827
Brumwell, Ann, Blackburn, widow. Nov. 1829
Bryars, John, Liverpool, tallow chandler. Aug. 1830
Bryce, John, Eccles, weaver. Oct. 1826
Bryden, John, Manchester, umbrella manufacturer. July 1828
Buchanan, John, Liverpool, mariner. A Dec. 1829
Buckley, Abel, Doghill, Oldham, stone potman. Aug. 1829
Ann, Bank Top, Ashton-under-Lyne, widow. Dec. 1828 (lst grant 1803)
Charles, Dobfield, farmer. Oct. 1828
Daniel, Lees, Ashton-under-Lyne, blacksmith. A Aug. 1828*
Elizabeth, Manchester. A June 1826
Ester, Ashton-under-Lyne. April 1829
James, Mount Pleasant, Oldham, spinner. A Nov. 1827
James, Sholver, Oldham. Feb. 1828
James, Great Bolton, hatter. June 1830
James, Manchester, carrier. Aug. 1830
James, Oldham, clogger. Dec. 1830
John, Mossley, innkeeper. A Jan. 1826
John, Rochale, woollen weaver. Feb. 1826
John, Stayleybridge, yeoman. Aug. 1826 (2nd grant 1831)
John, Church St., Middleton. Dec. 1826
John, Upper Mill, Saddleworth, gent. Oct. 1827 (lst grant 1819; 3rd grant 1858)
John, Quick Edge, Saddleworth, cotton spinner. Oct. 1829
John, Shelderslow, cotton spinner. April 1830
Lewis, Oldham, cotton spinner, A April 1828
Philip, Kenches, Saddleworth, clothier. Jan. 1829
Rebecca, Liverpool, widow. Dec. 1830
Robert, Lees, cotton spinner. A June 1827
Samuel, Lilley Lanes, Ashton-under-Lyne, farmer. May 1826
Sarah, Thurstonclough, co. York. A Jan. 1826

Buckley, Thomas, Belfield, Rochdale, farmer. A April 1826
William, Uppermill, Saddleworth. Sept. 1827 (2nd grant 1859)
William, Stakehill, Middleton, gent. July 1830
Budge, Ellen, Little Bolton, widow. Oct. 1828
Buht, John, of the merchant ship Kingston of Liverpool, mariner. Oct. 1826*
Bulcock, Giles, Blackburn, gent. Feb. 1827
Bull, William, Manchester, shopkeeper. June 1830
Bullen, Hugh, Liverpool, distiller. March 1829
Joseph, Liverpool, tobacconist. Oct. 1827 (lst grant 1824)
Robert, Liverpool. Sept. 1829
Thomas, Kirkby, farmer. Feb. 1830
Bulley, Anna Parker, Boston, America, spinster. A Dec. 1830
Bulmer, George Donald, Liverpool, gent. A April 1829
Samuel, Toxteth Park, stable keeper. A April 1828
Bullock, Ann, Wigan, spinster. Feb. 1829
Ferdinando, East Challon, esq. A Aug. 1830
George, Liverpool, upholsterer. A Jan. 1830
James, Manchester, cabinet maker. A April 1828
James, Wigan, brazier. A April 1828
Robert, Little Bolton, clerk. July 1828
Roger, Roundabout Barn, Upholland, yeoman, May 1829
Bullough, William, Salford, publican. A Feb. 1830
Bulock, Thomas, Hoarstones, Goldshaw Booth, yeoman. Feb. 1829*
Burchall, James, Ashton-in-Makerfield, pavior. Aug. 1828
Burdikin, John, Manchester, victualler. Dec. 1830
Burgess, Edward, Liverpool, shoemaker. Sept. 1830
John, Much Woolton, butcher. Feb. 1830
Sarah, Liverpool, spinster. Feb. 1826
William, Ashton-under-Lyne, joiner. A Sept. 1828
Burns, George, Manchester, bookkeeper. A Aug. 1827
Solomon, Liverpool, mariner. Aug. 1829
William, Warrington, gent. Feb. 1827 (2nd grant 1833)
Burroughs, William, Liverpool, brewer. A July 1826
Burrows, James, Parr, sawyer. A June 1826
Robert, Manchester, butcher. March 1827
Samuel, Liverpool, mariner. A Oct. 1829*
Thomas the younger, Ince-in-Makerfield, fustian manufacturer. May 1826
Thomas, Ince, Wigan. A and Tuon March 1827
Thomas, Ince, yeoman. June 1828
Burslem, William, Manchester, pickmaker. A Aug. 1826
Burton, Peter, Crumpsall, oil and vitriol manufacturer. March 1827
Richard, Salford, brickmaker. Oct. 1830
Bury, Eliza, Chorley, spinster. A July 1829
George Frederick, Manchester, solicitor, March 1827
John, Clayton Mills, Manchester. June 1830
John, Salford. July 1830
Lawrence, Over Darwen, yeoman. Aug. 1827
Mary, Rochdale, spinster. A Aug. 1828
Robert, Worsley, Eccles, weaver. Oct. 1826
Selina, Rochdale, spinster. A Aug. 1828
Thomas, Nabbs Horse, Tottington. A Aug. 1827
Bushell, Daniel, Liverpool, gent. Sept. 1828
Jane, Middleton, spinster. A Jan. 1827*
Lydia, Liverpool, widow. May 1828

Buszard, Marston, Lutterworth co. Leics., banker. Nov. 1826
Butler, Benjamin, Bolton-le-Moors, joiner. April 1828 (1st grant 1793)
Butt, Edward, Liverpool, painter. A Aug. 1829
Butters, James, Liverpool, mariner. A June 1830*
Butterworth, Ann, Middleton, widow. May 1828
Benjamin, Royton Lane. April 1829
Edmond, Lower Swain Rd., Rochdale, farmer. May 1830
Henry, Sunnyside, Higher Booths, calico printer. Nov. 1830 (2nd grant 1880)
James, Holebottom, Oldham, tin-plate worker. June 1826
James, Manchester, publican. A July 1828
James, Milkstone, Rochdale. June 1829
John, Banks, Todmorden, weaver. May 1829
John, Manchester, pawnbroker. Aug. 1829
John, Lower Lomas, stonegetter. March 1830
Joseph, Wardleworth, woolstapler. March 1830
Mary, Manchester, widow. A Sept. 1829
Robert, Tonge Bridge, Rossendale, labourer. A Feb. 1827 (2nd grant 1836)
Robert, Pilsworth, farmer. Sept. 1827
Samuel, Middleton, innkeeper. March 1829
Stephen, Worsthorne, stonegetter. Jan. 1829
William, Clough House, Rochdale, yeoman. July 1827
William, Horwich, farmer. Oct. 1828
Buxton, Alice, Lower House, West Derby, widow. April 1829
Benjamin, Tothill St., Westminster, last of Liverpool, gent. April 1826
Edward, Liverpool, earthenware dealer. Aug. 1826
Thomas, Manchester, baker. May 1826
Buzley, Thomas, Cadiz, Spain, merchant's clerk. A March 1830
Byard, George, Liverpool, seaman. A Feb. 1830
Byrom, Henry, Golborn, Winwick, husbandman. Feb. 1827*
Natham, Risley, Winwick, farmer. Aug. 1830 (2nd grant 1860)

CADDICK, Alice, Great Crosby, widow. Sept. 1829
John, Great Crosby, cordwainer. A Oct. 1826
Cairnon, Robert, Haslingden, draper. A Jan. 1826
Caistor, Thomas, Burnage, gent. April 1829
Calcott, Elizabeth, Winwick, spinster. A June 1827
Calderbank, Thomas, Liverpool, painter, plumber and glazier. Aug. 1830
William, Adlington, yeoman. Nov. 1830
Caldwell, Joseph, Martinscroft, farmer. A.Nov. 1827
Mary, Croft, widow. A Oct. 1829
Callie, Samuel, Wigan, draper. A Aug. 1827
Callon, Sarah, Liverpool, widow. June 1829
William, Liverpool, gent. A March 1830 (lst grant 1821)
Callow, Sarah, Liverpool, spinster. A June 1828
Calvert, Ann, Pendleton, spinster. May 1829
James, Bacup, mechanic. A Aug. 1828
John, Liverpool, innkeeper. March 1826*
Margaret, *see* Forbes
Samuel, Liverpool, bookkeeper. May 1827
Cammack, Edward, Scarisbrick, yeoman. Oct. 1827
Campbell, Mary, Manchester, widow. March 1828
William, Oldham, draper. Nov. 1829
Cannell, Margaret Eliza, Everton. A Feb. 1830*

Cannell, Thomas Egerton, Liverpool, gent. March 1829
Cannon, William, Atherton, yeoman. March 1826
Carbishley, William, Manchester, publican. A Oct. 1830
Cardale, William, Bedford Row co. Middlesex, esq. Aug. 1827*
Carey, Elizabeth, Liverpool, widow. Oct 1826
Cargey, Robert, Liverpool, spirit merchant. Oct. 1829
Carlile, James, Sunning Hill, esq. April 1829
Carlow, Richard, Walton Lodge, Walton-le-Dale, esq. Nov. 1830
Carlton, Sabbath Church, Salford, whitesmith. July 1827
Carpenter, Patrick, Liverpool, victualler. A April 1827
Carr, Betty, Manchester, widow. A Nov. 1828
John, Chorlton-cum-Hardy, husbandman. June 1826
John, Leyland, farmer. May 1829
Sarah, Liverpool, widow. Dec. 1829*
Carrley or McCawley, Peter, Liverpool, mariner. Aug. 1826*
Carroll, Patrick otherwise Peter, of the merchant ship Perneth of Liverpool, mariner. A March 1828*
Carruthers, Sarah, Askham, Westmorland. A July 1829
Carson, Alexander, Liverpool, merchant. March 1828
John, Liverpool, mariner. Aug. 1829
Carter, David, Garston, labourer. A Jan. 1827
Edward, Bury, clogger. Oct. 1828 (2nd grant 1844)
or McCarter, Francis, Liverpool, gent. Nov. 1827 (lst grant 1825)
John, Salford, bookkeeper. July 1826
John, Birchenley, Colne, farmer. A June 1830
John Sigourney, Boston, America, last of Liverpool merchant. A Sept. 1827
Joseph, Newton, yeoman. June 1828
Leonard, Chorlton, Manchester, stonemason. Jan. 1826*
Thomas, Manchester, cabinet maker. Oct. 1826 (1st grant 1822)
Thomas, Whitchurch, saddler. A Dec. 1829
William, Glazebrook, yeoman. Dec. 1826
William, Hurst Cross, joiner. A July 1828
Cartner, George, Liverpool. Oct. 1826 (2nd grant 1842)
Cartwright, Hannah, Liverpool, widow. Jan. 1830
Mary, Roby, widow. Feb. 1828
William, Chorlton Row, gent. Dec. 1830
Cash, John, Orford Lane, Warrington, farmer. A Sept. 1827
John, Goostrey, co. Lanc. *[sic]* , farmer. Nov. 1827
Samuel, Heaton Norris, tanner. June 1827
Thomas, Penketh. March 1830
Casidy, Thomas, Liverpool, feather dealer. A March 1830
Cass, James, Rooden Lane, blacksmith. A Jan. 1829
Casson, Esther, Liverpool, spinster. A Oct. 1828
Henry, Bolton-le-Moors, gent. Feb. 1827
Cathrall, Charles, Lees, Oldham, publican. Jan. 1827
Catlow, Alice, Haughton, spinster. July 1828
George, Haughton, hatter. Dec. 1826
Catterall, John, Manchester, corn dealer. A March 1826
John, Liverpool, gent. Dec. 1829
Peter, Upholland, yeoman. Feb. 1828
Thomas, Chorley, publican. A Sept. 1827
Cattrall, Samuel, Liverpool, master mariner. Dec. 1826 (1st grant 1811)
Caunce, Nancy, Golborne, spinster. March 1827

Caunce, William, Leigh, schoolmaster. Aug. 1828
Cave, James, Liverpool, watchmaker. A Dec. 1830
  Thomas, Ince, farmer. Aug. 1828
Cawley, Samuel, Liverpool, gent. Dec. 1829
  Thomas, Oldham, yeoman. Sept. 1830
Cawson, Betty (heretofore Betty Veary), Liverpool, widow. A July 1829
  James, Liverpool, watchmaker. A June 1829
Chadderton, Ellen, Manchester, widow. A Sept. 1829
Chadwick, Adam, Golborne. Oct. 1828
  Ann, Westhoughton. A Feb. 1826
  Ann, Hulme, Manchester. Oct. 1830
  Betty, Much Hoole. April 1826
  Edward, Park Hall, Ashton-under-Lyne, cotton manufacturer. Jan. 1830
  Elias, Swinton, esq., Dec. 1828 (1st grant 1825)
  Elizabeth, Burgh, Chorley, spinster. Jan. 1826*
  Elizabeth, Kirkdale, widow. May 1827*
  Elizabeth, Patricroft, spinster. July 1830
  Hannah, Walton, widow. Nov. 1826
  James, Platting, Rochdale, woollen weaver. A Feb. 1826
  James, Stonyhurst, Mitton, co. Lanc., gent. A 1826*
  James, Wigan, broker. A Dec. 1827
  James, Ashworth, woollen weaver. A May 1828
  James, Eagley, Little Bolton, smallware manufacturer . A Aug. 1830
  Jemima, Heights, Accrington, widow. A July 1827
  John, Hoghton, farmer. A March 1826
  John, Hades, Rochdale, yeoman. May 1826
  John, Francil, Rochdale, yeoman. Jan. 1828
  John, Liverpool, bookkeeper. April 1828
  John, Captain Fold, yeoman. Nov. 1828
  John the elder, Oldham, yeoman. Feb. 1830
  Martha, Coldwell Brow, Spotland. Jan. 1826
  Mary, Ashton-under-Lyne, widow. Jan. 1826
  Mary, Burgh, Chorley, spinster. A Jan. 1826
  Mary, Dumplington, Eccles. Aug. 1830
  Rachel, Billinge, widow. A May 1828
  Richard, Middleton, cotton manufacturer. Nov. 1827
  Robert, Lower Hey Mill, Rochdale. Jan. 1829
  Samuel, Small Bridge, dyer. A Feb. 1829
  Samuel, Manchester, warehouseman. Oct. 1829
  Thomas, Chorlton Row, bookkeeper. July 1830
  Thomas, Royton. A Oct. 1830 (2nd grant 1837)
Chaffer, John, Buckclough, Whalley. March 1830
Chaffers, Henry James, Quebec, merchant. A Sept. 1829
  Richard Unsworth, Nassau, New Providence, N. America, officer. A Sept. 1829
Chaldwell, William, Chorlton Row, shopkeeper. April 1828
Chaliner, Mary, Liverpool, widow. A and Tuon Aug. 1830
Chalk, Martin, Liverpool, mariner. A Feb. 1830*
Chalmers, Erskine, James, Liverpool, master mariner. A Nov. 1826*
Chambers, James, Salford in Todmorden, gingham manufacturer. A Jan. 1830
  Jonas, Todmorden, printer. July 1829
  Joseph Robinson, Everton, victualler. June 1829
Chamley, Elizabeth, Liverpool, widow. Oct. 1828
Chandley, Edward, Warrington, painter. A March 1828

Chandley, Henry, Warrington, last of Jamaica. A March 1828
Channing, John, Bedford Square, Middlesex, esq., Oct. 1828
Chantler, Samuel, Pendleton, gent. July 1826; Jan. 1827
Thomas, Pendleton, hop dealer. May 1829
Chapman, George, Liverpool, mariner. A Sept. 1830*
John, Broughton, servantman, A July 1829
Thomas, Manchester, skinner. Dec. 1828
Charles, Betty, Liverpool, spinster. Jan. 1829
Edward Stephenson, Liverpool, merchant. Aug. 1828
Hans, Liverpool, merchant. A Jan. 1830
John, Halsall, yeoman. June 1826
Richard, Manchester, tailor and draper. A Dec. 1830
Charlesworth, Thomas, Manchester, innkeeper. Aug. 1827
Charlton, Henry, Little Hulton, yeoman. A Aug. 1827
James, Manchester, agent. Oct. 1830
William, Little Hulton, farmer, Feb. 1826
Charnley, Margaret, Harpurhey. Oct. 1827
Charrier, Peter Samuel, Liverpool, minister of the Gospel. Sept. 1826 (2nd grant 1856)
Charters, William, Liverpool, builder. Dec. 1829
Chatburn, David, Liverpool, shipwright. A Sept. 1828*
Chatterton, Mary, Liverpool, spinster. June 1829
William, Liverpool, innkeeper. Aug. 1828
Cheadle, John, Liverpool, baker. Feb. 1829 (1st grant 1798)
Cheesbrough, John Orred Shewell, Laughton, Lincs. June 1830
Cheetham, George, Stayley Bridge, cotton spinner. Oct. 1826
John, Hooley Hill, Manchester, surgeon and apothecary. A Nov. 1826
John, Salford, block cutter. A June 1829
Cheshire, Thomas, Liverpool, linen draper. March 1827
Chester, James, Warrington, victualler. March 1826
Matthew, Great Crosby, clerk. June 1829
Chesters, Sarah, Liverpool, spinster. A March 1829
Chetham, James, Heaton Norris, gent. A Jan. 1827
Chippindale, John, Salford, excise officer. May 1828
Chisnell, John, Knowsley, farmer. Dec. 1827
Chorley, Charles Gray, New Orleans, Louisiana, merchant. Oct. 1830
Susanna, Pendleton, widow. A June 1829
Chorleton, John, Liverpool, mariner. May 1826*
Chorlton, Edward, Withington. March 1826
Mary, Kersley, widow. A and Tuon May 1829
Thomas, Lostock, Eccles, yeoman. Jan. 1826
Chrimes, Joseph, Warrington, cooper. Feb. 1829
Christian, Robert, Liverpool, cooper. A Sept. 1829
Chubbard, Hillis, Kensington, West Derby, widow. March 1826
Cillbanks, Henry, Liverpool, shipwright. A May 1830*
Clague, John, Liverpool, mariner. Jan. 1826*
Clancy, John, Liverpool, warehouseman. A July 1830
Clapham, John, Manchester, watchmaker. A March 1828
Clare, William, Haslingden, joiner. A July 1827
Clark, John, Warrington, yeoman. Aug. 1828*
John, Manchester, bookkeeper. A Dec. 1829
Thomas, Liverpool, gent. Dec. 1826 (1st grant 1815)
William, Liverpool, spirit dealer. A Jan. 1830

Clarke, James, Broughton St., Salford, cooper. Nov. 1826
John, Liverpool, mariner. March 1827*
John, Ashfield House, Lancs., esq. June 1830
John, Liverpool, carpenter. Will and Tuon Sept. 1830
Johnson, Warrington, victualler. Sept. 1829
Michael, Liverpool, mariner. Oct. 1828*
Sarah, Wavertree, widow. A May 1828 (2nd grant 1842)
Thomas, Manchester, yeoman. July 1826
William Bryan, Manchester, officer of excise. Sept. 1829
Clarkson, Bella, Liverpool, widow. Jan. 1826
James, Hulme. March 1826
James, Salford, gardener. Feb. 1830
John, Hacking Hall, Billington, farmer. Jan. 1830
Joseph, Manchester. Aug. 1827
Robert, Liverpool, bandbox manufacturer. A July 1827
William, Upholland, labourer. A Jan. 1826*
William, Longton, cheesefactor. May 1826 (1st grant 1822)
Claude, Lewis, Liverpool, merchant. March 1828
Clay, Henry, Liverpool, esq. July 1828
Robert, Liverpool, flour dealer. A Sept. 1829
Clayton, Ann, Lowton, widow. Feb. 1830
Betty, Slipper Hill, Foulridge, farmer. Feb. 1830
George, Lostock, cotton spinner. Dec. 1829
Henry, Winwick, yeoman. May 1827
Henry, Lathom, farmer. March 1829
Isaac, Ashton-under-Lyne, cotton spinner. Feb. 1829
James, Hooley Hill, butcher. Jan. 1830
James, Kinknall, Culcheth, gent. Aug. 1830
Joseph Prior, Leyland, esq. Nov. 1830 (1st grant 1801)
William, Blackburn, shopkeeper. Dec. 1828
William, Wigan, last of Cartmel, gent. March 1829
William, Anglezarke, farmer. May 1830
Cleator, Daniel, Liverpool, officer in the Customs. March 1827
Clegg, Abraham, Grange, Oldham, merchant. July 1826. Original to York.
Abraham, Higher Hethersall, farmer. A Jan. 1828
Alice, Manchester, widow. A Aug. 1826
Ann, Manchester, widow. April 1826
Benjamin, Oldham, yeoman. March 1829 (1st grant 1819)
Edward, Milnrow, innkeeper. May 1827
James, Rochdale, innkeeper. A Feb. 1826
James, Newchurch, Rossendale, yeoman. A June 1827 (2nd grant 1847)
James, Toad Lane, Rochdale, card maker. Sept. 1828
James, Standlees, Ashworth, farmer. March 1829
Jennet, Martholme. A Oct. 1829
John, Barnes Green, Blackley, yeoman. April 1826*
John, Winwick with Hulme, victualler. June 1826
John, Sheffield, Rochdale, yeoman. A Aug. 1827
John, Rochdale, innkeeper. March 1829
Jonathan, Whittle-le-Woods, print cutter. March 1828
Joseph, Peplow Hall, esq. A and Tuon April 1828
Joseph, Roundthorn, Oldham, cotton weaver. A Feb. 1829
Joseph, Mumps, Oldham. A July 1829
Mary, Salford, feme covert. A Dec. 1829

Clegg, Mary Ann, Rochdale, widow. A Sept. 1829
Samuel, Spotland, yeoman. Nov. 1827
Samuel, Rochdale, grocer. Jan. 1830
Samuel, Broadway, St. Thomas Southwark co. Surrey, surgeon. A April 1830
Clemens, James, Isle of Man, Lieutenant in the Army. A Dec. 1827 (2nd grant 1832
Joseph, Worsley, miner. Aug. 1827
Clements, John, Liverpool, gent. July 1826
Cleobury, William, Manchester, victualler. Sept. 1829
Clewarth, James, Urnwick, Winwick. A March 1829
Cleworth, Peter, Atherton, cotton manufacturer. July 1826
Cliff, George, Great Bolton, shopkeeper. May 1826
Richard, Liverpool, surgeon. A Jan. 1826
Thomas, Droylsden, calico printer. A March 1830*
Clough, Ann, Manchester, widow. A March 1827
Esther, Manchester, widow. Nov. 1826
Gervase, Abram, yeoman. April 1828
Isaac, Manchester, stone cutter. A June 1826*
John, Rooden Lane, butcher. A Oct. 1826
John, Manchester, gent. April 1828; Dec. 1828 (1st grant 1812, 4th grant 1831)
Richard, Trubsmithy. Nov. 1828
Robert, Ashton-in-Makerfield, yeoman. April 1829
Robert, Failsworth, weaver. April 1830
William, Liverpool, yeoman. March 1828 (1st grant 1814)
Clowes, Jane, Manchester, widow. A Nov. 1827; March 1830
John, Manchester, confectioner. March 1830
Thomas, Chowbent, shopkeeper. July 1828
Cluff, Mary, Prescot, widow. Dec. 1827
Coar, William, Worston, Clitheroe, husbandman. Sept. 1826
Cobham, Alice, Liverpool, gentlewoman. Oct. 1830
Elizabeth, Tib Lane, Manchester. Sept. 1826
Cock, Thomas, Tottenham, co. Middlesex, gent. April 1829
Cocker, Abraham, Wigan, yeoman. Jan. 1827
Elizabeth, Croft, Little Bolton, widow. A Oct. 1830
James, Birtshaw, Crompton, yeoman. Feb. 1827
James, Bolton-le-Moors, yeoman. A April 1829
James, Duckworth, farmer. April 1829
John, Cowlishaw, cotton spinner. Jan. 1828
John, Little Bolton, whitster. March 1828
John, Walton-le-Dale, husbandman. A May 1828
Cockill, Stephen, Audenshaw, yeoman. Nov. 1829
Cockroft, John, Bacup, shopkeeper. Sept. 1826
Cocks, Joseph, Wood St., Salford, yeoman. May 1826 (2nd grant 1835)
Cockshutt, George, Worston, Whalley, farmer. July 1830
Cogswell, Job, Rochdale, innkeeper. Oct. 1829
Colbert, William, Liverpool, mariner. July 1829
Colborne, Margery, Bath St., Liverpool, spinster. A Dec. 1826
Colclough, Thomas, Liverpool, mariner. A Dec. 1828
Cole, Samuel, Liverpool, victualler. A April 1829
Colfox, Hugh, Liverpool, mariner. A Oct. 1828*
Collier, Alice, Worsley, widow. March 1827
Elizabeth, Atherton, widow. Jan. 1829
Jane, Worsley, weaver. June 1827
Richard, Patricroft, grocer. A March 1828

Colligan, James, Liverpool, victualler. July 1830
Collin, Hannah and Martha, Openshaw. A joint will. July 1827
Collinge, Betty, Goodin Lane, Heywood, spinster. Dec. 1829
James, Meadows, Bircle cum Bamford, farmer. March 1826
James, Rawtenstall, shopkeeper. Dec. 1826
John, Parkfield, Middleton, weaver. Nov. 1828
Mary, Collinge Fold. A June 1828
Robert, Siddall Moore, yeoman. Jan. 1829
Collingwood, Thomas, Blackburn, stonemason. Aug. 1830*
Collins, Jane, Liverpool, widow. A Sept. 1829; June 1830
Morris or Maurece, Liverpool, mariner. Jan. 1827*
Peter, Liverpool, warehouseman. A May 1829
William, Liverpool, labourer. A Nov. 1830
Collinson, John, Oldenoat, Oldham. March 1827*
Robert, Wilpshire, farmer. A Dec. 1826
Collis, Benigna, Fairfield, last of Armley, co. York, spinster. A Oct. 1830
David, Fulneck, Leeds, co. York, teacher. A Oct. 1830
Colquhoun, John Wilkinson, Liverpool, merchant. Dec. 1830
Colquitt, William, Liverpool gentleman. Jan. 1827
Compton, James, Barton-upon-Irwell, weaver. A July 1827*
Connee otherwise Conway, Frederick, Liverpool, mariner. A Oct. 1827*
Conning, Catherine, Liverpool, widow. A Sept. 1829
James, Liverpool, tailor. A April 1830
John, Liverpool, gent. Feb. 1828
Connolly, Joseph, Liverpool, cooper. A March 1828*
Connor, Thomas, Cork, Ireland, mariner. June 1828
Consterdine, Robert, Middleton, farmer. July 1829
Conway, Frederick, *see* Connee
George, Rochdale, wool seller. Aug. 1829
Mary, Toxteth Park, spinster. A May 1827*
Peter, Liverpool, file cutter. April 1828
William, Liverpool, mariner. A Aug. 1830*
Cook, Isaac, Bolton-le-Moors, weaver. A Nov. 1830
Robert, Padiham Green, Hapton, farmer. April 1826
Sarah, Longford, spinster. A Dec. 1827
Tabitha, North Meols. A Sept. 1828
Cooke, Abraham, Denton, hatter. May 1827
Alice, Denton, widow. May 1826
Ann, Moorside, Flixton, widow. July 1830*
Elizabeth, Middleton, feme covert. Aug. 1829
Elizabeth, Hooley Hill, widow. Nov. 1830
James, Salford, drysalter. June 1830
John, Liverpool. March 1827
John the elder, Mellor, yeoman. Oct. 1830
Joseph, Greenacres Moor, Oldham, weaver. June 1830
Mary, Patricroft, widow. March 1830
Sarah, Liverpool, widow. Dec. 1826
Thomas, Rowe Green, Eccles, yeoman. July 1827*
William, Worsley. Aug. 1827
William, Middleton, gent. Jan. 1830*
William Goddard, Denton, hat manufacturer. Oct. 1829
Cookson, Anthony, Penwortham, farmer. April 1830
Catherine, Holmes, Tarleton, widow. April 1829

Cookson, Robert, Manchester, coach proprietor. A May 1829
Thomas, Cronton, blacksmith. May 1827
Coombes, Mary, Walton Hall, Liverpool, housekeeper. Jan. 1828
Coop, Betty or Elizabeth, Cheetham. May 1830
Cooper, Alice, Walton-le-Dale, spinster. April 1826
Elizabeth, Liverpool, nuncupative will, Feb. 1830*
James, Liverpool, block maker. A Jan. 1827
James, Manchester, gent. April 1830
John, Wigan, gardener and seedsman. July 1827
John, Wigan, farmer. A July 1829
John, Bickerstaffe, farmer. A Oct. 1829
Joseph, Salford, letterpress printer. July 1829
Joseph, Quarlton, farmer. Jan., 1830 (1st grant 1821)
Leonard, Pendleton, merchant. Jan. 1828
Martha, Manchester, widow. Sept., 1827
Mary, Balderstone, Rochdale, widow. A Feb. 1826
Richard, Over Darwen, blacksmith. Feb. 1829
Richard, St. Helens, butcher. Nov. 1830 (2nd grant 1850)
Sarah, Chorlton Row, spinster. Aug. 1829
Thomas, Blackburn, weaver. May 1830*
Thomas, Manchester, labourer. A Oct. 1830*
William, Rumworth, farmer. A Jan. 1826
William, Liverpool, draper. A Oct. 1827
Cooten, Ann, Tarleton, widow. March 1829*
Cope, James, Madeley, co. Staffs., gent. April 1830
Copeland, Michael, Liverpool, publican. Feb. 1829
Copley, John, Liverpool, mariner. A Sept. 1826*
Copp, John, Ashton-under-Lyne, manufacturer. June 1826
Coppock, Mary, Manchester, widow. A Dec. 1829
Corby, Joseph, *see* Howe
Cordwell, Elizabeth, Manchester, dressmaker. Nov. 1830
William, Park House, Pendlebury, labourer. A Dec. 1828 (1st grant 1823)
Cork, Sarah, Warrington, widow. Jan. 1830
Corless, Margaret, Salford, widow. Aug. 1829
Corns, Lawrence, Manchester, victualler. A Oct. 1826
Corran, Margaret, Liverpool, widow. A Nov. 1830
Corrin, Samuel, Liverpool, cooper. A April 1827*
Corris, Caesar, Peeltown, Isle of Man, merchant. June 1827
Corry, Bridget, Preston, feme covert. A Aug. 1829
Cotgreave, Frances, Warrington, widow. March 1828
Cotham, Winifred Maria, Eccleston. A and Tuon Nov. 1829 (later grants 1839, 1846 and 1848)
Cottam, John, Moss Lane, farmer. Aug. 1828
Thomas, of the Prince Regent of Liverpool, mariner. A Aug. 1826*
Cotter, John, Toxteth Park, plasterer. May 1830
William, Liverpool, joiner. June 1827 (2nd grant 1832)
Coulthard, George, Liverpool, mariner. A March 1830
Counce, William, Horwich, warehouseman. June 1830
Coup, Mary, Stoops, Habergham Eaves, spinster. Feb. 1828
Coupe, Ann, Osbaldestone, widow. A Nov. 1826*
Ann, Mawdesley, widow. April 1828
John, Holden, Haslingden, farmer. A Oct. 1827
Richard, Chapel Lane, Hoghton. Jan. 1826

Coupland, James, Ormskirk, yeoman. A Jan. 1829
Margery, Scarisbrick, spinster. May 1829
Court, Thomas, Blackburn, weaver. April 1828
Covell, James, Liverpool, bookkeeper. April 1826
Coventry, Edward, Liverpool, parish clerk. Jan. 1826
Jenny, Liverpool, spinster. April 1829
Ralph, Liverpool, rope maker. Dec. 1828
Cowban, James, Blackburn, grocer. June 1828
Cowburn, John, Livesey, farmer and grocer. March 1827
Cowell, William, Wigan, yeoman. Aug. 1830
Cowen, Edward, Liverpool, cooper. A Feb. 1830*
Cowley, William, Fairfield, architect and builder. Sept. 1826
Cowpe, Jenny, Pippins Bank, Bacup, spinster. A April 1828
John, Newchurch, Rossendale, weaver. Jan. 1826*
Thomas, Mellor, yeoman. April 1827 (1st grant 1819*)
Cowper, Solomon, Blackleach, Saddleworth, stonemason. A Aug. 1826
Cowsill, William, Manchester, bricklayer. Oct. 1827
Cox, James, London, gent. A June 1826
Coxhead, Alice, Ormskirk, widow. Dec. 1830
Crabtree, Abraham, Liverpool, umbrella manufacturer. March 1830
George, Top of Ridge, Burnley. March 1828
Hannah, Todmorden, spinster. Nov. 1826
Henry, Liverpool, dyer. April 1830
John, Denton, Manchester, husbandman. Aug. 1826
John, Ashton-under-Lyne, joiner. Feb. 1830
Cramer, *see* Creamore
Crampton, Mary, Little Bowland, spinster. Aug. 1830
Cramsie, John, Manchester, bricklayer. A Jan. 1830
Crane, Emma, Liverpool, widow. Nov. 1826*
Joseph, Liverpool, gent. March 1827
Craston, Edward, Oldham St., Manchester, shoe dealer. Jan. 1830
Craven, Elizabeth, Liverpool, widow. Oct. 1829
William, Bolton-le-Moors. March 1827
Crawford, Ralph, Preston, gent. Oct. 1829
Crawshaw, James, Tottington, schoolmaster. Aug. 1826
Jonathan, Church, calico printer. A Nov. 1828
Creswell, Ralph, Manchester, gent. A Nov. 1828
William, Manchester, gent. Jan., 1828 (2nd grant 1839)
Crichton, John, Manchester, butcher. A Dec. 1828
Crick, Alice, Liverpool, widow. Nov. 1828
Crighton, George, Manchester, machine maker. A Mar. 1827
Crisp, Mary, Liverpool, spinster. A May 1827
Critchley, Grace, Westby, widow. A June 1826
Thomas, Whiston, farmer. Aug., 1830 (2nd grant 1848)
Critchlow, Robert, Litherland, victualler. Sept. 1829
Croasdale, Henry, Livesey, husbandman. Aug. 1829
Croft, Henry, Liverpool, soap boiler. Oct. 1827
James, Lower Darwen, yeoman. Sept. 1830
John, Manchester, merchant. A Dec. 1828
Thomas Dobson, Wigan, surgeon. Nov. 1828
Crompton, Ann, Oldham. A Aug. 1830
David, Liverpool, hatter. A Aug. 1827
Henry, Westhoughton, yeoman. Dec. 1829

Crompton, James, Tongue Hall, farmer. A Dec. 1828
Robert, Farnworth. July 1827
Robert, Salford, gent., Aug. 1828
Sarah, Bolton, widow. Feb. 1829
Stamford, Liverpool, gent. A Oct. 1830
Thomas, Bolton-le-Moors, butcher. A Jan. 1826
Thomas, Manchester, gent. Nov. 1826 (1st grant 1822)
Thomas, Bury, organist. Aug. 1827
William, Bury, sexton. Nov. 1828 (2nd grant 1860)
William Richard, Rose Hill, Bolton-le-Moors, paper maker. A Feb. 1827
Cronkshaw, John Lower Eaves, Tottington Higher End, Bury, weaver. A Jan. 1826
Crook, Hugh, Brindle, farmer. Oct. 1828
Joseph, Blakow Hill, Barrowford Booth, yeoman. Sept. 1826
Robert, Longworth, Bolton-le-Moors, farmer. A March 1830
Crookall, Thomas, Wrightington, farmer. Oct. 1827
Crooke, James, Manchester, drysalter. July 1830
Nicholas, Liverpool, warehouseman. Nov. 1827
Cropper, Abraham, Hargreave Fold, Rossendale, yeoman. Aug. 1827
James, Further Hill, Rossendale, farmer. Oct. 1826
Matthias, Mawdesley, farmer. A Aug., 1827 (2nd grant 1846)
Crosby, Robert, West Derby, shoe maker. June 1829
Crosdale, Mary, Little Bolton, spinster. Feb. 1827
Crosfield, Samuel, Manchester, woollen clothier. July 1830
Croshaw, Thomas, Pilsworth, farmer. March 1830
Crosier, Robert, Chorlton Row. July 1827
Cross, Elizabeth, Hardshaw, Windle, spinster. A March 1826
Elizabeth, Hardshaw, widow. March 1826
Ellen, Winwick, widow. Aug. 1826
Henry, Kearsley, shopkeeper. Dec. 1829
Jane, Lily Hill, Pilkington, last of Darcy Lever, widow. Oct. 1827
John, Liverpool, timber merchant. A Feb. 1827
Mary, Hardshaw, spinster. March 1826
Nicholas, Hardshaw, shoemaker. A March 1826
Ralph, Langtrey, Standish. April 1829; Nov. 1829
Richard, Ulnes Walton, husbandman. Oct., 1828
Tabitha, Liverpool, spinster. Will and Tuon Feb. 1830
Thomas, Liverpool, yeoman. Oct. 1826 (2nd grant 1876)
William, Hardshaw, labourer. A Jan. 1826
Crossland, Robert, Liverpool, innkeeper. Sept. 1826
Crossley, Betty, Chorlton Row, spinster. Oct. 1826
Charles, Newhey, Rochdale, Oct. 1827
James, Newroad, Rochdale, woollen manufacturer. July 1826
John, Catley Lane Head, yeoman. Oct. 1828
John, Bullshead, Whalley. Jan. 1830
Thomas, Moston, farmer. A March 1826 (2nd grant 1852)
Croston, Mary, Bickerstaffe, spinster. Feb. 1827
Crouchley, James, Poulton. A May 1826
James, Poulton with Fearnhead, farmer. May 1826
Peter, Poulton with Fearnhead, farmer. A May 1826
Crow, Edward, Liverpool, officer. July 1828
Hugh, Liverpool, mariner. June 1829
Crowder, Mary, Stand Lane, widow. A Nov. 1829
Crowther, Betty, Water Foot, Rossendale, spinster. Jan. 1828 (2nd grant 1844)

Crowther, Emmanuel, Manchester, common brewer. A Jan. 1826
James, Liverpool, gent. March 1830
Nathaniel, Liverpool, mariner. A Nov. 1826
Nelly, Bacup, spinster. July 1826*
Ruth, Liverpool, widow. Nov. 1826
Cruse, John, the merchant ship Clyde, Liverpool, mariner. A March 1828*
John, Liverpool, mariner. March 1828*
Crye, William, Liverpool, mariner and cooper. A May 1828
Cudd, James, Liverpool, mariner. A July 1829
Richard, the brig Neptune, Liverpool, second mate. A Aug. 1827*
Cuite, William, Manchester, bookkeeper. April 1829
Culcheth, Ralph, West Leigh, gent. Sept. 1829
Cullingworth, Elizabeth, Manchester. A Aug. 1830
Culshaw, James, Aughton, gent. March 1830
James, Lathom. April 1830*
John, Lathom, yeoman. Aug. 1826
John, Burscough, wheelwright. Oct. 1826
Cumberbeach, Charles, Senterns Well, Openshaw, hatter. Oct., 1827
Cumming, Henry, Liverpool, merchant. July 1829
James, Liverpool, merchant. May 1827
Cummins, John, Liverpool, victualler. Jan. 1830
Cunliff, Betty, Enfield, Whalley, widow. May 1827
Joshua, Littlemoorhend, Whalley, yeoman. July 1830
Cunliffe, Alice, Middle Hulton, spinster. A May 1829
James, Manchester, widower. A and Tuon July 1826
John, Liverpool, contractor for docks. A Nov. 1827
Curphey, Richard, Liverpool, cooper. March 1828
Curran, Margaret, Liverpool, widow. March 1826
Curry, James, Liverpool, bookkeeper. July 1828
William, Pemberton, glazier. Oct., 1829
Curte, Ann, Chorlton Row, widow. April 1829
Curtis, Thomas, Manchester, fustian shearer. A Jan. 1829
Cutler, Richard, Blackburn, shoemaker. Oct., 1829

DAGNAL, Rachel, Eccleston, spinster. A Jan. 1829
D'Aguilar, Joseph, Liverpool, merchant. Dec. 1829
Margaret, Liverpool, widow. June 1829
Dakin, Frances or Fanny, Liverpool, widow. March 1826
Dale, Joseph, Blackwater St., Rochdale, clogger. A Nov. 1826
Thomas, Manchester, shoemaker. July 1828
William, Heaton Norris, bleacher. A Jan. 1830
Daller, George, Birch of Zell, Switzerland, last of Manchester, merchant. Sept. 1826
Daltera, Jane, Liverpool, widow. Feb. 1826
Dalton, Robert the elder, Manchester, last of Oldham, manufacturer. July 1826
Sarah, Liverpool, last of Middlewich, widow. Feb. 1827
Dandy, Ann, Bretherton, widow. A March 1826
Daniel, William, Manchester, dyer. A May 1828
Daniels, Mary Louisa, Liverpool, spinster. July 1830
William, Cadishead, yeoman. Oct. 1828
Danson, Ellen, Liverpool. A July 1826
Derbyshire, Charles, Rio de Janeiro, Brazil, agent. A March 1830
James, Manchester, hat finisher. March 1828
Darden, William, Haddock, Winwick, collier. A Sept. 1830

Darlington, Benjamin, Manchester. April 1828
Darnbrough, William, Clitheroe, innkeeper. Nov. 1830
Darnton, Sarah, Manchester. A Nov. 1828*
Darwell, Ann, Broughton, Manchester, widow. A Dec. 1829
Darwin, James, Sephton, yeoman. Aug. 1826
Davenport, James, Parade St., Rochdale. Aug. 1826
Jemima, Chorlton Row, widow. Jan. 1829
John, Toxteth Park, gent. April 1828
John, Chorlton Row, gent. Sept. 1829
John, Whitefield, Prestwich. Jan. 1830
Joseph, Rochdale. A June 1827
Peter the elder, Redvales, Bury, wheelwright. Nov. 1830*
Thomas, Radcliffe, farmer. Dec. 1826
Thomas, Manchester or Withington, gent., Sept. 1827
William, Tyldesley with Shakerley, farmer. Feb. 1829
Davidson, John, Chorlton Row, stonemason. May 1828
Davies, Ann, Liverpool, widow. A Jan. 1829*
Ann, Liverpool, widow. Nov. 1830
Bridget, the Lunatic Asylum, Lancaster, spinster. A Jan. 1827 (2nd grant 1834)
Daniel, Liverpool, coachmaker. July 1826
David, Salford, shoemaker. A Oct. 1826
Edward, Liverpool, gent. July 1830
Hannah, Liverpool, spinster. A May 1829
James, Great Crosby, warehouseman. Aug. 1829
John, Liverpool, turner. A Aug. 1826
John, Manchester, druggist. A Feb. 1829
John, Liverpool, mariner. A May 1829
John, Liverpool, yeoman. May 1829 (1st grant 1822)
John, Wavertree, gent. July 1829
John, Liverpool, mariner. A Oct. 1829
John, Liverpool, shoemaker. Dec. 1829*
John, Liverpool, master mariner. March 1830
John, Outwood, Prestwich, weaver. March 1830
John, Liverpool, butcher. A Oct. 1830*
Joseph, Liverpool, rag merchant. Dec. 1826
Joseph, Davyhulme, Eccles, weaver. June 1827
Joseph, Liverpool, officer in the excise. A May 1828
Joseph, Liverpool, bricklayer. July 1828 (2nd grant 1831)
Lowrey, Liverpool. April 1829
Martha, Liverpool, spinster. A March 1826 (2nd grant 1834)
Martha, Brownlow Hill, Liverpool. A Feb. 1830
Mary, Liverpool, widow. March 1829
Owen, Liverpool. May 1830
Peter, Manchester, gent. June 1829
Richard, Bolton-le-Moors, joiner. A Dec. 1827
Richard, Liverpool, picture frame maker. March 1830 (2nd grant 1834)
Thomas, Liverpool, gent. July 1828
Thomas, Toxteth Park, yeoman. Nov. 1830
William, Liverpool, timber merchant. A Jan. 1826
William, Lathom, yeoman. Sept. 1827*
William, Liverpool, mariner. A May 1830*
Dawes, Matthew Con, Bolton-le-Moors, common brewer. Oct. 1828
Dawson, Elizabeth, Edge Hill, Liverpool, spinster. March 1826

Dawson, Elizabeth, Chester, last of Liverpool, spinster. A March 1830
James, Bacup, Rossendale. Dec. 1826
James, Liverpool, cooper. June 1827
Jeremiah, Rooden Lane, Prestwich. Jan. 1827
John, Bury, yeoman. Dec. 1828
John, Windsor Place, Pendleton, gent. May 1830
Joseph, Bolton-le-Moors, weaver. A June 1826
Peter, Liverpool, shipwright. July 1828
Rachel, Rooden Lane, Prestwich, widow. Jan. 1830
Robert, Heskin, Eccleston, husbandman. March 1826
Samuel, Springmill, Oldham, cotton spinner. A Nov. 1827
Sarah, Clitheroe, widow. Feb. 1830*
Thomas, Rochdale, manufacturer. A April 1827
Thomas, Rochdale, innkeeper. Dec. 1827
Thomas, Liverpool, surgeon. April 1829 (2nd grant 1844)
William Primo, Liverpool, mariner. Jan. 1826*
Deakin, George, Heaton, Leek, yeoman. July 1830
Dean, Alice, Great Harwood. A March 1828
Ann, Alston, widow. Dec. 1828*
Betty, Blackburn. A May 1827
Elizabeth, Manchester, spinster. June 1826
James, Manchester, gent. Oct. 1827
Mary, Broughton, spinster. Sept. 1829
Peter, Manchester, commission agent. A Jan. 1829
Thomas, Liverpool, mariner. A Nov. 1826
Thomas, Accrington, house carpenter. Feb. 1827
Thomas, Middleton, weaver. Oct. 1830
William, Edge Hill, Liverpool, gent. April 1828
Deane, Edward, Prescot, gent. A Nov. 1827
Dearden, Charles, Hulme, gent. May 1828
Simon, Brick Field, Rochdale, yeoman. March 1830
Thomas, Walshaw, Bury, cotton weaver. A May 1829
Thomas, Lees, Ashton-under-Lyne, cordwainer. Aug. 1830
Deardin, Joshua, Rochdale, captain in the Lancashire Militia. Jan. 1829
Mary, Manchester, widow. March 1828
Deighton, Lucy, Halliwell, Deane. A Nov. 1829*
Delany, John, Liverpool, bookkeeper. Oct. 1826
Delap, Robert, Liverpool, gent. Jan. 1827
Delisser, Ellis, Liverpool, gent. Jan. 1829
Dempsey, John, Manchester, labourer. A Feb. 1826*
Dennett, Ellen, Birchley, Billinge, spinster. July 1827
Dennison, Alexander, Toxteth Park, master mariner. Nov. 1829*
Robert, Dover St., Piccadilly, co. Middlesex, coal merchant. March 1829
William, Mill St., Liverpool, merchant. Aug. 1830
Dent, John, Burnley, innkeeper. July 1827
Denton, Deborah, Liverpool, widow. April 1828
Valentine, Bolton, victualler. Dec. 1830
Derbishire, Richard, Ashton, gent. July 1829
Derbyshire, James, Tyldesley, weaver. A Dec. 1829*
Mary, Westhoughton, widow. Feb. 1830*
Thomas, Lower Darwen, yeoman. A May 1829
Devaynes, Jane, Liverpool, widow. Sept. 1827
Dewhurst, Alice, Blackburn, spinster. Aug. 1830

Dewhurst, Ann, Sark Hill, Blackburn, singlewoman. Oct. 1827*
Edward, Manchester and Salford, calenderer. Feb. 1826
Hugh, Ingol Lodge, Ingol, gent. Dec. 1830
James, Mellor, farmer. A Nov. 1828 (2nd grant 1837)
James, Blackburn, yeoman. March 1830*
Jane, Blackburn, spinster. A Aug. 1827
Joseph, Ashton-under-Lyne, weaver. April 1827
Mary, Blackburn, spinster. A July 1828
Thomas, Chorley, designer. A Dec. 1830
Dickey, Ann, Liverpool, widow. July 1829
Dickenson, James, Liverpool, grocer and flour dealer. May 1826*
Dickins, Elias, Castleton. May 1828
Dickinson, James, Liverpool, sailmaker. June 1830
James, Manchester, bricklayer. June 1830*
Jane, Liverpool, spinster. March 1829*
Lawrence, Formby. Oct. 1827
Mary, Ormston Lodge, Barton-upon-Irwell, spinster. A Nov. 1826
Ralph, Liverpool, victualler. Oct. 1826
Rebecca, Upholland, widow. A July 1826
Dickson, James, Liverpool, merchant. A July 1827
James, Liverpool, merchant. A Nov. 1828
Diggles, Ann, Liverpool, feme covert. A March 1829 (2nd grant 1854)
James, Bolton, manufacturer. June 1827
James, park gardener and tenant on Earl Wilton's estate (Heaton Park). Nov. 1827*
Peter, Bolton-le-Moors, manufacturer. A Dec. 1830
Robert, Harrington, Liverpool, gent. April 1829
William, Prestwich, farmer. Feb. 1826
Dillen, Joseph, Liverpool, mariner. March 1827*
Dipnall or Dispnall, Henry, Liverpool, mariner. A Nov. 1826
Ditchfield, Charles, Hindley, manufacturer. A April 1826
Peter, Hindley, gent. April 1830 (2nd grant 1871)
William, Newton. March 1828
Dixon, George, Bolton-le-Moors, cabinet maker. A Nov. 1828
James, Little Bolton, machine maker. Dec. 1827
Michael, Liverpool, mariner. A Sept. 1828*
Richard, Haslingden, school master. Aug. 1827
William, the ship Walter Scott, sailor. A March 1830*
Dobson, Cuthbert (commonly called John), Hulme, gent. Feb. 1826
Richard, 41st Regt. of Foot, sergeant major. A and Tuon May 1828
Dodd, Margery, Great Bolton, widow. Feb. 1826
Dodson, Robert, Bolton-by-the-Sands, gent., Jan. 1830
Domville, William, Warrington, carpenter. A Dec. 1828
Donathan, Thomas, Nassaw, New Providence, N. America, merchant. A Sept. 1830
Donbavand, Thomas, Liverpool, bookkeeper, Aug. 1828
Thomas, Orford, yeoman. Oct. 1828
Donelly, Peter, Liverpool, tailor and draper. A April 1827
Donovan, John, Liverpool, ship agent. A Jan. 1828
Doran, Felix, Liverpool. Jan. 1828
Mary, Liverpool, widow. May 1829
Dorning, Joseph, Culcheth, yeoman. A Oct. 1828
Douglas, James, Island of Jamaica, last of Wigtown, North Britain, esq. Nov. 1826
Douglass, William, Liverpool, mariner. A Sept. 1829
Dovey, William, Liverpool, anchorsmith. May 1826

Dow, John, Chorlton Row, traveller. A Sept. 1828
Downes, John, Reddish, yeoman. Feb. 1829
Downward, Charles, Manchester, grocer. A Dec. 1829
Doyle, James, of the H.M. Margaret, Liverpool, mariner. A Oct. 1827*
Dracup, Rachel, Salford, widow. A March 1828
Dransfield, Richard, Oldham, cotton spinner. A March 1829
Draper, William, Maghull, farmer. May 1829
Drew, William, Warrington, draper. A Feb. 1830
Drinkwater, John, Everton, gent. Nov. 1829
Driver, Henry, Manchester, shopkeeper. Nov. 1829
Dronsfield, Robert, Hopkin Mill, cotton spinner. A Sept. 1828 (1st grant 1822)
Drury, Hannah, Salford, widow. Nov. 1829*
  Robert, Rumworth, labourer. A May 1828
Ducker, John, Liverpool, joiner. Jan. 1827
Duckworth, James, Lower Darwen, weaver. Jan. 1826
  James, Clitheroe, farmer. A April 1828
  John, Haslingden, woollen weaver. April 1828
  John, Flaxmoss, weaver. May 1828
  Joseph, Hopwood, shopkeeper. A March 1829
  Lawrence, Stubbins Lane, Tottington Lower End, Bury, weaver. A Sept. 1826 (2nd grant 1856)
  Richard, Wigan, yeoman. May 1828
  Robert, Bury, innkeeper. Dec. 1828
  Thomas, Hargreaves, Rossendale, bleacher. March 1827 (2nd grant 1834)
  Thomas, Blackburn, innkeeper. Oct. 1827*
Dudson, William, Little Heaton, publican. A March 1830
Duerden, Robert, Sabden, Pendleton, farmer. Sept. 1829
Duff, James, Manchester, drysalter. July 1826
Duffey, Francis, Liverpool, mariner. A July 1828
Dugdale, Isabella, Liverpool, widow. May 1827
  John, Great Harwood, yeoman. Sept. 1826
Dumbell, Thomas, Rochdale. May 1828
  William, Liverpool, saddler. Nov. 1829
Dumvill, Nathaniel, Hollinwood, Prestwich, husbandman. Oct. 1826
Dunbabin, Daniel, Warrington, publican. A March 1826
Duncan, George, Liverpool, mariner. A Dec. 1830*
Duncuft, James, Hollinwood, merchant. A April 1826
  John, Collier Hill, Oldham, yeoman. Feb. 1829
Dunderdale, Mary, Walton-le-Dale, spinster. A April 1829
Dunne, William, Liverpool, officer in the Customs. A Aug. 1828
Dunning, Grace, Chorlton Row, widow. A Oct. 1830
Dunstan, Thomas, Salford, governer of the New Bailey prison. Dec. 1826
Durning, William, Edge Lane, West Derby, esq. Sept. Oct. and Dec. 1830
Dusnap, John, Ollerseat, Glossop, co., Derby, farmer. A Dec., 1829
Dutton, Charlotte, Hulme, spinster. Oct., 1826
  John, Golborne, Winwick, farmer. March 1826
  Joseph, Manchester, machine maker. March 1826
  Samuel, Seymour St., Liverpool, clerk in the Customs. A June 1826
  Thomas, Mill Hill, Little Bolton, gardener. March 1826
  William, Liverpool, gent. A Jan., 1828
Duxbury, Betty, Halliwell, Deane. A Oct. 1826
  James, Tottleworth, Rishton, yeoman. Aug. 1830
  Ridehalgh, Lower Colne, innkeeper. May 1828

Dwyer, Mary, Liverpool, widow. March 1826*

EARLAM, John, Partington, yeoman. March 1829
Earle, John, Liverpool, corn and flour dealer. A Jan. 1828
Earnshaw, Abraham, Shawforth, Rochdale, cotton weaver. July 1830
James, Pilkington, yeoman. Oct., 1828
Richard, Liverfold Herley, Rochdale, weaver. Oct. 1830
Thomas, Liverpool, engraver. March 1829
East, Robert, Yate Bank, Blackburn, farmer. A Feb. 1830
Eastham, Richard, Rochdale, cabinet maker. A Dec. 1828
Eastwood, Robert, Cuerden, yeoman. Sept., 1828
William, Blackburn, coal merchant. A Oct., 1829*
Eatock, Timothy, Horwich, gent. May 1830
Eaton, Joseph, Wrightington, publican. Aug., 1828
Margaret, Warrington, spinster. June 1829
Mary, Liverpool, spinster. June 1826
Roger, Manchester, confectioner. Jan., 1827
Eatough, Thomas, Churchkirk, innkeeper. A June 1826
Ebrey, William, Manchester, yeoman. Feb., 1827
Eccles, Bella, Liverpool, servant. Feb., 1829
Edmund, Blackburn, weaver. A June 1828
Elizabeth, otherwise Betty, Blackburn, widow. April 1826
Hesketh, Liverpool, cooper. A April 1829
Joseph, Liverpool, plumber. Nov., 1827
William, Over Darwen, cotton manufacturer. A June 1830
Eccleston, Jonathan, Liverpool, potter. A Oct., 1826
Eckersley, Joseph, Astley, farmer. A Nov., 1827
Peter, Tyldesley, last of Oulton Park, yeoman. Jan., 1830
Thomas, Clifton, Eccles, servant. Feb., 1827
Ecroyd, Samuel, Frierhill, Accrington. May 1826*
Eddowes, Mary Ann Esther, Manchester, spinster. Oct., 1826
Eden, Thomas, Scarisbrick, yeoman. April 1829
Edensor, William Johnson, Manchester, merchant. A May 1829
Edge, Hannah, Buxton, co. Derby, widow. Sept., 1830
James, Spitalfields, London. A June 1826*
Richard, Chowbent, Atherton, cordwainer. Jan., 1830
Edleston, Daniel, Livesey, yeoman. May 1826
Esther, Windle, widow. April 1826*
John, Blackburn, yeoman. A June 1826
John, Dilworth, yeoman. May 1830
Edmondson, William, Townley Park, labourer. Jan., 1829
Edmundson, John, Blackburn, yeoman. June 1829 (1st grant 1823*)
William, Chirge, yeoman. Oct., 1828
Edwards, Ann, Liverpool, servant. June 1827
Betty, Coniston, servant. March 1830
Edward, Liverpool, surveyor. Aug., 1826
Edward, Liverpool, mariner. A Aug., 1826 (2nd grant 1834)
Edward, Liverpool, porter. Dec., 1830
Frances, Collyhurst, Manchester, spinster. Sept., 1830
Henry, the brig Mary, Liverpool, mariner. Aug., 1827*
Henry, Manchester, smallware manufacturer. Dec., 1829
Jane, Harrington, Liverpool, widow. A Oct., 1830
John, Blackley, gent. Oct., 1827

Edwards, John, Liverpool, hosier. A Dec., 1829
John, Liverpool, ironfounder. A Aug., 1830
Mary, Liverpool, widow. Jan., 1828
Owen, Salford, joiner. June 1830*
Shem, Warrington, tailor. April 1829
William, Liverpool, yeoman. Aug., 1826*
William, Wavertree, yeoman. Sept., 1828
William, Manchester, merchant. Jan., 1829
Eggleston, Ann, Chatburn, widow. A Jan., 1826
John, Rochdale, excise officer. A April 1829
Eglinton, Richard, Manchester, gent. A Dec., 1826
Eley, George, Toxteth Park, stonemason. March 1826. Original will to York
Ellenthorp, Richard, Shorrockhey, gent. A Oct., 1828
Ellill, William, Blackburn, gent. May 1830
Ellingthorp, Mary, Pleasington, widow. Oct., 1827
Ellinthorpe, Joseph, Everton, gent. July 1829 (2nd grant 1850)
Elliott, Thomas, Liverpool, gent. Nov., 1830
William, Manchester, pawnbroker. Aug., 1829
Ellis, Edward, Liverpool, cooper. April 1829 (2nd grant 1837)
Jane, Trent, Colne, feme covert. April 1829
John, Liverpool, cowkeeper. May 1826 (2nd grant 1838)
Peter, Liverpool, mariner. Feb., 1830*
Sarah, Liverpool, widow. A April 1828
William, Liverpool, tide waiter. Aug., 1829
Ellison, Charlotte, Liverpool, spinster. July 1828
George, Huyton, yeoman. April 1830
James, Bickerstaffe, yeoman. May 1828
John, Winstanley, farmer. A Feb., 1826
John, Liverpool, gent. March 1826
John, Liverpool, boat builder. Aug., 1827
Joshua, Windle, husbandman. Oct., 1828
Margaret, Widnes. A June 1828
Richard, Liverpool, victualler. A April 1827
Richard, Liverpool, gent. April 1829
Else, John, Church Lane, Castleton. Nov., 1830
Elson, Samuel, Coldhurst, Oldham, yeoman. July 1826
Eltoft, John, Burnley, gent. Aug., 1826
Elton, Jane, Edenfield, Bury, spinster. A Aug., 1826*
Emberton, Daniel, Barton-upon-Irwell, victualler. A Oct., 1826
Emerson, Esther, Blackford Bridge, Bury, widow. A Aug., 1826
James, Blackford Bridge, Bury, weaver. A May 1826; Sept., 1826
Emett, Michael, Liverpool, Wesleyan methodist preacher. Aug., 1829
Richard, Liverpool, farrier. June 1826
Enfield, Mary, Nottingham, widow. June 1830
Entwisle, James, Bolton-le-Moors, weaver. A Nov., 1826
John, Brindle, yeoman. Dec., 1827
John, Chapel Field, Prestwich, weaver. A Nov., 1829 (2nd grant 1841)
Moses, Edgeworth, labourer. A April 1829
Thomas, Manchester, warehouseman. A Feb., 1829
Thomas, Windy Harbour. April 1829
Entwistle, Richard, Wigan, gent. March 1828
Thomas, Turton, farmer. Nov., 1828
Ercks, Henry, Liverpool, sugar refiner. A Oct., 1827

Ernest, Henry, Liverpool, mariner. March 1828*
Eshworth, Edmund, Salford, coal dealer. Dec. 1826*
Etchells, Richard, Heaton Norris, artist. July 1830
Ethelston, Charles Wicksted, Fellow of Collegiate Church, Manchester and rector of Worthenbury. Sept. 1830
Evans, Charles, Manchester, painter. Dec. 1830
Edward, Cornhill, Liverpool, labourer. Sept. 1826
Elizabeth, Warrington. Oct. 1828
Evan, Liverpool. Feb. 1827
Evan, Liverpool, liquor merchant. July 1828
Hugh, Liverpool, mariner. Jan. 1828
John, Liverpool. Dec. 1828
John, Manchester, yeoman. March 1830
John, Liverpool, mariner. A Oct. 1830*
Margaret, Liverpool, spinster. April 1827
Mary, Liverpool, widow. A May 1829
Paul, Liverpool, cork cutter. Nov. 1829
Peter, Liverpool, warehouseman. A Aug. 1828
Richard, Manchester. July 1827
Samuel, Liverpool, cooper. A Jan. 1829
Thomas, Manchester, house painter. Jan. 1828
Thomas, Stayley Bank, Ashton-under-Lyne, gent. Sept. 1829 (2nd grant 1869)
Thomas, *see* Richardson, John
Thomas Jenkins, Liverpool. A May 1829
William, Liverpool, mariner. A Feb. 1830
Evanson, Bridget, Derby, spinster. June 1830
Dorothy, Derby, spinster. April 1830
William, Warrington, grocer. A Oct. 1827
Everard, Patty, Liverpool, spinster. Nov. 1827
Everington, John, Lower Cleggs Wood, farmer. A Feb. 1829
Everson, John, Liverpool, victualler. Nov. 1826
Evison, Samuel, Salford, pattern maker. Oct. 1830
Eyles, George, Liverpool, mariner. A Aug. 1830*
Eyres, Joseph, Liverpool, butcher. March 1826

FAIRBROTHER, Robert, Salford, agent. April 1827
Thomas, Bradshaw, Bolton, innkeeper. A May 1827
Fairclough, Ann, Knowsley, widow. April 1827
Ann, Ormskirk, widow. Sept. 1830
Ellen, Ormskirk, widow. A Aug. 1828
Hugh, Leyland, bricklayer. June 1830
James, Hindley, joiner. May 1826
Mary, Ormskirk, spinster. Dec. 1830
Robert, Liverpool, merchant. A June 1827
Thomas, Tarleton, farmer. Dec. 1828
William, Scarisbrick, yeoman. Sept. 1826
William, Scarisbrick, husbandman. A Nov. 1827
William, Blackrod, carpenter. A May 1828
Fairhurst, Hugh, Liverpool, druggist. A July 1830
John, Warrington, cabinet maker. Sept. 1830
Joseph, Warrington, painter. June 1830
Fairweather, Robert, Liverpool, banker. A July 1828
Falder, Jonathan, Liverpool, linen draper. A April 1828

Falkener, James, Green Lane, Droylsden, hatter. A May 1827
Falkner, Edward, Fairfield. Jan. 1826 (2nd grant 1857)
James, Stretford, yeoman. March 1827
Fallows, Margaret, Stretford, spinster. July 1829
Philip, Manchester, weaver. A July 1828
Fargher, William, Liverpool, shipwright. Jan. 1830
Farington, Henry, Polygon, Manchester, esq. June 1827
Farmer, Thomas, Manchester, shopkeeper. April 1830
Farn, Joseph, Manchester, labourer. A Feb. 1827*
Farnworth, John, Heath Charnock, farmer. Jan. 1830
Mary, Astley, widow. Oct. 1829
Richard, Astley, yeoman. March 1830
Farquhar, Rose, Liverpool, widow. March 1826
Farrall, Thomas, Cheetham, coachman. Sept. 1826
Farrand, Robert, Oldham, ironmonger. Sept. 1826
Roger, Chorlton Row, gent. March 1830
Farrar, Francis, Billinge. A March 1829*
James, Standlane, Prestwich, gent. Aug. 1827
John, Billinge, check manufacturer. A March 1827
Ralph, Liverpool, fisherman. Dec. 1827
Farrimond, George, Orrell, yeoman. Nov. 1827
James, Billinge, delfman. July 1830
Jane, Wigan, spinster. Jan. 1826
Farrington, Henry, Pennington, yeoman. Nov. 1827
Richard, Lathom, gent. March 1826
Faulkner, Henry, Liverpool, broker. A Nov. 1828
John, Manchester, joiner. June 1827
John, Flixton, weaver. March 1830*
Nancy, Oldfield Road, Salford. Dec. 1828
Fawcett, Mary, Manchester. A March 1826
Miles, Liverpool, teacher of music. A Sept. 1828
Richard, Oldham, gent. March 1828
Thomas, Oldham, clerk. Jan. 1830 (1st grant 1818)
Fayrer, Edward, Liverpool. March 1827*
Fazackerley, Henry, Townrow, West Derby. March 1827
Fazakerley, Jane, Barbold [*sic*], co. Lanc. widow. May 1826
John, Sollom, Tarleton. June 1830
Mary, Simons Wood, widow. Aug. 1828
Nicholas, Lincolns Inn, co. Middlesex, esq. A Jan. 1830
Thomas, Liverpool, porter. Nov. 1827
William, Pemberton, shoemaker. Feb. 1829
Fearnhead, Mary, Astley, singlewoman. Feb. 1828
Fearnley, Peter, Ashton-in-Makerfield, yeoman. Dec. 1826
Fearns, George, Liverpool, cooper. Nov. 1829
Silvanus, Ashton-under-Lyne, yeoman. Oct. 1828
Fearon, John, Liverpool, doctor in divinity. Feb. 1826 (1st grant 1823)
Fee, John Farrell, Liverpool, victualler. A July 1829
Fell, Henry, West Houghton. June 1827
John, Liverpool. May 1829
Richard, Bolton-le-Moors, cotton spinner and dealer in cotton yarns. April 1826
Robert, Salford, shopkeeper. A Dec. 1826
Susannah, Liverpool, widow. April 1829
Thomas, Tarleton, farmer. A June 1827

Felton, John, Cheetham, gent. A Dec. 1828
Fenn, William, Farnworth. June 1827
Fenton, Alexander, Liverpool, mariner. A July 1829
Dorothy, Chadwick. April 1829
Roger, Birtle cum Bamford, woollen weaver. A June 1830
Fereira, Rodrigues Bernardo, Maranhao, Brazil, merchant. Feb. 1828
Ferguson, John, Bolton-le-Moors, surgeon. A Nov. 1830
Peter, Liverpool, mariner. A Oct. 1830*
Thomas, Liverpool, mariner. A April 1828
Fernley, Hannah, Manchester, widow. Sept. 1826
Fielden, James, Square, Walsden, weaver. April 1829
Fielding, Ann, Royton. A Feb. 1827*
Elizabeth, Bottom of Lane, Rochdale, shopkeeper. A May 1827 (2nd grant 1850)
Henry, Clitheroe, bookkeeper. Dec. 1830
John, Besom Hill, Oldham. A July 1829
Thomas, Pleasington, weaver. Feb. 1826
Fields, James, Manchester, grocer. March 1830
Fiestel, Simon, Manchester, clothes dealer. Oct. 1827
Files, James, Rainford, farmer. May 1829
Finney, Margaret, Warrington, widow. June 1830
Samuel, Ince, weaver. Nov. 1828
Firth, Mark, Dobroyd. A Nov. 1827*
Fish, Edmund, Eccles, victualler. Oct. 1827
Elizabeth, Eccles, widow. A Sept. 1826
Fisher, James, Copy Nook, weaver. June 1828
James, Oldham, innkeeper. Nov. 1830
John, Liverpool, merchant. June 1826 (1st grant 1791)
John, Bretherton, farmer. Dec. 1830
Nicholas, Little Bolton, shopkeeper. Jan. 1830
Rebecca, Rivington, widow. Aug. 1827
Robert, the ship P. Regent, Liverpool, mariner. A March 1828*
Thomas, Liverpool, gent. Sept. 1830
William, Standish, yeoman. Nov. 1828
Fishwick, Webster, Burnley, gent. Jan. 1826
Fitchett, James, Orford, gent. March 1828
Fitton, James, Low Crompton, Prestwich, cotton weaver. A July 1827
James, Spotland Tops, woollen weaver. Dec. 1827
John, Middleton. May 1827
John, Tonge, Prestwich, yeoman. A Feb. 1830
Fitzpatrick, Daniel, Liverpool, mariner. A Sept. 1827*
Fleetwood, Henry, Little Crosby, farmer. April 1829
John, Tarbock, beer brewer. Aug. 1830
Fleming, Ellen, Liverpool, widow. Nov. 1827
James, Liverpool, captain of the Thomas Parsons. A Sept. 1827
James, Liverpool, mariner. A Nov. 1827
Joseph, Blackburn, weaver. A Jan. 1829
Mary, Liverpool, pawnbroker. July 1827
Rooke, Manchester, yeoman. Nov. 1828
Flesher, Catherine, Liverpool, widow. A April 1828
Fletcher, Alice, Redvales, widow. March 1828
Betty, Hollinwood, shopkeeper. June 1829
Charles, Manchester, cotton spinner. March 1829

Fletcher, Elizabeth, Liverpool, widow. A March 1829
Elizabeth, Bury, widow. A Oct. 1830
James, Bottom of Moore, Oldham, innkeeper. Jan. 1829
James, Totting, Bury, farmer. A Dec. 1830
John, Unsworth, Prestwich, yeoman. Oct. 1826
John James, Oldham, hat manufacturer. A Feb. 1829
Joseph, Strangeways, gent. June 1826
Joseph, Newton. March 1828
Samuel, Winton, Eccles, boat builder. June 1830
Stephen, Ainsworth, publican. A Nov. 1827
Thomas, Liverpool, gent. A Nov. 1827
Thomas, Rochdale, sexton. July 1829 (2nd grant 1851)
Thomas, Bury, shoemaker. A and Tuon July 1830
William, Liverpool, tea dealer. A Nov. 1827
Flint, Elizabeth, Leek, co. Staffs. A June 1829
Focke, Maria Eleonora, alias C.E. [*sic*] late wife of Clarel Focke, Geertrinden Burgh, major in the service of the King of the Netherlands. A May 1827
Fogg, Ann, Liverpool, spinster. July 1829
Ellen, Davyhulme, spinster. A Nov. 1830
Rhoda, Pennington, Leigh, shopkeeper. July 1830 (1st grant 1822)
Thomas, Great Bolton, gent. April 1826
Thomas, Haughton, publican. March 1828
William, Bolton-le-Moors, solicitor. A April 1826
Folds, Sarah, Liverpool, spinster. Feb. 1829
Foley, Hugh, Liverpool, coach driver. June 1828
Forbes otherwise Calvert, Margaret, wife of David Forbes, Douglas, Isle of Man, merchant. May 1828
Ford, Catherine, Liverpool, spinster. Feb. 1826
William, West Derby, yeoman. Feb. 1826
William, the Ardent of Liverpool, merchant. A Aug. 1826*
Foretick, Salvator, Liverpool, merchant. A Aug. 1826*
Formby, Henry, Aldcliffe. May 1826*
Jane, Liverpool, widow. Jan. 1827
Forrest, John the elder, Pleasington, yeoman. May 1826
Forshaw, Edward, Much Hoole, yeoman. Sept. 1829
John, Bickerstaffe, yeoman. May 1830
Nathaniel, Liverpool, warehouseman. March 1826
Forster, Hugh, Bromborough, co. Chester, master of the brig Sarah, Liverpool. Jan. 1830
Robert, Bold, widower. A Nov. 1826
Sarah, Bold, spinster. A Oct. 1826
Thomas, Liverpool, confectioner. A Jan. 1827
William, Bold, yeoman. April 1826
Forsyth, Robert, Manchester, publican. July 1830
Foster, Alice, Standish. Feb. 1827
Elizabeth, Penketh, spinster. A Oct. 1828
Henry, Newborough, Lathom, shopkeeper. A July 1827
John, Liverpool, surveyor. May 1827 (later grants 1836, 1853 and 1855)
John, Bury, surgeon. A Dec. 1827 (2nd grant 1882)
John, Rainford, yeoman. April 1828
John, Milnthorp, Heversham, hoopmaker. A and Tuon March 1829
John, Liverpool, porter. A Dec. 1830*
Melicent, Billington (wife of George Foster, plasterer). April 1828

Foster, Peter, Penketh, mariner. June 1826
Robert, Salford, shopkeeper. A Nov. 1827
Robert, Liverpool, coachmaker. May 1828
Foulds, James, Atherton, clogger. A July 1828
Foulkes, Elizabeth, Liverpool, spinster. April 1829
William, Salford, common brewer. March 1830
Fowler, John, Walton-le-Dale, yeoman. May 1829
William, Shevington, yeoman. June 1826*
Fox, Ann, Audenshaw. Nov. 1826
Anthony, Sandy Lane, Royton, heald knitter. Nov. 1828
Edward, Salford, draper. A March 1828
John, Edgeley, Manchester, yeoman. A Jan. 1826
Margaret, Liverpool, widow. April 1829 (2nd grant 1852)
Martha, Port St., Manchester, widow. A Oct. 1826*
Foxley, Samuel, Strangeways, brewer. A Oct. 1826
France, John, Blackburn, gent. March 1828
William, Lostock, Bolton-le-Moors. A Nov. 1829*
Francis, Thomas, Liverpool, waiter. A July 1830*
Francisco, John, Liverpool, cooper and seaman. March 1830*
Franke, Ambrose, Manchester, porter dealer. Feb. 1829
Frekleton, Elizabeth, Manchester. A July 1827
French, Elizabeth, Toxteth Park, widow. A Jan. 1828
Frith, Betty, Warrington, widow. March 1828
Froggitt, Benjamin, Rushton, Manchester, joiner. A Jan. 1826
Frost, David, Hulme, gent. Dec., 1826
Lawrence, Liverpool, merchant. Sept. 1827* (*c.f.* Cheshire wills)
Fryer, Richard, Manchester, agent. May 1827
Furniss, John, Liverpool, victualler. May 1830

GALLAKER, Thomas, Liverpool, mariner. A Aug. 1827*
Gallemore, George, Pough Kepsy, co. Dutchess, New York, brewer. A Jan. 1827*
Galley, Sarah, Liverpool, widow. Feb. 1830
Galloway, James, Liverpool, mariner. A Dec. 1826*
Galway, Isabella Letitia, Liverpool, spinster. April 1828
Gamon, Mary, Liverpool, spinster. July 1830
Gandy, John, Warrington, hosier. April 1829
Thomas, Salford, doctor of physic. Dec. 1830
Gardener, Thomas, Liverpool, painter. March 1830 (1st grant 1816; then Gardner)
Gardner, Mary, Liverpool, widow. A Jan. 1827
Samuel, Salford, gent. Feb. 1826
William, Leasgill, Westmorland, esq. Jan. 1826
William, Manchester, victualler. A Sept. 1826
Garnett, John, Liverpool, attorney. A Aug. 1826
John, Bold, farmer. Nov. 1826 (2nd grant 1853)
Joseph, Rochdale, last of Liverpool, cabinet maker. Oct. 1830
Thomas, Salford, engraver. Oct. 1827
Thomas, Liverpool, soapmaker. Dec. 1829
William, Manchester, stonemason. A Feb. 1829
Garrard, Alice, Westhoughton, spinster. Oct. 1827*
Garrett, Philip, Liverpool, ropemaker. Aug. 1828
William, Manchester, yeoman. Jan. 1826
Garsden, James, Over Darwen, farmer. A Feb. 1829
Garside, Joseph, Ashton-under-Lyne, druggist. Jan. 1829

Garside, Samuel, Ashton-under-Lyne, whitesmith. May 1830
Garstang, Richard, Manchester, warehouseman. Nov. 1827
Garth, Ralph, Little Bolton, yeoman. June 1827
Gartside, Harriet, Preston, spinster. Aug. 1828
Henry, Cross Hall, Chorley, gent. A June 1827
John, Hanging Lees, Rochdale, labourer. A Jan. 1829*
Simeon, Brimmy Croft, West Riding co. York, yeoman. Sept. 1826
Gaskarth, Thomas, Yorkshire St., Wardlesworth, spirit merchant. March 1826
Gaskell, Alice, Wigan, widow. A and Tuon July 1826; March 1827
Ann, Parr, Prescot, spinster. A March 1826
Edmund, Orrell, Wigan, yeoman. Sept. 1827*
Elizabeth, Widnes, widow. Sept. 1829
Henry, Wigan, ironmonger. May 1827 (1st grant 1818)
James, Carr Mill, St. Helens, corn dealer. April 1826
James, Ashton-under-Lyne, badger. Nov. 1829
John, Parr, joiner. A March 1826
John, Warrington, sail canvas manufacturer. Oct. 1827; June 1830
Joseph, Liverpool, publican. Feb. 1827; Dec. 1828
Roger, Warrington, gent. Aug. 1827
Sarah, Parr, Prescot, spinster. A March 1826
Thomas, Warrington, last of Burtonwood, gent. Dec. 1829
William, Liverpool, cart owner. Dec. 1828*
Gaskill, Samuel, Manchester, victualler. May 1827
Gatley, Peter, Manchester, carter. Jan. 1829
Gatliff, James, Liverpool, chief mate. A Jan. 1827
Gauthorp, Robert, Manchester. Oct. 1828
Gawith, George, Liverpool, brewer. A Sept. 1829
Gawthorp, Joseph, Gibhill, farmer. A March 1828
Gee, Ann, Audenshaw, spinster. May 1827
Esther, New House, Castleton, widow. Sept. 1828
James, Hollinwood, Oldham, hat manufacturer. March 1830
John, Brinscall. Sept., 1828
John, Barton-upon-Irwell, yeoman. Feb. 1829
John, Hollinwood, Oldham, hat manufacturer. June 1830
Josiah, Debucca, Africa merchant. A Dec. 1828
Margaret, Barton-upon-Irwell, spinster. Dec. 1830
William, Heywood, gent. Nov. 1828
Gellebrand, John, Manchester, bookkeeper. Nov. 1829
Gent, Edward, Chorley, tailor. A Nov. 1826
John, Manchester, bookkeeper. Aug. 1826
Gerard, John, Liverpool, boot maker. A Aug. 1826
Thomas, Brinsup, Deane. Nov. 1830
Gerrard, Alexander, Anglezark, yeoman. Feb. 1826
Ann, Winstanley, widow. Feb. 1826
Elizabeth, Atherton, spinster. A Jan. 1829
Hugh, Whittle-le-Woods, yeoman. May 1826
John, Tyldesley, yeoman. July 1828
John, Atherton, farmer. Feb. 1829
John, Little Hulton, Deane, shopkeeper. Jan. 1830
Richard, Whittle-le-Woods, farmer. Jan. 1827
Richard, Rainhill, then Eccleston, last of Prescot, gent. April 1827 (2nd grant 1870)
Sir William, New Hall, baronet. Jan. 1827

Gerrard, William, Rumworth, Deane, yeoman. Dec. 1827
Gibbon, James, Manchester, shopkeeper. A Jan. 1828
Gibson, David, Salford, draper. Aug. 1827
Henry, Accrington, yeoman. March 1827*
James, Manchester, publican. A April 1830
John, Haggate, Briercliffe, weaver. May 1829
Kate, Everton, widow. A April 1829
Robert, Mayerscroft, co. Lanc. A Sept. 1830
Wood, Liverpool, merchant. May 1830
Gilbertson, Jane, Ripon, co. York., spinster. Jan. 1830
Mary, Ripon, co. York., spinster. Jan. 1830
Thomas, Burnley, chemist. A Jan. 1830
Gilbody, Ann, Eccles, spinster. A April 1828
Giles, George, Liverpool, tax collector. A Dec. 1830
Gill, Benjamin, Liverpool, coachman. Sept. 1826 (2nd grant 1850)
George, Liverpool, ship chandler. April 1829
John, Liverpool, grocer. June 1827
John, Salford, last of Darlington, co. Durham, innkeeper. July 1829 (2nd grant 1831)
Mary, Bolton, widow. Jan. 1827
Thomas, Liverpool, doctor of physic. A Oct. 1830
Gillbanks, Henry, Liverpool, shipwright. A May 1830*
Gilliard, Jane, Manchester, an infant. A Jan. 1827
Gillibrand, Thomas, Gillibrand Hall, esq. Jan. 1830
Gillis, John, Edge Hill, gent. Nov. 1830
Gillow, John, Liverpool, gent. Sept. 1829
Gleadhill, James, Oldham, cotton manufacturer. A Sept 1829 (2nd grant 1844)
Glease, James, Wigan, yeoman. April 1829
Gleave, Joseph, Manchester, bookseller. Aug. 1828
Robert, Manchester, stationer. A Aug. 1830
Wright, Liverpool, grocer. Aug. 1826
Glendening, William, the ship William Park of Liverpool, mariner. A Aug. 1828*
Glover, Charlotte, Ormskirk, widow. A Feb. 1828*
Elizabeth, Liverpool, widow. March 1830
Ellen, Little Woolton. A June 1830*
Henry, Hardshaw, Windle, clockmaker. May 1829
Isaac, Blackburn, esq. April 1830 (1st grant 1812)
James, Liverpool, victualler. March 1829
James, Wigan, warper. A Dec. 1830
James Irvin, Manchester, yeoman. Oct. 1826
Joseph, Liverpool, ropemaker. April 1830
Thomas, Liverpool, watchmaker. A July 1829
William, Hardshaw, schoolmaster. Aug. 1828
Gobin, Joseph, Burscough. July 1826
Godbert, Margaret, Ormskirk. May 1828
Margery, Hutton, widow. April 1826
Goddard, Jane, Ashton-under-Lyne. A April 1829
Godfrey, Daniel, Liverpool, gent. Oct. 1827
Mary Isabella, Preston. Aug., 1828; Sept. 1828
Thomas, Rusholme, schoolmaster. Jan. 1828
Goldie, Joseph, Liverpool, esq. Jan. 1826
Golightly, Ann, Liverpool, widow. Oct. 1830
Goodall, James, Manchester, carder. March 1826

Goodear, John the elder, Newton, gent. March 1827
Goodfellow, Robert, Salford, gent. Dec. 1828
Goodier, Samuel, Manchester, warehouseman. A Sept. 1828*
  William, Salford, cooper. April 1828
Goodison, Roger, Manchester, butcher. A May 1829
Goolden, Edmund, Catch End Lane, Eccles, yeoman. Dec. 1826*
  Jacob, Dumplington, Barton-upon-Irwell, weaver. May 1826*
Goore, Ann, Harrington, Liverpool, spinster. Feb. 1827
  James, Liverpool, cart proprietor. June 1830
  William, Liverpool and West Derby, esq. Feb. 1830 (2nd grant 1854)
Gordon, Alexander, Atherton, draper. March 1826
  Joshua, Linacre, Liverpool, merchant. Jan. 1829
  Robert, Liverpool, mariner. Dec. 1829*
  Samuel, Oldham, gent. A April 1830
Gore, James, Wrightington, farmer. June 1828
  McHannah, Liverpool, cart owner. May 1830
  Thomas, Rochdale, last of Heaton Norris, gent. Feb. 1830
Goring, Anthony Tristram, Rio de Janerio, Brazil. Aug. 1830
Gorse, Hannah, Haddock, widow. A June 1827*
Gorst, Samuel, Liverpool, biscuit maker. May 1827
  William, Liverpool, gent. A June 1829
Gorstige, Benjamin, *see* Lowe
  William, North Meols, farmer. A Aug. 1827
Gorton, Abraham, Blackburn, innkeeper. Nov. 1829
  John, Marl Earth, Castleton, weaver. Nov. 1826
  Nathan, Lower Place, Rochdale, cotton weaver. July 1827*
  Ruben, Salford, publican. Oct., 1830 (2nd grant 1843)
Gosling, Joseph, Haughton, innkeeper. A July 1830
Goulbern, James, Altcar, farmer. A Sept. 1828
Goulborne, Thomas, Manchester, joiner. A Oct. 1830*
Gould, Harriet, Ardwick, Manchester, spinster. A July 1830
  Mary, Ardwick Place, Manchester, widow. Nov. 1829
Gouldie, John, Liverpool, carpenter. A Feb. 1828*
Gouldin, John, Shevington, yeoman. April 1827
Goulding, William, St. Helens, miller. A May 1827
Gourlay, Margaret, Liverpool, widow. A March 1829
Grace, John, Halewood Green, Childwall, farmer. Sept. 1826
Gradwell, William, Ormskirk, gent. June 1828
Graham, James, Low Hill, West Derby, hide merchant. July 1827
  John, Chorlton Row, millwright. March 1830 (2nd grant 1839)
  Thomas, Manchester, collector of Excise. July 1830
Grainger, Thomas, Liverpool, butcher. A Feb. 1827
Grant, Charles, Barwood Lee, Bury, merchant. A June 1826
  Patrick, Nassau, New Providence, N. America, ship builder. A March 1826
Grason, Thomas, Bolton-le-Moors, yeoman. Sept. 1830 (2nd grant 1831)
Gratly, William, Liverpool, currier. A July 1828
Gratrix, John, Manchester, colour maker. A Feb. 1827
Gray, John, Liverpool, mariner. A Dec. 1826
  John, Manchester, cotton and yarn dealer. July 1827
  Joseph, Hulme, butcher. A Oct. 1830
Grayson, James, Croston, yeoman. May 1828
  William, Rainford, weaver. Nov. 1829
Greatorix, William, Manchester, retail brewer. A Nov. 1829

Greatrix, William, Cross Bank, publican. A March 1828
Greaves, Ann, Prescot, widow. May 1829
Betty, Crompton, widow. A Sept. 1828
Catherine, Liverpool, widow. April 1830 (2nd grant 1847)
Champion, Salford, schoolmaster. A Nov. 1826*
James, Brook Bottom, gent. A Aug. 1828
Jane, Balderstone. June 1827*
John, Thorpes, yeoman. Feb. 1828
John, Mossgrove, husbandman. Nov. 1828
William, Liverpool, livery stable keeper. Dec. 1830
Green, Agnes, Chorley, widow. Oct. 1827*
Alexander, Wigan, yeoman. Aug. 1829
Christopher, Culcheth, yeoman. May 1829
Esther, Horwich, widow. A Nov. 1828*
George, Great Lever, farmer. May 1828
Hatton, Warrington, clerk. May 1830
James, Liverpool, victualler. A Sept. 1830
Job, Reddish, cattle dealer. July 1830
John, Liverpool, pavior. March 1826
John, Culcheth, yeoman. March 1828
John, Lambran, yeoman. Oct. 1828
John, Chorlton Row, engineer. May 1829
John Josephus, Manchester, hosier. April 1829
Sarah, Warrington, spinster. Aug. 1828
Sarah, Liverpool, widow. A Feb. 1829
Thomas, May 1826
Thomas, Leigh, cotton manufacturer. Nov. 1827
Thomas, Westhoughton, yeoman. Nov. 1829*
William, Westhoughton, yeoman. July 1827
William, Prescot, timber merchant. Jan. 1829
Greenall, Richard, Eccleston, Knowsley, yeoman. A June 1829
Greenhalgh, Adam, Bolton-le-Moors. A Dec. 1828; Dec. 1830
Alice, Ainsworth, widow. April 1829
Elizabeth, Great Crosby, widow. Feb. 1828
John, Heywood, pawnbroker. A Nov. 1827
John, Ainsworth, farmer. March 1829
Margaret, Little Bolton, widow. June 1830
Mary, Manchester. Nov. 1828
Robert, Harwood, innkeeper. A Jan. 1830
William, Affeside, Tottington, farmer. A April 1827
William, Chapel House, Rochdale, publican. June 1827
William, Buckley Fold, Bury, yeoman. Nov. 1830
Greenhall, William, Haydock, collier. A April 1827
Greenough, John, Wigan, manufacturer. A Oct. 1827
John, Manchester, schoolmaster. A July 1828
Margaret, Ormskirk, spinster. July 1828
Margaret, Wigan, widow. Dec. 1830
Greenup, Mary, Liverpool, spinster. Feb. 1829
Greenwood, Alice, Liverpool, widow. May 1826
Alice, Water Foot, Rossendale. June 1830*
Ellen, Botthorne, Great Marsden. Aug. 1827
alias Kershaw, James, Shawcross, Rochdale, farmer. May 1827
John, Delph, Saddleworth, gent. May 1826 (2nd grant 1837)

Greenwood, John, Blackhouse Lane, Bury, farmer. Dec. 1827
John, Brownbirks, Whaleley, farmer. March 1830
John, Polefield, Manchester, merchant. Aug. 1830
Joseph, Little Moss, farmer. A Oct. 1829
Richard, Lower Darwen, farmer. Sept. 1827
Richard, Rochdale. Sept. 1828
Greetham, Benjamin, Liverpool, ropemaker. Jan. 1826
Gregory, John, Liverpool, pawnbroker. April 1830
Jonathan, Hax Moss, Aslingden [*sic*], yeoman. A Dec. 1830
Martha, Ormskirk. March 1828
William, Westhoughton, weaver. Aug. 1827
Gregson, Eliza, Liverpool, last of Southport, spinster. May 1830
Harriet, Liverpool, spinster. A Oct. 1830
Jabell [*sic*], Moss Brook Lodge, Widnes, spinster. Jan. 1826
John, North Meols, yeoman. Feb. 1827
Mary, Manchester, spinster. March 1830*
William, a private in the 91st Regt. who died in Jamaica. A June 1829
William, Liverpool, victualler. A May 1830
Gresley, William, Liverpool, surgeon. July 1826
Gresty, James, Chorlton-cum-Hardy, farmer. A Feb. 1827
Greswell, Francis Hague, Denton, clerk. A Feb. 1830
Grierson, Elizabeth, Liverpool, widow. Aug. 1828 (1st grant 1808)
Griffith, Mary, Oldham. A Oct. 1830
Thomas, Warrington, porter dealer. Feb. 1830
Griffiths, Edward, Liverpool, merchant. A Dec. 1828
Hannah, Manchester, widow. July 1826*
Griffith, Liverpool, mariner. A June 1827*
Griffith, Liverpool, ship carpenter. A Dec. 1830*
John, Manchester, brickmaker. May 1827
John, Liverpool, blacksmith. Feb. 1829
Joseph, Manchester, gent. Aug. 1827
Owen, Liverpool, mariner. July 1830
Thomas, Liverpool, warehouseman. A Oct. 1827
Grime, John or James, Salford, cabinet maker. A April 1829(1st grant 1811)
John, New Gate, Shuttleworth. July 1829
Ralph, Little Lever Hall, farmer. Oct. 1826
Richard, Euxton, blacksmith. Sept. 1830
Sarah, Salford, widow. Dec. 1827
Thomas, Scoutfold, Bury, yeoman. July 1826
Thomas, Bradshaw, weaver. A Feb. 1827 (2nd grant 1837)
Thomas, Blackburn, weaver. April 1827
Grimshaw, Elizabeth, Manchester, spinster. Oct. 1829
John, Swinton, Eccles, gardener. A Dec. 1827*
John, Droylsden, weaver. July 1830
Joseph, Hartleys, Manchester, farmer. Jan. 1826 (2nd grant 1833)
Joseph, Newton Heath, farmer. June 1830
Nicholas the elder, Higham, Forest of Pendle, gent. Feb. 1826
Sarah, Manchester, spinster. Feb. 1826
Grindrod, John, Ravenshore, Tottington, shoemaker. A Oct. 1827
John Clegg, Rochdale. May 1828
Mary, Chorlton Row, widow. Jan. 1826
Grisenthwaite, Joseph, Skelmersdale, farmer. A Aug. 1826
Grocock, Benjamin, Hollinwood, Oldham, yeoman. Jan. 1826

Groves, John, Manchester, painter. May 1827
Growros, Kendrick Willhalm, Liverpool, mariner. A July 1828
Grundy, Benjamin, Astley, weaver. A April 1827
David, Tildesley. Sept. 1827
Dennis, Little Heaton, Prestwich, weaver. Jan. 1826
Francis, Rainford, June 1830
George, Everton, gent. April 1827
George, Manchester, publican. July 1827
Grace, Manchester, widow. June 1827
James, Liverpool, salesman. May 1827
James, Little Leaver, Bolton, paper maker. Aug. 1830
John, Barton-upon-Irwell, farmer. Sept. 1829
John, Outwood, Pilkington, gent. Feb. 1830
John, Ringley Bridge, co. Lanc., shopkeeper. Nov. 1830
Joseph, Westhoughton, innkeeper. March 1826
Lydia, Lupton St., Great Bolton, widow. July 1827
Robert, Hurst, Ashton-under-Lyne, cotton spinner. A Jan. 1826
Samuel, Chorlton Row, farmer. Oct. 1830
Thomas, Worsley, Eccles. July 1828
Guest, Ann, Blackburn. Sept. 1827
Christian, Golbourn, spinster. July 1829
George, Liverpool, cow keeper. A Dec. 1830
Robert, Rivington, farmer. A Feb. 1829
Gulliford, Joseph, Manchester, gent. Jan. 1830
Gunnery, Ellen (formerly Webster), Grove House, Liverpool. A June 1830
Gutridge, Thomas, Haydock, yeoman. Nov. 1830
Guy, Jane, Liverpool, widow. A Aug. 1826*
Gwin, Margaret, Liverpool, spinster. A Nov. 1830
Gwyther, Brownlow, Hale, widow. July 1826

HACKEN, James, Winewall, Colne, farmer. Feb. 1829
Hacking, Ann, Cheetham, widow. Oct. 1828
James, Manchester, roper. March 1828
Hackney, Ann, Manchester, spinster. July 1827
Haddock, Margaret, Tarlscough, Ormskirk, widow. Nov. 1829*
Hadfield, Edward, Staley Bridge, corn dealer. Nov. 1830
John, Tom Bottom, Ashton-under-Lyne, farmer. A Aug. 1828
Joseph, Chorlton, labourer. July 1828
Thomas, Eccleston, cotton manufacturer. Will and Tuon April 1830
Hadwen, Joseph, Liverpool, gent. A Sept. 1826
Hagen, John, Liverpool, mariner. A Oct. 1828*
Hague, Joseph, Lords Court, Oldham, weaver. Nov., 1826
Haigh, James, Close, Rochdale, bachelor. A Dec. 1829
Joseph, Liverpool, woollen draper. Sept. 1826
Haighton, Alice, Blackburn, widow. Dec. 1830
Haining, John, Manchester, draper. A Feb. 1830
Hale, John, Maghull, husbandman. A April 1829
John, Leigh, shopkeeper. Dec. 1829
Halewood, George, Middleton Wood, farmer. Sept. 1829
John, Upholland. A June 1829
William, Liverpool, miller. April 1829 (1st grant 1824)
Halket, David, Toxteth Park, shipowner. Nov. 1829
Margaret, Liverpool. A Dec. 1829

Halkyard, Edward, Oldham surgeon. Sept. 1827
Hall, Ann, Blackburn, widow. July 1827
Benjamin, Failsworth, yeoman. April 1827
Christopher, Salford, cotton and twist commission agent. Jan. 1826
Elias, Manchester, coal dealer. Aug. 1826
Elizabeth, Manchester, spinster. Oct. 1828
Elizabeth, Toxteth Park, widow. Aug. 1830
Emery, Salford, widow. A Dec. 1828
Frances, Manchester, spinster. Oct. 1828
George, Manchester, linen draper. A June 1826
George, Manchester, billiard room keeper. March 1829
James, Moorhole, Middleton, yeoman. April 1826
James, Newton, printer. Nov. 1827
James, Cowhill, Chadderton, weaver. A March 1829
Jane, Littlewood, Bury, widow. Aug. 1826
John, Oldham, joiner. A Dec. 1826*
John, Liverpool, labourer. A May 1827
John, Chorley, dyer. A June 1827
John, Tonge, Prestwich, weaver. Nov. 1828
John, Liverpool, glazier. May 1829 (1st grant 1797)
Joseph, Failsworth. A Oct. 1827*
Joseph the elder, Liverpool, pavior. Jan. 1830*
Joseph, Staley Bridge, innkeeper. Nov. 1830
Lawrence, Blackrod, yeoman. Jan. 1830
Lawrence, Barlow Fold, Bury, shopkeeper. March 1830
Mary, Salford, widow. A May 1827
Mary, Manchester, widow. March 1829
Neddy, Rosbottom, clothier. Jan. 1828 (1st grant 1802; original to York)
Richard, Barbadoes, master mariner. April 1827
Richard, Toxteth Park, gent. April 1828
Robert, Davis, Bury, farmer. A Aug. 1827
Samuel, Manchester, liquor merchant. July 1830
Thomas, Wigan, attorney-at-law. A Oct. 1826
Thomas, Rainford, joiner. Dec. 1826
William, Rochdale, shopkeeper. A Jan. 1826
William, Liverpool, mariner. A March 1826
William, Chesham, Bury, yeoman. Nov. 1827
William, Winwick, shopkeeper. July 1829
William, Salford, gent. Nov. 1830
Hallam, John, Manchester, warehouseman. Jan. 1830
Hallas, Robert, Ardwick, dyer. March 1830
Halley, William Paul, Liverpool, agent. A March 1826
Halliday, Alexander, Manchester, porter dealer. A June 1829
Elizabeth, Liverpool. A Nov. 1826
Halliwell, Ellen, Gantley Lane, Billinge, widow. Oct. 1828
George, Bury, groom. March 1830
James, Lincolns Inn, esq. Oct. 1827
James, Bedford, weaver. May 1830
John, Turton, yeoman. Aug. 1826
Margaret, Chorley, spinster. Dec. 1826 (2nd grant 1831)
Matthew, Middle Hulton, collier. May 1828 (1st grant 1781)
Peter, Ince-in-Makerfield, farmer. April 1828
Thomas, Tyldesley, bricklayer. April 1828

Halliwell, William, Manchester, ironmonger. Oct. 1827
Hallsal, Cuthbert, Liverpool, pawnbroker. June 1829
Hallsworth, Henry, Salford, smallware weaver. A Oct. 1826*
Halsal, Daniel, Windle, farmer. A June 1830
Halsall, William, Warrington, liquor merchant. A Nov. 1826
Halstead, George, Oldham, innkeeper. May 1830
James, Colne Field, weaver. A June 1828
Hamblet, Mary, Warrington, widow. April 1827
Hambleton, Mary, Cheetham, widow. Oct. 1829
Hamer, Charles, Chelbourne, Rochdale, yeoman. Oct. 1829
James, Rochdale, innkeeper. Jan. 1826
James, Bolton-le-Moors, weaver and farmer. A Jan. 1827 (2nd grant 1832)
James, Mount Green, Rochdale, yeoman. May 1827
John, Manchester, coal dealer. April 1827
John, Salford, weaver. April 1829
Samuel, Bury, cordwainer. Jan. 1828
Thomas, Harwood, farmer. Sept. 1828
Thomas, Greengate Hill, Middleton, farmer. A Dec. 1830
Hamilton, James, Rochdale, tinplate worker. Oct. 1826
James, Liverpool, merchant. A April 1827 (1st grant 1811)
James, Liverpool, mariner. A Nov. 1827*
Nancy, Rochdale, spinster. A March 1827
Robert, Liverpool, mason. Feb. 1828
Samuel, Liverpool, currier. Jan. 1826
Walker, 23 Brompton Row, Middlesex, esq. Nov. 1828
William, Grays Inn, Middlesex, gent. June 1829
William, Liverpool, joiner. A June 1830
William Augustus, Liverpool, esq. A Jan. 1826
Hamlet, John, Bedford. Feb. 1828
Hammond, Andrew, Liverpool, mariner. April 1826
Francis, of H.M. 37th Regt. of Foot, Cork in Ireland. A April 1827
James, Whitesmithy Bar, Cheetham Hill, nailor. July 1829
Mary, Higginshaw, Royden. A Nov. 1829
Philip, Liverpool, mariner. A Nov. 1826*
Sarah, wife of Francis Hammond of H.M. 37th Regt. of Foot. A June 1827
Hamnet, James, Crumpsall, twist dealer. Aug. 1828
Hampson, Charlotte, Cheetham, spinster. A June 1829
Esther, Cadishead, spinster. A Sept. 1828
George, Broomhouse Lane, Eccles, weaver. A March 1829
Henry, Manchester, manufacturer. A July 1827*
James, Ashton-under-Lyne, gent. A July 1826
James, Stretford, widower. A and Tuon March 1829
James, Horwich, farmer. A July 1830
John, Stretford, farmer. Jan. 1826
John, West Derby, labourer. A March 1827
John, Stretford, yeoman. June 1827
John, Didsbury, yeoman. Nove. 1827
John, Lostock. Jan. 1828
John, Stand Lane, carrier. A July 1829
Joseph, Stretford, farmer. April 1829
Joseph, Wavertree, farmer. April 1829 (2nd grant 1843)
Matthew, Radcliffe, farmer. Jan. 1829
Nancy or Ann, Blackburn, widow. June 1826*

Hampson, Richard, Rumworth, weaver. A Jan. 1826
Richard, Rumworth, weaver. A Jan., 1826
Robert, Cheetham, watchmaker. Dec. 1828
Robert, Manchester, shopkeeper. Jan. 1829
Thomas, Heaton, farmer. A Jan. 1828
Thomas, Crofts Bank, Barton-upon-Irwell, shopkeeper. May 1829
Thomas, Cadishead, weaver. June 1829
Thomas, Outwood, Prestwich, farmer. Oct. 1830
William, Westleigh, yeoman. A March 1829
William, Limehurst, farmer. Oct. 1829
Hancock, Ann, Shetford [?]. A July 1828
Ellen, Farnworth, widow. Oct. 1828
John, Liverpool, merchant. A Sept. 1827; Sept. 1830 (1st grant 1821)
Richard, Monton, Eccles, cotton merchant. April 1827
Handforth, Daniel, Manchester, publican. A Sept. 1829
Handley, Elizabeth, Liverpool. Jan. 1829
George, Chorlton Row, preacher. A Aug. 1828
Handy, William Bevington, Liverpool, mariner. Sept. 1830
Hankey, James, Tarbock, yeoman. Aug. 1828
Hankin, Susan, Ormskirk. A June 1826
Thomas, Lathom, yeoman. July 1828
Hankinson, Alice, Cheetham, widow. A Oct. 1826
Elizabeth, Chorlton Row, widow. Oct. 1827
James, Rixton, Warrington, yeoman. A Jan. 1830
Mary, Barton-upon-Irwell, spinster. A Nov. 1827
Richard, Cheetham, publican. April 1829
Hanley, John, Liverpool, master mariner. Aug. 1828
Richard, Liverpool, mariner. A Sept. 1827
Hanmer, John Marsden, Liverpool, surgeon. Nov. 1828
Thomas, Liverpool, gent. Oct. 1828
Hanna, Ellen, Liverpool. A Feb. 1830
Hannahs, Robert, Manchester, joiner. Sept. 1826
Hanson, Christopher, Roughlee Booth. July 1828 (2nd grant 1852)
John, Lane Side, Great Mearley, yeoman. May 1828
Samuel, Fold, Oldham, warehouseman. A Aug. 1829
Hanway, James, Liverpool, ship broker and passenger agent. Sept. 1829
Harbottle, Michael, Manchester, gent. April 1829
Hardcastle, Francis, Boars Head, Bolton-le-Moors. A June 1826
John, Bolton-le-Moors, innkeeper. Aug. 1829 (2nd grant 1835)
Hardey, Thomas, Didsbury, yeoman. May 1829
Hardie, Henry, Manchester, doctor of medicine. A Jan. 1827
Hardiker, Deborah, Sollom, Tarleton, spinster. July 1827
Harding, George, Liverpool, wine merchant. A Oct. 1829
Thomas, Manchester, shop keeper. Jan. 1829
Thurstan, Liverpool. Aug. 1829
William, Ashton-under-Lyne, shoemaker. June 1827 (2nd grant 1846)
William, Liverpool. May 1830
Hardman, Giles, Clifton, farmer. April 1829
Hannah, Broad ith Lane, Spotland, spinster. Aug. 1827
James, Radcliffe Bridge, tailor. Sept. 1829
James, Barton, cotton carder. A Feb. 1830
James, Steephouse, Branwood, Rochdale, yeoman. July 1830
James, Walmsley, Bury, fulling miller. Nov. 1830
Mary, Clubhouses, spinster. Aug. 1828

Hardman, Richard, Radcliffe, butcher. A Jan. 1826
Richard, Liverpool, wine merchant. Nov. 1826
Richard, Lathom. A June 1829
Robert, Radcliffe Bridge, weaver. A March 1828
Hardwick, Ann, New Richmond, Pendleton, widow. Oct. 1826
Robert, Liverpool, gent. April 1829
Hardy, Anthony, Mossley, Ashton-under-Lyne, joiner. July 1829
Charles, Didsbury, gardener. A April 1826
John, Manchester, joiner. A Feb. 1826
Joseph, Manchester, sawmaker. A Jan. 1828
Hare or Hure, George, Failsworth, shoemaker. A Nov. 1830*
Robert, Liverpool, shipwright. A March 1827
Hargreave, Henry, Carr Hall, Haslingden, gent. Oct. 1828
Hargreaves, Alice, Bacup. Jan. 1828*
Alice, Spear Brow, Blackburn, widow. Dec. 1828*
George, Haslingden, shopkeeper. July 1827
George, Chapel Hill, Rossendale, yeoman. Aug. 1829
Henry, Chatburn, yeoman. Feb. 1827
Henry, Newchurch, Rossendale, gent. May 1830
James, Liverpool, brewer. May 1828 (1st grant 1813)
James, Brenning Croft, Leyland, weaver. A March 1829
James, Blackburn, schoolmaster. A July 1829
John, Scatcliff, Accrington. Nov. 1826
Lucas, Mellor, gent. Sept. 1830
Margaret, Downham, spinster. A March 1830
Mary, Holden, Haslingden, spinster. May 1826
Nancy, Billington, widow. A April 1828
Nancy, Chapel Hill, Rossendale. A Jan. 1830*
Richard, Manchester, publican. Aug. 1826
Richard, Strood, co. Kent, clerk. Feb. 1829
Robert, Scarisbrick, stonemason. May 1828
Susannah, Stafford, widow. March 1826
Thomas, Oak Hill, Blackburn, gent. A June 1826
Thomas, Colne, joiner. June 1827 (1st grant 1803)
Thomas, Chorlton Row, gent. April 1828
William, Southport, gent. Dec. 1826
Winter Ainsworth, Liverpool, brewer. Nov. 1827
Harley, Robert, Liverpool, timber merchant. Nov. 1828
Harlin, John, Kirkdale, Walton-on-the-Hill. A Sept. 1829
Harold, Nancy, Liverpool, spinster. Sept. 1828
Harper, Ann, Liverpool, widow. June 1829
Elizabeth, Cheetham, widow. May 1826
Robert, Ditton, joiner and victualler. April 1829
Harris, John, Manchester, cordwainer. Feb. 1828
Mary, Bury. A April 1826*
Thomas, Liverpool, mariner. A June 1827*
William, Manchester, shopkeeper. Nov. 1827
Harrison, Catherine, Ambleside, feme covert. Feb. 1828
Dorothy, Manchester, spinster. A Dec. 1828
Edward, Liverpool, shopkeeper and widower. A Oct. 1826*
Elizabeth, Tarleton, widow. Sept. 1826
Ellen, Woodhouse, weaver. July 1828
Henry, Liverpool, painter. A May 1826 (1st grant 1822)

Harrison, James, Liverpool, book binder. Sept. 1826
James, Manchester, cotton spinner. Sept. 1826 (2nd grant 1848)
James, Warrington, chair maker. May 1827
James, Bolton-le-Moors, cotton spinner. A Sept. 1828
James, Warrington, gent. A Sept. 1830
John, Alt, Ashton-under-Lyne, yeoman. Jan. 1827
John, Poulton, importer of linen and manufacturer. Jan. 1829
John, Little Hoole, yeoman. April 1830
Joseph, Woodhouse, weaver. A July 1828 (1st grant 1803)
Joseph, Liverpool, warehouseman. A Sept. 1829
Peter, Liverpool, cow keeper. A Nov. 1827
Ralph, Hollingsworth, farmer. A Aug. 1830*
Robert, Toxteth Park, gent. Jan. 1826; June 1830
Robert, Blackburn, weaver. Aug. 1826
Sarah, Manchester, spinster. A Dec. 1828
Sarah, Chorley, last of Southport, widow. Feb. 1830
Thomas, Tarleton, yeoman. June 1826
Thomas, Liverpool, master mariner. Sept. 1826
Thomas, Spring Valley, Isle of Man, esq. March 1827
Thomas, Manchester, yeoman. April 1829
Thomas, Warrington, gent. A Oct. 1829
Thomas, Fairfield, Manchester, shoe maker. Nov. 1830
William, Liverpool, spirit dealer. Feb. 1827
William, Worsley, weaver. Feb. 1827
William, Winstanley, labourer. A Sept. 1827
William, Winstanley, labourer. A June 1828
William, Wilmorleach, weaver. Aug. 1828
William, the ship Reliance, Liverpool, mariner. A Dec. 1828
William, Liverpool, mariner. A May 1829
William, Liverpool, mariner. A Oct. 1829
William, Barrowford, farmer. A Jan. 1830
Harrocks, Hannah, Liverpool, widow. A Jan. 1828
Harrop, Ann, Dodcross, Saddleworth, widow. May 1830
Hannah, Tame Water, Saddleworth. A Nov. 1828
James, Grass croft, yeoman. A Aug. 1826
James, Ashton-under-Lyne, cotton stretcher. A Feb. 1827*
John, Shaws, Saddleworth, clothier. April 1826
John, Hollingwood, weaver. A Feb. 1828
Thomas, Manchester, cotton dealer. Nov. 1827
Harrox, Thomas, London, last of Liverpool, gent. April 1827
Hart, Ann, Halliwell, widow. Oct. 1829
James, Coppull, farmer. A Oct. 1830
John, Liverpool, porter. A Nov. 1826*
John, Wigan. A June 1829
Priscilla, Liverpool, widow. Jan. 1828
Ralph, Great Bolton, innkeeper. April 1830
Sarah, Manchester, widow. Jan. 1830*
Uriah, of the cutter Margaret, Liverpool, surgeon. June 1827
Harte, Samuel, Cadishead, weaver. Feb. 1827
Hartell, Grafton, Liverpool, victualler. Feb. 1830
Hartley, Alice, Manchester, spinster. Oct. 1828
Anthony, Leghale, Trawden, weaver. May 1830
Barnett, Leyland, weaver. Oct. 1829

Hartley, Christopher, Westhoughton, chapman. Feb. 1826
George, Liverpool, victualler. Feb. 1830
Jane, Rochdale, spinster. Oct. 1827
John, Lower White Lee, Pendle, gent. March 1827
John, Blackburn, yeoman. Aug. 1829
Martha, Hulme. A May 1826
Martha, Colne, spinster. A Nov. 1828
Richard, Manchester, publican. July 1829 (2nd grant 1847)
Richard, Bradley, Great Marsden, gent. May 1830
Thomas, Moorend, weaver. June 1828
William, Lane Ends, Little Marsden, heald manufacturer. Aug. 1830
Haselden, Charles, Wigan, whip maker. Feb. 1829
Haskayne, John, Altcar, farmer. Nov. 1830
Haslam, Alice, Harwood, widow. Jan. 1828*
Ann, Great Bolton, spinster. Sept. 1830*
John, Chorley, grocer. March 1826
Thomas, Chesham, Bury, esq. March 1827
Haslehurst, Thomas, Manchester. A Jan. 1826
Hassall, William Thomas, Manchester, pawnbroker. A Nov. 1830
Hastie, Sarah, Manchester, widow. June 1830
Hastings, Grace, Liverpool, widow. March 1826
Hatch, John Godfrey, Liverpool. Nov. 1826*
Richard, Brindle, husbandman. A Jan. 1827*
Hatfield, Hannah, Travis Mill, spinster. March 1828
Hatton, Edward, Dalton, shoe maker. A March 1829
Emma, St. Helens, spinster. A April 1827*
George, Warrington, butcher. Aug. 1826
Jane, Crosby, widow. Sept. 1828
John, Warrington. A March 1827
Joseph, Warrington, butcher. Jan 1828
Richard, Warrington, innkeeper. A Aug. 1828
Thomas, Liverpool, liquor merchant. Feb. 1829
Haughton, John, Levenshulme, yeoman. Aug. 1826
John, Middleton, clerk. A Jan. 1829
Timothy, Manchester, fustian cutter. Aug. 1830
Haw, William, Liverpool, mariner. A Oct. 1828
Hawker, Nicholas, Ainsworth, weaver. A April 1828
Hawkins, Thomas, Liverpool, gent. April 1827
Hawkshead, William, Heskin, gent. May 1826
Hawkyard, Betty, Ashton-under-Lyne. Nov. 1826
Hawley, Robert, Salford, letter press printer. A May 1830*
Haworth, Edmund, Edgeside, Rossendale, farmer. Sept. 1829
Edmund, Tan Pitts, Rishton, yeoman. Dec. 1829*
George, Top of Bank, Rossendale, yeoman. May 1827
George, Chatterton Hey, Bury, gent. Dec. 1827
George, Wear, Rossendale, yeoman. Oct. 1828
George, Bacup, glazier. Jan. 1829
George, Leeches,Shuttleworth, Bury, yeoman. April 1829
Henry, Tunstead, Rossendale, weaver. Dec. 1827
James, Meadowhead, Rossendale, weaver. July 1826
James, Manchester, machine maker. Nov. 1830
Jane, Blackburn. A Sept. 1828
John, Freetown, Bury, labourer. A March 1827*

Haworth, John, Clayton-le-Dale, blacksmith. Sept. 1827
John, Walshaw Lane, Tottington, shoemaker. Dec. 1830*
Lawrence, Park House, last of Holden, Haslingden, gent. March 1829
Mark, Shadworth, shop keeper. July 1829
Matthew, Liverpool, bootmaker, Oct. 1826 (2nd grant 1838)
Matthew, Bury, weaver. A March 1827*
Peggy, Newchurch, Rossendale, spinster. A April 1826*
Peggy, Cockham, spinster. A Jan. 1828
Richard, Cross, Rossendale, yeoman. March 1826
Robert, Liverpool, gent. June 1827
Susannah, Bank Lane, Walmsley, Bury, spinster. June 1827
Susannah, Everton, widow. Oct. 1830
Thomas, Pilkington, labourer. A March 1827*
William, Henburn Bridge, innkeeper. A Sept. 1829
Hay, Alexander, Warrington, minister of the Gospel. Aug. 1827
Haydock, Henry, Blackburn, book keeper. A Sept. 1826
James, Hulton, gent. A July 1827
Nancy, Sevenacre Brook, Blackburn, spinster. A Aug. 1830*
Hayes, Ann, Liverpool, spinster. A Jan. 1826*
Daniel, Liverpool, gent. Nov. 1829
Elizabeth, Liverpool, widow. A Oct. 1827
Elizabeth, Liverpool, widow. March 1828
Elizabeth, wife of Charles Hayes, Dock St., Sulcoates, co. York, surgeon, A June 1829
Hannah, Sankey, spinster. May 1829
Jane, Great Sankey, widow. A June 1828
John, Wigan, coachman. A May 1828
John the elder, Olberdeston, yeoman. A Dec. 1829
Martha, Aughton, spinster. Feb. 1830
Sarah, Manchester, spinster. A April 1826
Sarah, Liverpool. A April 1830
Thomas, Liverpool, victualler. A Aug. 1828
Hayhurst, James John, Blackburn, attorney-at-law. A Nov. 1829 (2nd grant 1833)
John, Clitheroe, wheelwright. Aug. 1827
William, Bank End, Whalley, cutler. June 1830
Hays, Esther, Westhoughton. April 1826
Hayton, Joseph, Mill St., Harrington, export surveyor of Excise. Sept. 1826
Hazeldine, John, Liverpool, master porter. March 1828
Hazelhurst, James, Liverpool, mariner. A May 1829
John, Liverpool, last of Island of Granada, West Indies, stonemason. A May 1829
Hazzlehurst, Elizabeth, Salford, fustian cutter. April 1826
Head, Joseph, Toxteth Park, joiner. Feb. 1829
Heald, Joseph, Charnock Heath, farmer. Jan. 1829
Healey, Elizabeth, Small Bridge, Rochdale, spinster. June 1826
John, Mean Wood Brow, Rochdale, farmer. A Oct. 1826 (2nd grant 1876)
John, Rochdale, cotton spinner. Jan. 1828
John, Wellfield Hall, yeoman. Oct. 1829
Mary, Spotland Bridge, Rochdale, widow. Tuon April 1827
Matthew, Manchester, oil merchant. Dec. 1828
Robert, Small Bridge, Rochdale, woollen manufacturer. May 1830
Samuel, Small Bridge, Hundersfield, woollen weaver. Feb. 1826
Samuel, Sumerseat, Bury, manager. July 1830
Heamer, Sarah, Salford, widow. Feb. 1829
Heap, Abraham, Whalley, farmer. Feb. 1826

Heap, Ann, Manchester, widow. March 1829*
Christopher, Barker Lane, Blackburn. A Oct. 1827
Edmund, Stanhill, Whalley, farmer. A Oct. 1827
Edmund, Yate Bank, yeoman. May 1828
James, Goodshaw, stonemason. June 1828
John, Livesey, Blackburn, yeoman. A March 1829 (2nd grant 1848)
John, Newellhead, Yate and Pickup Bank, yeoman. Sept. 1830
Joseph, Stayley Bridge, auctioneer. Sept. 1829
Joshua, Burn, Crompton, yeo. July 1827
Martha, Barker Lane, Blackburn, spinster. A Oct. 1827
Mary, Barker Lane, Blackburn, spinster. A Oct. 1827
Robert, Ashton-under- Lyne, wine merchant. A Feb. 1828 (1st grant 1824; 3rd grant 1837)
Thomas, Hurst, Ashton-under-Lyne, yeoman. Nov. 1829
Heaps, John, Haigh, Wigan, farmer. Dec. 1829
Hearsnep, John, Aughton, yeoman. March 1828 (1st grant 1828)
Heath, James, Cheetham, gent. May 1826
Robert, Clitheroe, clerk. April 1826
Heatley, Peter, Whittle-le-Woods, gent. A July 1827
William, Manchester, woollen draper. May 1827
Heaton, Atherton, Wigan. Feb. 1826
Betty, Higher Lane, Prestwich, spinster. Aug. 1830
Evan, Scarisbrick, yeoman. A Aug. 1829
George, Salford, innkeeper. A Dec. 1829
James, Liverpool, bookkeeper. A March 1827
John, Adlington. Feb., 1828 (1st grant 1808)
John, Wigan, plumber and glazier. A Sept. 1828
John, Chorley, spinster [*sic*] . Nov. 1829
John, Asmall Lane, Scarisbrick, gent. Sept. 1830
Lambert, Halliwell, yeoman. A Sept. 1829
Mary, Wigan, widow. March 1827*
Noah, Bolton-le-Moors, chapman. March 1830
Richard, Ashton-in-Makerfield, hinge maker. May 1828
Thomas, Balladin Brook, Tottington, cotton spinner. A Aug. 1827
William, Leyland, innkeeper. Nov. 1828
William, Lawton, Winwick, weaver. March 1829
Heawood, James, Balderstone. Oct. 1828
Heckle, James the elder, Liverpool, cooper. Aug. 1829
Heelis, Edward, of H.M. ship Lively, a common seaman. A April 1826
Elizabeth, Liverpool, widow. A Dec. 1829
Thomas, Rumworth, gent. July 1827
Heginbottom, Eliza, Ashton-under-Lyne, spinster. A March 1827
James, Ashton-under-Lyne, esq. April 1826
Mary, Ashton-under-Lyne, spinster. Jan. 1829 (2nd grant 1843)
Samuel, Ashton-under-Lyne, esq. April 1829
William, Oxhey, Saddleworth, clothier. March 1829
Hellyer, John, Liverpool, victualler. July 1826
Helsby, Helen, Hardshaw, widow. Jan. 1828
Samuel, St. Helens. March 1827
Hemingway, John, Piccadilly, watchmaker. Aug. 1828
Henderson, James, Liverpool, merchant. A May 1827
Mary, Wavertree, spinster. Oct. 1828

Hendrick, William, Liverpool, last of Kingston, Island of Jamaica, bookkeeper. A Jan. 1828*
Henry, Margaret, Liverpool, widow. June 1829
Peter, Liverpool, mariner. A July 1830*
Phoebe, Brookhouse, Eccles, spinster. Feb. 1826
Henshaw, John, Halewood, farmer. Dec. 1829
Mary, Manchester, spinster. A Jan. 1830
William, Ashton-under-Lyne, hatter. A March 1827
Henthorn, John, Manchester, last of Thwaite, Coniston, gent. Jan. 1827
Joshua, Crompton Fold, stonemason. Dec. 1828
Mary, Heyside, Royton, widow. A March 1829
Herdman, Gawin, Lancaster, ironmonger. March 1830
Heron, Peter, Liverpool, mariner. A Feb. 1830*
Hesford, Ellen, Cadishead, spinster. A April 1826
Hesketh, Charles, Liverpool, tailor and draper. Dec. 1830
James, Simonswood, yeoman. April 1829
John the elder, Leyland, yeoman. Aug. 1826
John, Maghull. Sept. 1826
Mary, Manchester, singlewoman. Jan. 1827
Robert, Liverpool. July 1827
Roger, Tulketh, esq. Aug. 1829 (1st grant 1815)
William, Davyhulme, farmer. Sept. 1826*
William the elder, Manchester, gent. April 1829
Heslop, John, Blackburn, officer of Excise. A March 1826
Hesmondhalgh, Edward, Dutton, farmer. July 1830
Hess, Samuel, Liverpool, silversmith. A July 1829 (1st grant 1803)
Hewan, John, Liverpool, master mariner. July 1830
Hewitt, David, Pendleton, gent. A June 1829
James, Whiston, farmer. A Aug. 1828
John, Reddish, wheelwright. A and Tuon April 1828
John, Manchester, attorney-at-law. A March 1829
Peter, Manchester, manufacturer. Sept. 1827
Samuel, Liverpool, mathematical instrument and rule maker. A June 1827*
Thomas, Prescot, farmer. A Aug. 1828
William, Knowsley, farmer. June 1828 (2nd grant 1832)
William Eaby, Manchester, tailor. May 1827
Hewson, John, Liverpool, master mariner. A Oct. 1828
William, Manchester, butcher. A April 1827
Hey, Alice, Whitworth, Spotland, spinster. May 1829
Benjamin, Pasmons, Rochdale. June 1830
Heyes, Ann, Manchester, widow. Feb. 1827
Ann, Sutton. Dec. 1830
Catharine, Wigan, widow. Jan. 1826
Elizabeth, Bentlanes, Eccles, widow. Nov. 1827
Elizabeth, Ormskirk, spinster. Jan. 1828
John, Croft, yeoman. Dec. 1826
John, Bickerstaff, yeoman. Sept. 1828
Mary, Ormskirk. A Nov. 1827
Richard, Scarisbrick, yeoman. May 1828
Thomas, Cadishead, Eccles, gent. May 1826
Thomas, Everton, gent. May 1828 (1st grant 1767)
Thomas, Scarisbrick, schoolmaster. March 1829
William, Bolton, blacking manufacturer. A Sept. 1827

Heys, David, Wheelton, stonemason. Oct. 1830
James, Horwich. April 1827
James, Haslingden, weaver. Dec. 1829*
James, Haslingden, common carrier. June 1830 (2nd grant 1837)
John, Wigan. Nov. 1826*
John, Hindley, farmer. Dec. 1827
John, Further Barn, Shuttleworth, yeoman. May 1828
John, Manchester, baker. Sept. 1828
Robert, Haslingden, labourer. A Nov. 1829
William of the schooner Sailsbury, Liverpool, mariner. A Dec. 1826*
Heywood, Alice, Manchester, widow. Feb. 1827
Benjamin Arthur, Manchester, banker. Jan. 1829
James, Cheetham, weaver. A June 1828
John, Cheetham, woollen manufacturer. April 1826
John, Liverpool, shoe dealer. A Aug. 1826
Joseph, Little Heaton, weaver. May 1827*
Joseph, Lever, shopkeeper. A July 1827
Thomas, Manchester, smallware manufacturer. Jan. 1829
Heyworth, James, Lane Head, Bacup, yeoman. May 1826
John, Height Barn, Rossendale, yeoman. May 1830*
Hibbert, Deborah, Chorlton Row, dressmaker. May 1828
James, Broughton Hall, Manchester, esq. May 1828
John, New York, Glossop, co. Derby, labourer. Feb. 1828
Richard, Southport, yeoman. March 1828*
Robert, Manchester, last of Douglas, Isle of Man, esq. April 1828
William, Newton, silkwarper. A Aug. 1826; Oct. 1828
William, Newton, weaver. A Oct. 1828
William, Heaton Norris, innkeeper. Oct. 1829
Hickson, James, Liverpool, cart owner. Oct. 1827
John, Liverpool, ship carpenter. A July 1827
William, Broad Green, West Derby, yeoman. Nov. 1827
Hickton, Elizabeth, Salford, spinster. A Dec. 1829
Higgin, Jane, Edge Hill, West Derby, widow. June 1829
John, Liverpool, merchant. Feb. 1827 (2nd grant 1844)
John, Holmes Chapel, Burnley. Aug. 1829
Higginbotham, Robert, Manchester, fustian weaver. Sept. 1826
Higginbottom, Henry, Tempest Hey, Liverpool, waiter. A Jan. 1830
John, Ashton-under-Lyne, gent. July 1829 (2nd grant 1851)
Joseph, Wogden Moor, Little Hulton, farmer. A June 1827
Higginson, Alice, Prescot, widow. A Oct. 1827*
John, Culcheth, farmer. Nov. 1826
Margaret, Chorlton Row, widow. April 1830
Mary, Warrington, widow. Jan. 1827
Richard, Manchester, butcher. Feb. 1827
Higham, Agnes, Upholland, spinster. Jan. 1830*
John, Upholland. Dec. 1828
Highfield, Charles, Liverpool, gent. Sept. 1826
Highton, James, Bolton-le-Moors. A Dec. 1828
William, Halsall, yeoman. June 1826
Hignett, Thomas, Salford, warehouseman. A June 1829
William the elder, Liverpool, flour dealer. July 1826*
Higson, James, Farnworth, weaver. A July 1827 (1st grant 1819)
James, Middle Hulton, yeoman. May 1828

Higson, Joseph, Heaton Norris, cotton manufacturer. Jan. 1828
Joseph, Heaton Norris. Feb. 1829
Hill, Alice, Marsh Green, spinster. April 1828
Edmund, Tongend, cordwainer. April 1828
George, Manchester, engraver. A Feb. 1828
Hannah, Gate Inn, Rochdale, widow. Nov. 1829*
James, Wrigley Brook, Bury, carpenter. A Feb. 1826
James, Manchester, fustian shearer. A Dec. 1826
John, Hardshaw, publican. April 1828
John, Tottington Lower End, Bury, hatter. Dec. 1828*
Jonathan, Manchester, fustian shearer. A Dec. 1826
Jonathan, Manchester, fustian shearer. A May 1830
Lydia, Tongend, Rochdale. Sept. 1826*
Richard, Rochdale, labourer. A April 1828
Richard, Gale, Rochdale. A Dec. 1829*
Robert, Manchester, linen draper. Aug. 1828
Robert, Gate, Littleborough, innkeeper. A June 1829
Robert, Gale, Rochdale. A May 1830
Samuel, Wigan, pawnbroker. Nov. 1829
Thomas, Roughbank, Rochdale. May 1826
Thomas, Burton Wood, yeoman. Aug. 1828
William, Melling, farmer. June 1826
William, Doncaster, methodist preacher. June 1827
William, 4 Spring Garden Terrace, co. Middlesex, esq. Jan. 1829
Hilton, Abraham, Greenacres Moor, Oldham, cotton manufacturer. A Feb. 1828
Abraham, Whitfield, farmer. March 1828
Andrew, Astley, Leigh, weaver. Oct. 1829
Ann, New Bank, Oldham. Feb. 1829 (2nd grant 1893)
Anthony, Laneside, Prestwich, weaver. Aug. 1829
Betty, Rushyfields, Crompton, cotton spinner. May 1826
Catherine, Upholland, widow. A May 1829
Jane, wife of James Hilton, Manchester, shoemaker. Aug. 1830
John, Liverpool, butcher. A May 1828
John, Oldham, shopkeeper. A July 1830
John, Bottom of Greenacres Moor, Oldham, cotton manufacturer. Aug. 1830
John, Liverpool, victualler. Aug. 1830
Joseph, Touchet Hall, Middleton, farmer. Feb. 1827
Mary, Preston, widow. Feb. 1826 (1st grant 1825)
Mary, Failsworth, widow. June 1827
Peter, Liverpool, wheelwright. March 1827
Peter, Upholland, victualler. A July 1827; May 1829
Peter, Ince-in-Makerfield, farmer. Jan. 1830
Ralph, Oldham, shopkeeper. A March 1826
Richard, Pendleton, plaisterer and painter. May 1827*
Sarah, Oldham, spinster. A July 1830
Thomas, Dalton, carpenter. Nov. 1829
Thomas, Crumpsall, weaver. Oct. 1830
William, Middleton, weaver. A April 1826*
William, Liverpool, miller. Dec. 1829
William, Coldhurst, Oldham, machine maker. Jan. 1830
Hinde, Robert, Liverpool, sailmaker. Nov. 1830*
Hindle, Alice, Whalley, widow. Dec. 1829*
James, Roading Fold, mason. Aug. 1828

Hindle, Margaret, Liverpool, widow. A March 1827
Ralph, Liverpool, gent. March 1830
Hindley, Ellen, Warrington, widow. A Sept. 1826
Margaret Bennett, Liverpool, widow. April 1827
Ralph, Pemberton, publican. A June 1830
Richard, Manchester, smallware manufacturer. Sept. 1830
Sarah, Warrington. A June 1827
Hindman, James, Preston, cotton manufacturer. Sept. 1827
Hinton, John, Liverpool, butcher. April 1827
John, Manchester, contractor. A May 1827
William, Liverpool, painter. A Dec. 1826
Hirst, Joseph, Blackburn. A Nov. 1828
Joseph, Manchester, staymaker. Nov. 1828
Martha, Salford, widow. Sept. 1827
Hitchin, Joseph, Chatburn, farmer. Feb. 1830
Hitchon, Peter, Read, farmer. Dec. 1827
Hitherton, Thomas, Largy, Kilsherdenall, co. Cavan, Ireland. April 1826
Hobson, William, Pendleton, Eccles, innkeeper. March 1830
Hodge, Richard, Scarisbrick, farmer. Sept. 1829
William, North Meols. A March 1826
William, North Meols. A March 1827
William, Skelmersdale, farmer. A May 1830
Hodgkinson, Adam, Westhoughton, weaver. A Feb. 1830*
Adam, Chowbent, Atherton, carpenter. March 1830
John, Toxteth Park, shipwright. Jan. 1830*
John, Atherton, bricklayer. A March 1830*
Joseph, Leigh, clerk. A Aug. 1826 (2nd grant 1850)
Hodgson, Ann, Manchester, widow. A July 1830
Elizabeth, Penketh. A July 1828
Elizabeth, Whitehaven, last of Liverpool, spinster. May 1829
Jane, Great Crosby, widow. Sept. 1828
Thomas, Liverpool. A Oct. 1828
Hodson, Ann, Chorley, widow. July 1828
Ellen, Ellerbeck, widow. March 1829
Hannah, Manchester, widow. Feb. 1828
John, Ellerbeck, esq. Aug. 1828
Susanna, Wigan. July 1828
William, Westhoughton, labourer. A Nov. 1828*
William, Liverpool, baker. Nov. 1830
Hogg, George, Liverpool, last of Kingston, Jamaica, master mariner. Dec. 1827
James, Crouchend, co. Middlesex and Randwick, co. Glouc., merchant Dec. 1828
Robert, Clifton, yeoman. Nov. 1826
Hoggarth, Agnes, Bolton-le-Moors, spinster. A July 1828
Hoghton, Edward, Shorrockford, Peckup Bank, farmer. Nov. 1829
John, Blackburn, yeoman. Dec. 1829*
Holbrook, William, Hulme, widower. A Aug. 1826
Holcroft, Elizabeth, Lathom. A Oct. 1828
Gilbert, Wigan, butcher. Feb. 1828
Thomas, Middleton, manufacturer. A Oct. 1828
Holden, Ellen, Manchester, widow. A and Tuon May 1829
George, Liverpool, joiner. Aug. 1826
Hannah, Holden Fold, co. Lanc., widow. A Sept. 1828

Holden, Henry, Shaw Chapel, Crompton, shuttlemaker. June 1826 (2nd grant 1838)
Isabel, Belthorne, co. Lanc., widow. March 1827
Isabella, Darwen, farmer. A Oct. 1828 (2nd grant 1852)
James, Highlands, Royton, yeoman. Feb. 1826; June 1826
James, Inghead, yeoman. Aug. 1828
John, Blackburn, machine maker. A Jan. 1826
John, Wayoth, yeoman. April 1828
John, Rainford, yeoman. Feb. 1829 (1st grant 1794)
Joseph, Lower Place, Rochdale, woollen weaver. A Aug. 1827
Richard, Parr, St. Helens, farmer. April 1829
Robert, High Lands, Prestwich, cotton manufacturer. A March 1829 (1st grant 1808)
Samuel, Liverpool, mariner. A May 1829
Simeon, Royton. A June 1829
Thomas, Blackburn, innkeeper. May 1827
William, Blackburn, yeoman. May 1830
Holdin, Simeon, Holdenfold, yeoman. March 1828
Holding, George, Waterside, Oswaldtwistle, farmer. May 1827
Holdstock, Thomas, Manchester, book keeper. Aug. 1828 (1st grant 1824)
Holford, Ann, Manchester, spinster. Aug. 1829
George, Manchester, gent. A Feb. 1826
Holgate, James, Nelson House, gent. Jan. 1828
Holker, Christopher, Crawshaw Booth, Rossendale, weaver. July 1830
Samuel, Bury, woollen manufacturer. A Nov. 1828
Holland, Elizabeth, Eccleston. Feb. 1829
George, Failswoth, labourer. Nov. 1828*
James, Manchester, carrier. A March 1826
John, Little Bolton, clerk. Jan. 1827
Mary, Manchester, widow. March 1827
Peter, *see* Mirtha
Roger, Birch House, Failsworth, merchant. Oct. 1828
Samuel, Rochdale, gent. Nov. 1827
Thomas, Skelmersdale, yeoman. Nov. 1827
Thomas, Manchester, gent. Aug. 1829
Holliday, Emy, Liverpool, widow. July 1830
Hollingworth, John, Fairfield, Manchester, inn keeper. A Sept. 1830
Thomas, Liverpool, timber merchant. July 1828 (1st grant 1824)
Hollinhurst, Robert, Penwortham, yeoman. A Aug. 1829
Hollins, John, Manchester, brass founder. A May 1828
Hollinshead, Jonathan Blundell, Liverpool. Jan. 1828
Holliwell, Peter, Liverpool, mariner. A March 1830*
Hollows, Charles, Whitefield, Prestwich, tailor. A Dec. 1828*
Holme, Catharine, Aintree, widow. March 1829
Edward, Liverpool, accomptant. Dec. 1829 (1st grant 1792)
Holmes, Henry, Liverpool, merchant. July 1827
Jane, wife of John Holmes, Liverpool, labourer. A Nov. 1826
John, Liverpool, labourer. Oct. 1826
John, Manchester, weaver. Sept. 1829
Richard, Wigan, yeoman. May 1826
Walton, Liverpool, hosier and laceman. Feb. 1828
Holroyd, Betty otherwise Elizabeth, Colne. A Aug. 1829
John, Manchester, gent. Aug. 1830
Holt, Ann, Mardyke, Rochdale, spinster. July 1830

Holt, Betty, Newbold, Rochdale. A April 1826
Charles, Higher Lane, Pilkington, gent. Nov. 1828
Edmund, Liverpool, joiner. April 1826 (2nd grant 1836)
Edward, Chorley, cotton weaver. June 1826
Elizabeth, Audenshaw, spinster. Nov. 1828
Francis, Chesham, Bury, farmer. Dec. 1826
Isabella, Manchester. Sept. 1827
Jacob, Wardleworth Brow, Rochdale, woollen weaver. April 1826
James, Haslington yeoman. April 1826*
James, Musbury, Bury, cotton weaver. A May 1827
Jane, Liverpool, widow. Sept. 1828*
Jeremy, Pigs Lee, Bury, tailor. A June 1829
John, Speakedge, Rochdale, cotton weaver. A Jan. 1826
John, Haslingden, manufacturer. March 1827
John, Low Clough, Whalley, gent. A Dec. 1827
John, Witton, yeoman. March 1829
John, Pilkington, weaver. March 1830*
Mary, Boothfold, Rossendale, widow. Oct. 1830
Oliver, Underwood, Spotland, dyer. Nov. 1830
Richard, Castleton, chapman. Feb. 1829
Robert, Hulme, dyer. Dec. 1826
Robert, Lower Place, Castleton, woollen weaver. Feb. 1828
Robert, Broadhalgh, Rochdale. April 1829
Robert, Bispham Hall, Billinge Higher End, esq. Dec. 1829; Nov. 1830
Thomas, Bentley, farmer. July 1828
William, Knothill, Rochdale. A Aug. 1826
William, Edenfield, Bury, yeoman. Nov. 1827*
William, Tottington Lower End, butcher. July 1828
Hooton, Henry, Billinge, delf master. A Sept. 1826
James, Billinge, delf master. Oct. 1826
Mary, Billinge, widow. July 1830
Hope, Jane, Liverpool, widow. Nov. 1828
John, Liverpool, stonemason. A April 1828 (1st grant 1813)
John, Barton, co. Lanc., weaver. Dec. 1828*
Mary, Liverpool, spinster. July 1828
Thomas, Prestwich, smallware manufacturer. Dec. 1830
William, Liverpool, gent. Sept. 1827
Hopkinson, Elizabeth, Rawtenstall. Feb. 1828*
Hopper, Ann, Bolton-le-Moors, spinster. A Jan. 1830
Hopwood, Elizabeth, Rochdale, widow. A Aug. 1828
Hannah, Heaton Norris, widow. Nov. 1829
John, Chorlton Row, merchant. Nov. 1829
Peter, Wigan, linen manufacturer. Dec. 1827; June 1828
Horn, Mary, Manchester. A Nov. 1828
Hornby, Breakill, Liverpool, bookkeeper. A April 1826
Charles, Liverpool, master mariner. June 1829
Dorothy, Liverpool. A July 1829
Mary, Liverpool, widow. A May 1830
Richard, Leagram, farmer. Sept. 1827
William, Liverpool, ropemaker. A Sept. 1829
Horrocks, Adam, Bradshaw, farmer. Feb. 1830
Adam, Helton, Bury. April 1830
James, Wigan, saddler. May 1828

Horrocks, James, Spotland, blacksmith. Oct. 1830 (2nd grant 1841)
John, Bolton-le-Moors, manufacturer. A March 1826 (2nd grant 1839)
John, Harwood, innkeeper. A Sept. 1826
John, Pennington, Leigh, farmer. Oct. 1830
Mary, Crescent, Salford, widow. March 1829
Samuel, Bolton-le-Moors, blacksmith. Sept. 1827
Samuel, Oldham, corn dealer. A July 1828
Thomas, Bolton-le-Moors, weaver. Sept. 1827
Thomas, Holcombe, Tottington, weaver. A Jan. 1828*
William, Four Lane Ends, Tottington, farmer. Aug. 1828
William, Rumworth, yeoman. May 1829
Horrox, Thomas, Atherton, minister and schoolmaster. Dec. 1827
Horsey, William James, Chorlton Row, packer. A Jan. 1828
Horsfall, Jane, Liverpool. A May 1827
Hosker, Robert, Liverpool, stone getter. Sept. 1830
Hough, James, Croft, Winwick, schoolmaster. Jan. 1829 (2nd grant 1852)
James, Culcheth, bleacher. July 1829
Samuel, Over Knutsford, last of Gorton, gent. May 1829
Houghton, David, Liverpool, weaver. March 1826
Elizabeth, Wavertree, spinster. May 1828
Ellen, Widnes, widow. July 1829 (Written on the same sheet as the will of Thomas Houghton, proved April 1829)
James, Scarrs, Little Marsden, farmer. Sept. 1826
James, West Derby, gent. Jan. 1828
James, Liverpool, turner. July 1829
John the younger, Low Hill, Walton-on-the-Hill. A Aug. 1826*
John, Newton, tanner. A Dec. 1828
Thomas, Ormskirk, gent. Feb. 1826
Thomas, Newton, miller. A Nov. 1826
Thomas, Widnes, watch tool maker. April 1829
Houlbrook, Elizabeth, Liverpool, widow. Sept. 1830
Houlcroft, Joseph, Pennington, cordwainer. July 1828
Joseph, Wrightington, farmer. Feb. 1829
William, Liverpool, white cooper. A Aug. 1828
Houlden, Ann, Rusholme. Feb. 1830
Houldgrave, Edward, Toxteth Park, gardener. Nov. 1826
Houldsworth, William, Liverpool, gent. June 1830
Hoult, Hugh, Rainford, yeoman. A July 1827
Houson, Joseph, Davyhulme, weaver. Jan. 1827*
Howard, Edmund, Healds Green. Chadderton, weaver. May 1827*
Edward, Liverpool, mariner. A July 1826
Edward, Liverpool, cabinet maker. Dec. 1829*
Elizabeth, Kent St., Liverpool, spinster. A March 1826
Elizabeth, West Derby, spinster. Jan. 1829
Henry, Liverpool, pilot. Nov. 1828
Hugh, North Meols, fisherman. A Aug. 1830
Jane, Rochdale, widow. Aug. 1830
John, Burtonwood, farmer. March 1827
Jonathan, Flixton, yeoman. Aug. 1830
Joseph, Heaton Norris, yeoman. March 1826
Margaret, Appleton, co. Lanc., spinster. Feb. 1826
Peter, Low Hill, West Derby, gent. Feb. 1827
Richard, Prestwich. Jan. 1826

Howard, Samuel, Burnley, gent. May 1830
Thomas, Manchester, warehouseman. A March 1829
Thomas, North Meols, husbandman. July 1829
Thomas, Eccleston, yeoman. Sept. 1829
Thomas, Tarleton, yeoman. June 1830
Thomas, Epworth St., Walton-on-the-Hill. A Dec. 1830
Howarth, Adam, Lostock, yeoman. Jan. 1828
Betty, Kearsley, Deane, widow. A Sept. 1827
Edmund, Hollins, Oldham, coal miner. Nov. 1827
Henry, Far Bank House, Wheatley Booth, farmer. Sept. 1826
James, Heap Brow, Bury, weaver. A April 1827
James, Linedred, weaver. June 1828
James, Broughton, Manchester, nurseryman and gardener. Sept. 1828
James, Middleton, labourer. A Feb. 1829*
or Haworth, James, Manchester, machine maker. Nov. 1830
John, Buershill, Castleton, manufacturer. Aug. 1830 (2nd grant 1831)
Jonathan, Middleton, weaver. May 1828
Richard, Tong, Rochdale. July 1830 (2nd grant 1859)
Robert, Milnrow. Jan. 1827
Samuel, Goodshaw, Rossendale, surveying general of Excise. Oct. 1828 (2nd grant 1837)
Thomas, Todmorden. A July 1827*
Thomas, Liverpool, file cutter. A May 1829
Thomas, Bolton-le-Moors, publican. A Dec. 1829
William, Manchester, cupper. A Jan. 1826
William, Little Heaton, Prestwich, weaver. July 1826
William, Middleton, weaver. July 1830
Howe, Joseph, Corby, last of Manchester, tailor. Sept. 1828*
William, Manchester, auctioneer. Oct. 1826
Howell, John, Ashton-in-Makerfield, yeoman. Oct. 1827
Howorth, Betty, Bury, grocer. A March 1827
George, Constable, Forrest of Rossendale, yeoman. Dec. 1827
George, Bridge End, Bacup, woollen manufacturer. Jan. 1828
James, Hight Lane, co. Lanc., shopkeeper. Jan. 1827
John, Top of Little Heaton, schoolmaster. March 1827
John, Coldvale Brow, Rochdale, miller. A Oct. 1826*
otherwise Lord, Sarah, Rochdale, pawnbroker. A July 1828
Howson, Robert, Manchester, warfinger. A May 1828
Hoyle, Isaac, Brotherod, Rochdale, farmer. A June 1829
John, Stonefold, Rossendale, yeoman. March 1828*
Thomas, Simonstone, weaver. A April 1828
Hubbersty, John, France, farmer. A Oct. 1828
Huddart, Henry, New South Wales, mariner. A March 1830*
Huddleston, Thomas, Maghull, esq. A Feb. 1829
Hudson, Edward, Manchester, merchant. A Feb. 1828
George, Manchester, surgeon. Oct. 1828
George, Liverpool, woollen draper. A May 1829
Mary, Ormskirk, widow. March 1829
Thomas, Heaton Norris, attorney. A July 1826
Hughes, Adam, Manchester, hatter. Nov. 1829
Daniel, Liverpool, labourer. Feb. 1828
Daniel, Broughton, farmer. July 1828
Edward, Liverpool, gent. Nov. 1827

Hughes, Elizabeth, Liverpool, widow. A April 1826*
Francis, Rochdale, victualler. July 1830
Hugh, Liverpool, victualler. A April 1830
Jane, Liverpool, widow. A Feb. 1827
John, Liverpool, gent. A July 1826
John, Liverpool, gent. Oct. 1827
John, Liverpool, shoemaker. May 1828
John, Portico, Preston [*sic* Prescot], Roman Catholic Minister. Dec. 1828
John, Eccleston, Prescot, glassman. A March 1829
John, Liverpool, slater and plasterer. A May 1829
Joseph, Liverpool, mariner. A Oct. 1826*
Joseph, Toxteth Park, mariner. Aug. 1828
Joseph, Liverpool, mariner. A April 1829
Phillip, Bolton-le-Moors, gent. Feb. 1829
Richard, Liverpool, mariner. A July 1828
Robert, the Neptune, Liverpool, cooper. A June 1826*
Roger, Everton, gardener. A Dec. 1827*
Sarah, Liverpool, widow. June 1826
Sarah, Manchester, widow. June 1827
Sarah, Harrington, widow. June 1828
Thomas, Barton, farmer. June 1828
Thomas, Liverpool, joiner and builder. Jan. 1829*
Thomas, Liverpool. Nov. 1830
Hulley, Squire, Rossbottom, Stayley Bridge, shop keeper. Sept. 1830*
Hulme, Dauntsey, Salford, esq. May 1828
Elizabeth, Stretford, widow. May 1830
Fleetwood, Scarisbrick, widow. Dec. 1830
Hannah, Withington, innkeeper. Feb. 1826
Jacob, Withington, publican. Jan., 1830 (2nd grant 1836)
James, Stretford, weaver. April 1826*
James, Manchester, alehouse keeper. May 1828
James the elder, Manchester, dyer. Dec. 1828 (1st grant 1824)
John, Pilsworth, farmer. A Nov. 1830
Joseph Wright, Medlock Vale, co. Lanc., esq. Oct. 1826
Peter, Stretford, yeoman. Jan. 1826
Richard, Ainsworth, farmer. March 1826
Thomas, Manchester, merchant. A Aug. 1826 (2nd grant 1835)
Thomas, Lees, shopkeeper. Aug. 1828
William, Huyton, yeoman. Nov. 1826 (later grants 1842, 1853)
Hulse, Elizabeth, Great Bolton, innkeeper. April 1828
Humphreys, John, Liverpool, victualler. Aug. 1827
John, Cropper St., Manchester, weaver. June 1829
Roger, Manchester, gent. March 1829
Hunt, Alice, Lostock, Bolton-le-Moors, widow. A May 1830*
Alice, Lostock, widow. Aug. 1830
Edward, Widnes, watch verge maker. March 1826*
Edward, Manchester, chapman. May 1826
James, Eccleston, farmer. A April 1826
Richard, Kenyon, farmer. April 1830
Robert, North Meols, yeoman. Aug. 1830
Thomas, Tottington Higher End, farmer. July 1828
Thomas, Aintree, innkeeper. Oct. 1830 (2nd grant 1923)
William, Liverpool, bookkeeper. Oct. 1829

Hunter, James, Liverpool, watchmaker. May 1826
John, Liverpool, baker. A June 1827
Robert, Mawdsley, yeoman. A Sept. 1829
Thurstan, Croston, farmer. Dec. 1830
William, Whallow [?Whalley]. Aug. 1828
Huntington, Edward, Cockermouth, co. Cumb., tailor. A April 1829
Joseph, Liverpool, officer in H.M. Excise. Jan. 1826
Hure, George, *see* Hare
Hurst, Benjamin, Boothstown, Worsley, weaver. Sept. 1828
Catherine, Bedford. Dec. 1827
Giles, Carr Bank, Atherton, cotton weaver. A March 1829*
Joseph, Oilmill, Undersfield, Rochdale, woollen weaver. May 1826
Joseph, Middleton, weaver. Oct. 1826
Mary, Manchester, widow. April 1828
Oliver, Manchester, weaver. March 1826
Samuel, Manchester, publican. Jan. 1827
Huson, William, Club Moor, co. Lanc. Aug. 1829
Hussey, Elizabeth, Warrington, widow. A Nov. 1829
Hutchinson, Bridget, Manchester, spinster. A March 1826
James, Liverpool, mariner. A April 1828
John, Liverpool, captain's clerk. A May 1827*
William, Manchester, ironmonger. Oct. 1829
Hutton, Ann, Everton, spinster. Feb. 1827
John, Eccleston, blacksmith. June 1828
Robert, the M.S. True Blue, Liverpool. A Sept. 1826
Hyde, Mary, Hartshead, spinster. Feb. 1828
George, Bank Top, Manchester, dyer. June 1826
John, Tonge, Prestwich, weaver. June 1826
Joseph, Manchester, bookkeeper. April 1828
Thomas, Salford, victualler. April 1829 (1st grant 1811)
Thomas, Salford Wood, turner. A June 1829
Hyson, William, cook on board the Albert, Liverpool. Oct. 1826*

IMER, Charles, Liverpool, merchant. A Aug. 1828
Ince, Samuel, Edge Lane, Oldham. April 1828
Inch, Margaret, Liverpool, widow. Feb. 1828
Margaret, Liverpool, spinster. A March 1830*
Ingham, David, Top of Green, Chadderton, yeoman. April 1830
James, Sandy Gate, Habergham Eaves, shopkeeper. Aug. 1826*
James, Crawshaw Booth, weaver. A Feb. 1827*
James, Salford, gent. Dec. 1828
Ingle, Ellen, Chowbent, Leigh, widow. April 1827
John, Broomhouse Lane, Eccles, yeoman. May 1830
Ingleson, Christopher, Manchester, spinner. Feb. 1830
Inglis, Robert, Manchester, draper. A April 1826
Inman, Edward, Liverpool, plasterer. May 1830
Thomas, Manchester, publican. A Oct. 1826
Inness, Edward, Liverpool, mariner. A July 1827
Ippolili, Charles, Moor St., Ormskirk, teacher in foreign languages. March 1830
Ireland, Thomas, Liverpool, gent. A April 1827
Irlam, Alice, Eccles, widow. A Nov. 1828*
Jane, Standish, widow. Nov. 1827
Mary, Wigan, spinster. Nov. 1826

Irlam, Mary, Grindle St., Manchester, widow. May 1830
Irving, Ann, Ormskirk, widow. March 1826
 Joseph, Liverpool, mariner. A July 1828
 Mary, Ormskirk, spinster. Aug. 1827
Isaac, Thomas, Liverpool, mariner. A Oct. 1826*
Isbester or Ivester, John, Liverpool, mariner. Dec. 1827
Isherwood, Abraham, Windley, weaver. A Aug. 1826*
 Elizabeth, Hindley, widow. May 1827
 George, Little Bolton, weaver. Feb. 1829
 Henry, Longworth Bank, Bolton, farmer. May 1828
 Henry, Ashton-in-Makerfield, shoemaker. A May 1830
 Henry, Ashton-in-Makerfield, schoolmaster. A and Tuon July 1830
 Isabella, Houghton, spinster. A May 1828
 James, Little Bolton, manufacturer. May 1826
 John, Rochdale, yeoman. July 1829 (2nd grant 1847)
 Robert, Ramsgreave, Blackburn. A May 1826
Ives, Edward Olto, Titchfield, co. Southampton, esq. Dec. 1829
Ivester, *see* Isbester

JACKMAN, Ann, Euxton. A July 1826*
Jackson, Aaron, Liverpool, warehouseman. March 1828
 Alice, Urmston, spinster. Sept. 1827
 Anthony, Manchester. March 1829*
 Betty, St. Helens, watch movement maker. June 1829
 Edward, Edge Hill, master and part-owner of the good ship Catharine. Oct. 1829
 Edward, Manchester, last of Camforth Lodge, Lancaster, gent. March 1830
 Elizabeth, Chorlton-cum-Hardy, spinster. May 1829
 George, Green Lane, Barton-upon-Irwell, yeoman. May 1827
 Hannah, Manchester, spinster. April 1826
 Isaac, Manchester, dyer. Nov., 1827
 James, Lancaster, steel manufacturer. June 1829
 James, Holt Hill, Whalley, weaver. Nov. 1829
 James, Nabbs, Walmsley, farmer. Feb. 1830
 James, Manchester, butcher. A Aug. 1830*
 Jane, Liverpool, spinster. June 1828
 Jane, Lancaster, spinster. A June 1830
 John, Warrington. April 1827
 John, Edenfield, yeoman. Feb. 1828
 John, Prescot, gent. July 1828
 John, Pendleton, cabinet maker. A Sept. 1828
 John, Manchester, bookkeeper. July 1830
 John, Liverpool, merchant. A Oct. 1830
 Joseph, Liverpool, esq. Dec. 1826 (1st grant 1815)
 Lawrence, Chorley, yeoman. July 1830
 Mary, Wigan, widow. Jan. 1826
 Mary, Tarleton, widow. Sept. 1830
 Moses, Liverpool, mariner. May 1827*
 Peter, Chorley, tallow chandler. March 1826
 Peter, Liverpool, master mariner. Dec. 1828
 Peter, South Haws, labourer. July 1829
 Samuel, Little Heaton, Prestwich, victualler. May 1827
 Sarah, Middleton, shopkeeper. Jan. 1830

Jackson, Thomas, Kearsley, joiner. Jan. 1830
Thomas, Liverpool, mariner. Dec. 1830 (2nd grant 1845)
William, Royton, gent. A Feb. 1826
William, Oldham, machine maker. March 1826
William, the ship Margate, merchant. A Nov. 1827*
William, Urmston, publican. March 1830
William, Childwall, victualler. July 1830
Jaeger, William, Liverpool, blockmaker. A Oct. 1826 (1st grant 1817)
Jagger, Thomas, Newton Heath, schoolmaster. A and Tuon July 1830
James, Betty, Liverpool, widow. A April 1828
Elizabeth, Cheetham Hill, widow. May 1829
Gabriel, Liverpool, master mariner. Aug. 1826
John, Cheetham, gent. March 1826
John, Liverpool, mariner. A and Tuon Oct. 1828
Jameson, Thomas, Ashton-in-Makerfield, yeoman. April 1830
Jancey, William, Liverpool, an infant. A Sept. 1827
Jandrell, Benjamin, Liverpool, tailor. May 1827
Janson, John, of M.S. Huskisson, Liverpool, mariner. A Nov. 1826*
Jarvis, Hannah, Standiford, co. Staffs., spinster. A April 1830
Jeagel, Matthew, of M.S. Cornwall, Liverpool, mariner. Jan. 1826*
Jee, Edward, Pipe Hill, co. Staffs., gent. Sept. 1829
Jeffs, Moses, West Derby, yeoman. Oct. 1830
Jenkinson, James, Liverpool, butcher. A Sept. 1829
Thomas, Burscough, gent. Dec., 1830
Jepson, Jane, wife of Henry Jepson, Blackburn, weaver. Sept. 1826
Thomas, Manchester, clogger. Aug. 1830
Jewison, Leonard, Manchester, tallow chandler. A June 1827 (2nd grant 1850)
Johnson, Ann, Astley, widow. A May 1828
Catherine, Liverpool, widow May 1827
Catherine, wife of Robert Johnson, Fazakerley, gent. A March 1829 (2nd grant 1854)
Catherine, Lydiate, widow. A April 1829
Charles, private in the 22nd Regt. of Foot. Sept. 1829*
Charles, Liverpool, mariner. Aug. 1830*
George, Liverpool, brewer. Feb. 1826
Henry, Fazakerley, farmer. A Nov. 1829
Hugh, Birkdale, yeoman. Feb., 1827*
James, Manchester, coal dealer. March 1826
James, Manchester, cooper. A Nov. 1827
James, Astley, victualler. Sept. 1828
James, Southport, yeoman. April 1829
James, Salford, publican. May 1829
James, Warrington, chandler. A Feb. 1830
Jane, Horridge, Deane, spinster. A June 1826
John, Warrington, shoemaker. Feb. 1826
John, Culcheth, weaver. March 1828
John, Manchester, carrier. Aug. 1828
John, Lever, tailor. A Sept., 1828
John, Bretherton, clerk. Feb. 1829
John, Chorlton Row, cotton spinner. Feb. 1830 (2nd grant 1859)
John, Worsley, yeoman. Feb. 1830
John, Liverpool, mariner. A May 1830*
John, Toxteth Park, yeoman. Oct. 1830

Johnson or Johnston, John, Liverpool, seaman. Nov. 1830*
Jonathan, Chowbent, Leigh, weaver. Feb. 1826
Joseph, Pendlebury, shoemaker. Aug. 1826*
Joseph, Liverpool, watchmaker. Aug. 1827
Joseph, Liverpool, gent. June 1828
Margaret, Manchester. Feb. 1829*
Margery, Prescot, widow. March 1830
Mary, Liverpool, widow. Oct. 1830
Nicholas, North Meols, yeoman. Feb. 1828
Peter, Liverpool, mariner. A Nov. 1826*
Peter, Liverpool, mariner. Jan. 1830*
Peter, Liverpool, mariner. A and Tuon Sept. 1830*
Richard, Liverpool, stable keeper. Aug. 1826
Richard, Winton, co. Lanc., farmer. A Oct. 1826*
Richard, Bickerstaffe, yeoman. Feb. 1827
Richard, Billinge, stonegetter. March 1827
Richard, Lathom, yeoman. Nov. 1827
Robert, Liverpool, brewer. Jan. 1826 (1st grant 1824)
Robert, *see* Johnston
Samuel, Everton, gent. Jan. 1826 (1st grant 1825)
Samuel, Horwich. March 1826
Samuel, Great Crosby, gent. Jan. 1829
Samuel, Whiston, yeoman. Aug. 1829
Simon, Liverpool, mariner. A Sept. 1829
Thomas, Little London, North Meols, farmer. Jan. 1830*
Tyrer Young, Liverpool. March 1829
William, Liverpool, mariner. May 1830*
William, Liverpool, labourer. Feb. 1827
William, Liverpool, mariner. A June 1829
William Heywood, Salford, calenderman. A April 1826
Johnston, John, see Johnson
otherwise Johnson, Robert, Liverpool, merchant. A Jan. 1826
William, of the brig Dido, Liverpool, mariner. A Feb. 1828*
William, Dumfries, mariner. Aug. 1828
Johnstone, William, Port Glassgow, North Britain, merchant. A Dec. 1829
Jolley, Edward, Linacre Marsh, gent. Jan. 1830
Jolly, Elizabeth, Liverpool, spinster. April 1826
Thomas, Standish, gardener. A Feb. 1827
Jones, Agnes, wife of Hugh Jones, Liverpool, timber merchant. April 1830*
Agnes, Liverpool. A April 1830*
Ann, Gilda Brook, Eccles, spinster. March 1829
David, Liverpool, labourer. Aug. 1829
Edward, Liverpool, watch case maker. June 1828
Edward, Liverpool, brewer. Feb. 1830
Edward, Salford, millwright. Nov. 1830
Elizabeth, Liverpool, widow. Oct. 1828*
Elizabeth, Liverpool, widow. Dec. 1829
Ellen, Liverpool, singlewoman. Feb. 1827
Ellen, Barton-upon-Irwell. A Jan. 1829
Evan, Mansfield St., Liverpool, gent. A Feb. 1826
Evan, Liverpool, draper. A April 1826
George, Orton, co. Huntingdon, gent. A June 1827
Hannah, Park Lane, Pilkington, widow. April 1828; Dec. 1828

Jones, Hannah, Warrington, spinster. A June 1829
Henry, Liverpool, dock gate man. Jan. 1830
James, Liverpool, mariner. A Oct. 1828*
James, Liverpool, sailmaker. May 1829
James, Gilda Brook, Eccles. Aug. 1829
Jane, Liverpool, spinster. July 1829
John, Chorlton, nursery and seedsman. Feb. 1827
John, Harrington, dock gate man. April 1828
John, Manchester, tailor. May 1828 (1st grant 1806)
John, Liverpool, mariner. A Aug. 1830*
John, Manchester, coach proprietor. Sept. 1830
Joseph, School Lane, Rochdale, gent. Dec. 1830
Martha, Liverpool, widow. A Feb. 1826
Mary, Liverpool. Nov. 1827*
Mary, St. Helens, spinster. May 1828
Mary, Liverpool, dressmaker. Dec. 1830
Matthew, Pilkington, weaver. A Feb. 1829 (1st grant 1805)
Nancy, Liverpool, spinster. March 1828
Oliver, Liverpool, linen draper. A Feb. 1830
Peter, Chorlton Row, bookkeeper. A Dec. 1828
Richard, Manchester, last of Liverpool, twine spinner. Aug. 1829
Richard, Manchester, baker. July 1830
Robert, Ravenhead, glass worker. Feb. 1826
Robert, of the Jamaica, Liverpool, mariner. A Sept. 1826*
Robert, Stone Hill, Walton-on-the-Hill, goldsmith. Sept. 1826
Robert, Liverpool, master carter. Dec. 1827
Robert, Liverpool, gent. A Aug. 1829
Robert, Liverpool, cooper. A Sept. 1829
Robert, Liverpool, gent. A Nov. 1829
Robert, Liverpool, carter. Sept. 1830
Robert, Bolton-le-Moors, publican. A Nov. 1830
Sarah, Liverpool, shopkeeper. May 1828
Thomas, Liverpool, drug grinder and plaster manufacturer. March 1826 (2nd grant 1840)
Thomas, Liverpool, flax dresser. A May 1829
Thomas, Liverpool, mariner. A Dec. 1829*
Thomas, Bootle, Liverpool, accountant. Feb. 1830
Thomas, Liverpool, optician. July 1830
Thomas, Bolton, gent. Oct., 1830
William, Liverpool, mariner. A Dec. 1826*
William, Everton, corn dealer. Jan. 1827 (2nd grant 1855)
William, Liverpool, mariner. A Jan. 1827
William, Liverpool, mariner. A April 1827*
William, Liverpool, seaman. A May 1827*
William, Burscough, yeoman. Jan. 1828
William, Liverpool, cabinet maker. Jan. 1829
William, Liverpool, carpenter. A Feb. 1829*
William, Liverpool, iron founder and victualler. July 1829 (2nd grant 1853)
Jowett, John, Heaton Norris, blacksmith. May 1827 (2nd grant 1846)
Samuel, Portwood, last of Reddish, gent. July 1830
Joy, Esther, Liverpool, widow. Aug. 1828
Joyce, Thomas, Liverpool, cooper. A Dec. 1829*
Joynson, John, Liverpool, mariner. A Aug. 1830*

Joynson, Samuel, Liverpool, tailor. Feb. 1829*
Jump, Mary, Tarleton, spinster. Feb. 1830
Ralph, Tarleton, yeoman. June 1828
William, Harrington, cowkeeper. April 1828 (1st grant 1817)
Justice, Elizabeth, Little Bolton, widow. A July 1827

KAGHEY, Margaret, Liverpool, spinster. April 1827
Kay, Ann, Bolton-le-Moors, widow. Oct. 1830
Catherine, Prescot. Jan. 1829
Edmund, Cobhouse, Walmsley, Bury, yeoman. May 1830
Edward, Tottington, weaver and shopkeeper. Jan. 1830
Elizabeth, Limefield House, Bury, widow. A March 1830
Ellen, Salford, last of Bury, widow. July 1827 (2nd grant 1843)
George, Manchester, coach proprietor. July 1828
George, Liverpool, millstone maker. Aug. 1828
George, Levenshulme. Oct. 1830
Hannah, Blakeley, widow. A March 1830
James, Moorside, Bury, weaver. Jan. 1826
James, Salford, cotton manufacturer. A Aug. 1826
James, Warrington, joiner. Aug. 1827
James, Rochdale, glue manufacturer. A Feb. 1830
James, Swinton, last of Monton, Eccles, yeoman. Oct. 1830
John, Pilkington, weaver. A June 1826
John, Cobhouse, Middleton, woollen manufacturer. A June 1826
John, Blackley, weaver. Feb. 1827
John, Brookshaw, Bury, woollen manufacturer. A Feb 1827
John, Bury, ironmonger. March 1827
John, Middleton, joiner. A Nov. 1828
John, Curzon St., Burnley, miller. A March 1829
John, Liverpool, teacher. March 1829
Maria, Chorlton Row, spinster. Dec. 1830
Mary, Bury, widow. Nov. 1830
Richard, Limefield House, Bury, esq. July 1827
Robert, Blakeley, weaver. A Feb. 1830*
Samuel, Bury, gent. Sept. 1830
Thomas, Woolrend, Saddleworth, slubber. Aug. 1826*
Thomas, Royton, weaver. July 1826
Thomas, Bury, shopkeeper. Dec. 1829
Thomas, Bassland, Walmsley, esq. June 1830; Nov. 1830
William, Bury, tailor. Oct. 1826
Kaye, Ann, Toxteth Park, widow. Aug. 1828
James, Hindley, yeoman. Nov. 1829
Kearney, Barnard, Liverpool, shoemaker. A July 1828
Kearsley, Ann, New Brook House. June 1829
Henry, Newton, bleacher. A Sept. 1828
Robert, Hindley, weaver. Oct. 1828*
Robert, Atherton, butcher. A April 1829
Keighley, Thomas, Manchester, attorney's clerk. Oct. 1828
Keirby, Samuel, Liverpool, labourer. Aug. 1829
Kellet, Mary, Westhoughton, widow. A Nov. 1828*
Kellett, Robert, Leyland, yeoman. Aug. 1829
Thomas, Burscough, yeoman. Dec. 1829
Kelly, George, Warrington, travelling draper. Sept. 1826

Kelly, Henry, Tew Brook, West Derby, farmer. A Dec. 1829
John, Liverpool, labourer. A Jan. 1829
John, Liverpool, shipwright. A Sept. 1829
Kelsall, John, Burtonwood, yeoman. Feb. 1828
John, Manchester, merchant. Sept. 1828
Robert, Manchester, publican. April 1830
Kemp, William, Liverpool, blacksmith. Dec. 1828*
Kendall, Adam, Liverpool, last of Cockermouth, mariner. July 1827
Thomas, Liverpool, furniture broker. Sept. 1826
Kendrick, Thomas, Walton, Liverpool, gent. April 1826
Kenna, Elizabeth, Manchester, spinster. A June 1828
Kennedy, Aulay, Liverpool, master mariner. A Jan. 1829
James, Manchester, cotton spinner. July 1829
Mary, Brownlow Hill, Liverpool, widow. Oct. 1829
Mary, Liverpool, spinster. Dec. 1830
Rachel, Upwood Cottage, Crumpsall, spinster. Nov. 1829
William, Chorley, surgeon. April 1828
Kent, Ann, Middleton, spinster. A Oct. 1827
Richard, Liverpool, merchant. April 1828 (1st grant 1790)
Samuel, Manchester, pawnbroker. June 1830
Simon, Oldham Rd., cotton weaver. March 1829
Kenworthy, Ann, Delph, widow. July 1828
James, Chorlton Row, dissenting minister. A July 1828
James, Castleshaw, Saddleworth, clothier. A Feb. 1829
John, Castleshaw, clothier. A June 1828
John, Ashton-under-Lyne, coal master. Oct. 1829
Joseph, Seelfold, clothier. April 1828
Mary, Ashton-under-Lyne, widow. July 1827
Mary, Charlestown, Ashton-under-Lyne, widow. June 1830
Kenyon, Charles, Wigan, joiner. A April 1828
Elizabeth, Liverpool. March 1829
Henry, Manchester, publican. Dec. 1830
James, Croft, Winwick, weaver. Jan. 1826
James, Failsworth, yeoman. Jan. 1827
James, Halsall, husbandman. Feb. 1827
James, Ashworth, Middleton. July 1830
John, Halsall, farmer. A Sept. 1826
John, Wigan, victualler. A April 1830
John, Whittle-le-Woods, yeoman. Sept. 1830
Mary, Leeds, co. York. A May 1829
Robert, Salford, clerk. A April 1828
Thomas, Halsall, husbandman. April 1829
Kerby, Richard, Formby, yeoman. March 1828*
Kerfoot, Richard, Dalton, yeoman. Feb. 1828
Kerney, Thomas, Pendlebury, collier. A Oct. 1829*
Kershaw, Alice, Stott Field, Royton, widow. A Dec. 1826
Ann, Ramsbottom, Bury. A March 1830
Betty, Church Stile, Rochdale, spinster. May 1828
Charles, Liverpool, carter. A Feb. 1826
Charles, Moorside, Wardle. Sept. 1826*
Edmund, Catches, Spotland, stonemason. Nov. 1829
James, Rochdale, carpenter. Oct. 1827
James, Blackley, shopkeeper. A June 1829

Kershaw, James, Wrigley Brook, Key Wood, Bury, gent. Aug. 1830
alias Greenwood, James, *see* Greenwood
John, School Lane, Rochdale, blacksmith. Aug. 1826
John, Ashton-under-Lyne, cotton spinner. Nov. 1827
John, Halewood, farmer. Dec. 1829
John, Standish cum Langtree, yeoman. Dec. 1830
Mary, Bardsleys, Crompton, widow. Feb. 1830
Philip, Oswaldtwistle, innkeeper. Dec. 1827
Samuel, Oldham, shopkeeper. A Feb. 1830 (2nd grant 1851)
William, Clay Lane, Rochdale, gent. A Sept. 1826
William, Calder Moor, Littleborough, yeoman. Oct. 1826
William, Charlestown, butcher. Aug. 1829
Kevan, Dolly, Great Bolton. Sept. 1826
Kewley, Elizabeth, Everton, widow. Aug. 1829
John, Liverpool, cooper. A June 1826 (2nd grant 1870)
Thomas, Liverpool, bookkeeper. A April 1826
Key, Andrew, Liverpool, mariner. A July 1829
Kidd, William, Prescot, druggist. A Jan. 1827
William, Widnes, sailcloth manufacturer. Feb. 1827
Kilbee, William Leonard, Manchester, police officer. A March 1829
Kilbrick, Peter, of the William Rathbone, Liverpool, cooper. A Sept. 1826*
Killey, Charles, Liverpool, joiner. A April 1826*
Killner, Samuel, Tildesley cum Shakerley, yeoman. July 1826
Kilshaw, Martha, *see* Birchall
Richard, Liverpool, watch case maker. A Oct. 1827*
William, Liverpool, watchspring maker. A Oct. 1827*
Kilvington, Ellen, Liverpool, widow. May 1829
Kinder, William, Water Houses, hatter. Oct. 1826
King, George, Liverpool, gent. A July 1827
John, Islington, engineer. A Oct. 1826
Thomas, of the Arowra, Liverpool. A March 1826*
Kingsley, Peter, Upholland, watch tool maker. April 1826
Kinsey, Frances, Manchester, widow. Oct. 1827*
Kippax, Elizabeth, Lathom, widow. Feb. 1826
Kirby, James, Liverpool, bookkeeper. Sept. 1828
John, Melling, farmer. Sept. 1827
Kirk, John Thomson, Chorlton Row, civil engineer. Aug. 1826
Kirkaldy, Robert, Liverpool, master mariner. Jan. 1830
Kirkby, Dorothy, Collyhurst, spinster. Oct. 1829
Kirkham, Ann, Liverpool, spinster. A Jan. 1829
James, Cheetham, gent. Jan. 1827
Jane, Liverpool, widow. Dec. 1827
Mary, Liverpool, spinster. Oct. 1829 (2nd grant 1831)
Kirkman, Esther, Liverpool, widow. A Jan. 1830
James, Little Bolton, gent. May 1828
Joseph, Farnworth, weaver. A May 1829
Mary, Manchester, widow. A March 1826
William, Great Bolton, cotton merchant. A Oct. 1826
Kirshaw, James, Anderton, farmer. A April 1829
Kissock, Margaret, Liverpool, widow. March 1827
Kitchen, Charles, Liverpool, seaman. Nov. 1830*
Jane, Liverpool, widow. A Jan. 1827
Thomas, Liverpool, merchant. Sept. 1828

Kitchen, William, Liverpool, officer in the Excise. A May 1826; Aug. 1830 (1st grant 1
Kitchin, James, Liverpool, gent. June 1830
Kite, James, Rochdale, cardmaker. Aug. 1830 (2nd grant 1838)
Knight, Benjamin, Ashton-under-Lyne, yeoman. Jan. 1829
Gregory, Litherland, gent. Oct. 1829
John, Salford, warehouseman. Nov., 1828
Joshua, Reddish, farmer. A March 1829
Lydia, Brindle, widow. A Dec., 1829
Richard, Stretford, yeoman. March 1826*
William, Hoghton, weaver. March 1826
William, Hollinwood, yeoman. Feb. 1829
Knoll, Samuel, Kersall Moor, Broughton, dyer. A Aug. 1826*
Knott, Daniel, Oldham, yeoman. June 1829
James, Lees, cotton manufacturer. Dec. 1826
James, Top of Heights, Ashton-under-Lyne, whitster. A Feb. 1828*
James, Boston, cotton manufacturer. June 1829
Knowles, Alice, Orrell, widow. A Feb. 1828
Bateman, Liverpool, tailor. A July 1826
Catherine, Blackburn, widow. Nov. 1830
Christiana, Liverpool, widow. A July 1826
Elizabeth, wife of Joshua Knowles, Tottington, calico printer. March 1829
Isabel, Over Darwen. Dec. 1827
Jane, Over Darwen. A May 1826*
Jane, Over Darwen, feme covert. A May 1828
John, Liverpool, bookkeeper. A Dec. 1826
John, Burscough, shopkeeper. Feb. 1827
John, Bold, yeoman. Aug. 1828 (former grants 1775, 1781)
John, Entwistle, farmer. A Oct. 1828
John, Lydiate, yeoman. Nov. 1829
Mary, Bispham, widow. Sept. 1827
Richard, Kensington, West Derby. April 1830
Robert, Liverpool. Feb. 1827
Thomas, West Derby, yeoman. June 1828
William, Liverpool. A March 1828
William, Manchester, publican. April 1828
William, Lane End, Hopwood, farmer. A May 1829
Knubley, George, Liverpool, master mariner. March 1830

LAITHWAITE, George, Atherton, cordwainer. Sept. 1829
Lake, Benjamin, Heaton Norris, hat manufacturer. A Feb. 1826
William, Liverpool, tailor. Aug. 1830
Lamb, John, London, last of Salford, gent. A June 1827
Joseph, Eccles, cordwainer. Aug. 1827
Mary, Manchester and Heaton Norris, spinster. March 1826
Mary, Manchester, widow. Nov. 1827
Sarah, Manchester, widow. April 1827
Lambert, Oswald, Cheetwood, Manchester, schoolmaster. A March 1827*
Lancashire, James, Tonge, tailor. Sept. 1828
John, Hebers, Middleton, farmer. Aug. 1826
John, Prestwich, gent. March 1827
John, Crumpsall, labourer. Oct. 1829
Thomas, Moston, farmer. Sept. 1828
Lancaster, Betty, Standish with Langtree, widow. June 1829

Lancaster, John, Blackburn, surgeon. Sept. 1827
Mary, Manchester. Oct. 1829
Mary, Manchester, widow. Jan. 1830
Philip, Blackburn, cordwainer. May 1830*
Lane, John, Manchester, gent. Dec. 1826
John, Manchester, plasterer. Dec. 1826
John, Manchester, gent. A May 1829
Lang, Ann, Accrington, widow. A Aug. 1829
Ann, Liverpool, widow. Aug 1829
John, Liverpool, printer. Oct. 1827
William, Bolton, linen draper. Oct. 1826
Langars, William, Liverpool, shipwright. A Nov. 1830*
Langford, Jonathan the elder, Withington, farmer. Feb. 1829
Langhorn, Sarah, Parkhouse, Crompton, widow. June 1830
Langhorne, William, Liverpool, musician. Jan. 1828
Langley, John, Manchester, stonemason. April 1827
Ralph, Liverpool, wheelwright. Jan. 1828
Langshaw, Thomas, Wigan, bookkeeper. A Oct. 1830
William, Sharples, yeoman. Jan. 1826
Langslow, Mary, Warrington. A June 1830
Langton, Robert, Chipping, yeoman. May 1829
Langworthy, William, Liverpool, attorney's clerk. A Jan. 1827
Larkin, Alice, Liverpool. A Oct. 1827
Latham, Ann, Salford, widow. Oct. 1828
Henry, Eccleston, farmer. A Sept. 1829
John, Wigan. A March 1830
Lydia, Liverpool, widow. Nov. 1828
Mary, Eccleston, spinster. Aug. 1826
Richard, Salford, brewer. March 1827
Robert, Heaton, Deane, farmer. A Sept. 1829 (2nd grant 1839)
William, Liverpool, last of Platt Bridge, Ince-in-Makerfield, gent. Aug. 1826
William, Liverpool, merchant. A May 1827
Latimer, Thomas, Liverpool, victualler. Dec. 1830
Laughrin, Michael, Hill St., Harrington, engineer. A July 1828
Lavender, William, Salford, gent. Feb. 1828
Law, George, Rochdale, merchant. March 1828 (2nd grant 1831)
Henry, Newbarn, Rochdale, woollen weaver. May 1830(1st grant 1814)
John, Dyke Green, Rochdale, farmer. Jan. 1826
John, Ormskirk, gent. March 1829
Samuel, Car, Rossendale, farmer. Feb. 1827
Sarah, Law House, Rochdale, widow. May 1830
William, Barrowford, yeoman. July 1827; Feb. 1829
Lawe, Mary, Lane Side, Spotland, widow. Sept. 1826
Lawler, John, Manchester, gent. Sept. 1829
Lawlor, David, Carishead, Warrington. A Feb. 1826
Lawrence, Edward, Liverpool, cooper. May 1829
Henry, Liverpool, gent. Oct. 1830
John, Liverpool. A Dec. 1826
John, Manchester, merchant. A Feb. 1829
Joseph, Liverpool, mariner. A Sept. 1827*
Lawrinson, John, Much Woolton, shoemaker. A March 1827*
Lawson, Alice, South Haws, North Meols, widow. April 1826*
Elizabeth, Manchester. A July 1829

Lawson, John, Liverpool, mariner. A July 1827*
William, Lower House, Habergham Eaves, farmer. March 1826
Lawton, Hannah, Royton. A Aug. 1827
James, Denshaw, Saddleworth, woollen weaver. A Jan. 1829
John, Heaton Norris, yeoman. Feb. 1827
John, Denshaw, Saddleworth, farmer. Sept. 1827
Samuel, Brown Hill, Saddleworth, merchant. Nov. 1827
Thomas, Orford, yeoman. March 1828
Lax, Thomas, Manchester, publican. A March 1826
Lay, John, Liverpool, chairmaker. Oct. 1830*
Laycock, Jane, Carry Bridge, Colne, widow. A April 1829
Layland, Alexander, Aspull, yeoman. Aug. 1830
Esther, Anderton, widow. A Oct. 1829
Henry, Salford, gent. June 1827
Henry, Hale, co. Lancs., schoolmaster. March 1829
James, Gleadehill, Euxton, gent. Aug. 1826
Leigh, Warrington, yeoman. Feb. 1826
Margaret, Wigan, widow. A July 1827*
Laytham, Thomas, Revige Four Lane Ends, Blackburn, yeoman. Feb. 1829*
Lea, Jane, Standish with Langtree, widow. May 1826
John, Bickerstaffe, blacksmith. Jan. 1829*
Peter, Lowton, shopkeeper. Nov. 1829
Richard, tide surveyor. March 1829
Samuel, Windle, tailor. A Dec. 1829
Leach, John, Bury, house painter. April 1828
Robert, Westhoughton, yeoman. March 1828
Robert, Lowerfield, Wardle, flannel weaver. Oct. 1829
Robert, Boardmans, Tottington, yeoman. Nov. 1830
Samuel, Wardlefold, Rochdale, shopkeeper. A July 1826
Simon, Over Darwen, grocer. Oct. 1826
Leadbeater, William, Liverpool, turner. A March 1827
Leang, James, Whitehaven, mariner. Oct. 1827
Leather, John, Hindley, Wigan, sawyer. Jan. 1830
Joshua, Prescot, shopkeeper. Oct. 1826
Mary, Hurst, widow. July 1828
Richard, Liverpool, gent. Feb. 1828
Thomas, Eccles, weaver. May 1828
Leaver, James, Exwistle, Burnley, farmer. June 1828
Sarah, Prescot, widow. A March 1829
Ledger, John the elder, Stratford, farmer. A June 1830
Ledson, Daniel, Melling, farmer. Dec. 1826
Lee, Charles, Davyhulme, gent. May 1828
Elizabeth, Liverpool, widow. April 1826
Elizabeth, Halebank, widow. Oct. 1826
Elizabeth, Warrington, widow. April 1827
George Augustus, Salford, cotton spinner. Aug. 1826
James, Liverpool, bookkeeper. May 1828
James, Prescot, yeoman. March 1830
John, Manchester, gent. March 1827
John, Haughton, Manchester. July 1827
John, Chorlton Row, maker up. July 1829
John, Hollings, farmer. July 1829
Margaret, Great Bolton, widow. May 1830

Lee, Margaret Rawsthorne, Cross Hall St., Liverpool, publican. Oct. 1826
Nathaniel, Liverpool, watchcase maker. Feb. 1829 (2nd grant 1840)
Peter, Pennington, Leigh, carrier. A March 1830
Thomas, Reddish. Aug. 1826
William, Liverpool, merchant. April 1826
Leech, Ephraim, Toxteth Park, joiner. June 1827*
George, Ormskirk, shoemaker. July 1827
Isaac, Roxbury, Oldham, cotton weaver. A June 1829
Isaac, Spotland Bridge, woollen manufacturer. A June 1830
James, Marld Earth, Rochdale, farmer. A April 1826 (2nd grant 1835)
John, Ashton-in-Makerfield, yeoman. A March 1826; Feb. 1827 (1st grant 1788)
Thomas, Ashton-in-Makerfield, hardware manufacturer. A Feb. 1827 1st grant 1822)
Leedham, John, West Derby, yeoman. Jan. 1830
Leeming, William, Great Bolton, machine maker. Sept. 1829
Lees, Abraham, Mount Pleasant, Oldham, cotton manufacturer. A Sept. 1830
Ann, Denneby, Rotheram, co. York. A March 1829
Betty, Cross Bank, Ashton-under-Lyne, widow. April 1826
Charles, Nova Scotia, North America. A June 1829
George, Twarl Hill, Ashton-under-Lyne, farmer. June 1827
George, Harst Brook, Ashton-under-Lyne, weaver. May 1828
Hannah, Oldham, widow. April 1829
Henry, Ashton-under-Lyne, draper. Oct. 1827
James, Crowthorn, Ashton-under-Lyne, weaver. Oct. 1826
James, Heyrod, Ashton-under-Lyne, yeoman. July 1827
James, Clarkesfield, Prestwich, esq. Dec. 1828
James, Hey Chapel, innkeeper. A Jan. 1829
Jane, Alkrington, Prestwich. A June 1830
John, Whiston, esq. March 1826 (1st grant 1812)
John, Rosbottom, Ashton-under-Lyne, yeoman. Dec. 1827*
John, Townfields, Oldham, fustian manufacturer. June 1828
John, Blackley, weaver. A Dec., 1828; Jan. 1829
John, Chorlton Row, Irish linen merchant. Feb. 1830
Jonathan, Oldham, cotton spinner. A Nov. 1827
Jonathan, Oldham, cotton spinner. A May 1830
Joseph, Clarksfield, gent. Oct. 1826
Joseph, Lane End, Chadderton, farmer. March 1828
Joseph, Ardwick, gent. Sept. 1829
Martha, Chorlton Row, spinster. Sept. 1830
Mary, Oldham Lane, Oldham. A Sept. 1830*
Robert, Audenshaw, farmer. A June 1830
Robert, Mellisons, Ashton-under-Lyne, gent. Dec. 1830
Sarah, Ashton-under-Lyne, widow. A March 1826
Sarah, Reddish, spinster. Oct. 1828
Sarah, Castle Hall, Dukinfield. spinster. Feb. 1830
Thomas, Salford, cotton merchant. Jan. 1828 (1st grant 1822)
William, Slate Lane, Ashton-under-Lyne, farmer. Oct. 1827
William, Mosley, Ashton-under-Lyne, shopkeeper. Nov. 1830
Leiceste, Ellen, Much Woolton. May 1830
Leicester, George, Manchester, victualler. May 1826
Leigh, Alexander, Wigan, gent. Sept. 1830 (1st grant 1772)
Benjamin, Atherton, weaver. Oct. 1829
Edward, Pennington Leigh, carrier. A Dec. 1827

Leigh, Elizabeth, Worsley. Aug. 1829
James, Liverpool, coachman. A Oct. 1827
James, Worsley, farmer. June 1828
John, Bury, last of Manchester, gent. June 1826
John, Blackburn, gent. Oct. 1828
John, Pemberton, labourer. Jan. 1829
John, Southport. Dec. 1829
Mary, Worsley, spinster. A April 1826
Mary, Southport, spinster. Jan. 1827
Robert, Liverpool, confectioner. May 1827
Robert, Westhoughton, yeoman. Oct. 1827
Samuel, Manchester, manufacturer. July 1828
Thomas, Salford, joiner. Jan. 1828
Thomas, Bank Quay, Warrington, yeoman. Aug. 1828
William, Manchester, pawnbroker. Jan. 1826
William, Liverpool, landing waiter. A Jan. 1827
William, Liverpool, scale board maker. Aug. 1827
William, Tarleton, labourer. March 1829
Wilson, Manchester, gent. A April 1828
Leighs, Joseph, Unsworth, farmer. A Jan. 1828
Lesh, John Richardson, Liverpool, mariner. A Oct. 1829
Lester, John, Hollinwood, collier. April 1826 (2nd grant 1846)
Joseph, Manchester, shoemaker. May 1827
Lettman, Edward, Liverpool, spirit dealer. Feb. 1827
Lever, James, Churchgate, Bolton-le-Moors, engraver. Oct. 1826
James, Bolton-le-Moors, publican. A April 1827
Thomas, Ainsworth, yeoman. Dec. 1828
William, Bolton-le-Moors, publican. A Feb. 1830
Lewin, Edmund, Liverpool, wine merchant. Nov. 1829
Lewis, Betty, Liverpool, widow. May 1829
Henry, Church Stretton, co. Salop, last of Puerto Cabello, S. America, gent. A April 1830
Mary, Liverpool, widow. Oct. 1829
Maurice, Manchester, salesman. A Aug. 1828
Owen, Liverpool, mariner. A Nov. 1826*
Thomas, Liverpool, confectioner. April 1826
Thomas, Liverpool, joiner. A March 1828
Thomas, Liverpool, butcher. March 1830
William, Liverpool, baker. Feb. 1827
Leyland, Henry, Ashton-in-Makerfield, yeoman. April 1829 (1st grant 1809)
John, Liverpool, hairdresser. May 1828
John, Ashton, farmer. A Oct. 1828
Richard, Green Ground, co. Lanc., farmer. June 1826
Richard, Anderton, farmer. A Jan. 1827
Thomas, Liverpool. June 1827
Thomas, Walton-on-the-Hill, esq. Jan. 1828
William, Hindley. A Dec. 1830
Lightbourne, James, Manchester, chapman. Dec. 1829 (1st grant 1747)
Lightfoot, Ann, Liverpool, singlewoman. A Aug. 1827
John, Manchester, servant. June 1829
Joseph, Warrington, yeoman. March 1830
Lignum, Andrew Manchester, doctor in medicine. Nov. 1826
John, Hale, last of Manchester, surgeon. Dec. 1826

Lilley, John, Ridgehill and Lanes, Ashton-under-Lyne, yeoman. March 1830
Lilford, Thomas, Lord Lilford, Baron of Lilford. Jan. 1826
Linaker, Mary, Runcorn, last of Farnworth, widow. May 1827
Lindley, John, Kearsley, weaver. June 1827
Lindsay, Mary, Liverpool widow. May 1830
Lingard, George, Manchester, victualler. A Oct. 1828
George, Winton, Eccles, yeoman. Sept. 1829
Lingley, Margaretta, Warrington, spinster. Nov. 1829
Linley, Matthew, Barton, publican. A Aug. 1826
Linnecar, Martha, Liverpool, widow. Dec. 1828
Linney, John, Audenshaw, weaver. Feb. 1826
Linquist, Andrew, Liverpool, seaman. Sept. 1829
Linstead, James, Liverpool. June 1827
Liptrot, Richard, Haulgh, Bolton-le-Moors, counterpane manufacturer. April 1829
William, Bispham, farmer. April 1829
Liptrott, Richard the elder, Wigan, yeoman. May 1830 (1st grant 1824)
Lister, John, Colne, yeoman. Feb. 1826
Litherland, Elizabeth, Upper Mill, Saddleworth. A April 1828
Ralph, St. Helens, shopkeeper. A March 1829
Lithgoe, John, Rainford, farmer. Feb. 1828
Litler, John, Liverpool, butcher. Feb. 1826
Litt, John, Liverpool, calico printer. May 1829
Little, James, Liverpool, tailor. A and Tuon April 1827 (2nd grant 1848)
Jenny, Manchester, widow. A July 1828
John, Bahia, Brazil, S. America, M.D. Dec. 1827
Littledale, George, Sandown Hall, Wavertree, esq. Dec. 1826
Isaac, Liverpool, broker. Sept. 1828
Littlejohn, Duncan, Liverpool, gent. A April 1829
Littlemore, George, Warrington, bookkeeper. A Aug. 1829
Littlewood, Sarah, Rochdale, widow. A Jan. 1826
Livesay, William, Withnell, Leyland, farmer. A June 1828
Livesey Edward, Inghams, Leyland, gardener. May 1827
Edward, Leyland, gardener. A July 1827
James, Marland, Castleton, blacksmith. Jan. 1828
Mary, Rylands, Hereford, formerly of Bath, widow. Sept. 1827
Richard, Over Darwen, grocer and draper. April 1830
William, Radfield Head, farmer. Sept. 1828
William, Bury, mechanic. A Nov. 1830
Livesley, Alice, Liverpool, widow. Dec. 1827
Livingston, John, Everton, merchant. Sept. 1828
Livsey, James, Manchester, coal miner. Aug. 1827
John, Wheelton, grocer. A Aug. 1828
Lloyd, Ann, Liverpool, widow. Jan. 1829
Edward, Liverpool, victualler. Dec. 1827
Elizabeth, Liverpool, spinster. A Oct. 1827
Hugh, Manchester, joiner. A June 1827*
John, Manchester, innkeeper. May 1826
John, Warrington. Nov. 1826 (former grants 1816, 1819, 1822, 1823; later grant 1831)
John, Manchester, dyer. A June 1828
Martha, Liverpool, widow. June 1830
Robert, Ince Hall in Makerfield, esq. Feb. 1827
Thomas, Liverpool, gent. A Feb. 1828

Lloyd, William, Liverpool, tobacconist. A Jan. 1827
Lockett, John, Newchurch, groom. Aug. 1828
Lodge, Alice, Lancaster, last of Penwortham (wife of Henry Lodge, yeoman), Sept. 1829
Lolley, William, Liverpool, needle and fish hook manufacturer. Oct. 1828
Lomas, Ann, Manchester, widow. A Feb. 1827
Charles Watson, Salford, pawnbroker. Sept. 1830
Robert, Bedford, gent. A Sept. 1828
William, Strangeways, calico printer. Feb. 1828
Lomax, Ann, Bury, widow. May 1830
James, Little Lever, cotton manufacturer. Sept. 1827
James, Great Sankey, yeoman. Nov. 1827
James, Bolton-le-Moors, publican. A May 1830
John, Manchester, merchant. Oct. 1827
John, Deane, farmer. March 1828
John, Horsecroft, Spotland, coal miner. A Dec. 1830 (1st grant 1795)
Joseph, Little Lever, cotton manufacturer. April 1827
Lawrence, Rochdale, yeoman. Aug. 1828*
Martha, Turton, spinster. Jan. 1827
Thomas, Bury, joiner. May 1828
Thomas, Stalybridge, grocer. June 1828
William, Farnworth, farmer. A Oct. 1826
William, Great Bolton, tailor. Sept. 1727
Longshaw, Thomas, Worsley, cotton spinner. May 1828
Longstaff, Robert, Warrington, officer of Excise. A and Tuon Feb. 1828
Longton, Thomas, Halsall, gent. A Feb. 1830 (1st grant 1819)
Longworth, James, Liverpool, builder and sawyer. Feb. 1830
John, Heaton, yeoman. Feb. 1826
Martha, Manchester, widow. May 1828
Lonsdale, George, Liverpool, gent. A July 1826
Lord, Betty, wife of John Lord, Hermitage, Crompton, weaver. Nov. 1829
Catherine, Standon Hall, Newcastle-under-Lyne, co. Staffs. A April 1829
Edmund, Walton-le-Dale, innkeeper. Dec. 1826
Edmund, Lower Mill, Rochdale, manufacturer. March 1828
James, Liverpool, broker. July 1828
Jane, Newton, Manchester. A July 1828
Jenny, Boothfold, Rossendale, widow. March 1828
John, Coat, Cliviger, farmer. March 1826
John, Chapel House, Ashworth, farmer. Nov. 1826
John, Wigan, sheriff's officer. Jan. 1827
John, Crawshaw Booth, Rossendale, weaver. June 1827
John, Heald, Bacup, yeoman. A June 1827
John, Manchester, surgeon. Aug. 1827
John, Hoyle Hey, last of Greens Mill, Rossendale, yeoman. Sept. 1828
John, Calliands, Butterworth, yeoman. Nov. 1828
John, Knothill, Spotland, yeoman. A July 1829 (1st grant 1809, 3rd grant 1854)
John, Bacup, yeoman. A June 1830
John, Deansgate, Manchester, publican. Sept. 1830
Lawrence, Boothfold, Rossendale, shopkeeper. Nov. 1826
Mary, Rochdale, feme covert. A Feb. 1828
Richard, Knothill, Rochdale, woollen weaver. A Oct. 1829
Robert, Rochdale, innkeeper. A Dec. 1828
Robert, the Unicorn, Radcliffe, farmer. Dec. 1830

Lord, Samuel, Laneside, Rochdale. June 1828
Samuel, Cow Clough, Spotland. June 1830
Sarah, *see* Howorth
Sarah, Shawclough, Rochdale, widow. May 1829
Simeon, Whitworth, Rochdale, yeoman. Aug. 1827
Simeon, Knothill, Spotland, farmer. A June 1829
Thomas, Todmorden, gent. June 1827
Thomas, Newton, Manchester. A Oct. 1827
Thomas, Vicars Moss, Rochdale, chapman. Aug. 1828
Thomas, Preston, yeoman. May 1829
Low, Jonathan, Rhodes, Middleton, bleacher. Aug. 1826*
Lowe, Ann, Newton-le-Willows, widow. Oct. 1829
alias Gorstige, Benjamin, Liverpool, labourer. April 1830*
Hamlet, Salford, gent. Feb. 1826 (1st grant 1816)
James, Abram, Wigan, farmer. A Jan. 1826
James, Liverpool, innkeeper. May 1828
James, Astley, yeoman. May 1829
Jane, Haigh. A Jan. 1829*
John, Shipley Hall, Ashton-under-Lyne, esq. Feb. 1830
Joseph, Manchester, tailor. Aug. 1828
Matthew, Liverpool, victualler. A May 1830 (2nd grant 1832)
Richard, Liverpool, flour dealer. April 1830
Samuel, Warrington, cotton weaver. Dec. 1826
William, Longsight, Manchester, warehouseman. Dec. 1826
William, Royton. May 1830
Lowndes, Charles, commonly called Charles Spencer Lowndes, Duke St., Edge Hill, esq. Nov. 1830
Lowry, John, Liverpool, mariner. A Jan. 1830*
Lowson, John, Wigan. Dec. 1826
Lowther, John, Liverpool, rigger. A June 1826*
Loxam, Elizabeth, Newburgh, Lathom, widow. March 1827
Lund, James, Haslingden, blacksmith. A April 1829
Mary, Haslingden, shopkeeper. Oct. 1829*
Thomas, Dutton, yeoman. May 1830
William, Leigh, last of Windsor, Toxteth Park, gent. Jan. 1830
Lunt, Alice, Bootle, widow. June 1828
Catherine, Altcar, spinster. A May 1830*
John, Liverpool, watchmaker. March 1830*
Richard, Toxteth Park, mariner. Oct. 1830
Lurtin, John, Liverpool, bookkeeper. A Oct. 1830
Lynch, James Christian, Liverpool, doctor of physic. April 1826
Patrick, Liverpool, draper and tailor. Dec. 1827
Lyon, James, Manchester, joiner. A March 1827
James, Abram, Wigan, farmer. Sept. 1829
Jane, Wigan, last of Billinge Chapel End, spinster. July 1830
John, Manchester, warehouseman. Oct. 1829
Joseph, Liverpool, mariner. A Feb. 1829 (1st grant 1799)
Martha, Salford and Pendleton, widow. May 1826
Ralph, Kirkby, yeoman. Dec. 1829
Thomas, West Derby, yeoman. July 1828
Lythgoe, Benjamin, Lodge Lane, farmer. A Nov. 1829
Ralph, Martins, co. Lanc., farmer. A Jan. 1830
Thomas, Liverpool, last of Roby. Sept. 1828

MCADAM, Mary, Liverpool, widow. July 1827
McCall, Jane, Liverpool, widow. Aug. 1829
McCan, Thomas, Manchester, draper and tea dealer. Aug. 1830
McCandlish, John, Openshaw, captain in the Navy. A Sept. 1830
McCarter, Francis *see* Carter
McCartney, John, Halkethleaths, Scotland and Liverpool, doctor of physic. Feb. 1830 (later grants PCC 1831 and PPR 1858)
McClean, Samuel, Liverpool, mariner. A Aug. 1829
McClintock, Peter, Liverpool, draper. A March 1826
McCollaugh, John, Manchester, gent. Sept. 1829
McConachy, John, Liverpool, mariner. A Sept. 1827*
McConnel, John, Manchester, cotton spinner. A March 1828
McCoppin, Alexander, Liverpool, carpenter. A Dec. 1827*
McCurdy, Alexander, Manchester, joiner. A April 1826
McDonald, Donald, Edge Hill, master mariner. July 1827; June 1829
Macdonald, James, Liverpool, woollen draper. March 1826
McDonald, James, Manchester, barber. A Aug. 1826*
William, Liverpool, mariner. June 1830*
McDowal, Samuel, Liverpool, merchant. June 1827
McDugald, John, Liverpool, mariner. A April 1830*
McFarlane, Peter, Bolton-le-Moors. May 1829
McFee, Archibald, Liverpool, baker. Feb. 1829*
McGhil, Alexander, Blackburn, linen draper. Aug. 1830 (2nd grant 1832)
McGinn, James, Liverpool, mariner. A Aug. 1830*
McGowan, Anthony, Warrington, linen draper. Oct. 1828
Macgowan, Felix, Liverpool, mariner. A Sept. 1830*
McGowan, Margaret, Liverpool, spinster. A March 1828
McGrath, Patrick, Liverpool, labourer. A July 1829
McGregor, Alexander, Everton, merchant. June 1829
McGurk, John, Crosshall st., Liverpool, foundry man. A March 1829
Machell, Janet, West Derby, widow. A Jan. 1828
McIlquham, Robert, Clitheroe, calico printer. A Jan. 1829
McIntosh, Henry, Manchester, land surveyor. A July 1827
McIntyre, Arthur, Newry, Ireland, coppersmith. A Nov. 1828
Mack, Robert, Liverpool, mariner. A July 1830*
Mackay, George, Windle, esq. June 1829
Robert, Edge Hill, officer in the customs. A Jan. 1827
McKee, David, Liverpool, tailor. June 1828
McKenzie, Jennet, Liverpool, widow. Feb. 1829
McKinnell, James, Manchester, merchant. A June 1827
Macknight, Jane, Liverpool, widow. A June 1827
McKnight, John, Liverpool, shipwright. A Aug. 1830*
Macknols, Ann, Cragg, Colne, widow. March 1830
Mackreth, Michael, Liverpool, mason. March 1830
McLean, Donald, Liverpool, merchant. Jan., 1828
Hector, Liverpool, mariner and carpenter. A Aug. 1830*
McMail, John, Liverpool, mariner. A Oct. 1829*
William, Liverpool, mariner. A Sept. 1829
McMellon, Richard, Bury, grocer. Nov. 1830
McMillan, John, Liverpool, painter. A June 1830
McMurdo, William Dick, Liverpool, merchant. Dec. 1828
McMurray, Catherine, Liverpool, spinster. Sept. 1826
John, Liverpool, mariner. A July 1830

Macnab, Archibald, Manchester, commission agent. A May 1830
McQuade, James, the civilian Brig [*sic*], mariner. A Dec. 1829*
McQuillan, Mary, Manchester, widow. A Oct. 1829
McViccar, Joseph, Liverpool, merchant. A March 1826
Maddocks, Mary, Bidston, last of Toxteth Park, spinster. May 1830
Maddox, John, Liverpool, painter. March 1830
Maden, George, Stack, Spotland. Aug. 1828
  Henry, Newchurch, Rossendale, woollen weaver. April 1829
  Henry, Maller Inglane, Goodshaw, Rossendale, weaver. June 1829
  Peggy, Tonge, Rochdale, spinster. A Nov. 1830
Magee, Cicely, wife of Bernard Magee, formerly Liverpool, late of Chorlton Row, draper. May 1827
Magie, Terence, Wigan, hawker. April 1830
Maguire, Hugh, Liverpool, smith. Dec. 1830
  James, Liverpool, an infant. A Nov. 1828*
  Peter, Liverpool, seaman. May 1830*
Maine, Margaret, Liverpool, widow. June 1826
Mains, Robert, Demerary, millwright. Dec. 1826
Mainwaring, Peter, Manchester, M.D. Oct. 1827 (1st grant 1786)
  Thomas, Liverpool, pawnbroker. A March 1829
  William, Liverpool, victualler. Jan. 1829
Makin, Betty, Great Bolton, widow. Jan. 1826*
  James, Preston, gent. A April 1830
Makinson, Evan, Horwich, farmer. Oct. 1829
  Nicholas, Blackrod, yeoman. July 1826
  William, Adlington, carpenter. Nov. 1829 (2nd grant 1834)
Mallalieu, Ellias, Delph, Saddleworth, yeoman. Dec. 1830*
  James, Hulme, merchant. Oct. 1827
  John, Salford, clothier. A April 1829
Malley, Elizabeth, Warrington. Dec. 1827
Mallinson, David, Burnage, gent. Nov. 1828
Malvy, John, Liverpool, mariner. Sept. 1830*
Manchester, Joseph, Bickerstaffe, husbandman. July 1829
  Timothy, Bickerstaffe, yeoman. June 1829
  William, Great Bolton, clock dresser [*sic*]. June 1830*
Manchnols, Edmund, Heyhead, Great Marsden, yeoman. June 1826*
Mandell, Isaac, Harrington, schoolmaster. Feb. 1826
Mangnall, John, Westhoughton. Feb. 1829
  John, Bolton-le-Moors, parish clerk. May 1829
Manley, Ellen, Atherton, feme covert. A June 1828
  John, Chowbent, nailmaker. A Sept. 1826 (2nd grant 1852)
Mansfield, George, the brig Mary, Liverpool, mariner. A Sept. 1827*
  Mary, Liverpool, widow. Sept. 1826
Manson, William, Liverpool, mariner. Feb. 1829*
Mansure, Ann, Manchester, spinster. Jan. 1828
  Elizabeth, Manchester, widow. Oct. 1827
Marginson, James, Houghton, Blackburn, labourer. A May 1829
Markland, Ann, Westhoughton, widow. A Nov. 1828*
  Peter, Ashton-under-Lyne, innkeeper. Nov. 1829
  Robert, Mabfield, Withington, esq. Aug. 1828
  Thomas, Hulme, Manchester, gent. Sept. 1826
  Thomas, Standish, farmer. A Nov. 1829
Marland, Jonathan, Hartshead, Ashton-under-Lyne, stonemason. April 1826

Marriott, Jonathan, Salford, salesman and shopkeeper. Nov. 1829
Mary, Manchester, spinster. A Dec. 1828
Samuel, Kinder, Glossop, co. Derby, yeoman. Feb. 1827
Marrs, John, Toxteth Park, miller. May 1830
Marsden, Ellen, Liverpool, widow. A June 1827
Hugh, Brindle, farmer. Jan. 1827
James, Tockholes, farmer. A July 1826
James, Oldham. A Oct. 1830*
Jane, Blackburn, A July 1827*
Jenny, Blackburn. A Dec. 1826*
John, Salford, yeoman. April 1828
John, Wigan, yeoman. April 1828
John, Brindle, yeoman. Sept. 1830
Robert, Salford, cooper. A and Tuon Feb. 1826
Thomas, Over Darwen. June 1828
William, Salford, machine maker. A Dec. 1828
Marsh, Henry, Liverpool, mariner. A Sept. 1830
James, Wigan, shopman. A July 1826
John, Wigan, gent. A Oct. 1826
John, Liverpool, cordwainer. A April 1827
John, Ashton-in-Makerfield, blacksmith. Oct. 1827 (1st grant 1822)
Peter, Liverpool, cabinet maker. April 1827
Richard, Bedford, Leigh, farmer. Nov. 1827
Marshall, Ann, Liverpool, widow. Aug. 1828
Edward, Birkdale, yeoman. Sept., 1826*
Humphrey, Manchester, publican. Aug. 1829
Jarvis, Manchester, gent. Feb. 1828
Mary, Longborough, co. Leicester. May 1830
Robert, Liverpool, gent. Feb. 1830
Simon, Liverpool, tailor. A Aug. 1829
Thomas, Formby, yeoman. March 1828
William, Birkdale, yeoman. Sept. 1828
Marsland, Edward, Manchester, merchant. A June 1830 (later grants PCC 1833 and PPR 1902)
Hannah, Oldham, widow. A Jan. 1826
Margaret, Oldham, widow. March 1826
Mary, Chorlton Row, spinster. A July 1830
Mart, Josiah, Manchester, grocer. A March 1827
Martin, Ellen, Liverpool, widow. A June 1827
James, Liverpool, merchant. June 1828
Joseph, Liverpool, gent. April 1828
Michael, Manchester, egg merchant. A May 1826
Richard, Walton-le-Dale, gent. May 1827
Richard, Walton-le-Dale, merchant. Nov. 1829
Thomas, Liverpool, officer in the Customs. Feb. 1827
William, Westminster, co. Middlesex. Feb. 1830
Martindale, James, Warrington, victualler. A July 1828
Marthew, John, Wigan, agent. A April 1828
Joseph, Manchester, grocer and slate dealer. March 1830
Thomas, Burscough, yeoman. May 1827
Mason, Adam, Great Sankey, yeoman. Dec. 1828 (1st grant 1804)
Isabella, Pendleton, widow. Nov. 1829
Jane, Liverpool, spinster. A April 1830

Mason, Samuel, Walton, co. Lanc., farmer. Oct. 1829
Thomas, Horwich, gent. Dec. 1830
William, Manchester, plasterer and painter. Nov. 1828 (2nd grant 1859)
Massam, James, Scarisbrick, yeoman. March 1826
William, Liverpool, excavator. A Feb. 1828
Massey, John, Manchester, calenderer. Feb. 1826
John, Liverpool, ship carpenter. Feb. 1828 (1st grant 1773)
John, Manchester, last of Vicars Hall, Worsley, cotton manufacturer. Dec. 1828
John, Lancashire Hill, Heaton Norris, hatter. Sept. 1830
William, Denton, yeoman. Jan. 1827
Masterman, Hannah, Stockton, widow. Dec. 1828
Mather, Alice, a servant in the family of Anthony Legh Keck of Haughton Grange, esq. June 1829
Ann, Toxteth Park, spinster. A Dec. 1826
Elias, Salford, publican. A June 1830
Emanuel, Manchester, victualler. Nov. 1828
Hugh, Pennington, Leigh, weaver. A Dec. 1828*
James, Manchester, gent. Aug. 1827
John, Great Bolton, weaver. Jan. 1826
John, Playmouth Hospital, mariner. A Dec. 1826*
John, Billinge, delf master. Dec. 1827
John, Walton-le-Dale, yeoman. March 1828
John, Radcliffe, cordwainer. March 1830
John, Blackrod, farmer. Oct. 1830
John, Longsight, shopkeeper. Nov. 1830
Miles, Radcliffe, weaver. July 1830 (1st grant 1820)
Peter, Manchester, sheriffs officer. Will and Tuon Nov. 1826 (1st grant 1824)
William, Manchester, bachelor. A Oct. 1828
Matthews, Ann, Manchester, widow. Jan. 1827
Philip, Liverpool, miniature painter. A June 1827
William, Liverpool, tavern keeper. A Nov. 1827
Maud, Sarah, Fairfield, Manchester, spinster. April 1830
Maurice, Thomas, Kirkdale, flour dealer. Aug. 1827
Mawdesley, James, Ormskirk, yeoman. May 1827
Mawdsley, Dorothy, Burscough, widow. Dec. 1829
Evan, Manchester, innkeeper. Jan. 1826
Hugh, Leghorn, Italy, merchant. A May 1830
James, Edge Hill, joiner. Feb. 1828
John, Aughton, esq. May 1829
Richard, Ormskirk, spirit dealer. A Sept. 1826
Thomas, Skelmersdale. April 1828
William, Burscough, yeoman. Dec. 1828*
Mawn, Meredith, Manchester, tea dealer. Dec. 1827
Mawson, Eleanor, Chorlton Row, widow. May 1826
May, John, Liverpool, cooper. A March 1828*
Mayall, Miles, Lees, carpenter. March 1829
William, Oldham, cotton spinner. A Nov. 1827
Maycon, John, Pendleton, deputy constable. April 1828
Mayer, Edward, Manchester, last of Hamburg, merchant. A April 1826
Mayers, Martha, Heaton Norris. Dec. 1828
Maymon, William, Pendleton, maker up of twist. A Dec. 1830
Maynard, Henry, Plymouth Dock, last of Liverpool, gent. July 1828
Mayo, Francis, Mount Pleasant, Oldham, gent. Jan. 1830

Mayo, John, New Barns, Pendlebury, farmer. Feb. 1826
Mayor, Margaret, Farington, widow. Jan. 1829
William, Chorlton Row, butcher. Oct. 1829
Meacock, Lettia, Mount Vernon, Liverpool, widow. Oct. 1827
Sarah, Liverpool, spinster. Aug. 1828
Meaden, Richard, Manchester, innkeeper. A Aug. 1829
Meadowcroft, Catharine, Tittleshaw, Tottington, widow. Feb. 1827
Charles, Spotland, farmer. A July 1829 (2nd grant 1856)
James, Boothstown, Eccles, weaver. Dec. 1826
Miles, Royton, cotton spinner. A Feb. 1826
Richard, Wavertree, gent. April 1827
Thomas, Bury, shopkeeper. A March 1830
Meadows, Christopher, Hindley, labourer. Jan. 1830*
John, Liverpool, attorney-at-law. A July 1828
Mary, Liverpool, widow. Feb. 1826
Mears, Mary, Liverpool, widow. Dec. 1829
William, Liverpool, tailor. Dec. 1827
Meates, William, the brig Dido, Liverpool, mariner. A Dec. 1827
Medcalf, Charles, Manchester. April 1826
James, Liverpool, mariner. A Feb. 1827
John, Chorlton Row, gent. July 1830
Richard, Middleton, carpenter. July 1829
Medcalfe, Margaret, Liverpool, victualler. May 1828
Meek, William, Liverpool, merchant. June 1828 (1st grant 1825; 3rd grant 1856)
Mellalieu, George, Manchester, manufacturer. A Oct. 1830 (2nd grant 1837)
Melling, James, Stand Lane, Pilkington, gent. March 1830*
Thomas, Liverpool, gent. A July 1829; March 1830
William, Upholland, husbandman. Oct. 1828
Mellodew, John, Meadow Croft, Bury, yeoman. A March 1829
Mellor, James, Salford, tin plate worker. June 1828
James, Royton, cotton manufacturer. Sept. 1829
John, Manchester, watchmaker. A Feb. 1827
John, Birkacre, Chorley, calico printer. April 1828
John, Droylsden, shoemaker. May 1829
Joseph, Rushulme, hosier. Oct. 1829
Martha, Manchester, spinster. Jan. 1827
Samuel, Lees, Ashton-under-Lyne, shopkeeper. Jan. 1829
Thomas, Liverpool, brewer. May 1829
Ursula, Horwick, widow. A Feb. 1828 (2nd grant 1846)
Melvell, Michael, Liverpool, seaman. Dec. 1829*
Mercer, Ellen, Liverpool, widow. Oct. 1829
Hannah, Liverpool, spinster. March 1829
John, Blackburn, weaver. Feb. 1829
Jonathan, Liverpool, officer in H.M. Customs. June 1830
Margaret, Rainhill, spinster. June 1827
Mary, Bakewell, co. Derby, widow. Aug. 1829
Richard, Blackburn, weaver. A Jan. 1828*
Samuel, Manchester, cotton merchant. Feb. 1830
Sarah, Parr, widow. A Dec. 1826
Meredith, James, Rochdale. A June 1826
William, Liverpool, carter. March 1830
Merry, Thomas, Bolton, solicitor. A June 1830
Merryweather, Mary, Stretford, widow. May 1830

Metcalf, Christopher, Salford, joiner and carpenter. A March 1826
Frances, Liverpool, spinster. A Dec. 1826
Metcalfe, Christopher, Liverpool, joiner. Aug. 1828
Middlehurst, Thomas, Ashton-in-Makerfield, yeoman. May 1827
Middleton, Jane, Adlington, widow. A April 1829
Midgley, Henry, Liverpool, merchant. A Sept. 1827
William, Liverpool, mariner. A Oct. 1827
Midwood, James, New York, America, merchant. A Nov. 1829
Joseph, Manchester, merchant. March 1830
Miles, Birch, Liverpool, gent. Feb. 1830*
Milford, Gawen, Liverpool, master mariner. A March 1829
Mill, Ann, Low Hill, Liverpool, widow. May 1828 (2nd grant 1840)
Millar, Mary Ann, Manchester, widow. April 1828
Miller, Henry, Liverpool, publican. Jan. 1828
Humphrey, Ulnes Walton, yeoman. June 1829
Isaac, Charlestown, Ashton-under-Lyne, clothier. Dec. 1830
Jacob, Hurst, shopkeeper. A April 1830
John, Manchester, apothecary and druggist. Dec. 1826 (2nd grant 1868)
John, Liverpool, seaman. March 1830*
Tabitha, Liverpool, widow. Nov. 1829
Thomas, Bridport St., Liverpool, gent. March 1830
William, Liverpool. Jan. 1827
Millett, Richard, Hopwood, Middleton, farmer. Dec. 1826
Millington, James, Ashton-in-Makerfield, farmer. Dec. 1830
Richard, Salford, silk weaver. Dec. 1826*
Millner, Mary, Chesterfield, co. Derby, widow. Jan. 1829
Mills, Abraham, Bridge Mill, Rochdale, cotton weaver. A July 1826 (2nd grant 1846)
Alexander, Manchester, farmer. May 1829
Ann, Northumberland St., Strand, co. Middlesex, spinster. A May 1829
Betty, Salford, widow. Aug. 1828; May 1829
George, Tong End, Rochdale, cotton weaver. A Jan. 1826*
George, Salford, yeoman. July 1827
George, Whitefield, gent. April 1829
Henry, Oldham, painter. Aug. 1826
Henry, Liverpool, shoemaker. A Dec. 1828*
James, Ladyhouse, Rochdale. June 1829
John, Court Hill, Oldham, farmer. Jan. 1827
John, Oxhey, Saddleworth, yeoman. Oct. 1830
Mary, otherwise Jane, Manchester, spinster. A Aug. 1826
Richard, Liverpool, gent. Dec. 1828
Samuel, Oldham, weaver. A June 1829
William, Marylebone, London, gent. July 1827
Milne, Abraham, Crompton, yeoman. Nov. 1828
Abraham, Ladyhouse, Rochdale, yeoman. Feb. 1830
Charles, Brunedge, Castleton, yeoman. Aug. 1827
Edmund, Shaw, cotton manufacturer. A April 1827
Edward, Manchester, liquor merchant. Nov. 1826
George, Shaw, yeoman. Jan. 1827
James, New Lower House, Oldham, weaver. May 1829
John, Moor Gate, Rochdale, yeoman. Aug. 1827
John, Crompton, yeoman. Dec. 1828
John, Haworth Cross, Rochdale, gent. Feb. 1829
John, Top o'th'Hill, Butterworth, yeoman. A May 1830

Milne, John, Butterworth, yeoman. A June 1830 (1st grant 1803)
Mary, Crompton, feme covert. A Dec. 1828
Phebe, Rochdale, widow. Feb. 1829
Rebecca, Park House, Crompton, widow. A and Tuon July 1826 (2nd grant PR 188
Richard, Rochdale. A Aug. 1827*
Robert, Liverpool, commission broker. A and Tuon Jan. 1828
William, Manchester, distiller. Dec. 1826
Milner, Elizabeth Wilkinson, Ashton-under-Lyne, spinster. Sept. 1829
James, Barton-upon-Irwell, gent. June 1830
James, Crown Court, Old Change, London. Oct. 1830
John, Liverpool, victualler. Jan. 1829
Ralph, Mellor, yeoman. Dec. 1830
Richard, Manchester, bookkeeper. A May 1826
Milnes, James, Warrington, liquor merchant. April 1829
John, Manchester. Sept. 1826
John, Broadway Lane, Oldham. A Oct. 1830
John, Manchester, provision dealer. Oct. 1830
Mirtha, alias Holland, Peter, Liverpool, mariner. A July 1828
Mitchel, Peter, Liverpool, seaman. Dec. 1830*
Mitchell, John, Middleton, manufacturer. A Oct. 1828
Mary, Chorlton Row. A Sept. 1827
William, Holt Town, Manchester, merchant. April 1826
Mitchinson, Elizabeth, Liverpool. A April 1828
Mitten, Miles, Wigan, butcher. May 1827
Mockitt, John, Liverpool, mariner. A May 1830*
Mocock, John, Toxteth Park, clerk in the Custom House. A Oct. 1828
Moffat, James, Liverpool, merchant. Dec. 1827
Moffitt, Matthew, Liverpool, stonemason. Jan. 1830 (lst grant 1793)
Mollineux, Benjamin, Rainford, farmer. May 1827
Molyneux, Edward, Haigh, farmer. Nov. 1827
Ellen, Mawdsley, farmer. A Dec. 1829
Henry, Ormskirk, yeoman. April 1830
Henry, Little Woolton, gent. July 1830
James, Little Woolton, yeoman. April 1826
John, Burscough, blacksmith. Aug. 1826
John, Liverpool, blacksmith. A March 1827
John, Liverpool, victualler. Sept. 1829
Mary, Liverpool. A Sept. 1827
Thomas, Aintree, yeoman. April 1826
William, Liverpool, esq. Sept. 1827
Moncaster, Elizabeth, Liverpool, widow. June 1829
Moneypenny, Henry, Liverpool, mariner. A Aug. 1826*
Monks, Joseph, Warrington, shopkeeper. Sept. 1826
Michael, Wrightington, farmer. A May 1827
Moon, Henry, Rio de Janerio, merchant. Sept. 1828
James, Eccleston, Croston, yeoman. March 1826
Mooney, Eliza, West Derby. A July 1829
Moorcroft, James, Ormskirk, cabinet maker.Oct. 1829
Moore, Ellen, Wigan, feme covert. A April 1828 (2nd grant 1850)
Henry, Manchester, butcher. A June 1827
John, Cross Bank, Eccles, farmer. A Feb. 1826
John, Pendleton, yeoman. April 1827
John, Wigan, carrier. Feb. 1828

Moore, John, Carrington, yeoman. Feb. 1829
Joseph, Manchester, publican. July 1830
Thomas, Chorley, bookkeeper. A March 1826
William, Liverpool, labourer. A Sept. 1829
Moores, William, Toxteth, brewer. A Nov. 1827
Moorhouse, Robert, Chamber, Oldham, gent. A Sept. 1829
Moors, John, Openshaw, pavior. March 1830
Mordaunt, Thomas, Lathom, farmer. A July 1826*
William, Dalton, Wigan, farmer. A Sept. 1826*
Moreau, Ann Cath., Liverpool, spinster. Feb. 1829*
Moreton, Mary, Anderton. A March 1828
Samuel, Manchester, maker up of goods. A Nov. 1829
Samuel, Liverpool, gent. Aug. 1830*
Morgan, George, Rochdale, coachman. A July 1828
Sarah, Manchester. A Dec. 1827
Morison, John Hall, Liverpool, surgeon. A Aug. 1826
Morley, Elizabeth, Kirkdale, widow. Aug. 1826
John, Great Bolton, hat manufacturer. June 1829
Morris, Edward, Little Halton, co. Lanc., shopkeeper. April 1826
Edward, Liverpool, mariner. A Aug. 1830*
Elizabeth, Liverpool, widow. A Feb. 1830
Ellen, Walton-on-the-Hill, widow. A April 1828
Hannah, Harrington, spinster. Nov. 1829
Henry, Halliwell, yeoman. Aug. 1830
James, the Bounty Hall, Liverpool, mariner. A Aug. 1826*
James, Breightmet, gent. Aug. 1827
John, Oldfield Rd., Salford, shopkeeper. Jan. 1827
John, Haslingden, shoemaker. April 1827
John, Hag Side, Radcliffe, farmer. June 1828
John, Edgeworth, yeoman. Dec. 1830
Joseph, Manchester, victualler. March 1826
Martha, Manchester, shopkeeper. May 1827
Mary, Manchester, widow. March 1829
Owen, 51 Fleet St., Liverpool. A Dec. 1829
Ralph, Golborne, farmer. Nov. 1828
Richard, Liverpool, mariner. July 1828
Robert, Liverpool, doctor of physic. Sept. 1828 (2nd grant 1831)
William, Upholland, yeoman. Aug. 1829
Morrison, John, Campobello, co. Charlotte, New York, formerly Liverpool, mariner. A Feb. 1826*
Mort, John, Manchester, innkeeper. A Nov. 1826
Mortimer, Mary, Salford, singlewoman. July 1828
Morton, Charles, Pilsworth, weaver. A June 1829
James, Liverpool, iron founder and soap boiler. A June 1826 (2nd grant 1836)
James, Pendlebury, publican. Oct. 1828
Joseph, Manchester, silversmith. April 1827
Richard, Moorside, Flixton, yeoman. Feb. 1828
Thomas, Manchester, publican. A Nov. 1830
William, Manchester, publican. A Feb. 1827
William, Chorlton Row, cotton twister. Feb. 1828
Moses, Phoebe, Much Woolton, spinster. A Sept. 1830*
Mosley, James, Liverpool, spirit dealer. May 1828 (1st grant 1819)
John, Bootle, farmer. May 1828

Moss, Daniel, Warrington, doctor of medicine. Nov. 1826
Elizabeth, Warrington, spinster. A Nov. 1826
Elizabeth, wife of Thomas Moss, Moss Brook, Widnes, esq. Feb. 1829
James, Pemberton, bricklayer. Jan. 1827
John, North Meols, parish clerk. A and Tuon April 1826*
John, Pemberton, farmer. March 1828
John, Longton, esq., Nov. 1828
Robert, Mossley, yeoman. March 1827
Susannah, Bickerstaff, spinster. Feb. 1828
William, Toxteth Park, gent. A July 1826
William, Manchester, last of Stretford, saddler. June 1827
Mossop, John, Liverpool, provision [*dealer*]. May 1829
Mottram, Jabez Clegg, Irwell House, Manchester, clerk. Oct. 1827*
Joseph, Salford, bookkeeper. A Jan. 1826
Peter, Manchester, draper. April 1828
Mould, William, Liverpool, coachman. Nov. 1830
Moulson, Ellen, Chester, last of Liverpool, widow. Jan. 1829
Mounsey, William, Chorlton Row, shopkeeper. Jan. 1828
Much, Mary, Liverpool, widow. A Nov. 1830*
Mudge, Charlotte Cole, Everton, spinster. May 1828
Mullin, James, Liverpool, shoemaker. A Aug. 1827
Mulliner, John, Manchester, cotton spinner. A Feb. 1826
Mullins, Jonathan, Liverpool, rag merchant. A Nov. 1828
Mullions, Robert, Liverpool, mariner. A May 1828
Munn, John, Prestwich, cotton manufacturer. A Nov. 1826
Murphy, Catherine, Liverpool, spinster. A Aug. 1828 (1st grant 1820)
Dennis, Isle of Man. Aug. 1828
Dennis, Liverpool, minor. A Aug. 1828 (1st grant 1817)
James, Liverpool, merchant. May 1830
John, Liverpool, merchant. A Oct. 1827; Aug. 1828
Mary, Liverpool, feme covert. A Aug. 1828 (1st grant 1820)
Mary, Liverpool, widow. Oct. 1828
Murray, James, Liverpool. Dec. 1827
James, Rochdale. A March 1830
John, Manchester, weaver. A June 1829
Margaret, Manchester, widow. May 1827
Roger Cowley, Liverpool, bookkeeper. Aug. 1828
Murry, Elizabeth, Cadishead, widow. April 1828
Musker, Robert, Bootle, farmer. May 1829 (2nd grant 1867)
Mutch, John, Liverpool, officer in the Customs. A Sept. 1830
Samuel, Liverpool, cooper. A Feb. 1830*
Myers, Margaret, Liverpool, spinster. Nov. 1829*
Myles, John, Eccles. March 1829
William, Liverpool Wesleyan minister. June 1828

NAIRN, Robert, Liverpool, surgeon. March 1826 (1st grant 1824)
Naylor, Isaac, Speke, farmer. A and Tuon Jan. 1827
James, Manchester, carver and gilder. Dec. 1827 (2nd grant 1880)
James, Wigan, check manufacturer. A Dec. 1830
John, Tarbock, file cutter. April 1829
Margaret, Manchester, widow. A Aug. 1829
Richard, Liverpool, innkeeper. Feb. 1827
Richard, Ormskirk, ironmonger. A March 1827

Naylor, William, Liverpool, last of Clifton, co. Glouc., esq. March 1830
Needham, Ann, Liverpool, widow. A Nov., 1829
Mary, wife of John Needham, Liverpool, shipwright. Nov., 1830
Mary, Liverpool. A Dec., 1830
Neil, John, Liverpool, master mariner. A Feb., 1829
Neild, Hannah, Manchester. A June 1830
Henry, Manchester, cotton merchant. Feb., 1827
Nelson, George, Liverpool, gent. A Feb., 1827
James, Liverpool, mariner. A Dec., 1830*
Peter, the Hardy, Liverpool, mariner. A Oct., 1826*
Peter, Heap, Bury, cotton carder. A Aug., 1828
Richard, Farnworth, farmer. A Oct., 1829
Thomas, Manchester, innkeeper. Nov., 1826
William, Liverpool, cook. A Jan., 1829*
Neville, Patrick, alias James, Liverpool, mariner. A Jan., 1827*
Newall, James, Warrington, miller. Oct., 1830
Jane, Littleborough, Rochdale, spinster. A April 1830
Jenny, Lower Townhouse, Rochdale. A April 1826; Jan., 1829
Lawrence, Lower Town House, Rochdale, merchant. Nov., 1828
Smith, Rochdale, woolstapler. March 1826
Newby, John, Liverpool. A Oct., 1827
Samuel, Liverpool. A Oct., 1827
Newcomb, George, Liverpool, mariner. Aug., 1829
Newell, Martha, Haggate, Burnley, widow. March 1830
Newman, Benjamin, Liverpool, mariner. May 1830*
Edward, Manchester, last of Barton-upon-Irwell, yeoman. June 1826
Newsam, Thomas, Liverpool, mariner. A Nov., 1830*
William, Manchester, lodging house keeper. A March 1826; May 1827
Newsham, Richard, Liverpool, dealer in earthenware. A Jan., 1829
Newton, Ann, Manchester, widow. April 1826
Ann, Alt Hill, Ashton-under-Lyne, widow. A May 1829
Catharine, Urmston, widow. Sept., 1829; Jan., 1830
Hump[h]rey, Liverpool, landing waiter. A Jan., 1830 (2nd grant 1848)
James, Ashton-under-Lyne, innkeeper. Feb., 1826
James, Ashton-under-Lyne, yeoman. July 1826 (2nd grant 1862)
James, Oldham, weaver. Feb., 1830*
John, Well oth Lane, Rochdale, cotton spinner. Oct., 1826
John, Withington, gent. June 1828
John, Stayley Bridge, yeoman. A Feb., 1829
John, the Colony of Demerary, last of Toxteth Park. June 1829
John, Ashton-under-Lyne, yeoman. A Oct., 1830*
John, Manchester, cabinet maker. A Oct., 1830
John Abney, Heaton Norris, yeoman. May 1828
Joshua, Lees, Ashton-under-Lyne, cotton spinner. Dec., 1830
Martha, Liverpool, widow. Sept., 1830
Robert, Lees, Ashton-under-Lyne, yeoman. Feb., 1826
Ruth, Chorlton Row, widow. Sept., 1829
William, Middle Hulton, farmer. Sept., 1829
William, Manchester, bookseller. Oct., 1830
Nicholls, Charles, Manchester, baker. A March 1828 (1st grant 1821)
Elizabeth, Manchester, spinster. Feb., 1830
Hannah, Manchester, widow. A Oct., 1827
Nichols, Ann, Salford, widow. A June 1830

Nichols, David, Hulme, cordwainer. March 1830
Thomas, Salford, gent. Feb. 1827
Nicholson, Arabella, Harrington, spinster. Jan. 1830
Elizabeth, Warrington, feme covert. A July 1828
Millicent, Liverpool. Sept. 1827
Peter, Orrell, nail manufacturer. Sept. 1827
Nield, William, Shaw Edge, Crompton, yeoman. May 1829
Noble, Henry, Bolton-le-Moors, stonemason. A Oct. 1826*
Noblet, Matthew, Billington, yeoman. Jan. 1826
Noblett, Robert, Brindle, innkeeper. A March 1827
Nodin, James, Manchester, labourer. Nov. 1826
Norbury, Hannah, Bootle St., Manchester, innkeeper. Dec. 1826
John, Hay Head, yeoman. Oct. 1828
Thomas, Croft, innkeeper. Aug. 1827
Norman, Isaac, Blackburn, pawnbroker. Jan. 1827
Thomas, Sutton. April 1826
Norris, George, Bretherton. Nov. 1829
Henrietta, Liverpool, widow. Oct. 1826
Henry, Halliwell, farmer. A Dec. 1829
Hugh, Liverpool, cooper. April 1827
Hugh, Penwortham, farmer. Oct. 1829
James, Everton, clerk in the Customs. Sept. 1826
John, Heskin. Feb. 1827
Margaret, Ormskirk, widow. Jan. 1829
Nathan, Heskin, farmer. April 1827
Richard, Liverpool, tailor. May 1826
Robert, Formby, yeoman. Dec. 1826
Sarah, Hardshaw, widow. April 1828
Thomas, Liverpool, mariner. A Feb. 1828*
North, Martha, Liverpool, widow. A Oct. 1826
Thomas Dunnington, Liverpool. Oct. 1829
Nowell, Abraham, Briercliffe, Burnley. July 1828
William, Knowsley, husbandman. April 1826
Nuttall, Ann, Bolton, shopkeeper. Oct. 1828
Betty, Edgeside, Rossendale, widow. A May 1827
Betty, Whitefield, spinster. A Nov. 1828 (2nd grant 1857)
Edward, Bury, bailiff. Nov. 1830
Elizabeth, wife of John Nuttall, Bury, esq. Feb. 1829
George, Tottington, weaver. Nov. 1830
Henry, Rochdale, yeoman. A Aug. 1827
Henry, Clough Folds, Rossendale, carrier. Dec. 1830
James, Smallshaw, Rossendale, farmer. April 1826
James, Bury, cabinet maker. Nov. 1828
James, Ernshaw Barn, Rossendale. June 1830
John, Gorsey Clough, Tottington Lower End, weaver. A July 1826 (2nd grant 1847)
John, Chorlton Row, pattern card maker. Jan. 1827
John, Bacup, butcher. Oct. 1829
John, Dove Bank, Little Lever, farmer. May 1830
Joseph, Ashton-in-the-Willows, cotton carder. A Oct. 1827
Nathaniel, Great Bolton, shopkeeper. June 1830
Robert, Bearshill, woollen weaver. April 1828
Thomas, Liverpool, car keeper. A Feb. 1829

Nuttall, William, Harwood, farmer. Oct. 1830
Nutter, Ellis, Sadlers, Goldshaw Booth, yeoman. Aug. 1829
John, Habergham, Burnley, private in the 10th Veterans. A Feb. 1826*

OAKES, Ann, Liverpool, widow. A Feb. 1826
Ellen, Atherton, widow. Feb. 1826*
James, Bolton, mechanic. A June 1828
Thomas, Liverpool, gent. A May 1828 (1st grant 1819)
William, Allerton, gardener. A May 1829
Oates, John, Liverpool, tailor. Oct. 1826
Oddie, John, Clitheroe, esq. May 1830 (2nd grant 1846)
Offington, Michael, Liverpool, seaman. Sept. 1826*
Ogden, Abraham, Manchester, publican. A Nov. 1828
Charles, Birch, Hopwood, shopkeeper. Feb. 1826
David, Oldham, saddler. A Nov. 1829
Elizabeth, Turton, spinster. Jan., 1828
James, Newton, Manchester, weaver. March 1827*
James, Blackley, innholder. Dec. 1827
James, Openshaw, weaver. Dec. 1827
James, Liverpool, bookkeeper. June 1829 (2nd grant 1839)
John, Failsworth, gent. May 1826
John, Ashton-under-Lyne, butcher. A July 1827 (2nd grant 1843)
Joseph, Failsworth, shopkeeper. Dec. 1827
Joseph, Cheetham, bookkeeper. A May 1828
Joseph, Oldham, shopkeeper. Dec. 1830
Joshua, Bolton-le-Moors, weaver. A Nov. 1829
Mary, Whittakers, Oldham, widow. March 1826
Mary, Oldham, widow. A Nov. 1826
Mary, Wavertree, spinster. Oct. 1830 (2nd grant 1846)
Peggy, Olderroot, Oldham, spinster. March 1828*
Richard, Liverpool, gent. A June 1828 (2nd grant 1846)
Robert, Middleton, joiner. Jan. 1826
Samuel, Sheeps Hey, Prestwich weaver. A Dec. 1827
Samuel, Bank Top, Oldham, cotton spinner. A June 1828
Sarah, Mount Pleasant, Oldham, widow. Aug. 1828
Thomas, Middleton, weaver. A Jan. 1827
Thomas, Edgworth, tailor. A Jan. 1829
Thomas, Oldham, hatter. A July 1830*
William, Manchester, shopkeeper. Feb. 1828
Oglethorpe, Joseph, Liverpool, victualler. A April 1829
O'Hara, Patrick, Stayley Bridge, tailor. A Dec. 1827
Okell, Margaret, Warrington, widow. Jan. 1828
William, Liverpool, merchant. A May 1826
Okill, William, Liverpool, cooper. A Jan. 1828
Oldfield, Benjamin, Heaton Norris, shopkeeper. Aug. 1828*
Charles, Windle, yeoman. March 1830
Jonathan, Worsley, boatman. A March 1830
Robert, Chorley, clothier. A Feb. 1827
Sarah, Heaton Norris, shopkeeper. June 1829
Oldham, Betty, Great Bolton, widow. Dec. 1826
Mary, Heywood, widow. Feb. 1830
Oldknow, Samuel, Mellor, co. Derby, esq. Feb. 1829
Olive, James, Coney Green, Radcliffe, farmer. April 1826 (2nd grant 1864)

Olive, Richard, Anisworth, grocer. A March 1829
Oliver, William, Manchester, joiner. A Oct. 1829
Oliverson, Margaret, Scarisbrick, widow. A and Tuon Oct. 1827
Ollier, Ann, Liverpool, singlewoman. Jan. 1827
Ollivant, Edward, Manchester, gent. A May 1827
Sarah, Pendleton, widow. March 1826
Omand, Magnees, Liverpool, master mariner. A June 1829
O'Neil, Margaret, Liverpool, widow. June 1827
Openshaw, Margaret, Horwich, widow. A July 1826
Nancy, Evans House, Wiswell, widow. May 1830
Samuel, Bury, hatter. A July 1828
Orford, William, Liverpool, merchant. A April 1830
William John, Liverpool, merchant. A Nov. 1829
Ormandy, James, Liverpool, joiner. A June 1827
Orme, James, Manchester. May 1827
Samuel, Liverpool, gent. A March 1827
Ormerod, George, Goodshaw Chapel, Rossendale, yeoman. Oct. 1828*
James, Heyhead, farmer. March 1828
James, Cloughfold, Rossendale, innkeeper. June 1830 (1st grant 1818)
John, Rochdale, gent. March 1826
John, Todmorden Edge, manufacturer. A March 1826
John, Henfield, Blackburn, innkeeper. A Dec. 1826
John, Bankside, Rossendale, merchant. May 1828
John, Bury, shopkeeper. Feb. 1829
Samuel, Cloughfield, Rossendale. Aug. 1827*
William, Hey Head, Gambleside, yeoman. April 1827
Ormesher, Edward, Rainford, farmer. A Feb. 1826
Ormisher, Henry, West Derby, yeoman. Feb. 1829
Ormrod, George, Hulme, market gardener. A April 1828
James, Chamber Hall, Bolton-le-Moors, cotton spinner. May 1827
James, Rixton cum Glazebrook, farmer. A Aug. 1829
Margaret, Turton, widow. Nov., 1826
Peter, Turton, co. Lanc., farmer. April 1830
Orred, Frances, Liverpool. Oct. 1826
George, Liverpool, gent. Feb. 1829
Orrell, John, Liverpool, saddler. July 1828
William, Halliwell, publican. A Oct. 1826
Ortt, Richard, Everton, clerk. Oct., 1828
Osborne, Elizabeth, Manchester, widow. A Nov. 1828
Ovens, Rebecca, Liverpool, spinster. April 1829
Overall, Mary, Prestwich, spinster. June 1830
Oversby, John, Liverpool, schoolmaster. A June 1830
Owen, David, Manchester, victualler. March 1828
John, Hulme, wheelwright. May 1826 (2nd grant 1851)
John, Oakfield, co. Lanc., gent. Nov. 1826
Joseph, Croft, Winwick, yeoman. Nov. 1829
Joseph, Childwall. Feb. 1830
Joseph Dodgson, Liverpool, clerk in the Customs. Nov. 1830
Thomas, Maghull. Jan. 1828
Thomas, Poulton, yeoman. Feb. 1828
William, Childwall, yeoman. Jan. 1827
William, Childwall, farmer. A Sept. 1827 (2nd grant 1849)
Owens, John, Liverpool, victualler. Feb. 1829

Oxendale, Richard, Longton, farmer. Dec. 1830
William, Longton, yeoman. April 1829

PAGE, Thomas Trent, Liverpool, gent. Aug. 1829 (2nd grant 1852)
William, Liverpool, victualler. A Dec. 1830
Paget, John, Liverpool, liquor merchant. A April 1827
Palethorpe, Ellen, Gedling, co. Notts. A Jan. 1827
Palmer, Samuel, High Crompton, bookkeeper. A Feb. 1826
Parcy, Mary, Liverpool, spinster. A Jan. 1826
Park, Richard, Wrightington, labourer. A May 1829
William, Wigan, ironmaster. July 1828
Parke, Ann, Highfield, widow. March 1828
Hannah, High Field, Liverpool, spinster. Dec. 1827
Thomas, Liverpool, merchant. A Dec. 1826
Parker, Ann, Liverpool, spinster. June 1830
Frances, Liverpool. A Oct. 1827
Francis, Liverpool, gent. A Dec. 1827
George, Blackburn, yeoman. Jan. 1828
George, Farrington, farmer. A July 1828
Grace, Ambwell, Foulridge. July 1829
Hodgson, Liverpool, mariner. A July 1827*
James, Bury, cloth dresser. A Oct. 1826
John, Haslingden Grange, weaver. A Sept. 1826*
Johnson, Bury, gent. Aug. 1830
Joseph, Low Hill Coffee House, Liverpool. Jan. 1828
Mary, Penwortham, spinster. March 1828
alias Parkinson, Richard, master of the Royal Navy. May 1826
Richard, Ince, yeoman. Jan., 1827; Nov. 1827
Robert, Bury, attorney-at-law. April 1830
William, Liverpool. A Feb. 1826
William, Tottington Lower End, weaver. A Feb. 1830
Parkes, Betty, Rochdale. A Nov. 1828
Edward, Hulme, gent. Feb. 1826
Parkinson, Alice, Salford. A Dec. 1827
Barton, Bardsea, yeoman. June 1826
Betty, Alston. Nov. 1828*
Charles, Bolton-le-Moors, ale house keeper. June 1829
Ellen, Shaws Brow, Liverpool, spinster. A Jan. 1828
John, Worsley, innkeeper. Jan. 1828 (1st grant 1812)
Peter, Liverpool, traveller. Nov. 1827
Richard, Liverpool, merchant. A March 1826
Richard, *see* Parker
Thomas, Shersin within Henheads, Rossendale, farmer. July 1828
Parr, Betty, Swinton, spinster. A Nov. 1829*
Edward, Liverpool, staymaker. Aug. 1830
Hugh, Prescot, gent. A Oct. 1827*
James, Liverpool, publican. Oct. 1830
Jane, Liverpool, widow. A May 1829
John Oughton, Liverpool, factor. A Feb. 1828 (2nd grant 1853)
Margaret, Liverpool, widow. Feb. 1827
Mary, Hopwood, spinster. A March 1829 (2nd grant 1842)
Mathew, Ormskirk, gent. A Sept. 1830
Richard, Barton-upon-Irwell, farmer. April 1830

Parr, William, Chadderton, publican. Feb. 1828
William, Ormskirk, auctioneer. Oct. 1829
Parry, Elizabeth, Liverpool, spinster. A June 1828
Fanny, Liverpool. A April 1830
Henry, Liverpool, mariner. A Oct. 1829*
Joseph, Liverpool, labourer. April 1827
Robert, Liverpool, gent. A Aug. 1827
Robert, Walton-on-the-Hill, labourer. Feb. 1828
Robert, Liverpool, gent. A Oct. 1828
Rowland, Liverpool, mariner. April 1829
Parsley, Thomas, Liverpool, innkeeper. A March 1830
Parson, John, Liverpool, gent. March 1829 (2nd grant 1837)
Parsons, Edward, Manchester, calico printer. Dec. 1826
William, Chorley, painter. A July 1830
Part, Thomas the elder, Pendleton, last of Astley, gent. Aug. 1829
Partington, Edmund, Whitehead, innkeeper. Nov. 1829
Elizabeth, Wood St., Middleton, weaver. Sept. 1826
John, Lostock, weaver. Feb. 1830*
Ralph, Liverpool, miller. A Jan., 1829
Pass, William, Manchester, filer and turner. A Feb. 1830
Patchett, Christopher, Tildesley, draper. Dec. 1829
Pate, John, Higham, farmer. June 1828
Richard, Ogden, farmer. June 1829
William, Burnley, cordwainer. Feb. 1829
William, Liverpool, victualler and clothier. A Dec. 1829
Patefield, Thomas, Hurdsfield, joiner and machine maker. Nov. 1826
Patten, Andrew, Hulme, iron liquor maker. A Jan. 1828 (1st grant 1815)
Elizabeth, Liverpool, widow. A Dec. 1830
John, Widnes, yeoman. April 1829
Patterson, Alexander, Liverpool, shipwright. A Aug. 1829
Allen, Liverpool, cooper. A June 1830*
Pattie, John, Liverpool, mariner. A June 1828
Pattison, Elizabeth, Warrington, spinster. A July 1827
John, Liverpool, gent. July 1830
Paul, Joseph, Salford, labourer. June 1829
Payn, James, Maidenhead, co. Berks., gent. Sept. 1830*
Payne, Mary, Liverpool, widow. Nov. 1827
Paynter, Richard, Manchester, gent. A June 1827
Peace, Benjamin Chappell, Manchester. A Nov. 1828
Peacop, John, Burnley, grocer. June 1828
Pearson, Elizabeth, Broad Oats, New Accrington. April 1828
George, Swinton, weaver. April 1830*
James, Liverpool, cow keeper. April 1829 (2nd grant 1868)
James, Pleasington, farmer. A May 1830
John, Liverpool, innkeeper. A June 1826
John, Kirkdale, gent. Oct. 1826
John, Warren Lane, Accrington, weaver. A June 1829
formerly Berry, Sarah, Monton Lane, widow. A Aug. 1827*
Thomas, Toxteth Park, gent. A Feb. 1828
William, Thoresby, farmer. A March 1828
Pease, George, Rusholme, servant. A April 1828
Peatfield, Robert, Pendlebury. Jan. 1828
Pedley, Mary, Chorlton Row. A Oct. 1829

Peel, Margaret, Bury, widow. Aug. 1829
William, Stand Lane, Pilkington, shopkeeper. May 1826
Peele, Peter, Liverpool, Navy agent. A June 1828
Peers, Alexander, Hollins Green, chapman. Feb. 1828
John, Culcheth, yeoman. April 1828
Joseph, Culcheth, husbandman. Sept. 1828 (1st grant 1769)
Mary, Warrington, widow. Oct. 1826
Richard, Liverpool, gent. March 1828
William, Liverpool, cotton broker. April 1826
Peet, John, Billinge, carpenter. Oct. 1829*
Pegg, Thomas, Manchester, bookkeeper. A May 1826*
Pegge, Sarah, Pemberton, widow. Oct. 1826
Pemberton, Charles, Liverpool, cabinet maker. Aug. 1830
Edward, Warrington. A June 1827
John the elder, Atherton, carter. Feb. 1826
Peter, Westleigh, weaver. March 1827*
Peter, Liverpool, mariner. A Oct. 1828
William, Liverpool, mariner. Jan. 1826
William, Liverpool, gent. May 1827
Pendlebury, Ann, Radcliffe Bridge. A July 1828
Betty, Lostock, widow. Feb. 1826
Betty, Bedford, Leigh, widow. A May 1829
Henry, Over Hulton, farmer. June 1828
James, Hindley, victualler. Jan. 1830
James, Chowbent, Atherton. Oct. 1830*
John, Lostock, Bolton, cotton spinner. A Feb. 1829
Ralph, Kersley, yeoman. Nov. 1827
Richard, Halliwell, farmer. A Oct. 1829
Robert, Horwich, weaver. Sept. 1829
William, Manchester, builder. Jan. 1826
Pendleton, Edmund, Prestwich, yeoman. May 1827
James, Salford, gent. April 1826
Margaret, Litherland, cowkeeper. April 1829
Robert, Litherland, labourer. Feb. 1829
Penketh, John, Hale, co. Lanc., farmer. Oct. 1827
Penkethman, George, Leigh, cordwainer. Dec. 1826
Penkett, Hannah, Liverpool. July 1829
Pennington, Elizabeth, Kendal, feme covert. A Feb. 1828
Elizabeth, Liverpool, spinster. May 1828
George, Worthington, yeoman. Dec. 1829*
Isaac, Blackrod, yeoman. Oct., 1826 (1st grant 1820)
John Richardson, Prescot, surgeon. July 1828
Margaret, Hindley, widow. Sept. 1826
Margaret, Warrington, widow. Nov. 1828
Mary, Billinge, spinster. May 1828
Penny, Elizabeth, Edge Hill, widow. June 1828
Penple, Florence Reine Joseph, Manchester, spinster. June 1830
Percival, Edward, Rochdale, spirit merchant. A Jan. 1829; Aug. 1829
Hugh, Castleton, dealer in malt. Oct. 1828
Mary, Rochdale, widow. Aug. 1829
Thomas, Warrington, shopkeeper. Nov. 1826
Perkin, James, Manchester, labourer. A Nov. 1830
Perkins, John, Liverpool, victualler. Feb. 1827

Perry, Charles, Pendleton, servant. Oct. 1827
Mary, Liverpool, widow. April 1830
Perryn, Richard, Standish, clerk. April 1826; June 1828
Petty, Alice, Colne, widow. Nov. 1828 (original to York)
Thomas, Billinge, butcher. Jan. 1830
Peyton, Jane Selina, Hulme, widow. July 1830
William, Liverpool, gent. May 1826
Phethean, John, Bolton-le-Moors, innkeeper. March 1829
Phibbs, Anne [Hannah *deleted*] , Liverpool, widow. June 1827
Phillips, Cordelia, Hulme, spinster. June 1828
Hannah, Warrington. A Jan. 1826
James, Liverpool, gent. May 1829
Walter, Manchester, last of Isle of Man, gent. Feb. 1829
Pickance, William, Liverpool, gent. A Nov. 1829
Pickavance, Joseph, Liverpool, flour dealer. May 1828
Pickering, John, Howarth, co. Durham, last of Eccleston, contractor. June 1830
William, Newton, farmer. Dec. 1829
Pickford, John, Shude Hill, Manchester, cordwainer. Nov. 1827
Pickles, James, Rishton, farmer. Feb. 1830
William, Todmorden, grocer. Nov. 1829
Pickston, Peter, Kirkhoms, co. Lanc., yeoman. June 1826
Pickton, John, Broughton, farmer. A Nov. 1829 (2nd grant 1830: Picton)
Robert, Newton, joiner. July 1828
Pickup, Abraham, Bank Lane, Walmersley, farmer. A Sept. 1826
Edmund, Bankside, Bury, widower. A Jan. 1830
George, Slack, Newchurch, weaver. March 1827
James, Edges, farmer. A Jan. 1829
Thomas, Liverpool, miller. May 1829
Picton, John, Broughton, farmer. Jan. 1830 (1st grant 1829: Pickton)
Pierce, William, formerly Liverpool, last of Tranmere Ferry, victualler. May 1829
Pierrepont, John, Liverpool, watchmaker. A Feb. 1826
Piggott, Judith, West Derby, spinster. May 1826
Pilkington, Alexander, Scoonhoven, Holland, Lieut. Colonel. May 1827
Betty, Houghton Nook, Altham, widow. A Jan. 1827
Erwin, Edgeworth, farmer. A March 1828
James, Jackson Fold, farmer. June 1828
John, Scarisbrick, farmer. A March 1827
John, Bolton-le-Moors, esq. Jan. 1829
Peter, Blackburn, yeoman. May 1828
Robert, Aughton, farmer. Nov. 1830
Thomas, Houghton, last of West Derby, farmer. Aug. 1829
William, Little Bolton. Dec. 1826
William, Aspull, weaver. A June 1827
Pilling, James, Bacup. May 1827
John, Manchester, currier and leather cutter. A Feb. 1826
Richard, Toadlane, Rochdale, bookkeeper. Aug. 1827*
Samuel, Finney Cote, Tottington Lower End, yeoman. Oct. 1830*
Pilshaw, William, Sharples, husbandman. Oct. 1829*
Pimbley, James, Aughton, farmer. Dec. 1826
Maximillian, Aughton, farmer. Dec. 1826
Pinnington, Ann, Billinge, spinster. A Aug. 1826
John, Liverpool, joiner. July 1828 (1st grant 1785: Pennington)
Thomas, Liverpool, auctioneer. May 1830

Pinnington, William, Winstanley, nailor. Feb. 1826
Pitt, Edward, Manchester, gent. A June 1830
Pixton, John, Manchester, shopkeeper. Feb. 1826
William, Lostock, butcher. Sept. 1827
Place, Charles, Warrington, glasscutter. A July 1829
Thomas, Liverpool, ropemaker. July 1830
Plant, George, Heaton Norris, baker. A July 1827
Richard, St. Helens, gent. April 1827
Thomas, Holmes Chapel, yeoman. Aug. 1828
Platt, Adam, West Derby, gent. A Nov. 1828
Ann, Bolton-le-Moors, widow. A March 1828
James, Rumworth, farmer. A Dec. 1828
Jeremiah or Jeremy, Liverpool, cotton broker. A May 1827; Sept. 1827*; Jan. 1830
John, Barracks, Saddleworth, cotton manufacturer. June 1826
John, Liverpool, victualler. Nov. 1826 (2nd grant 1833)
John, Ormskirk, yeoman. Feb. 1827
John, Liverpool, victualler. July 1829
Joseph, Stayley Bridge, carrier. A Feb. 1826
Mary, Worrockhallfoot, Saddleworth, widow. A Jan. 1826*
Matthias, Wood Park, Ashton-under-Lyne, coal miner. Feb. 1827
Ralph, Ormskirk, yeoman. March 1827 (1st grant 1793)
Roger, Breightmet, yeoman. May 1828 (1st grant 1824)
William, Liverpool, gent. June 1828; Dec. 1829 (3rd grant 1835)
William, Liverpool, gent. A Dec. 1828
Plumb, Dorothy, Eccleston, Croston, widow. July 1826*
Plumley, James, West Derby, tailor. A Sept. 1828
Plumpton, Mary, St. Helens, last of Sutton, spinster. July 1830
Peter, Horwich, last of Wigan, joiner. May 1830
Plunkett, Christopher, Toxteth Park. A Oct. 1829
Frances, Dublin, widow. A Jan. 1827*
Polding, William, Croxteth Park, yeoman. March 1828
Pole, Charles, Liverpool, merchant. Dec. 1826
Pollard, Jonathan, Manchester, cotton spinner. Nov. 1826
Matthew, Lower Bradley, Great Marsden, yeoman. Jan. 1828
Pollit, Jacob, Waterhouses, Ashton-under-Lyne, weaver. A May 1828
Ralph, Little Hulton, farmer. A June 1829
Thomas, Bury, gent. Jan. 1828 (2nd grant 1836)
Pollitt, Amos, Brooksmouth, Bury, painter. April 1826
Ann, Heaton Norris, widow. Dec. 1826
Daniel, Warrington, auctioneer. Nov. 1830
Edmund, Ashworth, farmer. A Jan. 1826
James, Pendleton, Eccles, gent. Jan. 1830
John, Bury, cotton manufacturer. Feb. 1827
Pontefract, Thomas, Delph, clothier. A Dec. 1828
Pool, Thomas, Manchester, earthenware dealer. May 1826
Poole, Elizabeth, Liverpool, spinster. A July 1826
John, Withington, coachman. A May 1829
John, Polygon, Ardwick, cotton broker. A Feb. 1830
Joseph, Liverpool, ironmonger. A Nov. 1830
Pope, Mary, Ormskirk. May 1826
Richard, Lytham, clerk. Sept. 1828
Robert, Ormskirk, cordwainer. May 1826

Pope, Thomas, Aughton. Feb. 1826
Thomas, Ormskirk, shoemaker. A Feb. 1830
Porter, Ann, Bury, spinster. Jan. 1828
Mary, Bury, widow. Aug. 1830
Samuel, Lees, yeoman. Nov. 1827
William, Manchester, farmer. A Jan. 1829
Porteus, Elizabeth, Cheltenham, widow. A Oct. 1827
Posnett, Benjamin, Wavertree, plumber and glazier. April 1830
Pott, Elizabeth, Newton, Manchester, spinster. A Oct. 1827*
John, Newton, Manchester, bachelor. A Oct. 1827*
Margaret, Newton, spinster. Jan. 1827
Samuel, Newton, Manchester. A Oct. 1827*
Potter, Arthur, Homer Hill, Bury, cotton spinner. Aug. 1828
Elizabeth, Manchester, spinster. A March 1826
Elizabeth, Rumworth, spinster. March 1827
Ellen, Camelfield Cottage, widow. Dec. 1829
George, Darley Hall, formerly Manchester, esq. June 1827
James, Ashton-under-Lyne, machine maker. A May 1827 (2nd grant 1871)
Potts, Jane, Manchester, spinster. A June 1829
William, Liverpool, mariner. Aug. 1828
Powell, Catherine, Liverpool, spinster. A April 1828
Elizabeth, Sankey, widow. A Oct. 1827
Evan, Liverpool, labourer. April 1826
Joseph, Liverpool, tobacco manufacturer. June 1829
Mary, Liverpool, widow. A Feb. 1827
Richard, Liverpool, brewer. A Nov. 1828*
Richard, Liverpool, cork cutter. A May 1829
Thomas, Manchester, shopkeeper. Oct. 1826
William, Bolton, publican. Nov. 1828
Pownall, Hannah, Unsworth, spinster. Oct. 1828
John, Manchester, coach proprietor. A Oct. 1826
John Williamson, Liverpool, mariner. A June 1827*
Joseph, Pennington, yeoman. Dec. 1828
Thomas, Bolee, Middleton, farmer. July 1830
William, Manchester, weaver. Nov. 1828
Pratchett, Ann, Manchester, widow. A Feb. 1830
Pratt, Margaret, Manchester, spinster. Aug. 1827
Prenton, Samuel, Liverpool, mariner. A Sept. 1829
Prescot, John, Chorley, innkeeper. Dec. 1830
Ralph, Tyldesley with Shakerley, labourer. A April 1826
Thomas, Ormskirk, shopkeeper. June 1828
William, Lathom, yeoman. June 1827
Prescott, Hannah, Prescot, spinster. March 1827*
William, Holme Wood, Tarleton, farmer. Feb. 1827
Preston, Elizabeth, Crawshaw Booth, Rossendale. A April 1829
John, Moss, Colne, farmer. Sept. 1829
John, Eccleston, Prescot, watchmaker. March 1830
Mary, Liverpool, spinster. June 1830
Robert, Liverpool, brandy merchant. A Aug. 1828
Robert, Manchester, innkeeper. March 1830
Rosannah, Manchester. A May 1827
William, Liverpool, distiller. June 1828
Prestwich, Martha, Heady Hill, Bury, widow. A Nov. 1828

Price, Elizabeth, Liverpool, widow. April 1830
Hannah, Liverpool, widow. May 1826
John, Liverpool, cart owner. July 1829
Thomas, Pendleton, Eccles, manufacturer. July 1826
Prickett, Ann, Liverpool, widow. June 1828
Thomas, Liverpool, victualler. Jan. 1827
Priestley, John, Church Stile, Rochdale, innkeeper. June 1829
Priestnell, Henry, Liverpool, pilot. A July 1826*
Prince, Benjamin, Whitchurch, maltster. Oct. 1828
Christopher, Paddington Lodge, Edge Hill, gent. Nov. 1827
Deborah, Cheetham. Nov. 1829
Pritchard, Edward, Everton, woollen draper. March 1830
John, Liverpool, cooper. A Sept. 1829
John, Liverpool, pilot. A July 1830
Proctor, William, Liverpool, mariner. June 1827
William, Liverpool, master mariner. Aug. 1830
William Fullideph, Prescot, minister of the Gospel. July 1826
Proudlove, James, Halliwell, farmer. Jan. 1829
Pryce, Edward, Salford, servantman. A June 1826
Richard, Manchester, joiner. Nov. 1826
Pugh, Ann, Liverpool, widow. June 1826
Pulford, George, Liverpool, cordwainer. A and Tuon June 1830; Oct. 1830
Pulman, Mary, Bradley Lane Head. A June 1826
Purchess, John, Gorton, stonemason. A July 1828
Pye, James, Liverpool, butcher. A Dec. 1828
John, Wavertree, miller. Oct. 1827
John, Liverpool, broker and auctioneer. Feb. 1829
John, Liverpool, labourer. A July 1829
Margaret, Liverpool. A Oct. 1827*
Thomas the elder, Westhend, Lathom, farmer. A Jan. 1830
Pyke, George, Liverpool, mariner. A Sept. 1830*

QUALTER, Elizabeth, Liverpool, feme covert. A Dec. 1828
Quarterley, James, Ribchester, clerk. June 1829
Quayle, Samuel, Liverpool, cooper. A Nov. 1827*
Quick, Andrew, Liverpool, mariner. A July 1829
Quilliam, William, Liverpool, gent. July 1826 (1st grant 1821; 3rd grant 1852)
Quin, Valentine, Great Bolton, muslin manufacturer. May 1830
Quirk, Philip, Toxteth Park, gent. Nov. 1828

RADCLIFF, Thomas, Bold, farmer. Sept. 1829
Radcliffe, Edmund, Oldham, gent. Aug., 1828 (1st grant 1745; 2nd grant 1805)
Edmund Stringfellow, Walton-le-Dale, clerk. April 1826
James, Saddleworth, clothier. A Dec. 1826
James, Blackburn, parish clerk. Oct. 1828
James, Bank, Oldham, hat manufacturer. Oct. 1829
John, Burnley, tinner and brazier. Feb. 1827
Joshua, Bowkhouse, Saddleworth, gent. A Sept. 1826
Margaret, Middleton, spinster. April 1826
Mary Ann, Denshaw, Saddleworth, spinster. Aug. 1826
Samuel, Saddleworth Fold, yeoman. Oct. 1827
Thomas Hayward, Bootle-cum-Linacre, esq. July 1829
William, Vineyard, Oldham. March 1828

Radcliffe, William, Bank, Oldham, hat manufacturer. Oct. 1829
Rainford, Ann, Halsall, widow. Aug. 1830
James, Dalton, yeoman. May 1829
John, Lathom, husbandman. April 1829
Raingill, Christopher, Manchester, tobacconist. Sept. 1829
Dennis, Manchester, tobacconist. Nov. 1829
Henry, Chorlton-cum-Hardy, farmer. Aug. 1830
Raisin, Thomas, Everton, coachman. A Nov. 1827
Ramsbottom, James, Liverpool, gent. Oct. 1827
James, Reeds, Rossendale, woollen weaver. Dec. 1827
James, Spotland, Rochdale, yeoman. March 1830
John, Redivales, gent. Nov. 1826
John, Tottington, last of Little Bolton, yeoman. Nov. 1829
Richard, Little Lever, husbandman. A Nov. 1827 (2nd grant 1879)
Ramsden, Ann, Clifton, widow. Sept. 1828
John, Liverpool, warehouseman. A Feb. 1826
Thomas, Clifton, agent. A Feb. 1826
Ramsey, Sarah, Liverpool, widow. A Aug. 1827
Randles, Elizabeth, Liverpool, spinster. Jan. 1830
Ranson, Catherine, Wigan, widow. Nov. 1829
Rasbotham, Peter, Alkrington, esq. Jan. 1830
Raspo, Alice, Chorlton Row, widow. A Oct. 1827
Ratcliff, Robert, Lostock, yeoman. April 1827
Ratcliffe, James, Manchester, brewer. Will and Tuon Nov. 1828
John, Manchester, dyer. Sept. 1827
John, Liverpool, flour dealer. A Nov. 1828
Margaret, Newton-in-the-Willows, widow. Jan. 1827
Nancy, Liverpool, widow. A March 1826*
Samuel, Openshaw, yeoman. Aug. 1829
Rathbone, James, Liverpool, shipbuilder. Oct. 1826
Ratliff, Mary, Rainhill, widow. A Aug. 1829
Ravenscroft, John, Nether Knutsford, formerly Salford, gent. Feb. 1828
Rawcliffe, James, Burnley, innholder. March 1828
Richard, Blackburn, warper. A Dec. 1830*
Rawlinson, Michael, Blackrod, farmer. March 1829
William, Liverpool, smith. A Feb. 1826
Rawson, James, Bury, weaver. Nov. 1828
John, Oldham. A Dec. 1829*
William, Astley, weaver. Sept. 1828
Rawsthorn, Henry, Pagheight, Accrington, weaver. July 1830 (1st grant 1813)
William, Ryehill House, Haslingden, woollen manufacturer. May 1829
Rawsthorne, Alexander, Blaguegate, Lathom, yeoman. Jan. 1828
John, Lathom, yeoman. Aug. 1827
Miles, Manchester. Dec. 1827
Rawston, Mary, Whitecroft, widow. June 1830*
Rawstron, James, Musbury, farmer. A Aug. 1828
Rayner, Martha, Ardwick, widow. A Nov. 1827
Thomas, Manchester, millwright. A Dec. 1828
Raynor, James, Ralph Green, Chadderton, weaver. June 1830
Read, Edward, Liverpool, tailor. A April 1829
Elizabeth, Liverpool, widow. May 1827
Sarah, Manchester, widow. A April 1828
Thomas, Standish, farmer. May 1828

Reade, Charles, Liverpool, gent. Aug. 1830
Rearden, William, Liverpool, mariner. Oct. 1830*
Reddish, James, Brookside, Oswaldtwistle, calico printer. A Sept. 1828 (2nd grant 1851)
Redfern, Joseph, Heywood, Bury, shopkeeper. May 1827
Redish, Thomas, Hale, yeoman. A Nov. 1828
Redmayne, James Wheldon, Liverpool, bookkeeper. Oct. 1828
Leonard, Great Bolton, clerk. Aug. 1829
Reece, Mary, Liverpool, widow. Feb. 1827
Reed, Ann, Liverpool, spinster. Nov. 1827
Peter, Liverpool, publican. A May 1826
William, Hulme, publican. A May 1828
Reichard, John Henry, Manchester, merchant. March 1827
Reid, Alice, Liverpool. A Oct. 1829 (2nd grant 1839)
John, Manchester, cotton spinner. A Aug. 1828
Nicholas, Liverpool, brewer. A Jan. 1826
Reilly, Thomas, Liverpool, feather merchant, last of Worcester, cabinet maker. April 1829
Rein, Charles William, Manchester, bookkeeper. Oct. 1828
Renales, Hendrick, Liverpool, mariner. Oct. 1827*
Render, Elizabeth, Hampsthwaite, co. York. A June 1827
Renshaw, Alice, Liverpool. A March 1829 (1st grant 1823)
Edward, Liverpool, ropemaker. A Feb. 1827
Henry, Liverpool, gent. A Dec. 1826
John, Liverpool, gent. A March 1826
Peggy, Cadishead, widow. Aug. 1826
William, Manchester, attorney. Nov. 1828
Reynolds, Adino Veysey, Roscommon St., Walton-on-the-Hill, tanner. A Dec. 1826
Ellis, Manchester, shopkeeper. A May 1827
Henry, Liverpool, surgeon. May 1830
John, Pemberton, weaver. A Nov. 1828
William, Liverpool, carter. Sept. 1828
Rhodes, Ann, Broadeth Lane or [*sic*] Caldwell Brow, co. Lanc., spinster. A May 1826*
Elizabeth, Salford, widow. Feb. 1826
Gregory, Liverpool, brazier. Sept. 1830
John, Three Lane Ends, Rochdale, yeoman. Oct. 1826
Samuel, Heap, shopkeeper. Dec. 1828
William, Brow, Saddleworth, clothier. June 1829
Rice, Ann, Low Green, Hindley, widow. Nov. 1826
Thomas, Linacre, farmer. Feb. 1828
Richards, Elizabeth, Manchester, widow. July 1829; March 1830 (3rd grant 1883)
Francis, Manchester, gent. July 1830
Joseph, Manchester, gent. June 1826
Richardson, Ann, Liverpool, spinster. A Feb. 1829
Ellen, Halebank, widow. A Oct. 1829
George, Liverpool, wine and spirit dealer. A Feb. 1829
Isaac, Manchester, shopkeeper. March 1827
James, Ardwick, bookkeeper. A Feb. 1826
James, Heywood, yeoman. April 1829
James, Manchester, gunsmith. Dec. 1830
John, Unsworth, yeoman. Sept. 1827
John, Liverpool, mariner. A July 1829

Richardson, John, alias Thomas Evans, Liverpool, mariner. A April 1830*
Joseph, Liverpool, vinegar merchant. May 1830
Mary, Halewood. July 1827
Mary, Liverpool, widow. A June 1829
Samuel, Tonge, Prestwich, gent. July 1827
Thomas, Rainhill, yeoman. Feb. 1827
Rickard, Stephen, Toxteth Park, master mariner. A Feb. 1828; June 1829
Rickman, Frederick, Liverpool, mariner. Sept. 1827*
Riddiough, John, Ormskirk, yeoman. April 1827
Riddle, Robert, the merchant ship Kingston, Liverpool, surgeon. Oct. 1826
Ridehough, Thomas, Warrington, officer of Excise. Jan. 1827
Rider, Ann, Cheetham. Feb. 1827
John, Gorton, Manchester, hatter. A Jan. 1828*
Robert, Cheetham, gent. Feb. 1827
Thomas, Manchester, joiner. March 1829
Ridge, Betty, Manchester, widow. Will and Tuon Oct. 1827
Ridgway, Joseph, Ashton-in-Makerfield, yeoman. June 1826
Sarah, Liverpool, feme covert. A June 1830 (2nd grant 1849)
Thomas, Chowbent, butcher. Oct. 1826
Riding, Joseph, Blackrod, calico printer. May 1827
Mary, Blackrod, widow. Feb. 1829
Ridings, Ellen, Rochdale, spinster. Oct. 1828
Esther, Pendleton, widow. March 1830
John, Middleton, weaver. Jan. 1829
Ridley, William, Liverpool, last of Jamaica, mariner. A Jan. 1828
Ridyard, Lydia, Warrington, widow. Feb. 1828
Rieley, otherwise Stockford, Liverpool, A March 1829*
Riely, Henry, Liverpool, mariner. June 1829
Rigby, Catherine, Huyton, widow. March 1829
Deborah, Liverpool, spinster. Feb. 1826 (2nd grant 1847)
Edmund, West Derby, esq. Feb. 1830
Henry, Winstanley, labourer. Feb. 1826
Henry, Halsall, yeoman. May 1830
Joseph, Swinton, gent. July 1830
Lewis, Skelmersdale. Jan. 1828
Rigbye, Harrock Hall, co. Lanc., clerk. May 1827
Robert, Liverpool, merchant. Feb. 1826*
Samuel, Sutton, shoemaker. July 1827
Thomas, Liverpool, cabinet maker. Feb. 1826
Thomas, Westleigh, manufacturer. Feb. 1827 (2nd grant 1848)
Thomas, Little Crosby, farmer. Nov. 1829
William, Cronton, yeoman. May 1830
William, Toxteth Park, esq. A June 1830
William, Risley, Culcheth, yeoman. Aug. 1830 (2nd grant 1832)
William, Wigan, gent. A Aug. 1830
Rigg, Esther, Liverpool, spinster. A May 1830
Right, Jonathan, see Wright
Rilence, Elizabeth, Appleton, Widnes, widow. Oct. 1827
Riley, Harry, Oldham, grocer. A Jan. 1827
Henry, Liverpool, mariner. A May 1829
James, Rossendale, weaver. Oct. 1826
John, Habergham Eaves, dyer. March 1826
John, Bents, Colne, cordwainer. June 1828

Riley, Reuben, Hurst St., Ashton-under-Lyne, cotton spinner. A Dec. 1826
Robert, Haslingden, hairdresser. May 1829
Rimmer, Ann, Formby, widow. Oct. 1828
Edward, Liverpool, gent. March 1827
Henry, Moss Lane, North Meols, yeoman. Aug., 1827
James, Liverpool, cooper. April 1828 (1st grant 1779)
Jane, Litherland, feme covert. A Aug. 1828
John, Formby, yeoman. Sept. 1828 (2nd grant 1846)
John, Lydiate, farmer. Nov. 1828
John, Newburgh, blacksmith. July 1829
John, Formby, yeoman. Nov. 1829
Martha, Liverpool. A March 1828
Richard, Formby. May 1827
Richard, Manchester, cooper. June 1827
Robert, Liverpool, ship carpenter. May 1826
Robert, Westward, North Meols. April 1830
Thomas, Formby, yeoman. March 1829
William, Town Row, West Derby, carter. A July 1826
William, Liverpool, cooper. A Sept. 1827
Ripley, Henry, Strangeways, Cheetham. Sept. 1830
Rishton, Edward, Elswick Lodge, gent. A April 1830*
John, Oakenhead Wood, Halsingden. A Dec. 1830
Ritson, Fletcher, Green St., Bolton. June 1826*
Sarah, Liverpool, widow. A Jan. 1827
Rix, James, Pendleton, Eccles, gent. Nov. 1830
Mary Ann, Manchester. Oct. 1829*
Roach, Constance, Birdholme, Chesterfield, co. Derby, widow. April 1828
George, Liverpool, merchant. March 1827
James, Liverpool, mariner. A Nov. 1827*
Robbins, Ann, Liverpool, widow. Dec. 1826
Robbs, James, Liverpool, last of Great Neston, merchant. Nov. 1826
Roberts, David, Tithebarn St., Liverpool, warehouseman. A Dec. 1826
David, Liverpool, cooper. A Aug. 1829
Edward, Bolton-le-Moors, shopkeeper. April 1830
Eleanor, Liverpool, widow. A April 1830
Elizabeth, Liverpool, spinster. Dec. 1826
Esther, Liverpool, widow. Oct. 1828*
Evan, Liverpool, ship cooper. A Oct. 1830*
Henry, Fence, Forest of Pendle, gent. June 1828
Henry, Liverpool, mariner. A March 1829*
Hugh, Liverpool, victualler. Feb. 1828
James, Bacup, yeoman. A Dec. 1829 (2nd grant 1878)
John, Liverpool, mariner. A Sept. 1828
John, Salford, gent. Oct. 1828
John, Manchester. Nov. 1828
John, Blakebey Nook, Saddleworth, clothier. Nov. 1829
John, Middleton, publican and farmer. Oct. 1830
John, Manchester, shopkeeper. A Dec. 1830
Martha, Liverpool, widow, Dec. 1826
Mary, Bolton-le-Moors. A Jan. 1828*
Peter, Liverpool, sailmaker. A May 1828
Richard, Liverpool, bricklayer. Sept. 1828
Richard, Upper Houses, Barley with Wheatley Booths, farmer. Feb. 1829

Roberts, Richard, Bacup, gent. Sept. 1829
Richard, Liverpool, mariner. A Aug. 1830*
Richard, Liverpool, master mariner. A Dec. 1830
Robert, Liverpool, watch finisher. A Sept. 1826
Robert, Liverpool, master mariner. Dec. 1827
Thomas, Burscough Bridge, innkeeper. A Aug. 1826
Thomas, Salford, packer. A Jan. 1827
Thomas, Liverpool, schoolmaster. A Jan. 1828
Thomas senior, Ardwick, farmer. A Feb. 1829
Thomas, Manchester, gent. Nov. 1829
Thomas, Liverpool. A June 1830
William, Liverpool, victualler. A June 1829
William, Liverpool, pawnbroker. Feb. 1830
William, Kirkby, farmer. April 1830
William, soldier in H.M. 49th Regt. of Foot. A June 1830*
Robertshaw, John, Coldweather House, gent. A Nov. 1829
Robertson, George, Liverpool, merchant. A Feb. 1829
Robinson, Ann, Liverpool, widow. June 1827
Ann, Turton. A March 1830
Christopher, Rochdale, woollen weaver. April 1828
Daniel, Stretford, farmer. June 1826
Emma, Liverpool, widow. Feb. 1826
Euphemia, Grange, widow. Sept. 1828
George, Manchester, draper. April 1827
Godsalve, Warrington, yeoman. March 1826
Harriet, Chorlton Row, spinster. A Jan. 1827
James, Lowton, yeoman. A Feb. 1826
James, Downham, cotton spinner. A and Tuon April 1827
Jane, Sutton, widow. Aug. 1828
John, Pendleton, bleacher. A April 1826*
John, Middleton, gent. A Jan. 1827.
John, Formby, yeoman. Jan. 1828
John, Habergham Eaves, joiner. Aug. 1828
John, Woodbrooke, merchant. Nov. 1828
John, Kirkby Kendal, weaver. July 1829 (1st grant 1822)
John, Liverpool, chairmaker. Dec. 1830
Joseph, Lower Tunshill, Butterworth. Sept. 1828*
Joseph, Liverpool, flax and hemp dresser. April 1829
Joseph, Bolton, manufacturer. A Feb. 1830
Joshua Kay, Harpurhey, gent. Dec. 1828
Margaret, Liverpool. May 1826
Mary, Edge Hill, widow. Oct. 1826
Mary, Manchester, widow. Feb. 1827
Richard, Hulme, porter. Aug. 1830
Samuel, acting master of H.M. schooner Pickle. A Oct. 1829
Sarah, Liverpool. A April 1828
Susanna, Deansgate, Manchester. March 1829
Thomas, Manchester, gent. Oct. 1826*
Thomas, Warrington, gent. April 1827 (1st grant 1806; 2nd grant 1825)
Thomas, St., Helens, grocer. Aug. 1827
Thomas, Higher Ardwick, gent. March 1828
William, Orrell, gent. Aug. 1826
William, Salford, shoemaker. June 1827*

Robinson, William, Clare Castle, Ireland, warehouseman. A Feb. 1828
William, Manchester, painter. Aug. 1828
William, Manchester, publican. A Dec. 1828
Robson, Elizabeth, Chorlton, widow. A and Tuon Oct. 1827
George, Manchester, coachman. A Oct. 1828
John, Manchester. A April 1828
Matthew, Manchester, coal dealer. A May 1829
Roby, William, Manchester, minister of the Gospel. Jan. 1830
Rockley, Ann, Rainford, widow. A Nov. 1828
Rockliff, James, Rainford, farmer. A Oct. 1828
Rodgett, Edward, Brindle, gent. Jan. 1828
James, Blackburn, cotton spinner. Oct. 1830
Roe, William, Liverpool, esq. June 1827
Roebuck, David, Manchester, wheelwright. A June 1829
Rogers, Henry, Bird in Hand, Rochdale. A June 1828
Mary, Sale, Ashton-under-Lyne, wid. Sept. 1827
Nathaniel, Westhoughton, gent. March 1826
William, Aspull, yeoman. Dec. 1828
Rogerson, Elizabeth, wife of James Rogerson, Liverpool, merchant, Sept. 1827*
James, Liverpool, victualler. Jan. 1828
John, Dumplington, Barton-upon-Irwell, cow doctor. Feb. 1827*
John, Blackburn, chemist and druggist. Feb. 1828
Mary, Thornley, Chipping. A April 1828
Robert, Patricroft, manufacturer. April 1830
Thomas, Liverpool, saddler. Aug. 1830
Roose, Edwin, Liverpool, merchant. A March 1828
Thomas, Liverpool, bread baker. Jan. 1828
Roper, Charles, Toxteth Park, bricklayer. April 1830
James, Toxteth Park, tallow chandler. Oct. 1826
James, Liverpool, plumber and glazier. Sept. 1827
John, Bedford, Leigh. A June 1826
Thomas, Newburgh, Lathom, tailor. March 1830
Rosbottom, Thomas, Charnock Richard, farmer. A Nov. 1826
Roscoe, George, Manchester, porter. A April 1828
Hugh, Pendleton, schoolmaster. A May 1830
Thomas, Widnes, farmer. June 1828
Roscow, Ann, Horwich, widow. Aug. 1829
Richard the elder, Grane, Haslingden, yeoman. June 1830
Roger, Tottington. May 1826
Rose, Abraham, Strangeways, calico printer. May 1828
Henry, Liverpool, yeoman. July 1828
James, Salford, gent. April 1827
James, the merchant ship John and Mary, Liverpool, mariner. A Dec. 1827*
James, Liverpool, surgeon and dentist. Nov. 1830
Micah, Manchester, gent. Sept. 1829
Thomas, Manchester, alehouse keeper. March 1829
Ross, Daniel, of the Colony of Berbice, S. America, planter. July 1828
George, Liverpool, brass founder and victualler. A May 1827*
Rossbottom, Peter, Westleigh, weaver. A Jan. 1828
Rossiter, William, Liverpool, mariner. A Nov. 1827*
Rotheram, Elizabeth, Edge Hill, West Derby. Nov. 1830
Rothwell, Betty, Musbury, Haslingden, widow. A Jan. 1827
Ellen, Tonge, widow. A June 1828

Rothwell, James, Middleton, dresser or weaver. Jan. 1827*
Jonathan, Newton, farmer. A Jan. 1829
Mary, Ormskirk, widow. Oct. 1830
Mary Ann, Manchester, spinster. March 1830
Nathaniel, Farnworth, farmer. May 1830
Peter, Over Hulton, farmer. May 1827
Peter, Rivington, yeoman. Jan. 1830
Thomas, Atherton, innkeeper. A April 1826
Thomas, Thornton, co. Lanc., publican. A Dec. 1826
Thomas, Little Bolton, gent. Oct. 1828
Thomas, Great Bolton, joiner. Jan. 1830
William, Hollins, Oldham yeoman. May 1827*
Roughley, Henry, Newton-in-Makerfield. Sept. 1830
John, Rainford. Jan. 1827
Mary, Rainford, widow. Aug. 1830
Peter, Windle, farmer. Feb. 1828
Roughsedge, Margaret, Rainhill. A May 1826
Robert Hankinson, Liverpool, clerk. Oct. 1829
Thomas, Great Sankey, yeoman. Sept. 1830*
Rourke, Michael, Liverpool, millwright. A March 1830
Rowbotham, Alice, Manchester, widow. April 1828
Rowbottom, John, Hunt Lane, Chadderton. A Aug. 1830 (2nd grant 1872)
Rowe, Dodson George, Liverpool, gent. Oct. 1830
Ellen, Liverpool. June 1826
George, May Place, West Derby, gent. Oct. 1830
Henry, Wigan, victualler. A July 1827
Thomas, Liverpool, police officer. A Jan. 1826
Rowland, Charles, Salford, gent. July 1829
David, Warrington, publican and butcher. Feb. 1826
John, Liverpool, brewer. Oct. 1827
Rowlands, Evan, Liverpool, schoolmaster. A June 1829 (2nd grant 1851)
Rowley, Peter, Bradfield, co. York., velvet dresser. A May 1827*
Rowlinson, Deborah, Warrington, widow. A Feb. 1829
Royden, Joseph the younger, Liverpool. A Nov. 1830
Roydes, John, Polly Green, co. Lanc. A March 1826 (2nd grant 1845)
Royds, Thomas, Willmers, co. Lanc. A Feb. 1829*
Roylance, Charles, Manchester, grocer. Aug. 1827
Samuel, Liverpool, gent. May 1830
Samuel, Liverpool, landing waiter. A March 1830
Royle, Ann, Bolton-le-Moors, weaver. A Jan. 1827
Jane, Manchester, widow. Oct. 1829*
Job, Flixton, weaver. July 1830
John, Kersall, Manchester, yeoman. A June 1827
Mary, Eccles, widow. June 1826
Nancy, Blackburn widow. A March 1828
Thomas, Urmston, yeoman. Sept. 1826
Thomas, Manchester, surveyor. Feb. 1830
Rudman, Joseph, Wall Bank, Rochdale, farmer. Nov. 1827
Ruscoe, Daniel, Whitchurch, co. Salop, gent. June 1827
Frances, Whitchurch, spinster. May 1827
Rushforth, Zacharias, Sharples, gent. June 1827
Rushton, George, Wackersall, farmer. May 1828
John, Pleasant St., Haslingden, linen draper. May 1826*

Rushton, Joseph, Bolton-le-Moors. Sept. 1828
Thomas, Lever Edge, Middleton, manufacturer. Feb. 1827
Thomas, Liverpool, hairdresser. May 1829 (2nd grant 1836)
Rushworth, James, Manchester, cabinetmaker. A Feb., 1829
Russell, Mary, Bolton-le-Moors. A Nov. 1826
Richard, Eccles, surgeon. A Jan. 1828
Rutherford, Robert, Bolton-le-Moors, joiner. Dec. 1830
Rutson, Fanny, Allerton Lodge, co.Lanc. May 1830
Rutter, James, Bretherton, weaver. A April 1829
Peter, Aughton, innkeeper. A April 1830
Rycroft, John, Liverpool, joiner. Jan. 1828
Ryder, James, Liverpool, gent. Jan. 1828
Ryle,Joshua, Carshalton, co.Surrey. Nov. 1828
Ryley, Jonathan, Bolton-le-Moors, publican. A Aug. 1827
Rymmer, James, Birkdale, North Meols, farmer. Dec. 1829

SADLER, Francis, Liverpool, gent. Oct. 1828
Sagar, William, Higham, yeoman. Jan. 1829
Sager, William, Todmorden, grocer. Dec. 1830
Salt, John, Manchester, hat manufacturer. Nov. 1828
Salter, Robert, Chowbent, bookkeeper. A Dec. 1827
William, Salford, watchmaker. Dec. 1828
Sampson, Mary, West Derby. Oct. 1828
Sandbach, James Watson, Liverpool, an infant. A Sept. 1828
Nathan, Manchester, farmer. June 1828
Sander, Ann, Keswick, Crosthwaite, co. Cumb., wife of John Sander. June 1830
Sanders, Jonathan, Liverpool, mailcoach guard. A April 1828
Sanderson, Ann, Warrington, widow. Jan. 1826
Sandford, Francis van, Radcliffe Hall, gent. Dec. 1830
Sankey, Mary, Bolton-le-Moors, widow. A Sept. 1830
Sarratt, Barton, Liverpool, joiner. A Nov. 1827
Satterfield, John, Liverpool, gent. Jan. 1830
Satterthwaite, Edward, Manchester, currier. April 1828
Margaret, Lancaster. June 1829
Saunders, Josiah Richardson, Ardwick Place, Manchester, merchant. Feb. 1828
Saxon, Betty, Queen St., Salford, widow. Nov. 1826
Robert, Langley, Middleton, weaver. Nov. 1830
Thomas Thornborough, Liverpool, hatter. Nov. 1830
Saxton, John, Top of Hebers, Middleton, weaver. A Nov. 1826; Aug. 1829
Scaife, Thomas, Liverpool, merchant. Nov. 1829
Scales, William, Liverpool, gent. May 1826
Scarisbrick, William, Liverpool, flour dealer. May 1827
Scarsbrick, Henry, Liverpool, gent. A June 1830
Schmid, John Daniel, Liverpool, merchant. Nov. 1826
Schofield, Alice, Wardleworth Brow, widow. A April 1826
Alice, Taunton, widow. A March 1830
Edmund, Dobcross, Saddleworth, butcher. July 1829 (2nd grant 1849)
Esther, Knat Bank, Bamford, spinster. Feb. 1830
George, Temple, Mill Bottom, Saddleworth, innkeeper. Sept. 1830 (1st grant 1825)
James, Milnrow, Butterworth. May 1826
James, Manchester, gent. Jan. 1828
James, Oldham, cotton spinner. Oct., 1828 (2nd grant 1843)
James, Stonepitfield, Rochdale, weaver. A Jan. 1830
James, Hollingreave, Saddleworth, Feb. 1830

Schofield, John, Delph, Saddleworth, yeoman. A March 1826*
Jonas, Openshaw, farmer. A May 1827*
Joseph, Liverpool. May 1828
Philip, Great Bolton, dyer. Jan. 1830 (2nd grant 1837)
Richard, Smith Fold, Little Bolton, farmer. May 1829
Robert, Lowerplace, Rochdale, shopkeeper. A Nov. 1830
Samuel, Taunton, weaver. Dec. 1826
Susey, Hollingrove, Saddleworth, spinster. Dec. 1829
William, Turkey Hall, Rochdale, woollen weaver. April 1827
William, Droylsden, weaver. May 1827
Scholes, Alice, Tetlow Fold, widow. May 1829
Betty, Deansgate, Great Bolton, widow. Feb. 1829
George, Tonge, yeoman. Oct. 1828
Hannah, Edgworth, widow. July 1828
James, Tetlowfold, Manchester, gent. Jan. 1826
James, Stakehill, Middleton, gent. A March 1830
John, Oldham, cotton spinner. A April 1829
Joseph the elder, New Windsor, Salford, gent. Nov. 1829
Lydia, Swinton, widow. Feb. 1827
Robert, Hopwood, weaver. Nov. 1827
Sarah, Oldham, spinster. A July 1829
William, Tonge, yeoman. A June 1829
Scholfield, Betty, Gooden Lane, Heywood, April 1826
Betty, Farnworth, Deane. Oct. 1829
Edward, Bamford, gent. July 1827
Ellis, Musbury, farmer. March 1829
Jacob, Heywood, cotton weaver. A April 1828
James, Littlecleg, Butterworth, yeoman. June 1830
John, Rochdale, last of Tonge End, yeoman. July 1826
John, Manchester, turner. A Sept. 1827*
John, Whams, Saddleworth. Nov. 1828
John, Salford, shopkeeper. Dec. 1828
John, Bacup, labourer. A Aug. 1830 (1st grant 1824; 3rd grant 1847)
Martha, Rochdale, spinster. April 1827
Samuel, Bolton-le-Moors. Nov. 1828
Scolfield, Alice, Carterplace, Haslingden, widow. April 1828
Scotson, William, Adlington, yeoman. Jan. 1827 (2nd grant 1856)
Scott, David, Liverpool, mariner. Sept. 1829
James, Flaxmoss, innkeeper. Nov. 1827
Jane, Southport. Oct. 1829
John, Liverpool, victualler of livery stable keeper. Jan. 1829
Jonathan, Liverpool, baker. July 1828
Peter Haffey the younger, Crabtree Lane, Liverpool. Jan. 1830
William, Manchester, gent. Oct. 1828
Scowcroft, Betty, Farnworth, widow. Oct. 1826
Betty, Tottington, spinster. Feb. 1828
Scragg, Hannah, Manchester, publican. Oct. 1828
Richard, Hulme, export officer. Feb. 1830
Scriven, Ann, Liverpool, spinster. April, 1830*
Seaman, Rebecca, Aigburth, widow. Aug. 1829; Oct. 1829
Seddon, Alice, Worsley, widow. A Feb. 1826
Alice, Liverpool, spinster. A April 1827
Ann, Whiston, last of Liverpool, widow. July 1830

Seddon, Ellen, Habergham Eaves, widow. June 1828
Helen, Ince Blundell, widow. Feb. 1827
John, Halliwell, farmer. Oct. 1827
John, Tyldesley, weaver. A May 1829
Margaret, Westhoughton, widow. A Aug. 1828
Thomas, Manchester, merchant. Nov. 1829
William, Heaton Norris, cotton spinner. April 1830*
Sedgwick, James, Manchester, linen draper. Nov. 1828
Thomas, Prescot, joiner. Dec. 1829
Seed, John, Walton-le-Dale, yeoman. Nov. 1827
William, Edge Hill, shopkeeper. April 1830
Seel, Samuel, Stayley Bridge, shopkeeper. April 1829
Sefton, Ann, Manchester, spinster. June 1826
Elizabeth or Betty, Manchester, widow. May 1826
John, Manchester, publican. June 1827
Nathan, Beardwood, Blackburn, farmer. June 1827
Segar, Jane, Formby, widow. Nov. 1827
Sellars, Barrett, Manchester, manufacturing chemist. March 1827
Sellers, Roger, Hollingworth, yeoman. Sept. 1829
Senner, James, Toxteth Park, master mariner. March 1828
Sephton, Ann, Newburgh, Lathom, spinster. Sept. 1829
Henry, Hardshaw, stonemason. March 1827
Henry, Prescot, shoemaker. May 1830*
John, Ormskirk, yeoman. May 1827 (later grants 1840 & 1846)
Richard, Ormskirk, farmer. June 1826*
Sergeant, John, Walton-on-the-Hill, gent. July 1830 (2nd grant 1838)
Sergent, William, Liverpool, mariner. A Oct. 1826*
Service, William, Liverpool, joiner. Nov. 1826 (2nd grant 1845)
Settle, Mary, Great Bolton, widow. June 1826
Sevil, Joseph, Netherlees, Ashton-under-Lyne, yeoman. Feb. 1828 (1st grant 1787)
Sevill, James, Royton, cotton spinner. A Jan. 1829
Seville, Mally, Silver Hill, Saddleworth, widow. Aug. 1828
Sewell, Henry, Blackburn, dealer in clothes. Jan. 1826
Shacklady, James, Liverpool, cowkeeper. June 1829
Shackleton, James, Old Accrington, shopkeeper. May 1827
William the elder, Manchester, tailor & draper. June 1826
Shacklock, Susanna, Liverpool, widow. A July 1828
Shaddick, John, John St., Bedford Row, co. Middlesex, esq. April 1826
John Gregory, John St., Bedford Row, esq. A March 1826
Shadrach, William, Liverpool, joiner. July 1829 (2nd grant 1836)
Shakelady, Robert, Lydiate, yeoman. Aug. 1827
Shakeshaft, John, Atherton, yeoman. A Oct. 1828
Shakledy, Henry, Maghull, innkeeper. Jan. 1826
Shallcross, Thomas, Toxteth Park, gent. Nov. 1827
Shankland, John, Manchester, shopkeeper. A Oct. 1827
Shapter, John, Liverpool, victualler. A July 1829
Sharp, John, Bretherton, last of Ulnes Walton, yeoman. Oct. 1830*
Sharples, Dianah, Church, widow. A March 1830
Ellen, Blackburn, widow. July 1827
James, Guide, Lower Darwen, yeoman. June 1829
John, Clayton-le-Dale, weaver. Jan. 1827
John, Little Bolton, counterpain manufacturer. May 1828
John, Chadderton, gent. July 1830

Sharples, Richard, Bolton-le-Moors, shopkeeper. A Oct. 1829
Thomas, Liverpool. April 1828
Sharratt, Richard, Warrington, Labourer. A May 1830
Sharrocks, Ellen, Bolton-le-Moors. A Jan. 1830*
Frances, Chorlton Row, spinster. A July 1828
William, Manchester, yeoman. April 1826
Shaw, Charles, Rivington, gent. June 1827
Charles, Delph, grocer. Dec. 1827
Daniel, Liverpool, labourer. April 1830
Gabriel, Wigan & Darwen, cotton dealer. April 1829
James, Hazlehurst, Ashton-under-Lyne, cotton spinner. Feb. 1827
James, Ardwick, victualler. Nov. 1827
James, Oxhey, Saddleworth, yeoman. Oct. 1829
Jane, Standish, widow. A July 1830
John, Churchtown, North Meols, gent. Jan. 1826*
John, Rivington, gent. Sept. 1826
John, Liverpool, seaman. Nov. 1826*
John, Bolton-le-Moors, bricksetter. Dec. 1826
John, Chowbent, yeoman. April 1827
John, Liverpool, pensioner. A Feb. 1829*
John, Liverpool, mariner. A Sept. 1829
John, Liverpool, esq. June 1830
John, Blackey Nook, Saddleworth, clothier. A Oct. 1830
Joseph, Broadmeadow, clothier. Dec. 1828
Margaret, Lees. A May 1826
Martha, Culcheth, spinster. Nov. 1826*
Mary, Everton, widow. A March 1830
Mary, Hart Common, Westhoughton, widow. Dec. 1830
Peter, Lumber St., Liverpool, saddletree manufacturer. June 1830
Ralph, Lostock, farmer. Sept. 1826
Richard, Ince Blundell, farmer. Sept. 1829
Thomas, Mantelow Gate, Saddleworth. Aug. 1830
William, Wigan, traveller. A Dec. 1826
William, Astley, blacksmith. Feb. 1827
Shawcross, James, Salford, auctioneer. A May 1829
John, Manchester, gent. Aug. 1828
Mary, Salford, widow. A Nov. 1828
Mary, Gorton, widow, A Sept. 1830
Mathew, Salford, pork dealer. A Jan. 1827*
Peter, Stretford, hay cutter. Dec. 1827
Thomas, Manchester, shopkeeper. A April 1827
Thomas, Manchester, bricklayer. A Oct. 1828*
William, Stretford, yeoman. Jan. 1830
Shawe, Jane, Cadishead, shopkeeper, March 1827
William, South Gate House, co. Middlesex, esq. March 1827
Shearer, William, Liverpool, gent. Feb. 1827
Sheldon, Alice, Manchester. A Dec. 1829*
Shelmerdine, James, Stayley Bridge, shopkeeper. April 1829
John, Bank Quay, Warrington, victualler. Feb. 1826
Shenton, William, Manchester, merchant. Oct. 1830
Shephard, Anne, Liverpool, spinster. Jan. 1828
Shepherd, Cicely, Sephton, widow. Feb. 1826
Frances, Middleton, widow. Oct. 1828

Shepherd, Henry, Liverpool, druggist, Feb. 1826
Henry, Parracklumb, Bacup. Aug. 1826
John, Coal Bank, Spotland, woollen weaver. Jan. 1826
John, Old Meadows, Rossendale, farmer. A Feb. 1827
John, Rochdale, draper. April 1827
Mary, Rochdale. Oct. 1828
Richard, Old Meadows, Bacup, farmer. Jan. 1828
Ruth, Bearshill, Spotland, widow. A Aug. 1827
William, Richmond Row, Liverpool. A Oct. 1830
Shepley, John, Cadishead, weaver. May 1828
Joseph, Stayley Bridge, yeoman. May 1828
Richard, Bolton-le-Moors, brushmaker. Jan. 1827
Sheppard, Anne, Litherland, widow. June 1826
Sheppeard, John, Heaton Norris, gent. Aug. 1829
Sherlock, James, Liverpool, merchant. A July 1830
Sherman, Margery, Skelmersdale, widow. Aug. 1830
Sherratt, John, Salford, ironfounder. Dec. 1827
John, Warrington, surgeon. A Oct. 1828
John, Prescot, gent. Nov. 1829
Richard, Warrington, grocer. Oct. 1827 (1st Grant 1815)
Sherrett, Joseph, Warrington, gent. Sept. 1827
Shewan, Samuel, Three Lane Ends, Saddleworth. Dec. 1828
Shields, Robert, Liverpool, brushmaker. April 1826
Shimmins, Caesar, Liverpool, carpenter. A Aug. 1826
Shore, Edmund, Spotland, yeoman. June 1827
John, Ardwick, Manchester, gent. Dec. 1826
John, Hollingworth, innkeeper. April 1828
Shorrock, Barnard, Over Darwen. Jan. 1826
Esther, Over Darwen, widow, A Dec. 1828*
Henry the elder, Mickle Key, co. Lanc., yeoman. May 1830
Thomas, Blackburn, weaver. Jan. 1828
Shotwell, Joshua, Liverpool, gent. April 1828
Shrigley, John, Delph, Saddleworth, tailor. A July 1827*
Shute, Elizabeth, Liverpool. A Feb. 1827
Shuttleworth, Alexander, Culcheth, yeoman. June 1830
Charlotte Hannah, Market Harborough, May 1826
Cornelius, Liverpool, surgeon. May 1826 (1st Grant 1822)
James, Tildsley with Shackerley, cotton manufacturer. May 1829
Thomas Starkie, Ashton, esq. May 1830
Sibberin, William, Tyldesley with Shakerley, farmer. May 1830
Sibson, Joseph, Bolton-le-Moors, excise officer. A May 1826
Siddall, John, Pilkington, weaver. A Sept. 1830*
Joshua, Manchester, surveyor. Aug. 1829
Siddel, Sarah, Walton-le-Dale, widow. March 1827
Sidebotham, John, Houghton, cotton spinner. July 1828
Sigley, John, Guide Lane, Ashton-under-Lyne, slater. Feb. 1826
Silbery, John, Liverpool, mariner. Dec. 1830*
Silva, Antonio de Louiza, Liverpool, merchant. A Feb. 1829
Silverwood, John, Liverpool, victualler. A Dec. 1829
Silvester, James, Manchester. A March 1828
John, Chorley, esq. Jan. 1827
Simcock, Ellen, Liverpool, spinster. Dec. 1826
Mary, Liverpool, A Jan. 1827

Simister, James, Droylsden, labourer. A Dec. 1827*
Thomas, Manchester, warehouseman & shopkeeper. May 1826
Simkin, Alice, Liverpool, widow. Feb. 1827*
Thomas, Salford, patten maker. Sept. 1826
Timothy, Manchester, yeoman. A June 1826
Simmons, Thomas, Toxteth Park, gent. Feb. 1829
William, Manchester, surgeon. July 1830
Simpson, Armstrong, Walton-le-Dale, yeoman. April 1826
Charles, Goldenhill, co. Staffs. Sept. 1829
Christopher, Manchester, dyer. March 1826
Edmund, Manchester, hatter, Feb. 1827
Henry, London, law stationer. A July 1829
John, Manchester, porter. A July 1827
Margaret, Liverpool, widow. July 1829
Nancy, Blackburn, A April 1826*
William, Liverpool, mariner. A March 1830*
Sinclair, Walter, Liverpool, seaman. Oct. 1829*
Singleton, Alice, Manchester, spinster. July 1829
Henry, Blackrod, farmer. A June 1830
John, Wigan, July 1830
Margaret, Blackrod, spinster. July 1830
Robert J. Bennett, Manchester, mariner. A July 1830
Samuel, Tildesley, shopkeeper. A Feb. 1826
Sives, James, Manchester, gent. Jan. 1826
Skearratt, Thomas, Liverpool, ironfounder. Sept. 1830
Skellorn, Emery, Knott Lane, Ashton-under-Lyne, weaver. A Jan. 1827
Skipton, George Hart, Liverpool, captain in the Army. A & Tuon April 1830
Slack, John, Salford, engraver. April 1828
Maria, Manchester, spinster. A June 1827
Mary, Little Hayfield, co. Derby, widow. July 1828
William, Keswick, co. Cumb., last of Ardwick, gent. Sept. 1830
Slade, Elizabeth, Desford, co. Leicester, spinster. May 1827
James, Dodford, co. Northampton, clerk. Jan. 1826
Slater, Andrew, Billington, farmer. A Nov. 1827
Edward, Walton-le-Dale, yeoman. April 1829
Elizabeth, Liverpool, widow, A March 1830
Henry, Manchester, publican, July. 1828
John, Ashton-under-Lyne, butcher. July 1829
Joseph, Woodhouses, Ashton-under-Lyne, manufacturer. Jan. 1827
Mary, Manchester. A Feb. 1826
Mary, Haslingden, widow. Aug. 1826
Mary, Liverpool, spinster. May 1827
Mary, Ashton-under-Lyne, spinster. Dec. 1830
Matthew, Ashton-under-Lyne, publican. A March 1829
Richard, Kidderminster, excise officer. A May 1827
Thomas, Clitheroe, whitesmith. A Dec. 1828
William, Burnley, publican. June 1829
William, Well Stile, Ashton-under-Lyne, yeoman. Dec. 1829*
Slingsby, John, Prestwich, June 1830 (2nd grant 1831)
Sloan, John, Haughton, weaver. Feb. 1827*
John, Liverpool, mariner. A June 1830*
Small, James, Liverpool, mariner. A Sept. 1827*
Smalley, Betty, Longton, widow. April 1828

Smalley, James, Chorley Moor, yeoman. Dec. 1827
John, Blackburn, innkeeper. A March 1829
Ruth, Manchester, widow. July 1826
William, Mellor, yeoman. May 1828
Smallwood, John Travis, Salford, gent. June 1829
Smeal otherwise Wright, Olive, Liverpool, widow. Feb. 1826
Smethurst, Ann, Manchester, widow. A Sept. 1829
Betty, Manchester, widow. Feb. 1827
Hobson, Stockbrook, Chadderton, gent. A Jan. 1826
Isaac, Blackley, yeoman. Nov. 1827
James, Clifton, surgeon. A May 1830
Richard, Bury, draper. Aug. 1827
Robert, Lane End, Prestwich. A Dec. 1828
Smith, Abraham, Manchester, yeoman. Oct. 1827
Alice, St. Helens, spinster. April 1828
Ann, Liverpool, widow. April 1826
Ann, Bradshaw, spinster. March 1828
Ann, Liverpool, widow. Aug. 1829
Ann, Upholland, widow. Oct. 1829
Ann, Salford, widow. A March 1830*
Anna, Sutton Coldfield, co. Warwick, widow. July 1829
Charles, Liverpool, mariner. A Feb. 1829*
Ebenezer, Rochdale, draper. Sept. 1830
Edward, Speke, wheelwright. A April 1827
Edward, Liverpool, labourer. Aug. 1829
Edward, Warrington, ironmonger. A July 1830*
Elizabeth, Warrington, feme covert. June 1828
Elizabeth, Wigan. Jan. 1830*
George, Atherton, spindlemaker. Jan. 1826
Henry, Liverpool, shipwright. A Oct. 1828
Horatio Sidney, Plunge, Bury, merchant. A Dec. 1826
Isaac, Rainford, pipemaker. Jan. 1829*
Isaac, Liverpool, gent. A June 1830
James, Newcastle-under-Lyne, co. Staffs, bookseller & stationer. June 1826
James, Greens House, Cliviger, farmer. A July 1826
James, Liverpool, mariner. A Oct. 1827*
James, Toxteth Park, master mariner. Dec. 1827
James, Southwark, co. Surrey. April 1829
James, Radcliffe Bridge, clogger. May 1829
James, Gorton, yeoman. Jan. 1830
James, Golborne, joiner. April 1830
James, Lowton, farmer. Oct. 1830
James, Bolton-le-Moors, shopkeeper & widower. A Nov. 1830 (2nd grant 1865)
James Haywood, Heaton Norris, overseer. A May 1830
Jennet, Liverpool, widow. A Dec. 1826*
John, Toxteth Park. A Jan. 1827
John, Stretford, farmer. A Jan. 1828
John, Trawden, Colne, cotton manufacturer. A Jan. 1828
John, Liverpool, merchant. July 1828 (1st grant 1807)
John, Astley, farmer. Jan. 1829
John, Salford, rag dealer. April 1829
John, Liverpool, seaman. May 1829
John, Fence House, Forest of Pendle, gent. Aug. 1829

Smith, John, Burnley, grocer. A Oct. 1829
John, Huncoat. Oct. 1829 (2nd grant 1841)
John, Stayley Bridge, auctioneer. A Dec. 1829
John, Woodend, Prestwich, weaver. Dec. 1829*
John Henry, Liverpool, seaman. A Oct. 1826*
Joseph, Salford, innkeeper. March 1826
Joseph, Whitecroft, Oldham. June 1830
Lydia, Haworth Fold, Habergham Eaves. June 1829
Mary, Ormskirk, spinster. July 1826
Mary, Dawson Croft, Salford, spinster. May 1829
Mary, Rumworth, widow. Aug. 1829
Mary, wife of Thomas Smith, Liverpool, bricklayer. June 1830
Nancy, Liverpool, spinster. Dec. 1826
Peter, St. Helens, cordwainer. A April 1828
Peter, Penwortham, yeoman. Dec. 1828
Philip, Failsworth, farmer. April 1826
Richard, Lower Haggate, Briercliffe, yeoman. April 1826
Robert, Manchester, millwright. A July 1827
Robert, Rochdale, tea dealer. Aug. 1827
Robert, Penwortham, shopkeeper. April 1828
Robert, Halsall, husbandman. Aug. 1828
Robert, Penwortham, farmer. A May 1830
Robert, Liverpool, mariner. A April 1830*
Roger, Chowbent, tailor. Sept. 1830*
Samuel, Atherton, weaver. Aug. 1829
Samuel, Pendleton, esq. Nov. 1829
Samuel, Odlham, bookkeeper. A July 1830
Samuel, Bury, machine maker. Aug. 1830 (2nd grant 1863)
Sarah, Chorlton Row. June 1827*
Sarah, Whittle-le-Woods. July 1827
Sarah, Lostock Hall, spinster. Dec. 1829
Solomon, Wardlesworth, musician. June 1829
Thomas, Ormskirk, yeoman. Oct. 1826
Thomas, Liverpool, wheelwright. Nov. 1827
Thomas, Salford, carter. A Nov. 1827
Thomas, Liverpool, tide waiter. A May 1828
Thomas, Bickerstaffe, plasterer. July 1828
Thomas, Booths Town, weaver. Aug. 1828
Thomas, Liverpool, coachman. Jan. 1829
Thomas, Middleton, farmer. July 1829
William, Atherton, nailmaker. Oct. 1826
William, Liverpool, plasterer. A March 1828
William, Manchester, pipe manufacturer. Nov. 1830
Smithurst, John, Chorley, cotton manufacturer. A Jan. 1830
Smylie, George, Warrington, tailor. April 1829
Snaith, Michael, Liverpool. A Oct. 1830
Snape, Ann, Billinge Chapelend, widow. Sept. 1829
William, Billinge, major - HM 63rd. Regt. of Foot. Jan. 1829
Snelham, John, Manchester, publican. A Oct. 1829
Snowdon, Thomas, Oldham, joiner. A Oct. 1828
Somner, Ellis, Wigan, victualler. July 1826
Sorson, Charles, Liverpool, cooper. A Jan. 1830*
Sothern, Benjamin, Worsley, agent. March 1827

Southart, Christopher, Liverpool, ropemaker. July 1827
Margaret, Liverpool. July 1827
Southern, Benjamin, Manchester, hairdresser. March 1829
John, Ditton, chapman.. A Aug. 1829
John, Bedford, last of Hundersfield, yeoman. Dec. 1830
Southerst, Thomas, New Inn, Crawshaw Booth, cotton manufacturer. June 1829
Southward, Ann, Great Crosby, widow. A May 1829
Southworth, Elizabeth, Orrell, widow. Sept. 1828
Hugh, Salmesbury, yeoman. April 1829
Mary, Upholland, widow. A June 1827
Richard, Upholland, mercer. A June 1827
Sowerby, Peter the elder, Liverpool, cheesefactor. June 1826
Peter, Liverpool, cheesemonger & provision merchant. A Aug. 1826*
Spakeman, Thomas, Bedford, yeoman. Sept. 1827
Sparkes, Elizabeth, Liverpool, widow. A June 1829
Sparks, Daniel, Liverpool, yeoman. June 1829 (1st grant 1806)
Jane, West Derby. A Dec. 1830*
Speak, Henry, Sharple, farmer. A Dec. 1829
Speakman, James, Flixton, yeoman. April 1830*
James, Liverpool, victualler. A Dec. 1830
John, Liverpool, cowkeeper. March 1828
Speedy, William, Liverpool, seaman. June 1828
Spence, William, Liverpool, gent. July 1826
William, the brig Perbriet, Liverpool, carpenter. A Sept. 1826*
Spencer, Alice, Childwall, spinster. A Feb. 1829 (2nd grant 1846)
Edward, Liverpool, cowkeeper. A Sept. 1829
Elizabeth, Haigh, widow. A Nov. 1827
Ellis, Longton, farmer. A May 1830
George, Kerdles, Rossendale, farmer. A July 1829
Isabel, Parkhill, Whalley. Sept. 1827
James, Haigh, farmer. A May 1827
James, Haigh, farmer. A Sept. 1829
Jenny, Ramsbottom, Bury, widow. Dec. 1829
John, Great Sankey, shopkeeper. March 1828
John, Lathom, farmer. Oct. 1829*
Margaret, West Derby, widow. A June 1828
Rachel, Tottington, Bury. A May 1828
Richard, Breightmet, farmer. Nov. 1826
Richard, Manchester, gent. Aug. 1828 (2nd grant 1832)
Robert, Liverpool, shopkeeper. April 1826
Thomas, Manchester, shopkeeper. Feb. 1830
William, Edgeworth, calico maker. Nov. 1827
William, Allerton, farmer. June 1830
Spilling, Samuel, Manchester, druggist. Nov. 1830
Sproat, Samuel, Liverpool, mariner. A Sept. 1829*
Sproston, Elizabeth, Liverpool, widow. A Oct. 1828
Stableford, Elizabeth, Chorlton Row, widow. A July 1827
Michael, Green Heys, Manchester, gent. Nov., 1827; Nov. 1828
Stables, Ellen, Liverpool, spinster. A Feb. 1828
Hannah, Bolton, milliner & dressmaker. July 1830
Stacey, William, Manchester, bricklayer. Oct. 1829*
Stafford, Esther, Denton, spinster. Nov. 1828
Thomas, Clayton, Manchester, collier. July 1826

Stananought, William, Much Hoole, yeoman. April 1827*
Standering, Robert, Stand Lane, Prestwich, weaver. A April 1828
Standish, Betty, Warrington. Jan. 1828*
John, Liverpool, carter. A Oct. 1827*
Martha, Liverpool, widow. Oct. 1829
William, Speke, Childwall. Aug. 1826
Standring, Ann, Rochdale, spinster. Oct. 1828
Charles, Hollant St., Spotland. tailor. March 1829
Elizabeth, Manchester, spinster. April 1830
Elizabeth, Hollinwood, spinster. May 1830
James, Rochdale, victualler. Dec. 1827
Samuel, Tenter House, Spotland, fuller. A Oct. 1826
Samuel, West Leigh, farmer. Oct. 1826
Stanistreet, Catherine, Liverpool, shopkeeper. May 1826
Samuel, Liverpool, cooper. A Sept. 1827*
Stanley, Alexander, Liverpool, last of Mount Vernon, West Derby. A Dec. 1826
Isabella, Manchester, widow. A July 1827
James, Brindle, clerk. May 1826
James, Blackburn, innkeeper. July 1829
Matthew, Liverpool, cart owner. A Dec. 1830
Robert, Liverpool, bookbinder. A Nov. 1829
Stansfield, Ashton, Accrington, surgeon. March 1826
Diana, Little Green, Middleton, spinster. March 1828
George, Bacup, butcher. Aug. 1829
James, Berks, Ashton-under-Lyne, widower. A March 1830*
John, Longclough, widower. A Feb. 1826
John, Hartshead, Ashton-under-Lyne. A Jan. 1827
John, Austerlands, Saddleworth, cotton spinner. Jan. 1830*
Stanton, Matthew, L'pool, boat owner & victualler. Will & Tuon May 1827; July 1827; F
Stanwix, Joseph, Liverpool, joiner. July 1826 (2nd grant 1840)
Starbrick, Henry, Liverpool, gent. June 1826
Starkie, John, Wheatley Lane, Forest of Pendle, yeoman. July 1830
Mary, Salford, widow. May 1830
Starky, Joseph, Redwalls, Bury, gent. A Feb. 1828 (1st grant 1770; (3rd grant 183
Statham, John, Withington, labourer. A March 1827
Staveacre, Alice, Little Heaton, widow. March 1829
Stavert, Elizabeth, Liverpool, widow. Jan. 1827
Stebbing, Robert, Liverpool, victualler. July 1830
Steel, Ellen, Liverpool, A Oct. 1826 (2nd grant 1832)
John, Liverpool, merchant. Jan. 1826
Sarah, Spotland Bridge, Rochdale. A Jan. 1830
Thomas, Liverpool, A Dec. 1826 (2nd grant 1832)
Steele, Catherine, Toxteth Park, widow. Sept. 1830
Thomas, Manchester, accountant. A May 1829
Stephens, Ann, Chorlton Row. Feb. 1828
Edward, Hollinwood, manufacturer. A Nov. 1829
Stephenson, Elizabeth, Upper Newington, Liverpool, widow. A Oct. 1826
Emanuel the elder, Blackburn, yeoman. Nov. 1826
George, West Derby, engineer. A Nov. 1830
Hannah, Liverpool, A Feb. 1830
Isaac, Manchester, corn & flour dealer. Oct. 1830
Jane, Longton, spinster. June 1829
Martha, Banister Hall, Walton-le-Dale, singlewoman. A May 1826

Stephenson, Mary, Wigan. A June 1826
Robert, West Derby, gent. Feb. 1828
Robert, Low Hill, joiner, Nov. 1829
Thomas the elder, Manchester, cordwainer. June 1830
Sterndale, Martha, Manchester, widow. June 1826
Stevenson, John, Tarlscough, Burscough, farmer. May 1830
Thomas Martin, Liverpool, mariner. A Aug. 1826*
Stewart, James, Manchester, ironmonger. July 1827
Stirrup, John, Salford, gent. May 1829
Stock, John, Heskin, yeoman. A April 1830
Roger, Chorley, attorney-at-law. Feb. 1829
William, Liverpool, cotton dealer. July 1829
Stockdale, Joseph, Liverpool, joiner. March 1829
Stockford otherwise Rieley, Sarah, Liverpool. A March 1829*
Stockport, William, Highwhitaker, Padiham, farmer. May 1830
Stoner, Thomas, Liverpool, publican. Nov 1830
Stones, James, Bolton-le-Moors, publican. A March 1826
Sarah, Blackburn, widow. Oct. 1829
Stoperton, James, Salford, hairdresser. Oct. 1827
Stopford, George, Manchester, cotton manufacturer. Jan. 1827
John, Audenshaw, shoemaker. April 1830
Joseph, Ashton-under-Lyne, yeoman. July 1828 (original will to York)
Samuel, Didsbury, yeoman. Nov. 1829*
Samuel, Chorlton Row, gent. Dec. 1830
William, Manchester, joiner. July 1826*
Stopforth, Henry, Liverpool, victualler. Nov. 1827
James, Shevington, yeoman. April 1826
James, Barton, yeoman. Nov. 1829
Storey, Elizabeth, Prescot, widow. June 1828
Storie, Robert, Liverpool, mariner. Feb. 1830
Storrow, Mary, Appleby, co. Westmorland. A March 1826
Story, Abraham, Liverpool, gent. Feb. 1827
Stott, Ann, Rochdale, spinster. A July 1829
Charles, Manchester, bookkeeper. July 1829
Charles, Haslingden, woollen manufacturer. June 1830
Edmund, Moorside, Bury, carter. Dec. 1830*
John, Brownwardle, Rochdale, yeoman. A Feb. 1826
John, Wardle, Hundersfield, yeoman. Oct. 1830
Joseph, Nathan Row, Oldham, coal miner. Oct. 1828
Josiah, Astley, carrier. Aug. 1828
Mary, Oldham, widow. A April 1828
Robert, Kercroft Nook, yeoman. Aug. 1828
Samuel, Brownwardle, Rochdale, yeoman. Feb. 1826
Sarah, Clayton, Droylsden, spinster. Dec. 1829
Sarah Watson, Benthouse, spinster. May 1829
William, Newchurch, cordwainer. A Oct. 1829
William, Lieutenant in H.M. 25th Regt. of Infantry, stationed at Barbadoes. A April 1830
Stout, John, Blackburn, June 1827
Richard, Blackburn, officer of excise. Oct. 1827
Strange, William, Rufford, farmer. Dec. 1830
Strawford, George, Manchester, print glazier. Jan. 1830
Street, Walter, Mossley, Ashton-under-Lyne, machine maker. June 1826

Street, Wilmot, Golborne, yeoman Feb. 1829
Stretch, John, Manchester, gent. June 1829
Joseph, Kirkdale, victualler. Aug. 1830
Strettell, Ann, Rochdale, widow. Dec. 1827
Strickland, John, Wigan, shoemaker. June 1829
Stringer, William, Manchester, victualler. Dec. 1830 (2nd grant 1857)
Stringfellow, Ann, Liverpool, spinster. A April 1827
Stuart, Janet, Prescot, widow. A Feb. 1829
Stubbs, Peter, Wigan, innkeeper. A Jan. 1826
Phebe, Bolton-le-Moors, widow. Nov. 1830
Sturgeon, William, Liverpool, mariner. A June 1829
Sudlow, John, Manchester, cabinet maker. Oct. 1829 (1st grant 1822)
John, Liverpool, labourer, A Nov. 1830*
Sugden, Mary, Liverpool, widow. Nov. 1829
Sullivan, Peter, Liverpool, mariner. A Oct. 1830*
Summerscale, Richard, Hollinwood, butcher. Feb. 1829
Sumner, Esther, Eccleston, spinster. Jan. 1830
John, Longton, husbandman, Aug. 1829
Thomas, Hardshaw, gent. Dec. 1830
William, Winwick, fustian manufacturer. A Dec. 1830
Sunbar, Peter, Liverpool, mariner. Oct. 1827*
Sunderland, Henry, Fearns, Rossendale, dyer. A Nov. 1830 (2nd grant 1850)
Sussum, Eleazar, supposed to be of Bolton. Dec. 1830
Sutcliffe, Abraham, Manchester, flour dealer. A Nov. 1828
Jacob, Middleton, weaver. A July 1827
James, Alderroot, Chadderton, joiner. April 1830
John, Milnrow, innkeeper. March 1828 (2nd grant 1834)
Martha, Knowlwood, Walsden, widow. A Sept. 1826
Oddie, Barrowford, Forest of Pendle, yeoman. May 1828
Robert, Doghillend, Crompton, weaver. A June 1830*
Thomas, Hubby Causway, Barrowford Booth, yeoman. Sept. 1829
William, Milnrow. Sept. 1828 (2nd grant 1864)
William, Springfield Cottage, cotton manufacturer. June 1829
Suthers, John, Mumps, cotton spinner. A June 1829
Sutton, Edward, Liverpool, custom house officer. A April 1829
Elizabeth, Wolston, widow. A & Tuon Jan. 1827 (2nd grant 1832)
Ellen, Hindley, spinster. A June 1827*
John, Liverpool, merchant. Feb. 1828
Peter, Parr, labourer. Sept. 1830 (2nd grant 1869)
Shaddock, Ulnes Walton, farmer. March 1829
William, Little Hoole, yeoman. Aug. 1827
Swainson, Ann, Colne. A June 1827
Swan, James, Olive Mount, Wavertree, esq. Oct. 1829
William, Liverpool, merchant. A Jan. 1829; Nov. 1829
Swarbrick, Mary, Southworth with Croft. Jan. 1827
Robert, Worsley, joiner. June 1830
William, mariner. A Aug. 1829
Sweeney, Hugh, Liverpool, outpensioner of Greenwich Hospital. A Oct. 1828*
Sweetlove, Sarah, Atherton. A July 1828
Swift, Ellen, Liverpool, spinster. A Oct. 1829*
John, West Derby, farmer. Nov. 1829
John, Liverpool, coach proprietor. March 1830
William, Liverpool, fishmonger. July 1827

Swinburn, Robert, Salford, butcher. May 1827
Swindells, Alice, Manchester, widow. A May 1828
Henry, Manchester, shopkeeper. Sept. 1829
John, Manchester, merchant. March 1826
Matthew, Pendleton, wheelwright. April 1829
Swindles, George, Heaton Norris, blacksmith. A Aug. 1828 (2nd grant 1831)
Swithenbank, Jeffrey, Manchester, tea dealer. A June 1830
Syddall, Charles, Manchester, coal banksman. June 1827
Ellen, Manchester Jan. 1827
John, Manchester, collier. A Sept. 1829
Joseph Lawton, Chorlton Row, clerk. Oct. 1829
Sydebotham, James, Toxteth Park, an infant. A Oct. 1827
Samuel, Liverpool, an infant. A Oct. 1827
Syers, Philip, Hale Bottom, yeoman. June 1828
Sykes, Hannah, Wardleworth Brow, Rochdale. May 1827
Hannah, Delph, Saddleworth, spinster. A Oct. 1827*
William, Hulme, baker. Feb. 1826

TAAFFE, Mary, Kensington, co. Middlesex, spinster. Feb. 1828
Taberner, John, Pemberton, farmer. June 1827
Phebe, Burtonwood, widow. May 1829
Taggart, Joseph, Liverpool, mariner. A March 1827*
Talbot, William, Wheelton, weaver. A July 1827
Talbott, John, Whittle-le-Woods, calico printer. March 1827
Tanner, John, Pilkington, innkeeper. June 1826
Tarleton, Richard, Liverpool, flour dealer. A April 1826
Tarlton, William, Liverpool, watchmaker. A May 1826*
Tarbuck, Mary, Liverpool, widow. A & Tuon May 1826*
Tate, John Silvester, Manchester, grocer & draper. Jan. 1829
Richard, Liverpool, gent. A July 1827
Tatlock, William, Liverpool, cooper. A Dec. 1828 (1st grant 1815)
Tattersall, James, Great Bolton, haircutter. Feb. 1828
William, Higher Ardwick, gent. April 1826
Taylor, Alice, Parbold. A July 1826*
Andrew, Hollinwood, weaver. A Aug. 1826*
Ann, Liverpool, widow. Feb. 1826
Ann, Manchester, last of Lees, widow. Dec. 1830
Bartholomew, Marton, farmer. May 1826
Bent, Spring Side, cotton manufacturer. Nov. 1829
Betty, Plattin, Castleton, widow. April 1828
Catharine, Spring Side, Ashton-under-Lyne, widow. Nov. 1826
Edmund, Milnrow. Jan. 1827
Edmund, Meanwood, Rochdale, yeoman. Aug. 1827
Edmund, Laneside, Prestwich, cotton spinner. Sept. 1827
Edmund, Barrowfields, weaver. June 1828
Edmund, Ogden, Butterworth, yeoman. A Sept. 1830
Edward, Liverpool, hairdresser. A Sept. 1826
Elizabeth, Spring Side, Ashton-under-Lyne, spinster. Sept. 1826
Elizabeth, Goose Green, Pemberton. A April 1828
Ellen, Grosvenor St., Chorlton Row, widow. July 1830
George, Whitworth, Rochdale, surgeon. A June 1830
Hannah, Ashton-under-Lyne, widow. Oct. 1828
Henry, Golborn, yeoman. April 1827

Taylor, Henry, Hindley, farmer. Dec. 1829
Hugh, Manchester, drysalter. Feb., 1827
James, Walkers, Saddleworth, gent. Jan. 1826
James, Whitworth, Rochdale, surgeon. July 1826
James, Cloughfold, Rossendale, woollen manufacturer. May 1827
James, Liverpool, esq. Sept. 1828
James, Manchester, gent. Nov. 1828
James, Liverpool, mariner. A Dec. 1828*
James, Little Bolton, weaver. June 1829
James, Worsthorn, yeoman. Aug. 1829
John, Glodwick, Oldham, dyer. July 1826
John, Hazlehurst, farmer. Dec. 1826
John, Manchester, gent. Dec. 1826 (1st grant 1803)
John, Clitheroe, cotton spinner. July 1827
John, Liverpool, joiner. A Oct. 1827
John, St. Bartholomew Close, London, surgeon. A March 1828
John, Longworth, farmer. A Aug. 1828
John, Glodwick, Prestwich, farmer. A Dec. 1828
John, Liverpool, gent. A Jan. 1829
John, Manchester, shopkeeper. A Feb. 1829*
John, Liverpool, draper. A May 1829
John, Heyside, Royton, cotton weaver. A June 1829
John, Salford, publican. Oct. 1829
John, Greenacres Moor, Oldham, cotton spinner. A March 1830
John, Thorp, Royton, farmer. June 1830
John, Withington, farmer. Dec. 1830
Joseph, Glodwick, Oldham, weaver. A March 1828
Joseph, Gravilhole, Thornham. Sept. 1828
Joseph, Oldham, innkeeper. Dec. 1828 (Earlier grants 1816 & 1818)
Joseph, Northgate, Oldham. Jan. 1829
Joseph, Liverpool, master porter. June 1829
Mally, Royton, widow. A April 1830
Mally, Boyton, [? Royton] , spinster. A Aug. 1830
Manesty, Moorlane, Bolton-le-Moors, gent. A July 1829
Margaret, Liverpool, widow. Jan. 1829
Martin, of merchant ships Bolivar & Julian, Liverpool, cooper. A Sept. 1830
Mary, Liverpool, spinster. Feb. 1828
Mary, Mountains, Rochdale, spinster. Aug. 1828
Mary, Hulme, spinster. Dec. 1828
Mary, Flixton, widow. Aug. 1829
Mary, Kersley, widow. Sept. 1830
Mary, Towfft, Knutsford, last of Blackburn. A Sept. 1830
Nicholas, Tarleton, husbandman. July 1827
Ralph, Thorpe St., Thurnham, Middleton. July 1826*
Ralph, Higher Shore, bachelor. A Sept. 1830
Richard, Liverpool, gent. Sept. 1826
Richard, Manchester, stonemason. June 1827
Richard, Tottington. Oct. 1827
Robert, Ashton-under-Lyne, wheelwright. A Jan. 1827
Robert, Liverpool, currier. July 1828
Robert, Bury, carrier. A July 1828
Robert Everleigh, Bolton-le-Moors, doctor of physic. March 1828
Samuel, Salford, cotton spinner. Nov. 1826

Taylor, Samuel, Lodge Stand, Prestwich, cotton manufacturer. Jan. 1827
Samuel, Snape Hill, Outwood, yeoman. Feb., 1827
Samuel, Salford, upholsterer. July 1827
Samuel, Wardleworth, weaver. Feb. 1828
Samuel, Bacup. Nov. 1828*
Sarah, Liverpool, widow. Aug. 1827
Thomas, White Smithy Bar, Manchester, surveyor. A April 1826
Thomas, Manchester, victualler. A Aug. 1828
Thomas, Manchester, leather currier. Nov. 1828
Thomas, Hollingwood, schoolmaster. Dec. 1828
Thomas, Oldham, joiner. June 1829
Thomas, Square, Todmorden, cotton weaver. Jan. 1830 (2nd grant 1833)
William, Bolton-le-Moors. April 1826
William, Padiham, blacksmith. Oct. 1826
William, Hebers, Middleton, weaver. Nov. 1826
William, Moss Gate, Crompton, weaver. A Nov. 1826
William, Cadishead, weaver. Dec. 1827 (2nd grant 1856)
William, Stand, Pilkington, esq. March 1828
William, Liverpool, gent. Aug. 1828 (2nd grant 1831)
William, Liverpool, master mariner. A June 1829
William, Wigan, yeoman. July 1829
William, Royton, cotton manufacturer. A May 1830
William Robert, Bury, schoolmaster. A Oct. 1828
Telfar, William, Wigan, draper. March 1828
Telford, James, Manchester, woollen manufacturer. A July 1826*
Mary, Liverpool, spinster. A Jan. 1829
Richard, Oldham, publican. A Oct. 1829
Tempest, Joseph, Rochdale, woollen manufacturer. A Aug. 1830
Terry, Charles, Chorlton Row, merchant. Feb. 1830
Tetlow, Alice, Hollinwood, widow. Dec. 1830
Edward, Thornham, husbandman. A July 1829
Thomas, Thornham, farmer. A May 1826
Thelwall, William, Manchester, builder. Sept. 1829
Thirlwell, George, Liverpool, mariner. A April 1829
Thistlethwaite, Ann, Manchester, confectioner. June 1829
Thomas, Henry, Liverpool, mariner. A Feb. 1828*
James, Chorlton Row, bookkeeper. March 1829
Jane, Manchester, spinster. Sept. 1827
Jane, Liverpool, spinster. A Feb. 1830
John, Liverpool, stable keeper. A March 1826*
John, Liverpool, esq. July 1828
Mary, Liverpool, dressmaker. April 1830*
Owen, Liverpool, pilot. May 1826
Richard, Hull, last of Manchester, gent. July 1829
Samuel, Manchester, publican. Jan. 1828
Sarah, Abbey Foregate, Shrewsbury, spinster. May 1829
Thomason, Richard, Manchester, fustian manufacturer. May 1826
Thompson, Alexander, Liverpool, mariner. June 1826*
Betty, Salford, widow. Will & Tuon July 1826 (2nd grant 1833)
Christopher, Liverpool, victualler. June 1829
James, Hurst Cross, Ashton-under-Lyne, yeoman. Oct. 1826
James, Hoghton, weaver. July 1828*
John, Manchester, common carrier. Feb. 1826

Thompson, John, Limefield, Ashton-under-Lyne, cloth dresser. A Feb. 1827
John, Liverpool, victualler. April., 1827
Nicholas, Hargreave, Padiham, agent. May 1830
Rebecca, Liverpool, widow. A June 1829
Richard, Manchester. A Oct. 1826
Robert, Lathom, bailiff. April 1827
Robert, Liverpool, mariner. April 1827*
Swinton, Liverpool, warehouseman. May 1826
William, Manchester, clock & watchmaker. A March 1827
William, Farnworth. Oct. 1827
William, Litherland, merchant. Jan. 1829
Thomson, Christian, Sloane St., co. Middlesex. A June 1829
Thorley, Thomas, Manchester, innkeeper. April 1828
Thorneley, William, Openshaw, hat manufacturer. Jan. 1827
Thorniley, Ellen, Heaton Norris, spinster. Feb. 1827
Thomas, Reddish, farmer. Spet. 1830
Thornley, Elizabeth, Park Field, Middleton, spinster. Feb. 1829*
Mary, Bolton. A Jan. 1828*
Thomas, Sharples, weaver. Oct. 1829
Thornton, John, Croston, farrier. Feb. 1826
Richard, Liverpool, merchant. A Nov. 1829
Robert, Manchester, bricksetter. A May 1827*
William, Colne Waterside, weaver. A March 1830*
Thorp, John, Walmsley, Bury, labourer. Nov. 1829
Joseph, Birks, Ashton-under-Lyne, cotton weaver. A Sept. 1826
Ralph, Bolton-le-Moors, warper. A June 1829
William, Manchester, manufacturer. Jan. 1829 (2nd grant 1834)
Thorpe, Esther, Pennington, spinster. March 1829
Thomas Dawson, Manchester, cotton merchant. A April 1826
Threlfall, Elizabeth, Eccleston, widow. July 1829
Henry, Lathom, yeoman. Aug. 1826*
Henry, Liverpool, mariner. Sept. 1828
John, Bolton, tailor. Oct. 1828
Thwaites, Lancelot, Bolton-le-Moors, ironfounder. May 1827
Tickle, George, Sutton, Prescot, carrier. A Dec. 1827
Peter, Eccleston, carpenter. Aug. 1828
Sarah, Tottington Lower End, widow. May 1830
William, Barton Wood, Warrington, shoemaker. A Nov. 1830
Tildesley, Mary, Tarleton. May 1829
Tilley, Thomas, Warrington, stonemason. Nov. 1829
Tillie, Elizabeth, Liverpool. Feb. 1826*
Tillotson, Robert, Colne, gent. A Oct. 1829
Tilsley, Elizabeth, Ormskirk, widow. Dec. 1827
Timperley, Isaiah, Chorlton with Hardy, yeoman. Nov. 1828
John, Little Hulton, shopkeeper. Nov. 1827; Oct. 1828
Tinker, James, Broughton, toll gate keeper. Jan. 1830
Tinsdale, Charles James, Bolton-le-Moors, grocer. A Aug. 1826
Tinsley, Henry, Knowsley. Jan. 1828*
John, Winwick, farmer. Jan. 1829
John, Abram, Wigan, yeoman. Oct. 1829
Thomas, Warrington, bachelor. A Oct. 1830
Tiplady, William Edmund, Oldham, apprentice. A Sept. 1830*
Tipping, Alice, Manchester, widow. Oct. 1828

Tipping, James, Chorlton Row, yeoman. Sept. 1827
 Thomas, Wigan, gent. Oct., 1827
Titley, Richard, Manchester, plumber & glazier. July. 1828
Todd, Edward, Edge Hill. Oct. 1829
 Robert, Leyland, weaver. Oct. 1826*
 Robert, Burscough, yeoman. A Nov. 1829
Toft, Aaron, Hollinsgreen, yeoman. April 1826
Tollitt, James, Liverpool, spirit dealer. Feb. 1827
Tomkinson, William, Manchester, gent. A April 1828
Tomlinson, George, Manchester, surgeon. April 1827
 Jane, Ardwick, widow. Sept. 1827*
 John, Bottom of Green acres Moor, Oldham, ironfounder. Nov. 1829
 Joseph, Rochdale, woolstapler. May 1826
 Thomas, Kendal, farmer. Feb. 1827
 William, Warrington, manufacturer. A March 1827
Tonge, Jabez, Pendleton. Aug. 1827
Toole, Edward, Liverpool, mariner. A Sept. 1829
Tootell, Jane, Whittle-le-Woods, spinster. April 1828
Tootill, Mary, Breightmet. A Nov. 1830*
 Thomas, Walshaw Lane, Bury, cotton weaver. A March 1830
Topp, Ann, Farnworth, widow. A Dec. 1828
 James, Farnworth, farmer. Dec. 1828
Topper, Mary, Blackburn, spinster. March 1828
Torbett, Ann, Liverpool, widow. April 1830
Torkington, Thomas, Haughton, Manchester. A April 1826
Tothill, Charles, Liverpool, officer in H.M. Customs. A Aug. 1826
Touchet, James, Manchester, merchant. June 1827
Toulmin, John, Liverpool, plumber & glazier. Feb. 1826
Towett, John, Heaton Norris, blacksmith. May 1827
Townley, Richard, Lancaster, gent. A June 1830
 Thomas, Manchester, merchant. A July 1827
Townsend, Joshua, Holme, Haslingden, gent. Jan. 1829
 Ralph, Manchester, stocking manufacturer. Sept. 1828
 William, Liverpool, widower. A Jan. 1829
Townshend, James, Billinge, farmer. Aug. 1828
Trafford, Elizabeth, Withington, spinster. March 1828
 William, Culcheth Hall, last of Pleremore, Chadderley Corbett, esq. Oct. 1829
Travers, Thomas, Lowton, cotton manufacturer. May 1826
Traverse, Henry, Hayton, publican. A April 1830
 James, Hardshaw, Windle, carpenter. Feb. 1826
Travis, Elizabeth, Blackley. A Sept. 1827
 James, Cowhill, Prestwich, yeoman. Jan. 1828
 James, Blackley, gent. March 1829
 Matthew, Manchester, gent. Feb. 1829
 Richard, Prestwich, whitster. Nov. 1829
 William, Inckfield Mill, Rochdale. July 1829
Traynor, Hugh, Liverpool, provision dealer. March 1829
Tristram, Dolly, Everton, spinster. Nov. 1827
Trotter, Isabella, Singleton, Prestwich, spinster. April 1828
 James, Liverpool, gent. April 1830
Trueman, George, Liverpool, gent. April 1826
Tudor, Alice, Liverpool, feme covert. May 1828
 Robert the elder, Liverpool, gent. Aug. 1830

Tudor, Robert the younger, Liverpool. A Sept. 1830
Tullock, John, Liverpool, master mariner. A April 1827
Tunstall, John, Blackburn, cotton warper. March 1830*
Turnbull, John, Liverpool, mariner. July 1829
Turner, Ann, Manchester, spinster. Jan. 1828
  Betty, Middleton, weaver. Nov. 1827
  Edmund the elder, Kersley, spinner. Aug. 1829
  Edward, Elton, bricklayer. Sept. 1829
  Henry, the barque Sir W. Scott, Liverpool. A May 1827*
  James, Rochdale, ropemaker. May 1826
  James, Barton-upon-Irwell, shopkeeper. April 1830
  James, Yorkshire St., Rochdale, butcher. June 1830
  James, Hoghton, yeoman. Sept. 1830
  John, Low Head, Spotland. yeoman. Sept. 1826*
  John, Mill Hill, Livesey, esq. Nov. 1826
  John, Davyhulme, Eccles, schoolmaster. July 1827
  John, Austerlands, Saddleworth, yeoman. June 1830
  Margaret, Penrith, co. Cumb. A June 1826
  Richard, Howarth Cross, Rochdale, cornfactor. A Sept. 1828*
  Richard, Warrington, gent. April 1829
  Richard, Liverpool, shipwright. A Dec. 1829*
  Susy, Rochdale, widow. Nov. 1829
  Thomas, Blackburn, calico printer. A March 1826
  Thomas, Cheadle, co. Staffs., esq. A July 1827 (2nd grant 1831)
  Thomas, Austerlands, yeoman. April 1828
  Thomas, Middleton, shopkeeper. A Jan. 1830
  Thomas, Barton, farmer. A March 1830
  Thomas Griffiths, Manchester, gent. March 1830
  William, Warrington, gent. June 1827; July 1828 (other grants 1799, 1810, 183
  William, Manchester, woollen manufacturer. A March 1828
Turtington, Jane, Chorley, widow. March 1827*
Tweedale, Sally, Oldham, straw hat manufacturer & dressmaker. April 1830
  Samuel, Shawclough, innkeeper. A July 1828
Tweedle, Hannah, Liverpool, spinster. April 1828
Twist, Jonathan, Breightmet, Bolton, weaver. A Dec. 1828
  Joseph, Liverpool, brazier. April 1830
Tyrer, Amy, Prescot, spinster. March 1830
  Henry, Liverpool, master mariner. Feb. 1827 (1st grant 1825)
  James, Ince Blundell, farmer. Jan. 1830
  James, Formby, yeoman. March 1830
  John, Formby, yeoman. April 1826
  Margaret, Liverpool, widow. May 1829 (2nd grant 1850)
  Ralph, Salford, tailor. Sept. 1830
  Richard, Blackrod, yeoman. April 1829
  William, Knowsley, yeoman. Aug. 1826 (1st grant 1811)
Tyson, Anthony, Liverpool, May 1827

UMPTON, Richard, Manchester, labourer. Nov. 1828
Underwood, James, Ormskirk, saddler. June 1826
  John, Liverpool, cowkeeper. March 1830
Unsworth, Edward, Wigan, publican. Nov. 1827
  Joseph, Scholes, shopkeeper. March 1828
  Mary, Liverpool, widow. May 1826

Unsworth, Mary, Liverpool, A May 1827
Richard, Ashton-in-Makerfield, miller. May 1826
Richard, Duxbury, miller. Dec. 1826 (1st Grant 1809)
Robert, St. Helens, cooper. Aug. 1827
Robert, Toxteth Park, cowkeeper. Nov. 1830
Upton, William, Prescot, tailor. May 1830
Urmson, Mary, April 1826
Usher, Jane, Liverpool, spinster. June 1830
Usherwood, John, Liverpool, coach wheelwright. July 1829
Uttley, James, Rochdale, butcher. A Dec. 1830

VAILE, John, Liverpool, seaman. A Oct. 1829*
Valentine, George, Eccleston, labourer. March 1826
William, Ormskirk, yeoman. Nov. 1828
Vandeburgh, Charles Frederick, Liverpool, doctor of medicine. Sept. 1828
Varley, Richard, Walton Lane, Bolton. Jan. 1827
Vaughan, John, Pall Mall, Liverpool, sugar baker. July 1828
William, Welch Whittle, Standish. June 1827
Veare, Robert, Manchester, dyer. A March 1828
Veevers, Sagar, Coal Clough, Habergham Eaves, gent. March 1828 (2nd grant 1834)
Verdon, Blackwell, Manchester, dyer. March 1827
Thomas, Liverpool, victualler. A June 1827
Vere, Ann, Liverpool, widow. Jan. 1829
Vernon, Edward, Liverpool, master mariner. A Nov. 1827
Thomas, Cheapside, London, gent. June 1828
Vertue, Timothy, Liverpool, boat builder. July 1829
Vose, Thomas, Burscough, yeoman. Aug. 1826
William, Rainhill, Prescot. A Dec. 1829

WADDINGTON, John, Walton-le-Dale, farmer. A May. 1828
Jonathan, Wrigley, shopkeeper. A Aug. 1827
William, Blackburn, farmer. May 1826
Wade, Elizabeth, Tottington. A Nov. 1829*
Wadkin, Elizabeth, Eccleston Low Steads, widow. May 1828
Wadsworth, Benjamin, Manchester, shopkeeper. A May 1827
Wainhouse, Elizabeth, Manchester, publican. Oct. 1829
John, Manchester, publican. A April 1827
Wainwright, Ann, Prescot, widow. Oct. 1826
Catharine, Ormskirk, spinster. March 1828
Ellen, Crumpsall, widow. A Oct. 1827
James, Liverpool, blacksmith. Jan. 1826; Feb. 1827
Richard, Liverpool, professor of music. May 1826
Robert, Liverpool, coach proprietor. Nov. 1830
William, Thames Bank, Westminster, coal dealer. Sept. 1826
William, Liverpool, publican. Feb. 1827
William, Hollins, farmer. A May 1828
William, Hulme, manufacturer. Oct. 1830
Waistell, John, Liverpool, cooper. A May. 1826
Sarah, Liverpool, widow. June 1828
Thomas, Liverpool, joiner. Sept. 1826*
Wakeford, Samuel Walford, Hulme, agent. A Jan. 1828
Walch, Henry, Parbold, weaver. May 1826
James, Over Darwen, yeoman. July 1828

Walch, Richard, Little Bolton, weaver. A April 1829
Thomas, Great Bolton, weaver. Jan. 1827*
Walkden, John, Urmston, yeoman. Nov. 1830
Sarah, Goals Mill, Prestwich, widow. A May 1826*
Walker, Alexander, Liverpool, brass founder. March 1830
Alexander, Manchester, labourer. A Aug. 1830
Ann, Manchester, spinster. April. 1827*
Ann, Sandy Lane, Pendleton, widow. Aug. 1828 (2nd grant 1842)
Benjamin, Tonge, Middleton, blacksmith. A June 1826
Catherine, Chorlton Row, widow. June 1828
Edward, Cronton, yeoman. Sept. 1826
Elizabeth, Chorlton Row, widow. Dec. 1828
George, Bury, cutter. A Feb. 1830
Henry, Salford, machine maker. April 1826
Henry, Downham. A May 1830
James, Manchester, joiner. A Oct. 1826
James, Lower Croft, Elton, whitster. A May 1829
John, Parr, gent. Oct. 1826
John, Manchester, widower. A Nov. 1827
John, Manchester, cotton merchant. March 1828
Jonathan, Fearned. Feb. 1828
Josiah, Ashton-under-Line, yeoman. Oct. 1828
Mary, Ashton-under-Lyne, linen draper. March 1827
Mary, Bury, spinster. A Jan. 1830
Nathan, Wigan, cotton manufacturer. Nov. 1828
Peter, Old Turks, Radcliffe, farmer. Jan. 1830
Quintin, Ashton-under-Lyne, Dec. 1828
Richard, Lovely Hall, Blackburn, farmer. A Oct. 1826
Richard, Manchester. Sept. 1830
Richard, Whitefield, Prestwich, yeoman. Sept. 1830
Robert, Unsworth, yeoman. Feb. 1830
Samuel, Manchester. A Feb. 1826
Samuel, Chadderton, labourer. A June. 1828
Silence, the Bridge, Prestwich, widow. Oct. 1830
Thomas, Liverpool, mariner. A Dec. 1827*
Thomas, Liverpool, liquor merchant. A Aug. 1828
Thomas, Aughton, gent. Feb. 1829
Thomas, Cheetham St., Rochdale, basket & skipmaker. A Feb. 1829
William, Manchester, barber. Aug. 1828
Walkinson, Edward, Sephton. April 1826
Wall, John, Oldham, joiner. A Dec. 1826*
or Wallis, Thomas, Wigan, butcher. A March 1829 (1st grant 1811)
Wallace, Gordon, Calcutta, last of Liverpool, gent. Oct. 1829; April 1830
Waller, Charles, Manchester, chapman. A July 1826
Wallis, Thomas, *see* Wall
Wallwork, Thomas, Holcome, fulling miller. June 1829
Thomas, Bury, joiner. A March 1830
Wallworth, William, Liverpool, last of Reading, co.Berks., gent. April 1828
Walmsley, Ann, Walton-le-Dale, widow. May 1829
Giles, Heaton Norris, farmer. July 1829
James, Bury, confectioner. A April 1828
John, Cuerden, weaver. A Sept. 1830
Mary, Bold, spinster. Feb. 1829

Walmsley, Sarah, Bury, widow. A April 1828
Susanna, Prestwich, spinster. A March 1830
William, Mellor, yeoman. May 1830
Walsh, Ann, Liverpool, widow. Oct. 1827
Joseph, Farnworth, blacksmith. A March., 1828
Thomas, Liverpool, earthenware & china dealer. Jan. 1827; June 1827
Walters, Joseph, Droylsden, farmer. Oct. 1826
Thomas, the merchant ship Huskisson, Liverpool, mariner. A Feb. 1828*
Walthew, Fanny, Edge Hill. A June 1829 (2nd grant 1839)
Walton, Edward, Fallowfield, Manchester, farmer. A Dec. 1828*
James, Davyhulme, Eccles, farmer. Jan. 1826*
Jane, Leyland, widow. A May 1827*
John, Liverpool, warehouseman. May 1826
John, Leyland, yeoman. Dec. 1826* (1st grant 1807*)
John, Leyland, farmer. A May 1828 (2nd grant 1846)
John, Liverpool, grocer. Aug. 1830
Robert, Liverpool, mariner. A Dec. 1829*
Roger, Leyland, weaver. A May 1827*
Thomas Blackburn, A July 1828 (1st grant 1810)
Wamsley, Sarah, Salford. A May 1830
Warberick, Robert, Liverpool, tide waiter. Jan. 1830
Warburton, Ann, Rusholme, spinster. Dec. 1828
John, Higher Woodhill, Bury. A Oct. 1829
Joseph, Heaton Norris, blacksmith. March 1830
Mary, Houghton, Winwick, spinster. A Sept. 1826
Mary, Houghton, Winwick, spinster. A Oct. 1826
Peter, Hulme, victualler. Aug. 1829
Samuel, Radcliff, carter. Nov. 1826
Thomas, Great Sankey. Jan. 1826
Thomas, Manchester. A July 1827
Thomas, Bedford, farmer. Dec. 1829
William, Roby, wheelwright. A May 1827
Warbutton, George, Turton, yeoman. Dec. 1828*
Ward, Betty, Roughley Gate, Oswaldtwistle. July 1830
Isabel, Liverpool, spinster. A March 1827
James, Didsbury, schoolmaster. A Jan. 1830
John, Liverpool, general agent. Jan. 1826
John, Little Bowland, yeoman. Oct. 1827
John, Mellor, yeoman. March 1829
Martha, Prescot, widow. March 1827*
Roger, Kidderminster & Stourport, both co. Worcester, dissenting minister. Feb. 1826
Wardell, Elizabeth, Liverpool, A Dec., 1827
Wardle, Dorothy, Manchester, widow. A Oct. 1827 (1st grant 1821)
John, Bury, bricksetter. June 1826
John, Manchester, fustian manufacturer. A Sept. 1826 (Former grants 1820 & 1821)
William, Manchester, shoemaker. June 1826
Wardley, John, Blackley, weaver. April 1827
Wareing, James, Little Crosby, husbandman. March 1829
John, Stayley Bridge, cotton spinner. April 1829
Waring, Henry, Chorley, wheelwright. A June 1826*
Thomas, Crossens, North Meols. May 1830
Warmby, William, Ashton-under-Lyne, machine maker. Feb. 1830
Warren, Anne, Liverpool, spinster. Oct. 1830

Washington, Agnes, St. Pauls Square, Liverpool, widow. April. 1830
Waterhouse, Joseph, Oldham, butcher. May 1830
Joshua, Oldham, yeoman. Nov. 1826*
Martha, Manchester . April 1829
Nicholas, Everton, broker. A Dec., 1828
Waterland, Thomas, Manchester, machine maker. A Aug. 1828
Waters, Ann, Manchester, spinster. Jan. 1827
Watkins, Thomas, Ardwick, esq. April 1827
Watkinson, James, Wigan, butcher. A March 1826
Thomas, Liverpool, porter. A Oct. 1826*
Watkis, William, Manchester, gent. A Sept. 1827
Watmough, Margaret, Liverpool. A June 1828
Robert, Liverpool, timber merchant. A March 1827
Watmouth, Mary, Upper Pit St., Liverpool, widow. Feb. 1830
Watmugh, John, Warrington, gent. Dec. 1827
Watson, Bingley, Liverpool, upholsterer. Dec. 1826 (2nd Grant 1849)
Collin, Liverpool, officer in the Customs. A July 1830
Henry, Cheetham Hill, esq. June 1826
Holland, Liverpool, esq. March 1829 ;Sept. 1829
John, Blackburn, gent. June 1826*
John, Liverpool, mariner. April 1828*
John, Clayton-le-Dale, farmer. Sept. 1828
John, Liverpool, mariner. A June. 1829
John jun., Toxteth Park, agent. Sept. 1829; Dec. 1829 (Later grants 1834 & 183
Thomas, Harrington, joiner. Feb. 1827
Thomas, Wigan, weaver. July 1829
Thomas, Ormskirk, woollen draper. A Dec. 1830
William, Manchester, hatter. A May 1827
William, Manchester, draper. A Sept. 1829
Waugh, Jane, Summerville, Manchester, spinster. A Oct. 1830
Webb, Benjamin Dungard, Chorlton Row, gent. June 1827; Dec. 1830 (3rd grant 1
Robert, Liverpool, victualler. June 1828
Webster, Betty, Liverpool, farmer. Aug. 1827
Ellen, *see* Gunnery
George, Didsbury, esq. Nov. 1829
John, Wigan, farmer. March 1826
John, Rainford, wheelwright. July 1827*
Margaret, Much Woolton, widow. Dec. 1826
Martha, Manchester, widow. A Nov. 1830 (2nd grant 1835)
Mary, West Derby, spinster. A Jan. 1827
Mary, Childwall, widow. A March 1830
Thomas, Liverpool, timber merchant. A Aug. 1827
Thomas, Childwall, yeoman. Jan. 1829
Thomas Sherlock, Liverpool. A Jan. 1828
Wedgwood, Betty, Liverpool, widow. Sept. 1827
Weems, Ebenezer, Liverpool, baker. March 1827 (2nd grant 1839)
Weir, Euphemia, Manchester, spinster. Feb. 1827
Wells, Joshua, Lathom, stonemason. Dec. 1827
Sleddon, Liverpool, mariner. A Oct. 1827*
Wellstood, William, Liverpool, master mariner. A June 1830
Welsby, Ann, Ormskirk, widow. May 1830
Welsh, Alice, Higher Constabley, Rossendale, spinster. Oct. 1829*
Eleanor, Manchester, widow. May 1830

Welsh, Hannah, Liverpool, widow. March 1826
Mary, Liverpool, shopkeeper. Sept. 1829
William, Manchester, common carrier. May 1827; Sept. 1828
West, Jane, West Derby, widow. Feb. 1827 (2nd grant 1869)
Jane, Clayton. A Oct. 1829*
Thomas, Eccleston, esq. July. 1828
Westcott, Benjamin, Liverpool, mariner. A Jan. 1829*
Westmore, Alice, West Derby, widow. A Oct. 1829
Jane, Liverpool, widow. Jan. 1828
Westmoreland, Samuel, Manchester. May 1829
Weston, Elizabeth, Manchester. July 1827
Jane, Manchester, widow. Jan. 1828
John, Wigan, portrait painter. Feb. 1829
Westwell, George, Copy Nook, Blackburn. Nov. 1828
Wetherall, Christopher, Salford. A Dec. 1830
Wetton, Benjamin, Manchester, publican. Dec. 1829
John, Manchester, coachmaker. Feb. 1830
Whaley, John, Liverpool, stonemason. Aug. 1827
Whalley, Ann, Blackburn, singlewoman. May 1829
Edward, Ormskirk, butcher. A Dec. 1827
Ellen, Little Harwood, widow. Sept. 1829
Giles, Clayton-le-Dale, weaver. A Dec. 1829 (1st grant 1822)
Henry, Heywood, Little Marsden, weaver. Nov. 1826
Peter, Chorlton, farmer. A March 1829
Robert, Rainford. April 1827*
Samuel, Salford, gent. April 1830
William, Eccleston, husbandman. Jan. 1827
Wharton, Henry, Ormskirk, tailor. Sept. 1829
Joseph, Liverpool, yeoman. A June. 1830
William Waterman, Liverpool, a Lieut. on halfpay in H.M. Navy. May 1829
Whatton, John, Liverpool, June 1830*
Wheeldon, Sarah, Manchester, feme covert. A Nov 1828
Wheeler, Charles, Manchester, letterpress printer. Sept. 1827
Henry the younger, Edge Hill, oilman. Dec. 1830 (2nd grant 1832)
Mary, Manchester, A Aug. 1827
Wheelhouse, Mary, Ardwick, widow. A May 1826
Wheelton, Joseph, West Derby, servant. March 1829
Whetnall, Alice, Liverpool, widow. A Jan. 1827
Whinfield, Thomas, Edenfield, mason. A May 1828
Whip, Richard, Barrowfold, Colne, yeoman. Feb. 1826
Whipp, Robert, Blackmoss, Whitley Booth, yeoman. Nov. 1829
Whistance, William, Herculaneum Pottery, Toxteth Park. May 1827
Whiston, Jane, Sutton, widow. A Dec. 1827
Whitaker, Ann, Newchurch, Rossendale, widow. Sept. 1829
James, Burnley Wood, farmer. Jan. 1826
James, Rochdale, butcher. Aug. 1828
John, Salesbury, yeoman. May. 1829
Joseph, Withington, manufacturer. A April 1826
Mary, Haworth, Bradford, co. York, spinster. Nov. 1826
Richard, Rossendale, printer. A July 1827
Richard, Holme Field, Rossendale, sizer. Oct. 1830
Robert, Rochdale, gent. Oct. 1830 (1st grant 1790)
Sarah, Liverpool, spinster. Dec. 1830

Whitaker, Simeon, Simonstone, stonemason. May 1826
Thomas, Ringley Bridge, blacksmith. A & Tuon Jan. 1827
Whitby, Bourne, London, bachelor. A Sept. 1827
Whitby, Robert, Manchester, flour dealer. A July 1826
Robert, Manchester, shopkeeper. April 1827
White, Alice, Edge Hill, widow. Feb. 1829
George, Liverpool, shoemaker. Nov. 1829
James, outpensioner no. 2939 of Greenwich Hospital. A Oct. 1827*
John, Liverpool, mariner. March 1828*
John, Salford, innkeeper. March 1829
Mary, Warrington, widow. July 1829
Mary, Liverpool, widow. Oct. 1829
Sarah, Manchester, widow. Aug. 1826
Sarah, Crabtree Lane, West Derby, widow. Nov. 1827
William, Manchester, plumber & glazier. A Jan. 1830*
Whitehead, Abraham, Strines, stonemason. A Nov. 1827
Ann, Liverpool, widow. A Aug. 1827
Charles, Burnedge, Rochdale, farmer. Feb. 1828
Charles Henry, Chorlton Row, warehouseman. A Aug. 1827
David, Collinge Croft, Oldham, weaver. March 1828
Edmund, Stanedge, Saddleworth, clothier. A Oct. 1829
Ellen, Wigan, widow. June 1826 (1st grant 1815)
James, Thorns Clough Mill, Saddleworth, woollen slubber. A Feb. 1827*
James, Bury, gent. April 1827
James, Harpurhey, weaver. A Sept. 1828 (2nd grant 1838)
James, Saddleworth, yeoman. Dec. 1828
James, Manchester, calico printer. June 1829
James, Blocklane, Oldham, shopkeeper. A Jan. 1830
John, Pemberton, gent. May 1826
John, Manchester St., Oldham, innkeeper. July 1826
John, Ainsworth, farmer. Aug. 1829
John Dicken, Saddleworth, woollen manufacturer. A Aug. 1830
Joseph Charles Frederick, Newton, clerk. A Feb. 1830 (1st grant 1825)
Mary, Flash House, Butterworth. May 1829
Peter, Manchester, cordwainer. A Dec. 1830
Richard, Harpurhey, weaver. June 1827
Richard, Liverpool, flour dealer. Dec. 1827
Robert, Manchester, broker. March 1829
Sally, Lockwoodhey, Saddleworth. March 1829
Sarah, Rochdale, feme covert. A April 1828
Thomas, Denton, farmer. A May 1828
Thomas, Saddleworth Fold, clothier. Sept. 1830
William, Quick, Saddleworth, carrier. April 1827
Whitelegg, Mary, Urmston, spinster, Nov. 1828
Thomas, Manchester, porter. Aug. 1830
Whiteley, John, Liverpool, pavior. Dec. 1829
Samuel, Liverpool. A May 1826*
Whiteside, Frances, Liverpool, widow. A Aug. 1827
Jennet, Liverpool, spinster. A Jan. 1829
Whitfield, James, Scarisbrick. A Feb. 1826
John, Liverpool, hosier. March 1830
Peter, Ditton. A March 1827*
Whithead, Ellen, Liverpool, widow. March 1826

Whitlow, John, Manchester, victualler. Oct. 1826
Thomas, Manchester, victualler. Feb. 1830 (1st grant 1820)
William, Liverpool, brewer. April 1827
Whitnall, Alice, Liverpool, widow. A Dec. 1826
Alice, Liverpool, widow. June 1827
Ann, Manchester. A April 1827
Whittam, Nathaniel, Liverpool, gent. April 1829
Whittaker, George, Hollinwood, weaver. A Feb. 1826*
James, Wardleworth. Dec. 1827*
James, Manchester, esq. July 1828
Mary, Oldham, widow. Nov. 1827
Philip, Carrion Crow, Oldham, yeoman. July 1826 (2nd grant 1847)
Richard, Rochdale, butcher. Feb. 1827
Robert, Bury, woollen manufacturer. March 1827 (1st grant 1802)
Thomas, Oldham, gent. April 1830
Whittenbury, Ann, Green Hayes, Manchester, feme covert. A Feb. 1828
William, Manchester, cotton merchant. A Jan. 1828
Whittington, George, Liverpool, joiner. Feb. 1829
Whittle, Edward, Brindle, farmer. Nov. 1828
Eleanor, Longton, last of Whittle-le-Woods. May 1826
Elizabeth, Lathom. Feb. 1826
Joash, Wheelton House, muslin manufacturer. May 1830
John, Longworth, yeoman. March 1826
John, Hillhouse, Brindle, farmer. Sept. 1828
John, Kirkdale, gent. May 1830
Nicholas, Westhoughton, yeoman. Dec. 1829*
Richard, Tarleton, schoolmaster. May 1828
Richard, Westhoughton, farmer. A June 1830 (2nd grant 1839)
Thomas, Brindle, weaver. A July 1827
Thomas, Brindle, bachelor. June 1829
William, Liverpool, victualler. Oct. 1826
William, Little Hoole, farmer. Sept. 1827
Whitwell, Elizabeth, Liverpool, last of Ardwick, widow. Sept. 1826
Whitworth, Ann, Whitworth, widow. Nov. 1827
Mary, Rochdale, widow. Jan. 1828
Richard, Royton, tinplate worker. Nov. 1828
Whowell, Mary, Horwich, farmer. A May 1826
Wiatt, Tryphesa, Everton, widow. April 1827
Widows, Thomas, Kenyon, yeoman. Aug. 1829
Wigan, Henry, Wigan, bricklayer. A Jan. 1830
William, Wigan, bricklayer. Feb. 1826
William, Wigan, bricklayer. A March 1827
Wigglesworth, Ambrose, Heyhead, Little Marsden, yeoman. July 1830
Wightman, James, Manchester, joiner & builder. Jan., 1828; June 1828
Wiglesworth, Betty, otherwise Elizabeth, Blackburn, widow. March 1830
Margaret or Peggy, Whalley, widow. April 1829
Wignall, Catherine, Liverpool, widow. Sept. 1828
John, Oldham, ironmonger. A & Tuon Jan 1828 (1st grant 1823; 3rd grant 1841)
Mary, Ormskirk, widow. June 1828
Thomas, Hesketh, shoemaker. A Nov. 1830
William, Worston, yeoman. A Aug. 1830
Wignell, Mary, Manchester, spinster. May 1826
Wikeley, John, Blackley, weaver. June 1827

Wilcock, Elizabeth, Liverpool, widow. June 1828
Lawrence, Chorley, yeoman. A March 1829 (1st grant 1789)
Robert, the Lady Combermere, Liverpool, mariner. A July 1826*
William, Liverpool, miller. A Aug. 1829
Wilcoxson, James, Manchester, callenderer, embosser & maker up. March 1829
Wild, Alice, Thornham, weaver. A July 1826
Betty Siddal, Toxteth Park. A Jan. 1830
Elnor, Shaw, Crompton, widow. Sept. 1828
James, Middleton, cotton weaver. A May 1828
Joseph, Fowleach, Oldham, weaver. June 1829
Richard, Langley Hall, Middleton. March 1830
Robert, Littlewood Cross, Bury, gent. March 1820 (2nd grant 1843)
Sarah, Side of Green Acres Moor, Oldham, spinster. A July 1830
William, Gigg, Bury, cotton spinner. Dec. 1829
Wilde, Ann, Black Clough, Crompton, widow. July 1828
Daniel, Newton, yeoman. Aug. 1830
Henry, Prestwich. A July 1827
James, Ashton-under-Lyne, cotton weaver. A May 1827
John, Broad Lane, Rochdale, coal miner. A Sept. 1826 (1st grant 1805)
John, Liverpool, captain & paymaster, 2nd Royal Lancashire Militia. May 1829
Mary, Laneside, widow, A Sept. 1827
Thomas, Manchester, innkeeper. Feb. 1830
William, Stayley Bridge, grocer. A March 1829
Wilding, Ellen, Longton, widow. May 1826*
James, Longton, weaver. May 1828
James, Ulnes Walton, farmer. A Feb. 1829
Joseph, Liverpool, master mariner. Sept. 1828 (2nd grant 1836)
Roger, Longton, yeoman. May 1826
Thomas the elder, Haslingden, parish clerk. Sept. 1829
William, Mawdesley, innkeeper. A May 1828
Wiley, James, Liverpool, victualler. July 1828
Wilkes, Sarah, Birmingham. A Sept. 1827
Wilkin, William, Wigan, spirit merchant. A Jan. 1830
Wilkinson, Henry, Blackburn, cordwainer. Aug. 1827
James, Chorlton Row, journeyman ironmonger. A April 1830
Jane, Liverpool, widow. Dec. 1830
John, Colne, linen draper. Nov. 1827
John, Trawden, Colne, weaver. Oct. 1828*
John, Near Trawden, Colne, weaver. Oct. 1828*
John, Liverpool, superannuated officer. March 1829
Rachael, Liverpool, widow. July 1826
Thomas, Lathom, farmer. Aug. 1828
Willacy, Christopher, Smithy Hoale, Livesey, farmer. June 1827*
Richard, Liverpool, cheese factor. April 1827
William, Toxteth Park, miller. Jan. 1829 (1st grant 1808)
Willan, Isaac, Gorton, schoolmaster. Dec. 1829
James, Manchester, druggist. Aug. 1826
Williams, David, Liverpool, blacksmith. A Sept. 1829
Edward, Sunny Side, Salford, dyer. A Aug. 1827
Edward, Liverpool, joiner. Dec. 1828*
Edward, the ship Alexander Lindo, Liverpool. A June 1830 (1st grant 1806)
Eliza, Chorlton Row, spinster. A Dec. 1827
Elizabeth, Liverpool, widow. A Feb. 1830

Williams, Elizabeth, St. Martins in the Fields, Westminster, spinster. A May 1830
Esther, Liverpool, widow. Dec. 1830
Godfrey, Liverpool, mariner. Nov. 1826*
James, the Finchett, Liverpool, mariner. Sept. 1826*
James, Liverpool, mariner. A April 1827*
or Williamson, John, the Lady Combermere, Liverpool, mariner. A July 1826*
John, Liverpool, victualler. June 1827
John, Liverpool, miller & boatman. Nov. 1828*
John the younger, Liverpool, joiner. July 1829 (2nd Grant 1842)
John the elder, Liverpool, joiner. Aug. 1829 (1st Grant 1821*)
John, Liverpool, bachelor. A Feb. 1830
Joseph, Liverpool. A July 1830*
Margery, Liverpool, widow. Sept. 1828
Martha, Liverpool, widow. March 1830
Mary, Walton-on-the-Hill. Jan. 1827
Owen, Duke St., Liverpool, plumber. A March 1830
Peter, Lathom, yeoman. April 1828
Richard, Liverpool, merchant. Feb. 1827
Richard, Liverpool, mariner. April 1827*
Richard, Liverpool, mariner. A May 1827*
Richard, Liverpool, fishmonger. April 1829
Richard, Netherton, farmer. Aug. 1830
Robert, Manchester, flax dresser. June 1829
Thomas, Liverpool, innkeeper. April 1828
William, Liverpool, publican. Sept. 1827
William, Liverpool, flour dealer. Dec. 1827*
William, Liverpool, spirit merchant. Aug. 1829
William, Hulme, innkeeper. July 1830
William Freke, Manchester, gent. A Sept. 1826
William Thomas, Chichester. March 1829
Williamson, Abraham the elder, Swinton, weaver. Feb. 1829
Alice, Liverpool, spinster. Sept. 1828
Ann, Longport, co.Staffs., widow. Nov. 1827
David, Rochdale, cornfactor. March 1830
Elizabeth, Warrington, widow. Jan. 1827
Elizabeth, Salford, pawn broker. July 1828
George, the fields, Ashton-under-Lyne, yeoman. Oct. 1826
George, Rochdale, cabinet maker. Dec. 1829
George, Pennington, husbandman. Aug. 1830
James, Stretford, shopkeeper. June 1827
James, Little Haughton, Worsley, weaver. April 1830*
John, *see* Williams
John, Southern St., Manchester, gent. Oct. 1826
John, Pennington. A Feb. 1827*
John, Manchester, merchant. June 1827
John, Ormskirk, clerk. May 1829
Margaret, Ardwick, widow. A Oct. 1830*
Matthew, Salford, export officer. Feb. 1827
Michael, Hulme, husbandman. July 1830
Roger, Ashton-under-Lyne, blacksmith. A July 1827
Sarah, Cheetham, spinster. Nov. 1827
Sarah, Liverpool, widow. A March 1830*
William, Ashton-under-Lyne, surgeon. Nov. 1826

Williamson, William, Liverpool, smallware dealer. A June 1829
Willicott, Thomas, Liverpool, victualler. A Oct. 1828
Willis, John, Wigan, cotton spinner. A Feb. 1829*
Wilman, Thomas, Liverpool, stonecutter. March 1828
Wilson, Alice, Wavertree. March 1829
Andrew, Ancoats St., Manchester, grocer. Sept. 1826
Andrew, Liverpool, cowkeeper. A July 1830
Christopher, Liverpool, victualler. Jan. 1826
Elizabeth, Liverpool, singlewoman. Sept. 1830 (1st grant 1824)
Elizabeth, Everton. A Dec. 1830
Ellen, Baxenden, Whalley, widow. Nov. 1828
Isaac, Trawden, yeoman. June 1828
Isaac, Bold, farmer. July 1828
Isaac, Liverpool, gent. Oct. 1830
James, the ship Molly, Liverpool, mariner. A Nov. 1826*
James, Poulton, gent. June 1829
James, Charles Town, shopkeeper. Aug. 1829
John, Liverpool, flour dealer. Dec. 1827
John, Swinton, merchant. Jan. 1828
John, Formby, widower. A May 1828
John, Liverpool, ship builder. A Jan. 1829
John, Winstanley, coal agent. June 1829
John, Liverpool, cheesemonger. May 1830
John, Mawdesley, yeoman. May 1830
Jonathan, Carlisle, last of Salford, yeoman. Nov. 1828 (2nd grant 1837)
Joseph, Pendleton, cotton spinner. Sept. 1826
Mary, Whalley, innkeeper. Feb. 1826
Mary, Hale, Childwall, spinster. June 1830
Mary, Ardwick, widow of Benjamin Wilson. Aug. 1830
Nanny, Manchester, spinster. A Aug. 1829
Richard, Oldham, stonemason. A Jan. 1829 (2nd grant 1848)
Robert, Liverpool, seaman. March 1827*
Sarah, Wigan. A July 1826
Sarah, Liverpool, spinster. A Aug. 1828
Susan, Baxenden, widow. A Aug. 1826
Thomas, Hale, co.Lanc, publican. April 1829
Thomas, Litherland, farmer. May 1829
Thomas, Hulme, blacksmith. A Dec. 1830
William, Eccles, weaver. A Feb. 1827*
William, Liverpool, gent. Feb. 1829
William, Liverpool, ropemaker & widower. A May 1830
Winder, William, Liverpool, warehouseman. May 1826
Windle, James, Ardshaw Clough, farmer. May 1828
Windsor, William, Manchester, stonemason. April 1828
Windus, John, Liverpool, watchcase maker. Aug. 1826
Winpenny, James, Manchester, cotton spinner. Jan. 1826
Winskell, Margaret, Liverpool, widow. Dec. 1826
Winstanley, Henry, Skelmersdale, nailor. A March 1828
James, Wigan, cordwainer. Jan. 1826
James, Billinge, shoemaker. A Oct. 1827
John, Aughton, farmer. A April 1828 (1st grant 1819)
Mary, Aughton, widow. Dec. 1826
Stanley, Liverpool, merchant. A June 1826

Winstanley, Thomas, Pemberton, nailer. Oct. 1827
Thomas, Upholland, farmer. A Dec. 1829
Winter, Thomas Forth, St. John's, Newfoundland, deputy commissary General of H.M. Forces. A April 1826
Winterbottom, Abel, Brock Bolton (Brookbottom in 2nd grant) shopkeeper.. A Feb. 1827; Jan. 1829
Benjamin the elder, Fernlee, Saddleworth, clothier. Jan. 1830
John, a soldier of the 54th Regt. of Foot. A Oct. 1826*
John, Knar, Saddleworth, yeoman. Dec. 1826*
John, Manchester. May 1830
John, Roebuckloe, Saddleworth, weaver. July 1830
Lydia, Brookbottom, Saddleworth, widow. Dec. 1828
Robert, Berches, Ashton-under-Lyne, yeoman. A Nov. 1829
Robert, Knar, Saddleworth, yeoman. Oct. 1830* (2nd grant 1831)
Winward, Ralph, Rumworth. A Jan. 1826
Samuel, Wigan, weaver. Aug. 1826
Witham, Robert, Pasture, Cliviger, gent. Sept. 1830
Withingham, John, Billington, labourer. Aug. 1828
Withington, Alice, Highfield, Pendleton, widow. April 1830
James, Pendleton, gent. July 1829
Peter, Culcheth Hall, Winwick. A April 1826 (2nd grant 1846)
Robert Barlow, Salford, gent. A Feb. 1830
Withnall, Margaret, Manchester, spinster. March 1827
Thomas, Pendleton, machine, clock & watchmaker. Jan. 1828*
Withnell, Sarah, Wigan, widow. A Oct. 1830
Thomas, Chorley, widower. Oct. 1828
Witter, Joseph, Halsall, cordwainer. June 1827
Wolfe, Thomas, Stoke-upon-Trent, co. Staffs, manufacturer. July 1826
Wolff, Sophia, Bath, spinster. A June 1830
Wolstencroft, John, Oldham, hatter. A Sept. 1829
Wolstenholme, Ellen, Liverpool, widow. May 1826
John, Liverpool, mariner. A July 1826 (1st grant 1822)
William, Bolton-le-Moors, weaver. A Oct. 1826 (2nd grant 1857)
Wood, Alexander, Orford Rd., Manchester, gent. A Oct. 1829
Bernard, Hapton, yeoman. Aug. 1829
Esther, Farnworth, servant. Oct. 1827
George, Openshaw, manufacturer. A Oct. 1827
George, Bolton-le-Moors, shopkeeper. Dec. 1828
George Darling, Manchester. Aug. 1826
James, Thurston Clough, Saddleworth, innkeeper. Feb. 1826
James, Hoghton, shoemaker. May 1826
James, Houghton, Middleton & Arbury. June 1828
James, Tain Barn, Castleton, farmer. A Aug. 1828
James, Harrop Green, Saddleworth, clothier. Aug. 1830
James, Burnley, apothecary. Nov. 1830
John, Oldham, surveyor. A Dec. 1827
John, Openshaw, weaver. July 1828
John, Liverpool, watchmaker. March 1829
John, Manchester, hairdresser. A Nov. 1829
Joseph, Hurst, Ashton-under-Lyne, brickmaker, June 1826*
Joseph, Warrington, pin manufacturer. A Oct. 1829
Joshua, Lady Barn, farmer. Sept. 1828
Martha, Manchester, spinster. A Oct. 1828

Wood, Mary, Blackburn, widow. July 1827
Peter, Chowbent, Atherton weaver. Jan. 1827*
Richard, Edgeworth, innkeeper. Nov. 1826
Thomas, Rochdale, gent. March 1826
Thomas, Manchester, manufacturer. A Oct. 1826
Thomas, Hollinwood, coal miner. March., 1829
Thomas, Hollinwood, coal miner. April 1829
William, Uppermill, Saddleworth, clothier. A May 1826
William, Closes, Tottington, yeoman. Dec. 1829
Woodburn, John, Liverpool, surgeon. May 1827
Woodcock, Ann, Walton-le-Dale, spinster. Sept. 1826
John, Halsall, yeoman. Sept. 1828
William, Holcomb, gent. June 1827
William, Netherton, farmer. A Nov. 1828
Woodend, Peill, Warrington, shopkeeper. Dec. 1829*
Woodfine, Elizabeth, Liverpool, widow. A Nov. 1830*
John, Liverpool, seaman. Dec. 1826
Robert, Toxteth Park, watchmaker. Feb. 1827
William, Liverpool, cooper. A Aug. 1827*
Woodiwis, Francis, Manchester, currier. Sept. 1830
Woodruff, William, Shone Fold, Levenshulme, farmer. A Dec. 1830
Woods, Ann, West Derby, widow. Dec. 1827
Ann, Ormskirk, widow. Dec. 1829
Charles, Liverpool, shipwright. Jan. 1826
Charles, Torbock, farmer. A April 1828
Edward, Simonswood, yeoman. May 1829
Elizabeth, Warrington, butcher. April 1830
Ellen, Great Bolton, widow. Aug. 1827
Ellen, Rainford, widow. March 1828
Ellen, Liverpool, widow. A Aug. 1828
Henry, Parr. June 1827
James, Euxton, yeoman. July 1826*
James, Walton-on-the-Hill, yeoman. Dec. 1826
James, Cabbage Hall, victualler. Sept. 1829
John, Garston, labourer. April 1826
John, Great Bolton, ironmonger. June 1826
Lawrence, Liverpool, mariner. A Nov. 1827*
Mary, Atherton, widow. A June 1828
Mary, Liverpool. Nov. 1828 (2nd grant 1857)
Nathan, Bolton-le-Moors, weaver. A Nov. 1826*
Richard, Ormskirk, innkeeper. A Jan. 1827
Robert, Walton-on-the-Hill, blacksmith. A May 1830
Thomas, a private of 1st Regt. in H.M. Service. A April 1827*
William, Liverpool, painter. Aug. 1826 (2nd grant 1838)
William, Liverpool, victualler. June 1827
William, Warrington, victualler & glass dealer. A March 1829
William, Manchester, machine maker. May 1829
Woodward, Charles, Sankey, yeoman. April 1826
John, Simonswood, yeoman. July 1828
Thomas, Liverpool, cooper. A Oct. 1827*
Woodworth, John, Oldham Rd., Manchester. Aug. 1829
Woodfall, James, Liverpool, cowkeeper. Dec. 1828
Thomas, Blackburn, joiner & timber dealer. Nov. 1829

Woolfenden, Joseph, Shaw Lane End, Rochdale, woollen manufacturer. Feb. 1827
Woolley, Betty, Brookbottom, widow. Feb. 1827
James, Houghton, hatter. April 1830
Jarvis, Manchester, bookkeeper. Aug. 1828
William, Mossley, grocer. A Feb. 1827
William, Stayley Bridge, gent. A Feb., 1827
Woosey, James, Lathom, wheelwright. A Sept. 1829
Richard, Liverpool, farmer. A May 1829 (1st grant 1819)
Richard, Liverpool, lawyer. A Feb. 1830
Thomas, Ormskirk, shopkeeper. A Jan. 1826
Wooton, Elizabeth, Oxford, spinster. Feb. 1830
Worden, James, Manchester, publican. June 1827; June 1829
Worrall, Ashton, Crumpsall, road surveyor. Oct. 1829
James, Old Lane, Chadderton. June 1827
Randle, Cocky Lane, yeoman. July 1828
William, Woodhouses, Ashton-under-Lyne, farmer. June 1827
Worsley, Edward, Swinton, yeoman. A Jan. 1829*
James, Heaton Norris, wheelwright. A June 1826*
James, Lowton, Winwick, yeoman. Feb. 1830
Richard, Bank Top, Manchester, horse breaker. Feb. 1829*
Roger, Ince-in-Makerfield, publican. A Nov. 1830
William, Tockholes, farmer. A Dec. 1827
Worswick, Thomas, Downham, weaver. Sept. 1830*
Worth, Thomas, Houghton, hatter. May 1828
Worthington, Charles, Manchester, gent. A April 1828
Edmund, Liverpool, bookkeeper. A May 1826
George, Audenshaw, gent. April 1828
Hannah, Manchester, widow. A Nov. 1830
Henry, Atherton, yeoman. Aug. 1827
John, Salford, farmer. A May 1829
John, Scarisbrick, yeoman. A March 1830
Martha, Rumworth, Deane. A Dec. 1826
Ralph, Little Green, Cheetham, dyer. Aug. 1829
Richard, Liverpool, plaisterer. Dec. 1829 (1st grant 1790)
Ruth, Rushulme. March 1829
Wragg, Ann, Holt Town, Manchester, widow. Aug. 1826
Francis, Chorlton Row, yeoman. Nov. 1830
Lydia, Cheetham, spinster. Feb. 1830
Peter, Manchester, engineer. A March 1826
Wrennall, Henry, Eccleston, farmer. July 1826
Wrenshaw, James, Wardleworth, Rochdale. A Jan. 1826
Wright, Elizabeth, Wigan, spinster. Oct. 1826
Elizabeth, Prescot, widow. Feb. 1828*
George, Oldham, innkeeper. Dec. 1826
Henry, Toxteth Park, farmer. July 1830
James, Crumpsall. July 1826
James, Much Woolton, printer. A Aug. 1826 (1st grant 1817)
John, Holmes, Tarleton, yeoman. A Aug. 1829
John, North Meols. A Sept. 1829
John, Kirkby, Walton, farmer. A May 1830
or Right, Jonathan, Naz-end, Colne, farmer. April 1830
Margaret, Bolton-le-Moors, widow. June 1830 (2nd grant 1871)
Margaret, Liverpool, spinster. A Oct. 1830

Wright, Martha, Broughton, widow. April 1829
Nanny, Hesketh, spinster. July 1829
otherwise Smeal, Olive, Liverpool, widow. Feb. 1826
Peter, Pestfurlong, Culcheth, yeoman. June 1830*
Richard, Liverpool, victualler. A Jan. 1829
Robert, Bold, farmer, July 1826
Thomas, Manchester, joiner. March 1827
Thomas, Mill Bottom, Prestwich, shopkeeper. A March 1827*
William, North Meols, farmer. March 1827*
William, Burtonwood, yeoman. Oct. 1828
William, Newton-in-the-Willows, farmer. A Dec. 1828
William, Hollinfare, Warrington, clerk. A April 1829
Wrigley, Ann, Brookbottom, Saddleworth, widow. A Jan. 1826
Constantine, Manchester, bricklayer. Oct. 1827 (1st grant 1811)
Edmund, Loadhill Platting, Saddleworth, labourer. A May 1826
James, Rochdale, yeoman. Feb. 1829
James, Bolton-le-Moors, victualler. Nov. 1830
John, Liverpool, cotton broker. March 1830
Joseph, Denshaw, Saddleworth, grocer. A March 1828
Mary, Bury, spinster. A Dec. 1826*
Mary, Oldham. Sept. 1827
Mary, Tumbo, Tonge, widow. Sept. 1828
Mary, Collyhurst, widow. Sept. 1829
Samuel, Oldham, hatter. A May 1829
Sarah, Delph, Saddleworth, widow. A Aug. 1828*
Thomas, Mosside, Tottington, weaver. Sept. 1830*
William, Liverpool, blacksmith. April 1827
Wroe, Esther, Hollinwood, widow. April 1829
Thomas, Eccles, tailor. Jan. 1827
Wyatt, Alice, Cheetham, spinster. A Oct. 1827
John, Cheetham, farmer. A May 1826
Mary, Almshill, Cheetham, spinster. Nov. 1830
Robert, Hooley Hill, silk manufacturer. A Feb. 1829
Wych, James, Denton, farmer. A June 1827
John, Ashton-under-Lyne, timber merchant. Aug. 1829
Wyke, John, Liverpool, shoemaker. A June 1827*
William, Liverpool, husbandman. A June 1827*
Wylde, Richard, Bolton-le-Moors, gent. June 1826
Wynn, Thomas, Manchester, fishmonger. Aug. 1830
Wynne, Charles, Salford, mechanic. July 1830

YARDLEY, Ann, Wednesbury, co. Staffs. A Dec. 1829
Yarker, Elizabeth, Ulverston, widow. A May 1828
Yate, Elizabeth, Liverpool, widow. Oct. 1829
Yates, Alice, Salford. Sept. 1828*
Charles, Liverpool, victualler. July 1828 (2nd grant 1835)
David, Manchester, esq. April 1827
Edmund, Standish, yeoman. May 1829
Elizabeth, Pennington, Leigh. A Feb. 1829
Esther, Whittlestonehead Lane, widow. Nov. 1827*
George, Liverpool, porter. May 1829
James, Rumworth, labourer. A Sept. 1827
James, Sheffield, co. York, coachman. A Nov. 1829

Yates, John, Liverpool, cooper. A Nov. 1826 (2nd grant 1848)
John, Toxteth Park, minister of the Gospel. Dec. 1826
John, Prescot, shopkeeper. A Sept. 1827
John, Mawdesley, wheelwright. A Nov. 1828
John, Chorley, farmer. A Aug. 1830
Joseph, Manchester, gent. July 1828; Oct. 1828
Mary, Manchester, widow. July., 1830
Rees, Liverpool, widower. Oct. 1829*
Robert, Over Darwen, farmer. A Oct. 1828
Thomas, Horwich, innkeeper. Nov. 1826
Thomas, Ainsworth, weaver. A May 1827
Thomas, Whitefield, weaver. Oct. 1827
Thomas, Radcliffe, last of America, calico printer. A July 1828
Thomas, Whiston, underlooker of coal mines. July 1830
William, Sephton, yeoman. Sept. 1828
Yeomans, Margaret, Liverpool, spinster.. A May 1827
Yorston, James, Manchester, machine maker. A June 1828
Young, James, Liverpool, mariner. May 1829

ZINCK, Henry Lawrence, Liverpool, merchant. A June 1830 (1st grant 1791)
Zuil, Mary Caroline, Liverpool, widow. May 1827

CHESHIRE WILLS

ABBOTT, Betty, Macclesfield, widow. Nov. 1830
Ackerley, Thomas, Great Boughton, gardener. July 1826*
Acton, William, Runcorn, gent. March 1827
Adams, Benjamin, Congleton, silk throwster. A May 1828
  Catharine, Neston. Dec. 1830
  Sarah, Chester, widow. A March 1828
Adamson, Elizabeth, Hartford, widow. A June 1826
  John, Sutton, yeoman. March 1827
Adkinson, Christopher, Stockport, patten maker. Jan. 1827
Adshead, Sarah, Mill Brook, Mottram, widow. June 1829
  William, Styall, Wilmslow. April 1830
Ainsworth, Benson, Heswall, gent. Jan. 1830
  John, Sutton, yeoman. May 1828
  Thomas, Bollington, stone merchant. Nov. 1827
Alcock, Jeoffry, Altrincham, yeoman. Sept. 1830
  Mary, Over, widow. July 1828
Aldersay, John, Broxton, Malpas, yeoman. Aug. 1826*
Aldersey, William, Chester, gent. June 1829
Aldred, Edward, Newton, Mottram, mechanic. Sept. 1827
Allcock, Cyrus, Congleton, yeoman. Sept. 1828
  Jeffrey, Congleton, victualler. May 1830
  Peter, Macclesfield, yeoman. March 1827*
Allen, Peggy, Altrincham, spinster. Nov. 1826
Allman, Ephraim, Leftwich, yeoman. Sept. 1827
Allstone, Thomas, Tarporley, gent. A Feb. 1830
Almond, William, Great Boughton, gardener. A June 1828
Alsop, Michael, Stockport, shopkeeper. May 1829
Amery, Charles, Little Sutton, gent. Feb. 1828
Andrew, John, Congleton, gent. March 1826
  Joseph, Dukinfield, hairdresser. A Dec. 1830
  William, Stockton Heath, Appleton, Lieut. in Royal Navy. June 1827 (1st grant 1822)
Andrews, Samuel, Weaverham, victualler. Dec. 1827
Ankers, William, Nether Knutsford, surgeon & apothecary. Feb. 1828
Anthrobus, Elizabeth, Dunham o'th' Hill, Thornton. July 1826*
Antrobus, Philip, Bollington, gent. March 1830
Antwis, William, Frodsham, gent. Nov. 1828
Armitage, Ann, Stockport, widow. Dec. 1828
Arnold, Josiah, Macclesfield, silk throwster. A Oct. 1829
  Peter, Rainow, farmer. March 1830
Arrowsmith, James, Stockport, last of Dunham Massey, cooper. May 1827
  Thomas, Kermincham, yeoman. Oct. 1829
Arundale, Hannah, Werneth, Stockport, spinster. A March 1827

Ashbrook, Elizabeth, Wallasey, widow. March 1829*
Ashley, Peter, Bredbury, Stockport, weaver. Sept. 1826
Ashness, Thomas, Macclesfield, silk throwster. June 1827 (1st grant 1825)
Ashton, George, Cholmondeley Park, farmer & cheesefactor. A March 1829
James, Latchford, Grappenhall, engineer. A Aug. 1826*
James, Macclesfield, yeoman. July 1828
James, Hollingworth. June 1829
Robert, Hyde, farmer. June 1829
Samuel, Roe Cross, Mottram, shopkeeper. May 1827
Samuel, Godley, farmer. July 1830
Astbury, Edward, Weelwood, Tarvin. June 1826
Thomas, Westwood, Tarvin, farmer. Oct. 1830*
William, Occleston & Newcastle-under-Lyne, last of Hatherton, farmer. Feb. 1827
Astle, James, Cheadle Bulkeley, butcher. June 1830
Astley, Charles, Stockport, timber merchant. A April 1829 (2nd grant 1833)
Martha, Stockport, spinster. May 1829
Aston, Edward, Frodsham, yeoman. March 1826*
Richard, Beeston, Bunbury, farmer. Nov. 1828
William, Frodsham, land measurer. Oct. 1826
Atherton, John, Altrincham, turner. April 1827
Atkinson, Elizabeth, Chester, spinster. Oct. 1827
Thomas, Congleton, stonemason. Aug. 1828
Austin, Thomas, Middlewich, tailor. May 1826

BAGALEY, Thomas, Rudheath, yeoman. Oct. 1827
Baggeley, Thomas, Stockport, gent. Sept. 1829
Baguley, *James, Bollington, farmer. June 1829*
John, Macclesfield, silk throwster. Oct. 1826
Bailey, John, Stockport, hosier. A July 1830
Baker, Ann, Chester, widow. A March 1830
Thomas, Marton, yeoman. Feb. 1828
Baldwyn, Edward, Saighton. Oct. 1828
Ball, Joseph, Bradley, husbandman. A Feb. 1829
Balmer, John, Acton Grange, farmer. Aug. 1829
Bamford, John, Stockport, painter. A Jan. 1826
John, Wilmslow, last of Macclesfield, gent. April 1828
Bancroft, John, Mottram, slater. March 1829
Joseph, Shipbrook, yeoman. July 1827
Band, Joseph, Mottram Longdendale, joiner. A Dec. 1826; Jan. 1828
Bann, Henry, Stockport, stonemason. April 1827
otherwise Goodwin, John, Macclesfield, labourer. June 1826
Bannister, John, Stockport, carpenter. A Nov. 1829*
Barber, John the elder, Macclesfield, gent. Jan. 1830
Thomas, Macclesfield, glazier. June 1828 (2nd grant 1851)
Bardsley, James, Dukinfield, farmer. April 1827
John, Stockport, feltmaker. Jan. 1830
Barker, Francis Edge, Chester, gent. Aug. 1827
John, Greasby, saddler. Aug. 1830
Samuel, Betley, Staffs., gent. April 1829
Barlow, Anne, Malpas, spinster. Aug. 1828
Francis, Nether Knutsford, plumber, glazier & painter. Feb. 1829
Henry, Macclesfield, silk manufacturer. Dec. 1829
Isaac, Wilmslow, yeoman. Feb. 1826

Barlow, John, Stockport, corn dealer. A Oct. 1830*
Joseph, Hurdsfield, yeoman. Oct., 1829
Samuel, Toft, farmer. Feb. 1826
Samuel, Sale, farmer. A Dec. 1828
Thomas, Appleton, timber merchant. April 1829
William, Great Warford, yeoman. July 1829
Barnes, Thomas, Lower Withington, husbandman. Sept. 1828*
Barnett, Joseph, Sandbach, shopkeeper. Oct. 1828
Thomas, Chester, yeoman. Aug. 1829
William, Macclesfield, gent. Feb. 1830
Barnshaw, Thomas, Macclesfield, stonemason. May 1828
Barratt, Thomas, Sharston Green, Northenden, farmer. A June. 1826
William, Audlem, timber merchant. Feb. 1829
Barrington, William, Stoke, Acton, gent. July 1830
Barrow, James, Timperley Lodge, gent. A April 1828
Joseph, Eaton, Tarporley, publican. Oct. 1827
Mary, Chester, spinster. Jan. 1828
Bartley, Thomas, West Kirby, yeoman. Dec. 1828*
Barton, George, Macclesfield, staymaker. A March 1826*
Sarah, Norbury, widow. Dec. 1826
Baskervill, James, Nether Alderley, farmer. March 1829
Baskerville, Martha, Butley, spinster. April 1830
Basnett, Thomas, Runcorn, labourer. March 1829
Bassnitt, Thomas, Stockport, gent. Oct. 1829
Bate, Ellen, Davenham, spinster. A March 1826
Bateman, Jane, Waverton, spinster. Feb. 1828
Martha, Chorley, spinster. May 1830
Thomas, Haslington. July 1826
Thomas, Wrenbury, yeoman. Nov. 1829
Thomas, Chester, cooper. Aug. 1830
Batt, Thomas, Macclesfield, silk throwster. A March 1829
Baxter, Henry, Etchells, gent. Sept. 1826
Bay, Abraham, Macclesfield, silk trimming maker. A Nov. 1828*
Bayley, Edward Schofield, Macclesfield, stationer. A May 1828
Elizabeth, Chester, spinster. Aug. 1829
James, Tilston Fearnal, farmer. Feb. 1827
James, Lime Handley, yeoman. June 1827
Marcus, Buglawton, yeoman. Jan. 1830 (2nd grant 1852)
Ralph, Morley, yeoman. A July 1827
Sarah, Park House, Gawsworth, widow. Jan. 1826; March 1830
Thomas, Church Hulme, innkeeper. Jan. 1828 (1st grant 1811)
Thomas, Macclesfield, button manufacturer. A Dec. 1829
Weston, Madeley, Staffs., esq. A Aug. 1826
William, Oulton Lodge, gamekeeper. A Oct. 1827
Beale, Richard, Biddenden, Kent, esq. A Sept. 1830
Beard, Barbara, Lower Bebington, widow. A Feb. 1826
Beaty, Henry, Cheadle Hulme, traveller. A Aug. 1826
Bebbington, George the elder, Wharton, butcher. Oct. 1830
Joseph, Acton, gardener. May 1829
Thomas, Nantwich, butcher. June 1826
Bebington, Hannah, Christleton, widow. Aug. 1826
Beckett, Esther, Chester, spinster. July 1830
John, Four Lane Ends, Bunbury, publican. A Nov. 1826

Beckett, Joseph, Marbury, yeoman. Jan 1828
Martha, Middlewich, widow. June., 1828
Thomas, Nantwich, gent. April 1827
Bedson, Margaret, Heswall, singlewoman. June 1829
Beech, Elizabeth, Congleton, spinster. A March 1828
John, Chester, gent. A March 1828
Samuel, Sandbach Heath, farmer. May 1829
Thomas, Chester, servant. Sept. 1828 (1st grant 1818)
Beecroft, Philip, Over Tabley, farmer. Nov. 1827
Beeton, Thomas, Northwich, formerly Witton, horse trainer. May 1830
Beevan, John, Stoke, farmer. Feb. 1827
Bellin, William, Chester, plumber & glazier. A & Tuon Nov. 1827
William, Chester, plumber & glazier. A April 1829
Bellis, Sarah, Newton co. Chester, widow. Dec. 1830
Bellyse, John sen., Audlem, surgeon. July 1828
Benison, Ebenezer, Stockport, chapman. Feb. 1828
Bennet, John, Kettleshulme, farmer. July 1826
John, Faddiley, yeoman. May 1828
Richard, Daresbury, stonemason. May 1828
Bennett, John Nevitt, Great Saughall, esq. Oct. 1830
Joseph, Hoylake, mariner. Sept. 1828
Margaret, Parkgate, widow. April 1827
Bennion, Owen, Nantwich, gent. Dec. 1829
Thomas, Barthomley, farmer. A Aug. 1827
Thomas, Barthomley, farmer. Oct. 1828
Benson, John, Wheelock, timber merchant. A Dec. 1826 (2nd grant 1837)
Bentley, George, Baguley, yeoman. Oct. 1829
Michael, Macclesfield, brewer's clerk. March 1826 (2nd grant 1833)
Benyon, Susannah, Chester, spinster. Aug. 1827
Berks, Henrietta, Chester, spinster. Jan. 1830
Berry, Ann, Daresbury, spinster. June 1826
Ann, Daresbury, spinster. A Jan. 1827*
John, Ringway, farmer. Sept. 1829
Joseph, Crowley, Over Whitley, yeoman. May 1826
Beswick, Catharine, Allostock, widow. May 1826
Elizabeth, Witton, widow. A June 1826
Samuel, Wharton, shopkeeper. March 1829
Bevin, William, Chester, draper. Aug. 1826
Billingham, William, Nether Knutsford, surgeon. Nov. 1830
Billington, George, Chester, surgeon. A Dec. 1827
Margaret, Stretton, widow. Aug. 1826
Bingley, George, Chester, glazier. Dec. 1827 (1st grant 1806)
Binns, Joshua, Dukinfield, cotton spinner. Oct. 1828
Birch, Margaret, Chester, widow. A April 1826
Martha, Macclesfield, widow. July 1826
Mary, Brombro, spinster. Feb. 1828
Birchinall, Matthew, Macclesfield, yeoman. Jan. 1830
Birchwood, Mary, Brimstage, widow. Aug. 1826
Bird, Henry, Saughall Massie, yeoman. Nov. 1829*
Joseph, Saughall Massie, yeoman. Aug. 1827
William, Hoose, fisherman. Aug. 1828
Birkin, George, Stockport, tailor. March 1829
Birtwistle, Peter, Gorstage, Waverham, farmer. April 1830

Blackshaw, John, Siddington, Prestbury, farmer. A Feb. 1826
Samuel, Nether Alderley, yeoman. Dec., 1827
Blake, George, Halton, surgeon. July 1830 (2nd grant 1853)
Joseph, Holt Hill, Tranmere, gent. March 1830 (2nd grant 1839)
Bleaze, Mary, Rostherne, widow. A Dec. 1828
Bloor, Jane, Cholmondley, widow. Aug. 1828
Matthew, Stublach, Middlewich, clerk. Oct. 1829
Bodden, Nathaniel, Chester, draper. Oct. 1826
Boode, Margaret, Leasowe Castle, widow. July 1826
Booth, Charles, Werneth, farmer. A July 1830
George, Capesthorne, servant. June 1830
Hannah, Disley, feme covert. A March 1829
Henry, Bebington, gent. A March 1826
John, Stockport, shopkeeper. Feb. 1826
John, Over Tabley, gardener. A March 1829
Mary, Grappenhall, widow. March 1827
Mary, Sandbach, spinster. Sept. 1830
Thomas, Congleton, A June 1829
Thomas, Werneth, Stockport, farmer. July 1830
Timothy, Macclesfield, butcher. A April 1829
William, Congleton, joiner & builder. June 1826
William, Stockport, cotton spinner. Nov. 1828
Boothby, John, Macclesfield, silk throwster. May 1829
Boothman, Benjamin, Wallasey, innkeeper. A Dec. 1830
Borel, Abram Henry, Timperley, gent. Oct. 1826
Borrow, William, Nether Knutsford, publican. June 1829
Bosley, Thomas, Duddon, yeoman. July 1830
Bostock, Jane, Congleton, spinster. May 1826
John, Broadbottom, Mottram, gent. Sept. 1826
Margaret, Church Coppenhull, widow. April 1827
Bottoms, Catherine, Marston, Great Budworth, widow. A Nov. 1827
Robert, Wincham, labourer. Oct. 1826
Boughley, Peter, Nantwich, publican. March 1829
Samuel, Nantwich, turner. March 1829
Boulton, James, Adlington, last of Sutton co. Chester, yeoman. July 1826
Boumphrey, Joseph, Gayton, Heswall, mason. June 1827 (1st grant 1824)
Bowcock, John, Wilderspool, skinner. March 1829
Bowden, Ann, Tranmere, widow. Aug. 1830
James, Over Lane, Over. Nov. 1826
Bower, Frances Clare, Buxton co. Derby, spinster. July 1826
John, Stayley Hall, farmer. Nov. 1828
William, Wilmslow, gent. Sept. 1827
Bowers, Henry, Chester, alderman. Jan. 1830
Robert, Chester, alderman. June 1829 (2nd grant 1845)
Bown, William, Macclesfield, gent. Dec. 1829
Boyd, James, Chester, slater. A Jan. 1830*
Braband, John, Newton, Middlewich, esq. Sept. 1828
Bracegirdle, John, Mobberley. Aug. 1828
Philip, Henbury, farmer. May 1826
Sarah, Mobberley. A May 1826
Braddock, James, Macclesfield, tailor. May 1826
James, Godley, Mottram, mechanic. A March 1827
John, Chester, yeoman. Dec. 1826

Bradford, Samuel, Chester, gent. Sept. 1828
Bradley, Charles, Rainow, slater. A Jan. 1827
David, Macclesfield, silk throwster. Oct. 1826
Ellen, Congleton, widow. May 1830
Richard, Portwood, Brinnington, cotton spinner. Nov. 1828
Brassey, John, Hampton, Malpas, farmer. May 1826
Bassington, Richard, Blackenhall, farmer. A Sept. 1830
Thomas, Blakenhall, farmer. Feb. 1830
Bray, James, Mobberley. April 1829
Brayne, Jonathan, Northwich, gent. A May 1826
Thomas Ives, Northwich, gent. July 1829 (1st grant 1796)
Breerton, John, Waverton. Jan. 1830
Brentnall, John, Congleton, yeoman. June 1828
Brereton, James, Fennywood, Little Budworth, farmer. Jan. 1826
John, Witton, labourer. March 1827
Mary, Preston-on-the-Hill, March 1829*
Samuel, Weston, Wybunbury, blacksmith. March 1827
Bridge, Robert, Kinderton, gent. Aug. 1828
Brierley, Margaret, Millington, widow. Aug. 1830
Brightmore, Benjamin, Stockport, maltster. Nov. 1827
Brindley, Elizabeth, Gawsworth, widow. Nov. 1827
Briscoe, Ann, Neston, spinster. A May 1827
Edward, Kelsall, farmer. Oct. 1827
Samuel, Kelsall, farmer. Dec. 1829
Thomas, Broxton, Malpas, gent. June 1829
Brittain, Jane, Chester, widow. Aug. 1829
Richard, Chester, minor. A June 1829
Robert, Hoole Bank, esq. Nov. 1828
Broad, Sarah, Betchton, widow. Nov. 1829
Broadbent, Rev. William, Latchford. Feb. 1828
Broadhead, Thomas, Rainow. Jan. 1829
Broadhurst, Isaac, Underbank, Stockport, builder. A & Tuon July 1829
James, Dudley, co. Worcs., grocer. A Aug. 1828
Johanna, Macclesfield, spinster. May 1826*
John, Birtles, last of Hough, Wilmslow, farmer. Jan. 1827*
John, Sutton, Prestbury, bread baker. A Dec. 1827 (2nd grant 1876)
Jonathan, Stockport, yeoman. Jan. 1828
Peter, Macclesfield, silk manufacturer. Jan. 1830 (2nd grant 1849)
Samuel, Chester, esq. A Feb. 1829
Broady, Thomas, Appleton, farmer. Aug. 1828
Brock, Thomas, Chester, esq. Jan. 1829 (1st grant 1785; later grants 1831 & 18
Brocklehurst, Joseph, Coopershaw, Kettleshulme. Oct. 1826
Thomas, Cogshall, tailor. Feb. 1829
Brockley, Samuel, Weston, Wybunbury, carpenter. Sept. 1826
Brooke, Margaret, Henbury, widow. Jan. 1827
Brookes, John, Chester, yeoman. July 1830
Brooks, John, Blakenhall, yeoman. Sept. 1827
Broome, Ann, Weaver Bank, Minshull Vernon, widow. Jan. 1827
Thomas, Sandbach, gent. Oct. 1829 (2nd grant 1833)
Broster, Mary, Bollington, spinster. Nov. 1826
Samuel, Prestbury, butcher. A March 1829
Thomas, Bollington, yeoman. May 1828
Thomas, Tarvin, yeoman. Sept. 1829

Broughton, Edward Delves, Teddington, Middlesex, esq. Nov. 1826
Brown, Ann, Chester, spinster. Aug. 1827
Anthony, Macclesfield, victualler. Aug. 1828
Daniel, Gurnett, Prestbury, labourer. Dec. 1829*
Elizabeth, Poulton-cum-Seacombe. Aug. 1829
Isaac, Knutsford, shoemaker. A Nov. 1827
Joseph, Chester, schoolmaster. Nov. 1826
Joseph, Chester, pawnbroker. Aug. 1827
Peter, Runcorn, victualler. Aug. 1827
Thomas, West Kirby, widower. A March 1829
Thomas, Hartington Upper Quarter, co. Derby, gent. Oct. 1829
Browne, David, Macclesfield, gent. June 1830
Richard, Middlewich, ironmonger. May. 1828
William, Northen Etchells, farmer. Nov. 1829 (1st grant 1824)
Brownhill, Anthony, Henbury, weaver. March 1830
Brownsword, Jonathan, Congleton, yeoman. Nov. 1826*
Bruce, Thomas, Leftwich, gent. Oct. 1826
Brundritt, Joseph, Dunham Massey, farmer. A Aug. 1826
Bryan, Mary, Mottram St. Andrews, widow. A April 1830
Bryans, Sarah Clough wife of Rev. Francis Bryans, Farndon. Nov. 1830 (2nd grant 1836)
Buckley, Catherine, Brereton, widow. Sept. 1826
George, Upton, Overchurch, yeoman. Oct. 1828
James, Siddington, yeoman. March 1829*
John, Betchton, yeoman. June 1827
John, Siddington, farmer. Oct. 1828*
John, Ashton, Tarvin, yeoman. July 1829
Lettice, Macclesfield, widow. Jan. 1826
Margaret, Byley-cum-Yatehouse, spinster. A Sept. 1830
Philip, Main Grass, Mottram, farmer. Jan. 1829
Phineas, Mottram. May 1828
Stanley, Macclesfield, bookkeeper. A Nov. 1827
William, Armfield, Mottram. July 1830
Bull, Samuel, Northwich, widower. A Jan. 1830
Bullock, Thomas, Gawsworth, yeoman. Sept. 1829
Bunnell, Mary, Chester, spinster. A Jan. 1829*
Burganey, Ann, Pulford, widow. A July 1828
Burgess, Ann, Chester, spinster. June 1830
Henry, Adlington, yeoman. May 1829
John, Delamere, gent. Feb. 1826
John, Nantwich. A Feb. 1827
John, Hale co. Chester, yeoman. Aug. 1827
Joseph, Timperley, farmer. A Jan. 1827
Maria, Partington, last of Knutsford, shopkeeper. Nov. 1829
Martha, Over Tabley, widow. July 1826
Mary, Stockport, widow. Jan. 1828
Richard, Eaton. A May 1828
Burgin, Ann, Nantwich, widow. A Aug. 1826
Burrows, Alicia, Chester, widow. Nov. 1828
Thomas, Marton, Whitegate, farmer. A June 1826
Butler, Elizabeth, Harthill, widow. March 1827
Joseph James, Chester, tallow chandler. April 1828
Buxton, John, Handforth-cum-Bosden, shopkeeper. A Feb. 1827
Bythell, Robert, Marshouse co. Chester, farmer. Feb. 1826

CADMAN, John, Great Warford, farmer. Nov. 1830
Caldwell, Ann, Nantwich, spinster. April 1826
Betty, Latchford, widow. A May 1829
James, Frodsham, tailor. Jan. 1826
Candelet, William, Stockport, broker & auctioneer. Feb. 1829
Capper, Henry, Handley, last of Gwaynynog, Denbs., gent. Sept. 1828
John, Brin, Cuddington, farmer. Oct. 1830
Carrington, Cornelius, Stockport, hatter. March 1826
Carter, George, Church Hulme, tailor. Jan. 1829
John, Chester, surgeon. April 1829
Martha, Kermicham, spinster. Nov. 1830
William, Lees, gent. Sept. 1826 (1st grant 1817)
Cartwright, Dorothy, Macclesfield, spinster. Aug. 1829
John, Hatton, labourer. May 1829
Cash, James, Stockport, sawyer. May 1827*
Chadwick, James, Hurdsfield, yeoman. Sept. 1826*
Mary, High Legh, spinster. Sept. 1826
Thomas, Cheadle Moseley, yeoman. May 1826
William, Leftwich, plumber & glazier. Oct. 1828
Challener, John, Bollington, Prestbury, quarryman. A Jan. 1830
Challinor, Elizabeth, Wrenbury, servant. April 1826
Chalton, John, Bromlow, co. Chester. Feb. 1826
Chandley, John, Cheadle Moseley, yeoman. April 1829 (1st grant 1789)
Joseph, Cheadle Bulkeley. April 1829 (1st grant 1802)
Chantler, Peter, Warburton, yeoman. Oct. 1827
Sarah, Grappenhall. A March 1830
Thomas, Middlewich, silk throwster. A April 1827
Chapel, James, Coppost Edge, Sutton, Prestbury, hatter. April 1829
Chappell, Mary., Macclesfield, A Jan. 1830
Charlesworth, Samuel, Minshull Vernon. June 1828
Charlton, Mary, Handbridge, Chester, widow. Jan. 1829
Charnley, Ellen, *see* Wickstead
Hannah, Marple, Stockport, widow. A Oct. 1827
Cheers, James, Barrow, gent. May 1828
Samuel, Barrow. Nov. 1827
Cheetham, Ellen, Newton, Mottram, widow. Feb. 1826
Joseph, Bosley, yeoman. May 1829
Joshua, Werneth, Stockport, farmer. June 1826
Samuel, Stockport, spindle maker. May 1828
Chesters, John, Leighton, farmer. June 1826
Chidloe, John, Aldersey, Prees, co. Salop, farmer. July 1830*
Chilton, Charles, Chester, banker. A Nov. 1827
Cholmondeley, George James, marquis of Cholmondeley, Cholmondeley House, Piccadilly, co. Middlesex. June 1827
Chorlton, George, Bollington, farmer. A Feb. 1830
Chrimes, Philip, Nether Knutsford, carrier. March 1826
Thomas, Crowton, yeoman. Oct. 1830*
Church, Sarah, Middlewich, widow. March 1829
Churton, Mary, Malpas, widow. March 1827
Clan, Jemima, Nantwich, widow. June 1827*
Clare, Margaret, Antrobus, widow. April 1828
Clark, Ann, Nantwich, spinster. Aug. 1828
Clarke, Ann, Congleton, widow. Sept. 1830

Clarke, John, Astbury, parish clerk. A April 1828
Mary, Altrincham, widow. Nov., 1828
Ralph, Hatton, yeoman. Sept. 1827
Samuel, Caldy, West Kirby, grocer & bread baker. A June 1830
Thomas, Marthall, publican. June 1826
Thomas, Altrincham, blacksmith. Sept. 1827
Thomas, Hawkins Lane, Rainow, blacksmith. March 1830
William, Audlem, builder. Aug. 1828
Clatton, Thomas, Stockport, wood turner. Oct. 1829*
Clay, Thomas, Dukinfield, iron moulder. A Dec. 1827
Clayton, Thomas, Chester, upholsterer. April 1827*
Thomas, Stockport, wood turner. Oct. 1829*
Clews, John, Hargreave, tailor. Sept. 1828
Thomas, Congleton, victualler. A May 1830 (2nd grant 1847)
Clough, Joanna, Great Neston, spinster. Feb. 1826
Clowes, John, Wybunbury, farmer. A Jan. 1826
Solomon, Gawsworth, farmer. A Aug. 1827
Clulow, Alice, Congleton, spinster. Nov. 1829 (2nd grant 1835)
Ann, wife of Joseph Clulow, Congleton, gent. Sept. 1830
John, Macclesfield, gent. Dec. 1830
Clutton, Richard, Pickforton, higgler. Jan. 1828
William, Chester, baker. Aug. 1826
Coksey, William, Dodcott cum Wilksley, Wrenbury, yeoman. May 1830
Colclough, James, Sandbach, gent. Dec. 1828 (1st grant 1819; 3rd grant 1833)
James, Sandbach, joiner & cabinet maker. A Jan. 1829
Coleclough, James, Sandbach, gent. Nov. 1830 (1st grant 1822; 3rd grant 1833)
Collier, John, Sale, yeoman. June 1830
Jonas, Windlehurst, Marple, farmer. A Dec. 1828
Robert, Bosden, yeoman. March 1826
Collins, Adam, Dukinfield, weaver. A Oct. 1829
Coltman, George, Chester, doctor of physic. April 1829
Colville, Mary, Castle Northwich, widow. May 1826
Cook, Mary, Sandbach. April 1826
Cooke, Ann, Lostock Gralam, spinster. Dec. 1826
John the elder, Nantwich, yeoman. May 1830*
William, Worleston Rookery, Nantwich, esq. July 1830
Cookson, William, Sale, yeoman. Sept. 1827
Coombs, Robert, Gatley, Stockport, Aug. 1828
Cooper, Abigail, Werneth, Stockport, widow. April 1830
Betty, Hague, Mottram, widow. July 1828
Hannah, Wildboarclough, spinster. March 1827
James, Wildboar Clough, yeoman. July 1828
James, Nantwich, brazier. Nov. 1830
John, Macclesfield Forrest, yeoman. March 1827
Samuel, Congleton, silk throwster. A Oct. 1829
Thomas, Appleton, farmer. Feb. 1829
Cope, Edward, Macclesfield, yeoman. Feb. 1826
Sarah, Wrenbury-cum-Frith, spinster. Jan. 1829
Coppock, Thomas, Stockport, ironmonger. Nov. 1828
Corbishley, Hugh, Wincle, day labourer. A April 1828
Corlett, Richard, Boughton, gent. Dec. 1828
Corner, Edward, Great Warford, yeoman. Sept. 1830
Cornes, Joseph, Elton, co. Chester, farmer. Jan. 1827

Cornes, Sarah, Nantwich, widow. Jan 1828
Cornforth, Joseph Birks, Macclesfield, watchmaker. June 1829
Cotgreave, James, Chester, gent. Aug. 1827
Cotter, Mary, Chester, widow. Dec. 1826
Cottingham, Jane Frances, Bebington, spinster. Oct. 1827
Thomas, Little Neston, gent. Oct. 1827
Cotton, Sir Robert, Salusbury, Combermere, bart. A Nov. 1826
Coumbs, Hannah, Baguley, Bowden. A May 1827
William, Carrington, tailor. A Sept. 1830*
Cowap, Ralph, Little Budworth, farmer. Oct. 1827
Cox, John, Newton, yeoman. Sept. 1829
Sarah, Halton co Chester, widow. Feb. 1826*
William Charles, Congleton, gent. May 1826
Cragg, Alan, Carrington, farmer. A Oct. 1828
George, Mobberley, yeoman. April 1830
Ralph, Trichinopoly, East Indies, private in 2nd Battalion of First Foot, widower. A May 1830
Crampton, William, Carrington, schoolmaster. Feb. 1827
William, Carrington, yeoman. A Jan. 1830
Craven, Robert, Brindley, gent. A June 1827
Crawford, Jane, Nantwich, widow. A Nov. 1828*
Joseph, Nantwich, cordwainer. A Nov. 1828*
Creamore, John, Barney Brook, Newhall, yeoman. May 1829
Crew, William, Congleton, farmer. Dec. 1829
Crewe, John Lord Crewe, Baron of Crewe. Oct. 1829
Critchley, Martha, Little Barrow, widow. May 1830*
Cross, John, Lymm, yeoman. A July 1828 (1st grant 1805)
John, Farndon, blacksmith. Aug. 1828
John, Lymm, yeoman. A Oct. 1829
Richard Townley, Adlington, esq. A Dec. 1829 (1st grant 1825)
Robert, Northwich, shopkeeper. Aug. 1829
Croudson, William, Antrobus, surgeon. A Sept. 1830
Crowther, Timothy, Frodsham, gent. April 1829
Crump. Thomas, Horton, Tilston. Dec. 1829*
Cummings, Elizabeth, Chester, widow. A Jan. 1826
Cutler, John, Dunham Massey, yeoman. April 1830

DAINE, Peter, Carrington, yeoman. March 1828
Dakeyne, Catherine, Dane Cottage, Astbury. A Jan. 1827
Dale, Moses, Macclesfield, gent. Feb. 1827
Thomas, Hinderton, blacksmith. April 1826
Dane, Gilbert, Bank Top, Wincle, yeoman. Oct. 1826
Daniel, Henry, Marthall, farmer. June 1827
Thomas, Norbury, yeoman. June 1828
Daniels, Dorothy, Chester, widow. June 1827
Joseph, Sandbach, yeoman. June 1828
Samuel, Over Peover, yeoman. Oct. 1827
Darbyshire, John, Ashton-upon-Mersey, farmer. A April 1826
Martha, Ashton-upon-Mersey, spinster. A April 1827
Mary, Lymm. May., 1826; April 1830
Darlington, Ellen, Moulton, spinster. Feb. 1828
George, Marbury, Great Budworth, farmer. Feb. 1830
Hannah, Little Peover, widow. Dec. 1827

Darlington, John, Newton, Frodsham, yeoman. May 1826
John, Burland, farmer. May 1830 (2nd grant 1857)
Peter, Barnton, gent. A April 1827
Richard, Middlewich, painter. Dec., 1826
Thomas, Middlewich, painter & glazier. Oct. 1827
Davenport, Charles, Stanthorne, miller. Sept. 1829
David, Broken Cross, Macclesfield, twister. Dec. 1828
Edward, Waterloo Rd., Stockport, hatter. A Jan. 1830
John the elder, Ashton-upon-Mersey. Feb. 1828
John, Crewe, Barthomley, yeoman. Jan. 1830*
Rev. Joseph, Acton, clerk. March 1829
Sarah, Nantwich, widow. May 1826
Thomas, Oldfield, Dunham Massey, gent. Feb. 1828
Thomas, Swanlow. Feb. 1829
William, Bramhall Hall, esq. Aug. 1829
Davidson, John, Chester, collector of Excise. Dec. 1828
Davies, Ann, Chester, married woman. A June 1827
Charles, Great Boughton, gent. Oct. 1830
David, Macclesfield, D.D. Feb. 1828
Elizabeth, Chester, widow. A Aug. ·1829
James, Bollington, yeoman. Sept. 1826
John, Allostock, yeoman. July 1828
John, Chester, grocer & tea dealer. Sept. 1828
John, Chester, gent. July 1830
Joseph, Chester, grocer. A July 1826 (1st grant 1825)
Mary, Flookersbrook, co. Chester, spinster. Jan. 1828*
Robert, Bollington, gent. A July 1830
Samuel, Chester, upholsterer. Jan. 1830
William, Weaverham, farmer. Nov. 1827
Davyes, Thomas, Chester, carver. A March 1827
Dawson, John, Sutton, Macclesfield, silk throwster. Aug. 1828
William, Moreton, last of Douglas, Isle of Man, yeoman. Jan. 1829
Dean, Benjamin, Chester, yeoman. Feb. 1826
Elizabeth, Weston, widow. March 1826
James, Congleton, last of East Indies, bombardier. A Aug. 1828
Jonathan, Macclesfield, joiner. Dec. 1829
Joseph, Over, weaver. Feb. 1827*
Ralph, Kelsall, yeoman. Jan. 1829
Robinson, Wallasey, farmer. Nov. 1827* (2nd grant 1852)
Samuel, Trafford, pavior. A June 1828
Thomas, Kelsall, farmer & mason. Oct. 1829
Dennil, John, Chester, proctor & public notary. Sept. 1826 (1st grant 1801)
Denson, Samuel, Wervin, farmer. May 1827 (2nd grant 1836)
Derbyshire, Rebecca, Drayton, co. Salop, spinster. A Feb. 1828
Dicken, Enoch, Norbury, cordwainer. Jan. 1826
Dickenson, Robert, Oldfield, Dunham Massey, yeoman. Nov. 1827
Dickinson, John, Sandbach, shoe manufacturer. Nov. 1830
Dilworth, Thomas, Mouldsworth, Tarvin, farmer. Oct. 1830
Dixon, Ann, Chester, widow. Nov. 1826
Samuel, Marple, tanner. Oct. 1826
Dobell, Benjamin, Witton, yeoman. July 1829
Martha, Malpas, widow. A April 1828
Dobson, Samuel, Hatherton, Wybunbury, yeoman. Oct. 1827*

Docker, Joseph, Hope Green, Adlington. June 1829
Dod, Thomas Crewe, Edge Hall, Malpas, esq. June 1827
Dodd, Ann, Chester, spinster. A Jan. 1830
Elizabeth, Nettledale, Pickforton, widow. Oct., 1827
Ellen, Chester, widow. A Dec. 1829*
John, Chester, skinner. Aug. 1827
Lydia, Hargreave, widow. A Oct. 1828
Mary, Cholmondley, Malpas. Aug. 1827
Richard, Guilden Sutton, farmer. April 1829
Dodge, William, Stockport, shopkeeper. Nov. 1826
Domville, Betty, Thelwall, spinster. Nov. 1827
Done, James, Bradford Mill House, farmer. July 1829
James, Tiverton, Bunbury, farmer's servant. A March 1830
John, Eaton, widower. A Jan. 1827*
Dooley, John, Ashley, yeoman. Sept. 1829
Doughty, Thomas, Bunbury, Feb. 1826
Dowers, John, Altrincham, exciseman. A April 1826
Downes, Edward the elder, Kettleshulme, last of Ardwick, yeoman. Dec. 18
Downs, Ann, Marple, widow. May 1830
William, Cheadle, crofter. June 1828
Doxon, James, London, merchant. A Sept. 1828
Drake, Eleanor, Chester, last of Ince, widow. March 1829; March 1830
Drinkwater, Mary, Altrincham, widow. Aug. 1830
Dumvill, John, Nether Knutsford, gent. Aug. 1828*
Duncalf, John, Congleton, silk throwster. Aug. 1826
Dunkerley, James, Chester, dissenting minister. A Jan. 1829
Dunn, Joseph, Hartford, land surveyor. July 1830
Durack, Sarah, Chester, spinster. May 1830
Dutton, Elizabeth, Brindley, widow. Oct. 1829
George, Little Budworth. May 1826*
Hannah, Chester, spinster. Oct. 1829
John, Kingsley, schoolmaster. March 1827
Joseph, Duddon, co. Chester, farmer. March 1830
Mary, Nantwich, spinster. March 1830
Robert, Thornton-in-the-Moors, farmer. May 1828
Samuel, Bickerton, farmer. Sept. 1826
Thomas, Duddon, Tarvin, yeoman. Nov. 1826
Thomas, Burwardsley, farmer. Dec. 1827
William, Top Brindley, yeoman. July 1830

EACHUS, James, Middlewich, yeoman. April 1830
Robert, Newton, Middlewich, ironfounder. Nov. 1827
William, Middlewich, printer. Oct. 1830
Eagles, Thomas, Tranmere, gent. June 1830 (1st grant 1800)
Earl, Thomas, Crowley, Great Budworth. July 1829
Earle, George, Macclesfield, innkeeper. Jan. 1827
Eaton, George, Comberbach, gent. A Dec. 1828
George, Lower Whitley. May 1829 (1st grant 1777)
James, Norbury, farmer. Feb. 1826
Joseph, Runcorn, labourer. Oct. 1829
Richard, Lea Mill, miller. April 1826
Thomas, Comberbach. A March 1828
William, Sandbach, surgeon. Feb. 1829 (2nd grant 1837)

Edge, Thomas, Bickley, Malpas, labourer. Sept. 1826*
Thomas, Haswell, co. Chester, labourer. A Feb. 1827
Edgerley, James, Lower Whitley, yeoman. April 1830
Edgerton, William, Stanthorn, farmer. Sept. 1829
Edmondson, William, Bridge Trafford, gent. Sept. 1826 (1st grant 1814)
Edwards, Ann, Woodside, spinster. A Feb. 1830*
Edward, Malpas, officer in the Excise. A May 1828
George, Great Boughton, gardener. A April 1828
John Goodman, Chester, gent. A Dec. 1826
Richard, Nantwich, gent. March 1830
Samuel, Alpraham, yeoman. Dec. 1827
Thomas, Macclesfield, innkeeper. A Dec. 1828
Thomas, Nantwich, publican. April 1829
Egerton, Philip, Malpas, baronet. Jan. 1830
Elderton, John, Lincolns Inn, Middlesex, gent. A June 1830
Ellis, Andrew, Frodsham, mariner. Oct. 1827
John, Stoke, co. Chester, farmer. A Sept. 1830
Joseph, Brombrow, farmer & miller. April 1826
Martha, Stoke, co. Chester, spinster. A Sept. 1830
William, Great Neston, clerk. Nov. 1829
Elwood, Richard, Nantwich, gent. July 1830
Emmerton, Sarah, Chester, spinster. Nov. 1826
Etchells, Harriet, Stockport, spinster. Dec. 1830
Evans, Leigh, Chester, gent. Nov. 1828
Roger, Handbridge, yeoman. Aug. 1828
Sarah, Chester, spinster. A Nov. 1828
Sarah, Chester, widow. A July 1830
Thomas, Chester, alderman. July 1828 (2nd grant 1839)

FAIRCLOUGH, Ann, Witton, widow. Sept. 1829
Thomas, Backford, yeoman. A Feb. 1826
William, Moor, Daresbury, publican. A July 1829
Fairfield, John, Congleton, yeoman. Dec. 1828*
Fallows, Philip, Stockport, gent. July 1826
Farrall, James, Congleton, labourer. A May 1827
Thomas, Frodsham, innkeeper. March 1826 (1st grant 1819)
William, Darnhall, Whitegate, farmer. June 1830
Faulkner, John, Deanrow, Wilmslow, labourer. Oct. 1826
Samuel, Sale, Ashton-on-Mersey. A Feb. 1827
Sarah, Tattenhall, spinster. Feb. 1830
Thomas, Wincham, farmer. Feb. 1828
Thomas, Runcorn, farmer. A May 1828
William, Duddon, Tarvin, labourer. Oct. 1828*
Fawcett, Rev. Stephen, Chester, D. Laws. June 1829
Feilden, Robert, Didsbury, Runcorn, esq. Nov. 1830 (2nd grant 1859)
Fenna, John, Wickstead Hall, Whitchurch, farmer. April 1828
Thomas, Tilston Hall, Bunbury, gent. June 1826
William, Wickstead Hall. A Dec. 1828
Fennah, George, Delamere, yeoman. June 1826*
Ferns, George the elder, Stockport, grocer. Feb. 1829
Filcock, Peter, Macclesfield, tallow chandler. A May 1826
Peter, Bosley, farmer. Oct. 1826
Filkin, Charles, Egerton, Malpas. A Dec. 1827

Filkin, John, Northwich, gent. Feb. 1830
Samuel, Overton, publican. A Feb. 1827
Finch, James, Halton, alehouse keeper. Sept. 1828
Finney, Mary Ann Lloyd, Wilmslow, widow. Oct. 1827
William, Etchells, Stockport, yeoman. A Oct. 1828*
Fish, Rev. William, Little St. Johns, Chester, clerk. A Oct. 1828*
Fleet, Charles, Lea Forge, labourer. Sept. 1828
George, Pickforton, Bunbury, mason. May 1827
Fletcher, George the elder, Partington, yeoman. June 1828
James, Newton, labourer. A July 1829
Samuel the younger, Macclesfield, silkman. July 1826
Foden, James, Congleton, yeoman. Feb. 1830
William, Marton, Prestbury, wheelwright. Feb. 1827
Ford, James, Sutton, farmer. July 1830
John, Barthomley, yeoman. Feb. 1829
Thomas, Lower Walton, yeoman. Oct. 1830
Forest, Ann, Lachford, widow. April 1830
Forrest, Joseph, Latchford, gent. Feb. 1827
Forster, James, Brombrow, tailor. Oct. 1828
Thomas, Lymm, farmer. Nov. 1829
William, Congleton, shoemaker. A May 1830
Foster, Alice, Bollington, widow. A Aug. 1826
Foulkes, Robert, Chester, gent. July 1826
Fowden, Samuel, Norbury, yeoman. June 1830
Fox, Acton the elder, Haslington, yeoman. May 1829
Elizabeth, Sandbach, widow. July 1826
Frankland, Ellen, Statham with Lymm, widow. A March 1827
Fraser, Jane, Charles Town, South Carolina, America, widow. A March 182
Freeman, Samuel, Chester, esq. April 1830
Frith, Aaron, Allostock, farmer. June 1827
Frodsham, James, Lymm, gent. May 1828
Frost, Lawrence, Upton, Macclesfield, last of Liverpool, merchant, June 1827; Sept.
Fryer, John, Dutton, yeoman. A Aug. 1828
John, Stockham, Runcorn. May 1829

GALLANT, Mary, Alpraham, Bunbury, widow. March 1830
Galley, Thomas, Church Coppenhall, yeoman. Feb. 1828
Gallimore, Thomas, Allostock, wheelwright. July 1828
Gardiner, Catherine, Morton, widow. A Oct. 1827
Rowland Charles, Macclesfield, brickmaker. May 1830
Gardner, Peter, Bruen Stapleford, farmer. May 1826
Richard, Malpas, gent. March 1829
Garman, William, Bosden, yeoman. June 1830
Garner, James, Hale, Bowden, farmer. A March 1829
John, Appleton, yeoman. Oct. 1827
John, Chester, gent. A May 1828
Josiah, Altrincham, yeoman. May 1829
Garnett, Rev. William, Tilston, clerk. A July 1829
Garratt, Harwar, Chester, currier. Oct. 1829
Garrett, John, Chester. Oct. 1827
Garside, Thomas, Tintwistle, farmer. A Jan. 1829
William, Woolley, Mottram, farmer. A Sept. 1827

Gaskell, Frances, Knutsford, spinster. A Nov. 1827
John, Nether Knutsford, clock and watchmaker. Dec. 1827
John, Worth, gent. Jan. 1828
Susannah, Over Tabley, last of Nether Knutsford, widow. July 1829
Thomas, Nether Knutsford, watchmaker. Nov. 1829 (2nd grant 1832)
Gaskin, Edward, Kelsall, farmer. A Jan. 1826*
Gatley, Edward, Stockport, yeoman. April 1826
Hannah the younger, Stockport, spinster. A Oct., 1830
Josiah, Hale, Bowden, yeoman. A Dec. 1829*
Peter, Nether Knutsford, butcher. Feb. 1830
Gee, Edward, Macclesfield, silk manufacturer. June 1826
Jonathan, Macclesfield, silk throwster. A May 1828
Gerrard, George Edward, Wimbolds Trafford, esq. June 1828 (1st grant 1794)
John, Witton, brazier. A July 1827
Mary, Waverham, widow. April 1829
Gibbons, Thomas, Chester, confectioner. Nov. 1826
Gibson, Richard the elder, Heatley Heath, Lymm, yeoman. Aug. 1830
Gill, Elizabeth, Chester, spinster. Oct. 1828
Gittens, Joseph, Weaver, farmer. Oct. 1828
Gleave, Samuel, Latchford, saddler. Dec. 1829
Thomas, Lower Peover, carpenter. A July 1828
William, Mere, farmer & maltster. A July 1826
Glen, Alexander, Seacombe. A March 1828
Glover, Peter, Nether Knutsford, yeoman. Feb. 1826
Randle, Ollerton, farmer. April 1828
Goddard, George, Bramhall, Stockport, ale seller. Dec. 1827
James, Stayley Wood, Mottram in Longdendale, weaver. Nov. 1829
Godwin, George, Macclesfield, silk manufacturer. Jan. 1827
Goodall, Thomas, Siddington, gent. Sept. 1828
William, Titherington, Prestbury, cotton manufacturer. A Oct. 1830*
Goodier, John, Ashton-upon-Mersey, farmer. Aug. 1826
Thomas, Cotton, labourer. May 1829
Goodison, William, Stockport, weaver. March 1826*
Goodwin, John, *see* Bann
Joseph, Fernilee, Hope, co. Derby, yeoman. A June 1828
Martha, Henbury, farmer. Feb. 1826*
Samuel, Stockport Etchells, farmer. A June 1829
William, Diglee House, Yardsly-cum-Waley. Jan. 1829
Goodyear, Samuel, Lach Dennis. March 1828
William, Sproston, farmer. Dec. 1826
Goose, Richard, Siddington, higgler & hawker. A July 1826
Gosling, Sarah, Macclesfield, spinster. Aug. 1827
Gough, Owen, Allostock, Great Budworth, wheelwright. June 1830
Goulbern, Thomas, Newton. March 1827*
Goulden, Betty, Davenham. April 1826
Joseph, Altrincham, victualler. A Sept. 1826 (2nd grant 1844)
Joshua, Mottram St. Andrew, farmer. Sept. 1827
Graham, John, Stockport, surgeon. Aug. 1828
William, Altrincham, cordwainer. Nov. 1830
Graisty, James, Mobberley, yeoman. April 1829
Granvil, Frances, Chester, widow. Sept. 1830
Gratrix, Edward, Altrincham, gent. A Nov. 1830
Joseph, Wilmslow, innkeeper. A April 1830

Greaves, James, Macclesfield, yeoman. Dec. 1827
William, Midgeley, Wincle, yeoman. May 1828
Green, Ann, Lords Fields, Shocklach. Oct. 1826
Hannah, Chester, spinster. A Nov. 1826
James, Ridley, gent. July 1829
James, Sandiway, gent. June 1830
James, Bullock Smithy, Stockport, gent. A Oct. 1830
Joseph, Poulton Lancelyn, formely Joseph Kent, Liverpool, esq. May 1829: Aug. 1830
Joseph, senior, Sandbach. Sept. 1830
Thomas, Tatton, Rostherne. May 1828
Greensmith, Hannah, Macclesfield, widow. Jan. 1826*
Greenway, William, Utkinton, Tarporley, yeoman. March 1830
Greenwood, Hannah, Runcorn, spinster. Sept. 1828
Gregory, Benjamin, Wheelock, Sandbach, gent. A Oct. 1830
Elizabeth, Frodsham. Sept. 1827
George, Plumbley, Great Budworth, labourer. Feb. 1826
Timothy, New Crane St., Chester, mariner. Aug. 1829
Griffith, Thomas, Chester, cowkeeper. July 1827 (1st grant 1805)
Griffiths, John, Chester, labourer. A Aug. 1827*
Grimes, Matthew, Tatton Mill, Rostherne, miller. Nov. 1829
Grimsditch, John, Park House, Butley, gent. April 1829
Grindrod, Alice, Chester, widow. May 1826
Gronow, Elizabeth, Shrewsbury, spinster. A Feb. 1830
Groves, Martha, Lower Peover, widow. A Nov. 1826
Grundy, Mary, Matley, Mottram, widow. A March 1826*
Thomas, Styal, Wilmslow, farmer. A March 1829
Guest, Thomas, Preston Brook, agent. A & Tuon April 1827 (2nd grant
Gyles, Esther, Nantwich, spinster. Sept. 1829

HACKNEY, Thomas, Somerford, gardener. March 1828
Hadkinson, Roger, Hattersley, farmer. A July 1829
Hale, Peter, Burland, gent. Oct. 1829
William, Paddiley, co. Chester, gent. Jan. 1830 (2nd grant 1838)
Hall, David, Macclesfield, gent. April 1830
Ellen, Weston, spinster. Dec. 1829
George, Furnace, co. Chester, coal agent. A Sept. 1830
Isaac, Dukinfield, shopkeeper. A June. 1829
James, Nether Knutsford, flagger. Oct. 1830
Joyce, Chester, widow. Jan. 1826
Mary, Appleton, widow. April 1829
Nancy, Hyde, Stockport, widow. May 1827
Richard, Crowley, co. Chester, yeoman. Feb. 1827
Sarah, Macclesfield, widow. May 1829
Thomas Bayley, Hermitage, esq. Dec. 1828
Halliwell, Margaret, Altrincham, widow. A Aug. 1828
Thomas, Altrincham, wharfinger. A Sept. 1827
Hallsworth, William, Hyde, hatter. Nov. 1829
Hallworth, James, Stockport, carrier. Nov. 1830
John, Bramhall, gent. Jan. 1830
Joseph, Bosden, collier. Feb. 1828
Thomas, Norbury, publican. June 1830
William, Norbury, Stockport, labourer. Jan. 1828

Halton, John, Carrington, yeoman. July 1827
Hambleton, John, Bosley, Prestbury, baker. A March 1830 (2nd grant 1856)
Thomas, Styall, Wilmslow, weaver. June 1829
Hammond, Ralph, Macclesfield, yeoman. Feb. 1827*
Hamnet, John, Stapeley, co. Chester, cheese factor. June 1826 (1st grant 1798)
John, .Bowden, yeoman. Feb. 1828
Joseph, Bowden, yeoman. Sept. 1827
Hamson, Abraham, Bredbury, yeoman. March , 1829
Thomas, Macclesfield, cordwainer. Nov. 1828
Hand, Thomas, Middlewich, gent. Jan. 1829
Handford, Amos, Kettleshulme. June 1828
Daniel, Cheadle Bulkeley, miller. Dec. 1828
Hankey, Peter, Grappenhall. Aug. 1830
Hankinson, George, Hale, Bowden, tanner. A May 1827*
John the younger, Hale tanner. A Oct. 1827*
John senior, Hale, tanner. A Oct. 1827
Mary, Hale, widow. June 1827
Hanson, Kitty, Macclesfield, widow. A Jan. 1828
Richard, Over Whitley, yeoman. Dec. 1826
Roger, Shocklach Oviatt. Dec. 1826
Hardern, Samuel, Macclesfield, silk twister. Oct. 1826
William, Macclesfield, silk manufacturer. A May 1829
Hardey, Betty, Oldfield, Dunham Massey, widow. Oct. 1829
John, Sinderland, Bowden, yeoman. A June 1829
Samuel, Altrincham, merchant. Feb. 1829
Harding, Mary, Church Minshull, spinster. Oct. 1829*
Samuel, Pott Shrigley, gent. Dec. 1827
Hardman, Samuel, Underbanks, Stockport, cordwainer. A Dec. 1828 (2nd grant 1833)
Hardy, George, Sinderland, Dunham Massey, yeoman. April 1827
Henry, Woodley, Stockport, hatter. A Nov. 1828*
Robert, Stockport, cotton manufactuer. April 1828
Harper, Jane, Grappenhall, widow. March 1830
John, Grappenhall, gent. A Dec. 1830
Nanny, Wildboarclough, widow. May 1830
Peter, Wildboarclough, bookkeeper. A March 1829
Harpur, George, rector of Whitechapel, Middlesex, formerly rector of Harthill. A Nov. 1826
Harris, James, Oldcastle, co. Chester, farmer. March 1830
Harrison, Ann, Northen, widow. April 1830
Benjamin, Werneth, yeoman. June 1827
Elizabeth, Mottram Moor, widow. Dec. 1829
Elizabeth, Chester, widow. Jan. 1830
Isaac, Stockport, innkeeper. Aug. 1828
John, Chester, gent. Aug. 1827
Richard, Over Whitley, yeoman. Dec. 1826
Richard, Bidston, gent. June 1827
Thomas, St. Martins Lodge, Chester, architect. Sept. 1829
Harrop, George, Dukinfield Lodge, co. Chester. June 1826
Thomas, Macclesfield, labourer. A Feb. 1830
Hart, Martha, Latchford, widow. April 1830
Susannah, Chester, servant. July 1828
Hartley, James, Cheadle Mosley, gent. March 1828
Harvey, John the elder, Hankelow Mill, Audlem, miller. Aug. 1827

Harvey, Joseph, Macclesfield, silk manufacturer. Nov. 1829
Haslehurst, John, Witton, pansmith. Nov. 1830
Haspell, Elizabeth, Sandiway, Weverham, widow. March 1829
Hassal, Thomas, Nantwich, gent. June 1829
Hassall, John, Brindley, Acton, yeoman. Sept. 1828
  Richard, Sound, co. Chester, farmer. March 1827
  Samuel, Wrenbury, farmer. Aug. 1830
Hassell, John, Hyde, gent. June 1827
Hatfield, Elizabeth, Lisbon, Portugal, spinster. A July 1828 (1st grant 1819)
Hatton, Hannah, Macclesfield, widow. A May 1827
  Peter, Preston o'th'Hill & Latchford, gent. Dec. 1830 (2nd grant 1844)
  Thomas, Deanrow, publican. May 1828
Haughton, Amos, Dukinfield, weaver. Oct. 1829
  Josiah, Stockport, gent. Feb. 1830
Hayes, Jonathan, Norley, Frodsham, yeoman. Oct. 1830*
  Joseph, Wybunbury, webster. May 1827
  Mary, Hatton, widow. Feb. 1830
  Samuel, Hatton, farmer. A June 1829
  William, Frodsham, gent. May 1827
  William, Backford, farmer. June 1827
Hayman, John, Fallybrom, Prestbury, farmer. A Jan. 1826
Haynes, Joseph, Boughton, Chester, gent. Dec. 1829
Hays, William, Davenham, yeoman. March 1827*
Hayward, Edward, Goldstone, Cheswardine, co. Salop, esq. Nov. 1827
  William, Nantwich, glove manufacturer. Nov. 1827
Hazelhurst, Elizabeth, Comberbach. July 1830
Hazlehurst, Ellen, Macclesfield, widow. A March 1826
  George, Runcorn, gent. Dec. 1829
  John, Seven Oaks, Over Whitley, yeoman. July 1827
  Samuel, Lower Whitley, Great Budworth, yeoman. A March 1829
Heald, Thomas, Lostock Gralam, farmer. Oct. 1829
Heap, John, Dukinfield, gent. A Oct. 1826
  Joseph, Moorgate, Stayley, clothier. Dec. 1829
Heapy, Lawrence, Macclesfield, clerk. Nov. 1828
Heath, Joseph, Withenshaw, gardener. Oct. 1839
Heathcote, Sarah, Macclesfield, widow. A Oct. 1828
Heatley, Elizabeth, Alpraham, Bunbury. Jan. 1826
Heginbotham, John, Cheadle Bulkeley, gent. July 1827
Hemmins, Thomas, Middlewich, last of Congleton, yeoman. July 1826
Henchman, Charles, Chester, clerk. A Oct. 1828
Heney, Patrick, Chester, broker. May 1827
Henshall, Betty, Sandbach, spinster. May 1827
  Hannah, Macclesfield, widow. Feb. 1830
  James, Newton, Middlewich. Jan. 1829
  Rebecca, Hollinworth Smithy, Prestbury, widow. A Aug. 1827
  Thomas, Nether Knutsford, husbandman. Dec. 1830
  William, Macclesfield, glass dealer. Jan. 1830
Henshaw, Daniel, Wilmslow, blacksmith. Oct. 1826
  James, Middlewich, esq. May 1829
  Joshua, Over Alderley, yeoman. Sept. 1826
  Samuel, Church Hulme, blacksmith. Sept. 1827
Heppard, James, Frodsham, cabinet maker. April 1826
  Thomas, Crowton, Waverham, yeoman. Jan. 1827

Hesford, Alice, Thelwell, spinster. Oct. 1826
George, Edgeley, Cheadle, farmer. A April 1829
Hetherington, Jane, Liverpool, last Birkenhead, wife of William Hetherington, gent. Feb. 1828
Hewett, Sarah, Higher Whitley, widow. July 1828
Hewitt, Daniel, Bridgemere, Wybunbury, yeoman. Oct. 1827
Francis, Knutsford. A & Tuon. Feb. 1827
John, Crowley, Budworth, farmer. A July 1828
Joseph, Barnshaw, Sandbach. Nov. 1828
Samuel, Chester, tailor. A March 1829
Samuel, Mere, co. Chester, wheelwright. Aug. 1830
Sarah, Nether Knutsford, widow. June., 1828
Thomas, Cuppin St., Chester, gent. Oct. 1826
Thomas, Knutsford. A & Tuon Feb. 1827
Heyes, Alice, Lower Bebington, spinster. Feb. 1829
Heywood, John, Northwich & Witton, clockmaker. Aug. 1828
Samuel, Stockport, gent. Jan. 1828
William, Timperley, yeoman. Sept. 1829
Hibbert, Mary, Macclesfield, widow. March 1829
Hickson, Charles, Ellesmere Port, publican. A Dec. 1828
Elizabeth, Chester, widow. July 1827
Ephraim, Ollerton, Knutsford, farmer. A Feb. 1827
Joseph, Hilbre Island, farmer. July 1829
Mary, Spurstow, Bunbury. Dec. 1830
Hickton, Mary, Stockport, last of Little Bolton, widow. Feb. 1830
Higginson, Mary, Mere, co. Chester, spinster. Sept. 1830
Highfield, John, Frandley, Sevenoaks, co. Chester, yeoman. May 1827
Hignett, John, Elton, gent. Nov. 1826
Joseph, Elton, Thornton-le-Moors, gent. Nov. 1828
Thomas, Bruen Stapleford, gent. Nov. 1826
Higson, John, Frodsham, carrier. A Oct. 1826
John, Frodsham, carrier. A Aug. 1828
John, Frodsham gent. A April 1830
Sarah, Frodsham, widow. A May 1827
Hilditch, Mary, Moss End, Smallwood, widow. March 1826
Thomas, Nantwich, gent. April 1829
Hill, Ann, Marple, widow. Oct. 1830
Elizabeth, Nantwich, spinster. March 1830
George Nesse, Chester, surgeon. April 1830
James, Prestbury, gent. Oct. 1828
Richard, Mottram, Longdendale, farmer. A Sept. 1829
Thomas, Hollingworth, farmer. May 1826
Hilton, Thomas, Little Neston, yeoman. Feb. 1828
William, Tarvin, yeoman. May. 1830
Hincks, Joseph, Chester, gent. Feb. 1830
Hinde, John, Weston. A Nov. 1830*
Liptrot, Weston. A Nov. 1830*
Mary, Weston, spinster. Nov. 1830 (1st grant 1810)
Robert, Ince, yeoman. A Nov. 1830 (1st grant 1744)
William, Ince, yeoman. A Nov. 1830*
Hiorns, Hannah, Congleton, widow. Oct. 1829
Hitchin, Jacob, Middlewich, draper. A Dec. 1829

Hitchin, Jonathan, Barrow, wheelwright, Jan. 1829
Hobson, Elizabeth, Chester. Sept. 1828
John, Odd Rode, Astbury. A March 1827
Thomas, Stockport, innkeeper. A Dec. 1830
Hockenhall, Mary, Dodds Green, Newhall, widow. April 1828
Thomas, Day Green, Hassall, farmer. March 1829
William, Kermincham, farmer. Feb. 1826
Hocknall, Elizabeth, Chester, widow. June 1826*
Hodgkinson, Esther, Middlewich, spinster. Nov. 1827
Margaret, Dunham Massey, spinster. Aug. 1826 (2nd grant 1844)
Peter, Moston, Warmingham, lock tenter. June 1827
Hodgson, Joseph James, Marple. July 1830
Hodkinson, John, Macclesfield, innkeeper. June 1830
Hodskin, Charles, Tattenhall, farmer. April 1827
Holbrook, Martha, Tabley, widow. Jan. 1827
Mary, Tabley, widow. Jan. 1827
Holford, Thomas, Middlewich, publican & blacksmith. Aug. 1827
Holland, James, Kinswood Green, Wrenbury, farmer. March 1830
Jasper, North Rode. Aug. 1830*
Margaret, Stockport, widow. Nov. 1828
Samuel, Over Peover, schoolmaster. May 1828
Thomas, Altrincham, gent. Dec. 1829
William, Chester, clock & watchmaker. A Aug. 1829
Hollingworth, George, Holehouse, Mottram, innkeeper. June 1827
Hollins, William, Over Tabley, yeoman. Feb. 1829
Hollinshead, Mary, Macclesfield, widow. Dec. 1829*
Hollinsworth, John, Keckwick, Runcorn, gent. A July 1830
Hollinworth, James, Agden, Bowden, blacksmith. A March 1826
Peter, Partington, Bowden, farmer. Aug. 1826
Holme, Seebera, Stockport, widow. July 1830
Holt, John, Little Heath, Dunham Massey, labourer. Aug. 1826*
John, Great Budworth, labourer. A Dec. 1826
John, Handforth-cum-Bosden, Cheadle, publican. A Nov. 1827
Joseph, Dunham Massey, labourer. A Oct. 1829*
Joseph, Ashton-upon-Mersey, labourer. May 1830
Sarah, Altrincham, spinster. Feb. 1830
William, Etchells, Stockport, weaver. Jan. 1826
Hooley, John, Great Peover, farmer. May 1827
Hope, Edward, Stockport, silk manufacturer. Aug. 1830
George, Nantwich. Feb. 1828
Mary Ann, Macclesfield, spinster. A Sept. 1829
Hopkins, John, Stockport, druggist. Sept. 1826
Samuel, Lea, co. Chester, gent. A Sept. 1828
Hopley, William, Marton, Whitegate, farmer. Sept. 1829
Hopwood, William, Torkington, weaver. April 1827
Hornby, John, Hornby Lodge, Delamere, yeoman. A Feb. 1829
Horsfield, James, Werneth, hatter. A Sept. 1828
John, Hyde, hatter. July 1828
Zachariah, Hyde, widower. A Oct. 1827
Horton, Margaret, Haslington, widow. July 1827
Hough, James, Middlewich, carpenter. Dec. 1826
James, Kerridge, Prestbury, millwright. May 1827
John, Newton, Middlewich, bricklayer. May 1826

Hough, Katharine, Tarporley, spinster. May 1826
Nancy, Bradshaw Hall, Cheadle Moseley, widow. Sept. 1827
Sarah, Haywood, Audlem, widow. Jan. 1826
Howard, Abraham, Portwood, Brinnington, cotton manufacturer. Feb. 1829
Betty, Frodsham, widow. A Oct. 1830
Eliza Dean, Portwood, Stockport, spinster. July 1830
James, Dukinfield, hatter. May 1829
James, Newton, Mottram, cotton spinner. Aug. 1830
Joseph, Middlewich, bricklayer. Feb. 1829
Robert, Dukinfield, shopkeeper. Aug. 1830
Sarah, Stockport. Dec. 1826
Thomas, Bowden, innkeeper. April 1827
Thomas, Portwood, Stockport, cotton manufacturer. A Aug., 1829; Feb., 1830
William, Latchford, yeoman. Feb. 1826
William, Altrincham, yeoman. Nov. 1827*
Howarth, Peter, Chorley, farmer. April. 1829
Howell, Sarah, Chester, widow. Dec. 1827*
Howlbrook, Robert, Macclesfield, silk manufacturer. A Nov. 1828
Hudson, Phoebe, Handforth-cum-Bosden, widow. July 1826*
Hughes, Ann, Chester, widow. March 1830
John, Latchford, cotton spinner. July 1826
John, Runcorn, yeoman. Oct. 1830
Sarah, Chester, spinster. A Dec. 1826
Hulley, Anthony, Chester, publican & coachman. Oct. 1826
Hulme, George, Middlewich, yeoman. April 1828
James, Congleton, yeoman. May 1830*
John, Moston, farmer. Feb. 1826
Jonathan, Ashton-upon-Mersey, surgeon. Jan. 1830
Thomas, Great Warford, Alderley, yeoman. Feb. 1826
Thomas, Bramhall, farmer. Nov. 1826
Hulse, Moses, Oulton Lowe, co. Chester, formerly Penisarnant, Llandegai, Caernarvonshire, farmer. A Dec. 1826
Humble, Michael, Birkenhead, esq. Nov. 1830
Humphreys, Jane, Chester, spinster. Jan. 1830
Humston, John, Threapwood, maltster. A July 1829
Hunt, Ellen, High St., Stockport. A May 1828
Frances otherwise Fanny, Baguley, widow. Oct. 1830
James, Macclesfield, May 1830*
Hunter, William, Chester, agent to Company of Cheesemongers, London. A Jan. 1827
Hurst, Elizabeth, wife of William Hurst, Knutsford. A March 1829 (2nd grant 1845)
John, Macclesfield, gent. A June 1828
Hussey, John, Over Peover, gent. A March 1828
Hutchinson, John, Macclesfield, silk manufacturer. Jan. 1829
Hutton, Ezra, Congleton, ironmonger. Oct. 1830
Huxley, James, Weaver, yeoman. A Oct. 1828
Lucy, Macclesfield, spinster. March 1829
Mary, Chester, widow. A June 1829
Hyde, Henry, Dukinfield, yeoman. A April 1829
John, Werneth, Stockport, bookkeeper. Oct. 1829

IKIN, John, Baddiley, husbandman. Feb. 1828
Ince, Peter, Macclesfield, officer in H.M. Excise. Aug. 1829
Inglefield, John, Higher Bebington, cordwainer. June. 1829
Irish, Samuel, Hough, co. Chester, husbandman. Jan. 1827

Isherwood, James, Bradshawe, Poynton, Sept. 1828

JACKSON, Ann, Macclesfield, spinster. A May 1828
Elizabeth, Heald Mill, Mobberley, widow. A Jan. 1827
Jane, Stanney, widow. June 1829
John, Stanneylands, co. Chester. Aug. 1830
John, Kelsall, Travin, farmer & pavior. Oct. 1830
Joseph, Brown Edge, Lymm, yeoman. Dec. 1827
Martha, Hatton, co. Chester, widow. Aug. 1826
Thomas, Moore, co. Chester, grocer & draper. Dec. 1829
Thomas, Witton, sexton. Feb. 1830
William, Baguley, yeoman. Jan. 1829
Jacson, Roger, Bebington, clerk. Feb. 1827
James, William, Newton, Middlewich, innkeeper. A Sept. 1828
Jameson, David, Oswestry, co. Salop, maltster. Jan. 1827
Jane, Latchford, widow. Sept. 1826
Jamieson, Walter, captain of the ship James McUrey of Glasgow. Dec. 1826
Jancey, John, Malpas, gent. March 1826
Janion, Robert, Runcorn, yeoman. Oct. 1828 (2nd grant 1839)
Janson, Thomas, Portwood, Stockport, cotton spinner. Feb. 1827; Jan. 1830
Jefferies, Edward Watkin, Chester, attorney. Aug. 1827
John, Threapwood, labourer. Jan. 1827*
William, Eccleston, co. Chester, stonemason. Feb. 1827
Jefferson, Thomas, Mouldsworth, farmer & miller. A Feb. 1829
Jeffes, Thomas, Little Leigh, clerk. Aug. 1826
Jenks, Rev. David, Aldbury, co. Hertford. Nov. 1829*
Jepson, Isaac, Great Warford, farmer. Jan. 1828*
Ralph, Cheadle Bulkeley, yeoman. Nov. 1827 (1st grant 1819)
Jodrell, Caleb, Great Warford, farmer. June 1828
Francis, Henbury, esq. May 1829
Johnson, Ann, Macclesfield, widow. July 1826
Benjamin, Congleton, joiner. March 1827
Charles, Minshull Vernon, farmer. Nov. 1829
Daniel, Alsager, widower. April 1826
Daniel, Nantwich, chemist. A Dec. 1827
Edmund, Lostock Gralam, yeoman. June 1830
Edward Henry, Chester, wine & spirit merchant. March 1830
Elizabeth, Goss St., Chester, spinster. April 1829
Elizabeth, North Rode, widow. Feb. 1830
James, Chester, farmer. A Nov. 1826
John, Chester, draper. April 1827
John, Macclesfield, gent. June 1827
John, Hassall Green, Betchton, yeoman. Sept. 1827
John, Pool, Acton, farmer. Jan. 1829
John, Hartford, gent. May 1829
Joseph, Tarporley. Sept. 1830
Richard, Utkinton, farmer. July 1829
Robert, Audlem, yeoman. July 1827
Samuel, Dukinfield, gardener. A Jan. 1827
Sarah, Rainow, spinster. April 1828
William, Congleton, woollen draper. Oct. 1827
Jolley, George, Buglawton, farmer. Nov. 1828
Jolly, William, Knutsford, shopkeeper. July 1827

Jones, Ann, Chester, widow. A Feb. 1828*
Edward, Nantwich, stationer. April 1828
Edward, Chester, labourer. July 1829
Elizabeth, Chester, spinster. A Jan. 1829
Elizabeth, Farndon. May 1830
Grace, Chester, widow. A Dec. 1828
Jane, Chester, widow. Nov. 1827
John, Capenhurst, farmer. May 1826
John, Capenhurst, farmer. March 1828
John, Chester, bricklayer. Nov. 1828
John, Frodsham, yeoman. March 1829
John, Chester, grocer. A June 1829
John, Bowden, labourer. A Sept. 1829
Lydia, Bowden, widow. Dec. 1827
Margaret, Wallasey, widow. Nov. 1828*
Martha, Chester, widow. Feb. 1829
Richard, Stanthorne Hill, co. Chester, esq. Oct. 1830
Robert, Chester, gent. Sept. 1826 (former grants 1810 & 1825)
Samuel, Wellington St., Chester, yeoman. July 1829
Sarah, Chester, widow. A June 1826*
Thomas, Farndon, farmer. March 1827
Thomas, Aldersey, Cuddington. June 1827
William, Dunham Massey, cordwainer. Nov. 1829
William, Chester, baker. May 1830
William, St. John St., Chester, servant. A Sept. 1830
Joynson, Elizabeth, Newton, Middlewich, widow. Aug. 1829
Robert, Sandbach, labourer. Sept. 1830

KAY, Thomas, Steven St., Chester. Oct. 1826
Keeling, William, Congleton, baker & confectioner. Jan. 1826
Kellett, Samuel, Bredbury, watch and clockmaker. A Nov. 1830
Kelsall, Margaret, Dukinfield, A April 1830
Thomas, Stockport, joiner. Oct. 1830
Kendrick, Thomas, Birkenhead, yeoman. Feb. 1828
Thomas, Chester. Oct. 1830 (2nd grant 1835)
Kent, Betty, Nantwich, spinster. Oct. 1826
John, Nantwich, widower. Feb. 1827
alias Green, Joseph, Poulton Lancelyn. May 1829; Dec. 1830
Kenwright, John, Runcorn, waterman. A Nov. 1829
Kerfoot, John, Chester, gent. Aug. 1828
Peter, Witton, bricklayer. A Aug. 1827
Kershaw, Hannah, Stayley, widow. A Sept. 1828
Hugh, Stayley, clothier A Sept. 1828
Thomas, Dukinfield, musician. May 1828
Kettle, Samuel, Elton, Warmingham, farmer. July 1830
Keyte, Richard, Nether Alderley, gent. June 1827
Kidson, William, Birkenhead, mariner. A Nov. 1830
Kilgrass, Thomas, Dunham Massey, labourer. April 1827*
William, Dunham Massey, plasterer. A Dec. 1827
Kinder, John, Newton Heath, shoemaker. Sept. 1829
Ralph, Stayley, Mottram-in-Longdendale, yeoman. April 1826
King, John, Frodsham, gent. Feb. 1829
Mary, Chester, spinster. Jan. 1830

Kinsey, Elizabeth, wife of Ralph Kinsey, High Legh, tollbar keeper. Oct. 1830
George, Rudheath Lordship, yeoman. Feb. 1830
John, Lostock Gralam, yeoman. June 1826
Ralph, Gatley. Nov. 1826
Kirk, John, Macclesfield, quarryman. A Dec. 1830
Kirkby, Matthew, Chester, linen draper. Nov. 1826
Kirkham, Ann, Chester, spinster. Nov. 1828
James, Wettenhall, farmer. Dec. 1829
Sarah, Bunbury, widow. A Feb. 1826*
William, Runcorn, merchant. Jan. 1829 (1st grant 1825)
Kirkpatrick, Joshua, Dukinfield, tailor. Dec. 1827
Kitchen, Sarah, Northen, spinster. Dec. 1828
William, Hansford cum Bosden, last of Millhouse, Adlington, yeoman, March 1830
Knight, John, Macclesfield, bleacher. A Feb. 1829
Mary, Gawsworth, widow. Nov. 1826
Knowles, James, Stockport, plumber & glazier. Jan. 1830
Peter, Latchford, gent. March 1826
Samuel, Congleton, publican. April 1827
William, Nether Tabley, tanner. Nov. 1827

LAMB, Elizabeth, Weaverham, widow. March 1830
Hannah, Stockport, widow. A June 1826
James, Stockport, cotton manufacturer. Sept. 1829
Langshaw, Mary, Chester, widow. March 1827
Large, Thomas, Bunbury, farmer. Sept. 1828
Latham, Elizabeth, Walgherton, Wybunbury, widow. Oct. 1828
James, Rainow, farmer. June 1830*
John, Macclesfield, watchmaker. April 1827
John, Nantwich, maltster & saddler. Dec. 1830
Richard, Northwich, whitesmith. A June 1830*
Rose, Macclesfield, widow. Sept. 1828
Latimer, Robert, Neston, draper. A Oct. 1827
Laverick, James, Chester, yeoman. A Nov. 1826
Lawton, Anne, Hollinworth, Mottram, widow. A May 1826
George, Lane, Stayley, clothier. April 1829
Samuel, Stockport, cotton spinner. Dec. 1828
Samuel, Bollington Cross, innkeeper. Jan. 1830
Thomas, Grappenhall, yeoman. March 1826
William, Marton, co. Chester, farmer. June 1826
William, Hough, Wilmslow, farmer. A Jan. 1830*
Lea, Ann, Siddington, widow. Nov. 1829*
Catherine, Chester, spinster. April 1830*
Isaac, Lower Withington, gardener. March 1829
John, Bickerton, gent. Feb., 1826; June 1826
Samuel, Bollington, Prestbury. July 1826
Leah, James, Macclesfield, yeoman. Dec 1826
Leather, John Bradshaw, Rostherne, yeoman. Sept. 1826
Stephen, Seacombe, labourer. Oct. 1830
Lee, Amy, Werneth, Stockport, singlewoman. Nov. 1827
George, Helsby, yeoman. April 1826
Richard, Chidlow, farmer. Oct. 1827
Sarah, Chester, widow. Jan. 1828
Leech, Bezaliel, Higher Bebington, gent. Dec. 1827

Leech, Richard, Over Peover, yeoman. Sept. 1827
Leet, Simeon, Chester, druggist. A July 1827
Legh, John, Northbury Booths, co. Chester, esq. Oct. 1826
 Peter, Lyme, esq. Sept. 1829 (1st grant 1792)
Leigh, Eleanor, Pulford, spinster. May 1828
 George, Middlewich, clerk. A July 1830
 James, Northen Etchells, farmer. Oct. 1828
 John, Godley, Mottram, hatter & farmer. Feb. 1828
 Randall, Arley Hall, Frodsham, gardener. May 1828
 Samuel, Hyde, Stockport, labourer. Feb. 1829
 Thomas, Brinnington, Stockport, farmer. Jan. 1829
 Thomas, Snelson, co. Chester. Jan. 1830
 William, Barnton, co. Chester, gent. April 1826
Lem, Mary, Chester, spinster. Oct. 1826
Lever, Jane, Dukinfield, widow. A March 1830
Leversage, Hannah, Bridgemere, widow. March 1827
Lewis, Edward, Trafford, labourer. A July 1827
 Edward, Hyde, labourer. Sept. 1828
 John, Helsby, yeoman. May. 1827
 John, Netherton, farmer. A Oct. 1827
 Margaret, Cuppin St., Chester, widow. Aug. 1829
Lewthwaite, Richard, Chester, anchorsmith. A Sept. 1830
Lidster, John the elder, Stockport, gent. A June 1826
 John, Stockport, check manufacturer. Feb. 1827
Lightbody, John, Mount House, Prenton, gent. Oct. 1830
Lightfoot, George, Congleton, yeoman. Aug. 1827
 Samuel, Broomhill, Barrow, yeoman. May. 1826
 Samuel, Hockenhull, farmer. May 1829 (2nd grant 1835)
Lindop, John, Chester, flour dealer. Aug., 1829
 Joseph, Chowley, co. Chester, farmer. July 1826
 Richard, Church Coppenhall, yeoman. June 1827
Linney, William, Chester, gent. A April 1830*
 William the elder, Chester, gent. A April 1830
Litherland, Mary, Tranmere, widow. May 1829
Litler, Thomas, Castle Northwich, labourer. A Jan. 1826
 Thomas, Castle, co. Chester. Sept. 1826
Little, Robert, Hoose, farmer. June 1828
Littlemore, James, Kingsley, Frodsham, tailor. July 1828
Livesley, Samuel, Castle Northwich, yeoman. March 1828
 Samuel, Over. March 1830*
Lloyd, Ann wife of John Lloyd, Aston, Nantwich, cheese factor. A March 1829
 Caroline Margaret, Chester, spinster. A May 1827
 Elizabeth, Thelwall. A March 1827
 Lucy, Crabwall, Chester, spinster. Sept. 1830
 Mary, Latchford. A July 1830
 Samuel, Chester, brewer. May 1829
Lockett, John, Congleton, attorney. Jan. 1827; Dec. 1827
 John, Wistaston, farmer. A July 1828
Lomas, Edward, Harropfold, Rainow, gent. Dec. 1826
 Edward, Waterhouse, Bollington, gent. Aug. 1829
 John, Stockport, tailor. A April 1826 (1st grant 1825)
 John, Buglawton, farmer. Nov. 1829
Longson, John, Stockport, shopkeeper. Aug. 1826

Longstaff, Edith, Cranage, Holmes Chapel, publican. A Jan. 1828*
Loundes, John, Congleton, baker & shopkeeper. Feb. 1829
Lounds, James, Somerford Booths, tanner. A Sept. 1829
Thomas, Eaton, Astbury. A Feb. 1829
Lovatt, Mary, Witton, widow. Oct. 1828
Low, Richard, Congleton, druggist. April 1828
Lowe, Charles, Moorland, Brereton-cum-Smethwick, farmer. Jan. 1830
James, Macclesfield, grocer. A Aug. 1829
Joshua, Wincham, yeoman. A May 1827
Peter, Lower Withington, yeoman. March 1827
Sarah, Macclesfield, widow. Feb. 1826
Thomas, Mosshouse, Church Lawton, yeoman. May 1826
Lowndes, Catherine, Peover, widow. A & Tuon Sept. 1827
Jacob, Mobberley, publican. A Aug. 1828
Matthew, Congleton. A Aug. 1827
Lowton, Thomas, Lansdown Place, Brunswick Square, Middlesex. esq. Oct. 1830
Lucas, John, Astbury, husbandman. A April 1830*
Samuel, Timperley, blacksmith. Aug. 1828
Luke, Charles, Oakmere, Delamere, farmer. A Dec. 1827
Lumb, John, Crowden Brook, Mottram in Longdendale, cotton spinner. Jan. 1828
Lunt, Phebey, Chorley, widow. Feb. 1828
Lupton, George, Altrincham, yeoman. May 1829
Lyon, Thomas, Upton, cordwainer. March 1829
Lyons, Mary, Hargreave, Tarvin, widow. A Jan. 1827
William, Hargreave, Tarvin, yeoman. Jan. 1827
Lythgoe, Peter, Latchford, farmer. Feb. 1829

MACQUEEN, Somerville, Nether Knutsford, esq. A May 1827; Oct. 1827
Maddock, John, Hatton, co. Chester. March 1829
Sarah, Witton, spinster. Nov. 1828
Thomas, Barton, co. Chester, labourer. Oct. 1828*
Maddox, Elizabeth, Over Poole, spinster. A April 1828
Mainwaring, James, Brombrow, esq. May 1827
John, Chester, gent. July 1828
Samuel, Tarporley, surgeon. May 1827
Sarah Susannah, Chester, widow. April 1830
Major, John, Cholmondeston, farmer. A April 1830
Malam, Thomas, Weston farmer. June 1830
Malbon, William, Dane Bank, Congleton, esq. June 1827
Malt, Elizabeth, Hatton, Wharton, widow. April 1829
Manifold, Elizabeth, Kingsley, widow. April 1826
Manley, James, Anderton, Great Budworth, carpenter. A Dec. 1827
James, Anderton, yeoman. Dec. 1828
Mary, Eaton, Tarporley, spinster. A May 1830 (2nd grant 1838)
March, Elizabeth, Chester, spinster. Feb. 1827
Marshall, Robert, Bramhall, yeoman. May 1830
Marsland, David, Handforth-cum-Bosden, yeoman. May 1827
Martha, Sale, widow. Dec. 1827*
Peter, Wood Bank, Bredbury, esq. Feb. 1830
Robert, Baguley, yeoman. Sept. 1829
Martin, Joseph, Altrincham, shoemaker. May 1826
Thomas, Marton, co. Chester, yeoman. Sept. 1827
Mason, James, Stockport, saddler. A Dec. 1828

Mason, John, High Lane, Marple, publican. A April 1828; Jan. & April 1830
John, Highlane, Marple, innkeeper. A Sept. 1830
Michael, Latchford, cotton spinner. Dec. 1828
Samuel, Chester, gent. June 1829
Sarah, Roe Park, Astbury, spinster. A Nov. 1827
William, Shaw Heath, Stockport, weaver. Jan. 1827
Massey, Catharine, Chester, spinster. March 1827
Edmund, Mottram St. Andrew, tanner. Sept. 1829
Farrer, Chester, spinster. Aug. 1830
Hannah, Lower Tabley, widow. Oct. 1826
Isaac, Nether Alderley, yeoman. Nov. 1827*
John, Pownall Fee, Wilmslow, shoemaker. A Jan. 1828
John, Etchells, weaver. A Aug. 1828
Margaret, Stockport, widow. Oct. 1826
Martha, Dutton, co. Chester. March 1830
Martha Maria, Chester, spinster. March 1826
Peter, Little Leigh, husbandman. Feb. 1826
Sarah, Broomhall, widow. A June., 1828
William, Chester, druggist & alderman. Nov. 1827
Massie, Robert, Mottram St. Andrew, yeoman. April 1826
Thomas, The Lodge, Nantwich, gent. A March 1829
Mather, Ellen, Latchford, spinster. Feb. 1830*
Samuel, Pointon, Stockport, shopkeeper. July 1828
Sarah, Mottram St. Andrew, widow. A Dec. 1827
William, Latchford, Grappenhall, auctioneer. A March 1826
Mathers, Richard, Hartford, gent. Feb. 1830
Mathews, Mary, Chester, spinster. May 1830
Maydew, Ralph, Sutton, co. Chester. Jan. 1829
Mead, Maria Elizabeth, Chester, widow. May 1828
Meanley, George, Chester, gent. Oct. 1829
Mee, Joseph, Cholmondeston, Acton, farmer. A Jan. 1827
Meek, Ephraim, Moss End, Smallwood, co. Chester, yeoman. Aug. 1827
Mellor, James, Rainow, yeoman. March 1829
John, Micklehurst, Mottram, clothier. A Feb. 1826
John, Chester, plumber. Aug. 1827
John, Sandbach, maltster & retailer of wines & spirits. A Nov. 1828
John, Thurstaston, farmer. March 1830
Joseph, Bickley, Malpas, miller. June 1827
Joseph, High Legh, farmer. May 1829
Thomas, Odd Rode, carpenter. Sept. 1828
Thomas Shaw, Chester, plumber. A Oct. 1829
Merritt, Charles, Cheadle Bulkeley, shuttlemaker. A Jan. 1829
Metcalf, John, Macclesfield, yeoman. June 1826
Miller, Thomas, Farndon. Nov. 1828
Millington, Joseph, Moore, co. Chester, labourer. May 1827
Millner, Richard, Newton, Frodsham, gent. Oct. 1827
Mills, John, High Leigh, yeoman. A Nov. 1828
Mary, Altrincham, widow. A Feb. 1829
Milne, James, Staley, Mottram-in-Longdendale, farmer. A May. 1830
Thomas, Boyerfold, Stayley, yeoman. Sept. 1829 (2nd grant 1832)
Milner, Sarah, Acton, Waverham, widow. Nov. 1830*
Thomas, Moore, co. Chester, farmer. May 1827
Minshall, James, Wharton, butcher. A April 1828

Moile, Richard, Hampton Hall, co. Chester, farmer. A July 1830
Thomas, Liverpool, last of Holt Hill, pawn broker. May 1830
Molineux, Rev. William, Abbots Grange, Chester, clerk. A Nov. 1830
Mollard, Joseph, Adlington, farmer. A June 1828
Monk, Ann, Chester, spinster. A March 1828
Esther, Parkgate, Neston. A March 1829
Moore, Hannah, Hale, co. Chester. May 1826
John, Sale, gent. A Oct. 1826
John, Old Beachin, co. Chester, farmer. Aug. 1830
Mary, Stockport, widow. A April 1827
Thomas, Blackenhall, Wybunbury, farmer. A Feb. 1828
Moores, Alice, Budworth, widow. March 1826
Joseph, Stockport, tailor. A Jan. 1827
Moorhouse, John, Hay, Tintwistle, Mottram, yeoman. July 1826
Moors, Peter, Little Leigh, labourer. A Sept. 1827
Moreton, Mary, Stretton. A Jan. 1830
Morrey, Mary, Woodley, Bredbury. A Oct. 1830
Moseley, Robert, Betchton, farmer, July 1826
Moss, Alice, Goit Hall, Stockport, widow. Sept. 1826
George Johnson, Macclesfield, button & silk manufacturer. Aug. 1829
James, Longlands, Matley, Mottram, farmer. A Dec. 1826 (2nd grant 1834)
Mossford, John, Tiverton, Bunbury. March 1827*
Moston, Josiah, Monks Coppenhall, labourer. Nov. 1826
Mottershead, Elizabeth, Stockport, widow. March 1829
John, Little Peover, farmer. Aug. 1826
Sarah, Etchells, Monton, widow. March 1830
Mottram, Joseph, Wilmslow, yeoman. Jan. 1830
Ralph, Burwardsley, Bumbury, labourer. A Feb. 1829*
Mountfield, Ralph, Norley, yeoman. Oct. 1828
Mousley, James, Rushton, Tarporley, farmer. June 1830
Mulliner, James, Shocklach, formerly Loppinton, co. Salop. gent. Will & Tuon May
Mary, Audlem, widow. May 1827
Murray, James, Stockport, shopkeeper. Feb. 1829

NALL, Leah, Dukinfield, spinster. Oct. 1826
Naylor, Robert, Booth Smithy, Little Budworth, blacksmith. A Sept. 1827
Sarah, Little Budworth, widow. June 1830
Neesham, James, Stockport, farmer. Dec. 1826
Neild, John, Bowden, corn dealer. Aug. 1826
Newall, John, Altrincham. A Feb. 1826
John, Over, waterman. April 1828
Richard, Mobberley. Jan. 1830
Newbold, Francis, Macclesfield, esq. A Sept. 1828
Newell, John Porter, Chester, gent. Jan. 1827
Newton, Elizabeth, Macclesfield, widow. Feb. 1828
Rev. James, Upper Tranmere, clerk. Feb. 1830
John, Denfield Hall, Rosthern, farmer. Jan. 1826
John, High Leigh, farmer. A Dec. 1828
John, Woodhead, Mottram-in-Longdendale, farmer. A Oct. 1829
Peter, Nether Knutsford, yeoman. Dec. 1828
Samuel, Tilston Fernal, Bunbury, gent. March 1827
Nicholson, Ellen, Stockport, widow. July. 1826
John, Macclesfield, gent. Nov. 1830

Nicklin, Mary, Twemlow, spinster. Aug. 1828
Nickson, John, Audlem, gent. Jan. 1827
Nield, Emanuel, Cuddington, yeoman. June 1830*
James, Back Lane, Macclesfield. June 1830
Joseph, Christleton, blacksmith. Jan. 1828
Matthew, Macclesfield, labourer. A March 1828 (2nd grant 1846)
Richard, Rudheath, yeoman. A Aug. 1828
William, Brook St., Chester, yeoman. Dec. 1829*
Nixon, Martha, Chester, widow. Feb. 1829 (2nd grant 1838)
William, Threapwood. Feb. 1829
William, Rainow, yeoman. April 1830
Norbury, Betty, Alderley, widow. March 1829 (2nd grant 1843)
Thomas, Nether Alderley, yeoman. Sept. 1826
Norcob, William, Peckforton, shopkeeper. July 1829
Norman, Thomas, Latchford. April 1828

OAKES, Jane., otherwise Jenny, Northenden, widow. Feb. 1829
Ralph, Crewe, Barthomley, farmer. A March 1826
William, Burton, farmer. Oct. 1826.
Oberry, John, Birkenhead, master mariner. July 1827
Ockleston, Esther, Whitley, Budworth, widow. A March 1826; Oct. 1827
Thomas, Bollen Hall, Wilmslow, yeoman. Jan. 1827
Ogden, Phoebe, Knutsford, spinster. Nov. 1829 (2nd grant 1846)
Thomas, Mottram-in-Longdendale, cotton spinner. A May 1829
Okell, Alice, Lymm. A April 1830*
James, Wincham, Great Budworth, farmer. Sept. 1830*
Samuel Harper, Grappenhall, an infant. A Oct. 1829; April 1830*
Thomas, Barrow, gent. Oct. 1828
William, Dutton Hall, farmer. Nov. 1828
William, Leftwich, merchant. A March 1830*
Oldfield, John, Macclesfield, whitesmith. A July 1828
Oldham, Ann, Bollin Fee, Wilmslow, widow. Sept. 1828*
Charles, Stockport, publican. A Feb. 1827
Charles, Werneth, gent. Aug. 1828
Ralph, Stockport, postmaster. A Feb. 1828
Thomas, Titherington, yeoman. A March 1829
Thomas, Portwood, Stockport, moulder. A June 1829
Oliver, Richard, Macclesfield, silk manufacturer. Feb. 1826
Orford, John, Chester, saddler. A April 1829
Joseph, Frodsham, yeoman. May 1829
Orme, John, Knutsford, shoemaker. March 1827
Joseph, Stockport, postman. Aug. 1826
Peter, Hoo Green, Mere, innkeeper. A Nov. 1828
Ormson, Jane, Antrobus, spinster. Oct. 1827
Mary, Higher Runcorn, spinster. A July 1830
Orred, Daniel, Chester, esq. March 1828
Orton, Elizabeth, Tattenhall, widow. Jan. 1827
Oulton, Nancy, Newton, Middlewich, feme covert. A May. 1828
Richard, Crewe, farmer. A Aug. 1826 (1st grant 1779)
Richard, Acton, gent. Dec. 1827
Overton, Ann, Audlem, widow. July 1830
Owen, John, Carrington, yeoman. Aug. 1830
Philip, Macclesfield, silk weaver. Feb. 1829

Owen, Richard, Northenden, carter. A Sept. 1828
Thomas, Stockport, weaver. A Aug. 1829
Oxton, Eliza, Spittle, feme covert. A May 1828

PACE, Samuel, Willaston, farmer. Sept. 1828
Painter, Thomas, Bickerton, yeoman. Jan. 1830
Palin, Stephen, Chester, gent. A March 1830
Palphreyman, Stephen, Call Green, Stockport, labourer. A Aug. 1827
Panton, Charles, Chester, gent. Sept. 1826 (1st grant 1800)
Parbert, Robert, Wincham, gentleman's servant. A July 1826
Parbot, Charles, Bradley, Malpas, yeoman. June 1830
Parkinson, Henry, Chester, wheelwright. Dec. 1826
Parr, Clara, wife of Thomas Parr, Appleton, esq. A Oct. 1827*
John, Runcorn, farmer. A June 1827
Peter, Neston, carrier. July 1826 (1st grant 1824)
Susannah, Neston, widow. A July 1826
Parratt, Sarah, Nantwich, spinster. Oct. 1829
Parrey, John, Norbury, farmer. Sept. 1829
Parry, Joseph, Shaftsbury co. Dorset, last of Chester, surgeon and apothecary Feb. 1828
Joseph, Alpraham, labourer, Dec. 1830*
Rowland, Rowton, farmer. Jan. 1828
Sarah, Chester, widow. March 1830
Thomas, Great Boughton. July 1826*
Parson, Joseph, Rowton, Christleton, yeoman. March 1827
Parsonage, Elizabeth, Trafford Hall, servant and spinster. A Sept. 1827
Richard, Bickley, yeoman. A June 1827
Samuel, Bickley, Malpas, yeoman. A June 1827
Parsons, William, Frodsham, surgeon. A June 1828
Parton, Thomas junior, Chorlton, farmer. Jan. 1827
Pass, Elizabeth, Nantwich, widow. A Aug. 1827
James, Nantwich, cooper. July 1827
Pattison, Nathaniel Maxey, Congleton, silk merchant. May 1828
Paulden, Nancy, Offerton, widow. Aug. 1829
Pearce, George Massie, Mottram St. Andrew, wine merchant. A Sept. 1827
William, Nantwich, gent. March 1828
Pearson, Elizabeth, Macclesfield, widow. July 1830
George, Sinderland, yeoman. March 1829
John, Altrincham, plumber and glazier. April 1830
Joseph, Chester, druggist. A July 1830
Mary, Macclesfield, widow. May 1828
Thomas, Macclesfield, gent. A June 1829 (1st grant 1822)
Thomas, Hampton, Malpas, gent. July 1830
William, Altrincham, shoemaker. March 1830
Pedley, William, Bruen Stapleford, yeoman. May 1829
Peers, Ann, Chester, spinster. Dec. 1828
James, Chester, upholsterer. April 1826
Richard, Ashton-upon-Mersey, yeoman. March 1827*
William, Chester, silk dyer. A July 1826
Peirson, John, Castle Hill, Hale, farmer. A Aug. 1830
Pemberton, Mary, Toft, Knutsford, widow. A Jan. 1827
Pendleton, Thomas, Bidston, bachelor. A Dec. 1828
Penk, George, Witton, cordwainer. A Sept. 1828

Penk, George, Witton, rock getter. Nov. 1829*
Pennell, Ralph, Wistaston, gent. June 1828
Pennington, Peter, Lyme, yeoman. Nov. 1830
Peover, James, Crowton co. Chester, yeoman. Oct. 1830
Percival, George, Dunham Massey, gardener and labourer. July 1828*
Isaac, Stockport, whitesmith and ironmonger. Feb. 1828
John, Adlington. Oct. 1830*
Thomas, Bosley, gent. Nov. 1826
Perreau, Elizabeth, Chester, widow. April 1828
Perrey, Richard, Holt Hill, Bebington, gent. Dec. 1828
Perrin, James, Somerford Booths, farmer. June 1828
Martha, Hurlestone, spinster. A March 1830
Randle, Wistaston. March 1827
Perry, John, Frankby, West Kirby. Aug. 1827
Perryn, Dorothy, Trafford Hall, widow. A Feb. 1827
Phillips, Edward, Handbridge, yeoman. Oct. 1828 (1st grant 1823*)
Phipps, John, Aston, gardener. A March 1828
Pickering, Ellen, Hale, Bowden, widow. May 1826
Robert, Little Sutton, innkeeper. A June 1829
Pickford, Abiezer, Kirkby Clough, Kettleshulme, yeoman. June 1830
James, Stockport, publican. Feb. 1827 (2nd grant 1847)
Mary, Adlington, Prestbury. A Dec. 1830*
Pickstone, Jane, Stockport, widow. Aug. 1830
Pierson, Elizabeth, Castle Hill, Hale, spinster. March 1826
Martha, Goyts Moss, Taxal. A April 1826
Thomas, Castle Hill, Hale, road surveyor. Feb. 1829
Pigott, Philip, Foulk Stapleford, Tarvin, tailor. July 1828
Pike, Richard, Nantwich, cordwainer. A Jan. 1828
Pimlott, Thomas, Macclesfield, cotton spinner. Sept. 1828
Pinnington, William, Aldersey, victualler. Feb. 1826
Pixtone, Joseph, Ringway, farmer. Oct. 1828
Plant, Ann, Holme Chapel, feme covert. March 1828
James, Hurdsfield, shoemaker. A Sept. 1828
Jane, Bramall, widow. June 1827
Thomas the elder, Brereton, yeoman. Aug. 1828
Platt, James, Hulton, yeoman. March 1828
William, Plumbley, Nether Peover, yeoman. A July 1830
Plumbley, Peter, Allostock, yeoman. Sept. 1830; Dec. 1830 (3rd grant 1841)
Podmore, Jane, Nantwich, widow. May 1830
Pointon, Richard, Odd Rode, wheelwright. Aug. 1829
Pollitt, Thomas, Stockport, innkeeper. June 1826
Poole, Rev. John Halsted, Marbury, clerk. Dec. 1830
Porter, James, Alcumlow, Astbury, farmer. Feb. 1827
Pott, Joseph, Over Alderley, farmer. May 1827
Potter, James, Nether Knutsford, surgeon. Jan. 1828
Potts, Benjamin, Congleton, tailor. A Oct. 1827
William, Timperley, Bowden, farmer. A July 1830
Powell, Ann, Tarvin, widow. A March 1827
Ann, Prestbury, widow. April 1830
Elizabeth, Chester, widow. A and Tuon May 1826*
Martha, Butley, Prestbury. A May 1829
Pownall, John, Mile End, Stockport, draper. A Feb. 1826
John Hale, gent. Feb. 1829

Pownall, John, Over Alderley, victualler. June 1830
Peter, Adlington, Prestbury, yeoman. Feb. 1830
Thomas, Marple, yeoman. July 1829
Powys, Mary, Knutsford, spinster. June 1829
Pratchitt, John, Nantwich, esq. March 1826
Prescott, Thomas, Runcorn, butcher. Dec. 1830
Preston, Samuel, Minshull Vernon, labourer. A Dec. 1830
Price, Benjamin, Keelendre, Ellesmere, farmer. May 1827*
Elizabeth, Abbey Court, Chester, widow. Aug. 1830
John, Chester. Jan. 1828*
Joseph, West Kirby, schoolmaster. A Sept. 1828
Priestnall, Samuel, Edgbaston St., Birmingham, saddler and collar maker. A April 1829
Thomas, Stockport, silk manufacturer. July 1827
William, Butley, Prestbury, carpenter. A April 1829
Prince, Hugh, Chester, cordwainer. April 1828
Paul, Hyde, shopkeeper. A Oct. 1830
Prissick, James, Tiverton co. Chester, maltster. April 1830
Pritchard, Elizabeth, Trafford, servant. A March 1827
James, Chester, corn dealer. Feb. 1826
John Brackley, Great Boughton, gent. A June 1828
Rebecca, Great Boughton, widow. May 1828
Prossor, Elizabeth, Chester, spinster. Sept. 1829*
Proudlove, Mary, Brownlowe, Astbury, widow. Sept. 1830; Nov. 1830
Pursell, Richard, Wrenbury-cum-Frith, farmer. Dec. 1830
Pyatt, George, Macclesfield, silk dyer. A Nov. 1829

QUINCEY, Martha, Marple, Stockport, widow. A Jan. 1830

RADCLIFFE, William, Stayley, clothier. A June 1826*
Radford, John, Congleton. July 1827
Ralphs, Mary, Chester, widow. Feb. 1827
Ramscar, James, Stockport, yeoman. Sept. 1828
Ratcliffe, Thomas, Edgley co. Chester, yeoman. March 1826*
Rathbone, John Witton. May 1829
Ravald, Elizabeth, Altrincham, spinster. Sept. 1829
Ravenscroft, George, Bostock, yeoman. Jan. 1826
Peter, Bostock, farmer. Oct. 1827
Rawlins, William the elder, Oldfield, Dunham Massey, yeoman. Jan. 1830
Rawstom, Henry, Stockport, whitesmith. Aug. 1829
Reade, Charles, Wybunbury, gent. A March 1827; May 1827
Redfern, Joseph, Gee Cross, Werneth, shopkeeper. Sept. 1826
Renshaw, James, Sale, yeoman. June 1829
Nancy, Park Gate, formerly Liverpool, widow. A July 1829
Samuel, Altrincham, plumber and glazier. May 1828
Rhodes, John, Torkington, yeoman. May 1828
William, Torkington Hall, yeoman. Feb. 1830 (1st grant 1806)
Richards, Joseph, Chester, coachman. April 1826*
Richardson, Ann, Stockport, spinster. June 1829
John, Beeston, gent. Nov. 1828
Mary, Cheadle, spinster. A Jan. 1826*
Mary, Stockport, widow. Feb. 1826
Peter, Tattenhall, farmer. Dec. 1827*

Richardson, Samuel, Dunham-on-the-Hill, yeoman. Aug. 1829
Thomas, Dunham-on-the-Hill, gent. June 1828
Rider, John, Great Warford, yeoman. Dec. 1828
Samuel, Aston, Runcorn, farmer. Oct. 1829
William, Brindley, farmer. June 1826
Ridgway, Thomas, Duddon co. Chester, gent. Nov. 1827
Rigby, Betty, Moulton, widow. June 1826
Isaac, Hurdsfield, Prestbury, shopkeeper. A Oct. 1830
John, Acton Grange, yeoman. March 1827 (1st grant 1808)
Martha, Hurdsfield, widow. May 1827
Thomas, Overton, Malpas, farmer. A Nov. 1826
Riley, Thomas, Portwood, Stockport, shopkeeper. A March 1828
Roberts, Catherine, Spurstow, Bunbury, widow. Nov. 1827
Edward, Macclesfield, liquor merchant. July 1828
Elizabeth, Chester, spinster. A Oct. 1827*
Elizabeth, Agden, Malpas, farmer. A March 1828
John, Boughton, flour dealer. Jan. 1828*
John, Brinnington, Stockport, calico printer. A July 1830
Mary, Moreton. April 1828
Samuel, Hollingsworth, Mottram, yeoman. March 1827
Thomas, Crabb Hall co. Chester, esq. Sept. 1827
Thomas, Frodsham, glazier. May 1828
Robinson, James, Hillgate, Stockport, publican. A May 1828
Jane, Mobberley, widow. May 1828
Peter, Twemlow, farmer. Oct. 1826 (2nd grant 1836)
Sarah, Gawsworth, spinster. March 1826
William the elder, Carrington, labourer. March 1828*
William, Duddon, farmer. July 1829
Robson, Margaret, Sandbach, widow. March 1827
Rodenhurst, Benjamin, Nantwich, banker. Sept. 1829
Rogers, Edward, Chester, publican. Sept. 1828
Samuel, Hatton Heath, Saighton, yeoman. June 1826*
Rogerson, Peter, Northen Etchells, widower. Oct. 1828
Rolison, Joseph, Upton, Chester, farmer. A Dec. 1827
Rose, Elias, Hurdsfield, Prestbury, farmer. A Sept. 1830
Ross, William, Congleton, silk weaver. A Aug. 1827
Rothwell, Ellen, Lymm, widow. May 1826
Rowbottom, Joseph, Marple, yeoman. April 1827
Rowcroft, John Bramhall, yeoman. July 1829
Rowe, Elizabeth, Malpas, last of Ashton-under-Lyme, Staffs., spinster. Nov. 1827
William, Hoose Heath, Knutsford, farmer. A May 1827
Rowland, Dorothy, Shipgate St., Chester, widow. Nov. 1829
Rowson, Joseph, Huddersfield co. Chester, yeoman. March 1830 (2nd grant 1837)
Margaret, Hurdsfield, widow. Dec. 1830
Roylance, Drinkwater, Nether Alderley, smith. Oct. 1828*
Royle, Edmund, Stockport, labourer. Dec. 1828*
James, Ashton-upon-Mersey, farmer. A March 1830
Jane, Malpas, spinster. Sept. 1828
John, Sale, yeoman. Feb. 1827
John, Stockport, timber merchant. April 1829
Jonathan Hamnett, Nashville, U.S.A., last of Altrincham. Nov. 1826
Martha, Sale, spinster. Dec. 1827
Thomas, Ringway, Bowden, farmer. Oct. 1826

Royle, Thomas, Brownley Green, Northenden. Feb. 1827
William, Carrington, farmer. June 1826
Royles, Samuel, Utkington, Tarporley, labourer. Oct. 1826*
Ruscoe, Daniel, Aston, Wrenbury, yeoman. Nov. 1829
George, Audlem, cabinet maker. March 1827
Margaret, Churton, Farndon, widow. July 1830
Russell, William, Chester, hostler. A Nov. 1826*
Rylance, George, Newton, Mottram-in-Longdendale, coach proprietor. Aug. 1829
Thomas, Hyde Hall co. Chester. April 1827
Ryle, John, Bankhouse, Bredbury, hat manufacturer. A April 1829 (2nd grant 1832)
John, Macclesfield, yeoman. Dec. 1829
Joshua, Over, publican. A June 1829

SADLER, John, Morton Wood, Prees co. Salop, farmer. Nov. 1826
Salford, John, Stockport, timber merchant. Nov. 1826
Salmon, Ann, Nantwich, spinster. A Aug. 1826
Elizabeth, Chester, spinster. May 1826*
Frances, Nantwich, widow. March 1830
Joseph Whittingham, Nantwich. Oct. 1826
Pansia, Nantwich, gent. Sept. 1826
Richard Lownes, Sandbach, clerk. June 1828
Sarah, Chester, spinster. May 1826; May 1826*
Rev. William, Nantwich, clerk. A April 1828
Salt, Charles, Macclesfield, victualler. A Jan. 1827
Salter, Edward, St. Martins in the Fields, Chester, gent. April 1830
Sandbach, William, Burton, Tarvin, esq. March 1829; April 1829
Sanders, Nathaniel, Timperley, gent. July 1828
Sanderson, Thomas, Astbury, yeoman. July 1827
Sandford, Theodora, Bowden, spinster. Aug. 1827
Savage, Ann, Styall, Wilmslow, widow. A April 1830
Hannah, Frodsham, widow. Dec. 1827
John, Overton, Frodsham yeoman. Sept. 1827*
Thomas, Frodsham, yeoman. July 1830
Saxon, Daniel, Wood, Stayley, Mottram, yeoman. Oct. 1826
Schofield, Robert, Dog Lane End, Dukinfield, yeoman. April 1826
Samuel, Warks Moor House, Disley, cotton spinner. June 1830
Scott, George, Portwood, Brinnington, timber dealer. July 1826
Scragg, Richard, Wistaston, farmer. A Aug. 1829
Sculley, John, Chester, merchant. Jan. 1826
Sefton, Mary, Over, widow. A Nov. 1828
Shakeshaft, John, Rosthern, shopkeeper. Jan. 1826
Thomas, Lymm, chapman. June 1830
Shallcross, John, Shallcross co. Derby, esq. A Sept. 1829
Josiah, Weaverham. Dec. 1830 (1st grant 1766)
Sharp, Isaac, Latchford, dissenting minister. July 1827
Sharratt, Thomas, Broad Lane co. Chester, yeoman. May 1830
Shatwell, John, Macclesfield, grocer. Nov. 1830
Shaw, Alice, Micklehurst, Mottram, widow. Jan. 1830
Ann, Congleton, spinster. Oct. 1828
George, Styall Green, yeoman. July 1827
George, Wheelock House, Sandbach, ironfounder. Feb. 1829
James, Bosley, Prestbury, farmer. Oct. 1830

Shaw, John, Mottram-in-Longdendale, publican. A March 1826
Mary, Macclesfield, widow. Nov. 1826
Ralph, Iddenshall, St. Werburgh, yeoman. Nov. 1830
Thomas, Eaton, Tarporley, yeoman. Dec. 1827
Shawcross, James, Ashton-upon-Mersey, yeoman. Sept. 1829
Sheen, Catherine, Tarvin. A Feb. 1826*
James, Tarporley, publican. May 1826
Shelmerdine, James, Sale, tailor. May 1827
Shepherd, Elizabeth, Dukinfield, spinster. Sept. 1828
John, Macclesfield. May 1827
Shepley, Aaron, Mottram, tailor. A Aug. 1827
Harriet, *see* Wagstaff
Sarah, Dukinfield, widow. A Oct. 1828
Sherratt, Charles, Odd Rode, farmer. Jan. 1829
Smith, Congleton, gent. A Nov. 1830
Shewell, John, Holt Hill, Bebington. A Dec. 1827 (2nd grant 1843)
Shingler, James, Aston, Budworth, yeoman. May 1829
Shone, John, Chester, carpenter. Jan. 1830 (1st grant 1799)
Joseph, Lowcross, Tilston, farmer. Oct., 1827
Shore, Elizabeth, Cheadle, spinster. Sept. 1827
Shorto, Margaret, Chester, widow. Jan. 1829
Shrigley, Matthew, Macclesfield, bricklayer. April 1828
Shufflebotham, Daniel, Nantwich, linen draper. A Oct. 1829
Shufflebottom, William, Congleton Edge, dealer in earthenware. A June 1830
Shuttleworth, Sarah, Marston, widow. A Nov. 1829
William, Marston, widower. A Dec. 1829
William, Stockport, painter. Jan. 1830
Sibson, Martha, Sandbach, spinster. April 1826
Siddall, John, Stayley Wood, cotton rover. A March 1828
John, Sale, farmer. June 1828
Siddelley, James, Hillgate, Stockport, joiner. Nov. 1830*
Sidebottom, James, Hollingworth, Mottram, cotton spinner. July 1827
Thomas, Mill Brook, Mottram, cotton manufacturer. April 1827
William, Broadbottom, cotton spinner. Nov. 1826
Silvester, William, Bridgemere, wheelwright. A June 1829
Simister, Samuel, Bredbury, farmer. Dec. 1827
Sarah, Green Lane, Romiley, spinster. Sept. 1826
Simon, John, Congleton, bricklayer. A Sept. 1827 (2nd grant 1843)
Simpson, Betty, High Legh. May 1827
John, High Leigh, farmer. A Jan. 1826
John, Chester, bricklayer. Oct. 1828
John, Cheadle, yeoman. Sept. 1829
John, Tarporley, currier. Nov. 1829
Joseph, Broxton, gardener. July 1827
Matilda, Guilden Sutton, widow. Oct. 1829
Samuel, Bradley, Malpas, farmer. Nov. 1829
William, Shocklach Oviatt, labourer. July 1826
Sinker, Richard, Kelsall, publican. May 1826
Skelhorne, Ann, Ashley, Bowden, widow. A Dec. 1830
Zebulon, Ashley, tanner. Dec. 1830
Skerrett, Alfred, Nantwich. July 1827
Skilback, John, Congleton, joiner. A Sept. 1826
Skrymsher, Elizabeth, Shrewsbury co. Salop, widow. A May 1830

Slack, Fanny, wife of Samuel Slack, Stockport, hosier. Dec. 1830
John, Ingersley, Prestbury, gent. A March 1830
Samuel, Stockport, hosier. March 1829
Thomas, Sutton, cordwainer. July 1828
Slater, John the elder, Nether Knutsford, yeoman. Dec. 1830
Mary, Old Withington, servant. Dec. 1830
Smallwood, Joshua, Marton, farmer. March 1830
Thomas, Macclesfield, dyer. June 1829
Smethurst, Ellen, Cheadle, spinster. A Nov. 1826
Smith, George, Dunham Massey, groom to the Earl of Stamford. Sept. 1828
Henry, Neston, tailor. A Aug. 1826 (2nd grant 1845)
Rev. John, Nantwich. June 1827
John, Brookhead, Cheadle, farmer. A April 1829
John, Runcorn, gent. A Sept. 1830*
Jonathan, Newton, Mottram, publican. May 1827
Mary, Parkgate. Sept. 1828
Nathan, Hattersley, weaver. Oct. 1829.
Samuel, Hoose, yeoman. June 1826*
Samuel, Eastham Ferry, innkeeper. April 1828
Samuel, Seacombe, yeoman. April 1828
Rev. Thomas, Tarvin, clerk. A May 1828
Thomas, Norbury, Stockport, weaver. A March 1829
Snape, Aaron, Bramhall, Stockport, ironmonger. A Feb. 1826
Moses, Bollington, Prestbury, publican. March 1830
Snelson, George, Nether Peover, farmer. A Dec. 1827
Thomas, Black Road, Macclesfield, carter. A May 1829 (2nd grant 1851)
Sothern, William, Weaverham, coal merchant. A Feb. 1830
Sowerby, James William, Mount Pleasant, Hampstead, esq. Aug. 1828
Sparkes, Margaret, Chester, widow. Nov. 1826
Sparks, Benjamin, Great Boughton, gardener. Aug. 1829
Sparrow, Robert, Norbury, gent. A Jan. 1826
Spearman, Martha, Nantwich, widow. Nov. 1828
Speed, Hugh John, Chester, tinplate worker. A April 1826
Spencer, Thomas, Acton, husbandman. May 1830
Spilsbury, George, Sutton, silkman. July 1826
Spurstow, George, Chester, apothecary. Dec. 1828)
George, Chester, linen draper. Dec. 1828)
These [*two*] wills were deposited in the office for safe custody. See Jan. [*no year*]
Stafford, Daniel, Works Moor, Disley, yeoman. Feb. 1827
Stanley, Joseph, Lower Withington, farmer. Jan. 1830
Mary, Liscard, widow. Sept. 1828
Stanton, Elizabeth, Greenfield, Thelwell, spinster. Aug. 1829
Stanway, Ralph, Rudheath, Davenham, yeoman. April 1827
William, Witton, carpenter. March 1828
Starkey, Henry, Macclesfield. Feb. 1829*
James, Macclesfield, farmer. A Nov. 1829
James, Witton-cum-Twambrooks, flatman. March 1830
Thomas, Aston co. Chester, yeoman. April 1830 (2nd grant 1835)
Staton, Sarah, Sandbach. Feb. 1829
Stavert, John, Brownell, Seacombe, gent. A March 1829 (2nd grant 1847)
Steele, John, Hough co. Chester, yeoman. June 1827
John, Nether Tabley, farmer. Jan. 1829; July 1829

Stelfox, Betty, Reddish, widow. A July 1829
Thomas, Witton, blacksmith. Sept. 1827
Stonehewer, Samuel, Macclesfield, shopkeeper. April 1829 (2nd grant 1837)
Stoneley, George, Macclesfield, publican. Oct. 1828
Stones, Frances, Stockport, widow. May 1829
Joseph, Great Budworth, yeoman. June 1828
Street, Joseph, Macclesfield, button maker. June 1828 (1st grant 1784)
Mary, Baguley. A Dec. 1828*
Stringer, John, Bramhall and Etchells, yeoman. Aug. 1828
Thomas, Macclesfield, timber merchant. Jan. 1829
Stubbs, Charles, Congleton, silk weaver. July 1829
James, Steam Mill St., formerly Steven St., Chester, miller. A Jan. 1830
Martha, Congleton, widow. A Feb. 1829
William the elder, Sproston Hall co.Chester, yeoman. Feb. 1826
Sudlow, John, Stockport, shopkeeper. June 1827
Sumner, Joseph, Preston-on-the-Hill, farmer. Jan. 1829
Richard, Wharton. A June 1828
Sunderland, Elizabeth, Occleston, Middlewich, spinster. A Jan. 1830
Sutton, James, Edgeley, shopkeeper. A Nov. 1826
Joseph, Kinderton Hall, farmer. Aug. 1826
William, Liscard, gent. Sept. 1828
Swain, Mary, Lostock Gralam, widow. June 1827
William, Sandbach, farmer. Sept. 1830
Swale, Christopher, Wilmslow, gent. A April 1828
Swan, Edward, Wilmslow, yeoman. Aug. 1829
Swanwick, Elizabeth, Macclesfield, gentlewoman. June 1828
Swetenham, Roger Comberbach, Somerford Booth. March 1826
Swettenham, John, Sandbach, grocer. March 1829
Swindell, John, Stockport, gent. May 1829
Swindells, Edward, Goose Lane, Macclesfield. July 1829
Elizabeth, Whaley Bridge, Taxall. A July 1830
Humphrey, Bosley co. Chester, farmer. Feb. 1830
John, Hurdsfield, silkman. A Feb. 1827
John, Woodford, farmer. Aug. 1828
Thomas, Romiley, shopkeeper. March 1829
Thomas, Elibank, Stockport, farmer. A July 1830
Swindles, William, Macclesfield, plaisterer. April 1828
Syddall, Esther, Altrincham, widow. A Dec. 1827
Sykes, Mary, Tintwistle. A Aug. 1826
Symcock, John, Nantwich, whitesmith. March 1827
Symms, John, Castle Northwich, yeoman. March 1827
Symons, William, Kelsall, innkeeper. July 1828

TAPLEY, Margaret, Chester, widow. June 1826
Tavo, Edward, Chester, mathematical instrument maker. June 1827
Taylor, Betty, Acton Grange, widow. June 1826
George, Nantwich, gent. Feb. 1826
George, Plumley, yeoman. March 1828
James, Over Knutsford, yeoman. July 1827 (2nd grant 1833)
James, Gee Cross, shuttlemaker. Feb. 1828
John, Stockport, cordwainer. April 1829
John, Handbridge, miller and widower. A May 1829
John, Betchton, yeoman. Jan. 1830

Taylor, Joseph, Dukinfield, weaver. A Jan. 1828*
Mary, Wrenbury, widow. Oct. 1826
Peter, Etchells, yeoman. Nov. 1828
Samuel, Wood Shutes, Audley, yeoman. Aug. 1826*
Sarah, Nantwich, widow. A Feb. 1827
Sarah, Mottram-in-Longdendale, widow. A Nov. 1830
Thomas, Worth, Prestbury, labourer. A June 1827
Thomas, Warburton, yeoman. Feb. 1828
William, Sproston, farmer. May 1826
Tew, Richard, Hatherton, Wybunbury, carpenter. Sept. 1826
Thelwall, William, Church Shocklach, farmer. A Aug. 1829
Thomas, Edward, Chester, innkeeper. June 1827
Joseph the elder, Acton, yeoman. Dec. 1830
Thomas, Austerson, Acton, gent. Nov. 1828
William, Hunsterson, Wybunbury, labourer. Oct. 1830
Thomason, Isaac, Timperley, Bowden, farmer. A July 1826
John, Over Peover, farmer. Nov. 1827
Thompson, James Henry, Holt Hill, Wirral, gent. A March 1829
Samuel, Mobberley, farmer. A Dec., 1828 (2nd grant 1842)
William, Leftwich, labourer. June 1830
Thorley, Jonathan, Bradwall, farmer. Jan. 1829
Thorneley, James, Stockport, last of Disley, gent. Jan. 1826
Thornicroft, Amy, Gawsworth. A Jan. 1828*
Matthew, Millend, Gawsworth, farmer. A March 1826
Thorniley, William, Bredbury Green, yeoman. Oct. 1826
Thornley, Jonathan, Bosley, farmer. March 1828
Thorp, William, Bramhall, farmer. March 1829
Thursfield, Thomas, Buerton, co. Chester, yeoman. June 1830
Tickle, Richard, Over Peover, yeoman. Sept. 1829
Tillard, James, Street End, Petham, co. Kent, esq. Jan. 1829
Timmis, James, Stapeley, Wybunbury, carpenter. A Dec. 1828
John, Wybunbury, tradesman & surveyor. May 1827
John, Barthomley, yeoman. June 1827
Timperley, John, Hale, tailor. Feb. 1830
Nathaniel, Hall, Bowden, farmer. A July 1830
Thomas, Hale, tailor. March 1827
Tinker, George, Werneth, Stockport, weaver. Nov. 1826
Tipping, Ann, Cross St., Chester, widow. Aug. 1827*
John, Cross St., Chester, innkeeper. Aug. 1826
Todd, Jane, Ince, widow. Sept. 1828
Tollett, James, Sandbach, yeoman. Oct. 1826
Tomkies, John, Over, timber merchant. Nov. 1828
Tomkinson, Ann, Reaseheath, co. Chester, widow. Oct. 1826
Tomlinson, Dorothy, Parkgate, widow. Jan. 1830
Esther, Chester and Parkgate, spinster. Nov. 1828
James, Malpas, gardener. A June 1829
Mary, Nantwich, spinster. Jan. 1827
Thomas, Realshaw, Warton, co. Chester, gent. Jan. 1826
William the younger, Nantwich, gent. July 1826
William, Royal Hotel, Chester, innkeeper. Oct. 1830
Tonna, Elizabeth, Flookersbrook, widow. June 1826*
Tooel, otherwise Towele, Terence, Seller St., Chester, yeoman. Nov. 1829
Topham, Robert the elder, Handbridge, Chester, skinner. Nov. 1830

Torkington, Joseph, Wilmslow, labourer. April 1830
Towers, John, Little Sutton, tailor. A June 1829
Townend, Elizabeth, Edgeley, Cheadle, spinster. Nov. 1830
Townsend, Frances Sarah, Chester, spinster. Feb. 1828
Gerrard, Chester, gent. Oct. 1826 (1st grant 1790)
Trafford, Thomas, Macclesfield, silkman. April 1830
Traves, Mary, Mottram-in-Longdendale, wife of John Traves. A Oct. 1829
Travis, Eleanor, Chester, widow. March 1829
Trelfa, Elizabeth, Bridge End House, Davenham, widow. Aug. 1827
Trevor, Rev. Thomas, vicar of Eastham, clerk. June 1828
Trimble, John, Halton, clerk. A March 1828
Tunnicliff, Obadiah, Macclesfield. Dec. 1829 (1st grant 1799)
Tunstall, James, Nantwich, gent. Oct. 1828
Turner, Charles, Stockport, gent. A Nov. 1827
Rev. James, Mottram, clerk. M.A. Dec. 1826
John, Chester, architect. A Feb. 1827
John, Somerford, yeoman. A April 1827
John, Astbury, yeoman. May 1827
John, Prestbury, tailor and shopkeeper. June., 1827
Kitty, Godley, widow. Nov. 1828
Reginald, Butley, farmer. June 1827
Sarah, Saltersford, Rainow. May 1829
Thomas, Rainow Low, yeoman. June 1828
Thomas, Godley, gent. A & Tuon July 1828 (2nd grant 1838)
Thomas the elder, Godley, gent. March 1829
Thomas the elder, Bollington, yeoman. Dec. 1829
Thomas, Gerards, Stockport. Dec. 1830
Turton, Martha, Huntington, co. Chester, widow. A Dec. 1827
Tushingham, Ralph, Hatton Heath, Waverton. Nov. 1826*
Twamlow, John, Congleton, cabinet maker. Sept. 1830
Robert, Altrincham, gent. July 1827
Twemlow, Thomas, Liscard, gent. A May 1826 (2nd grant 1883)
Tylston, Elizabeth, Chester, widow. Oct. 1828 (1st grant 1767)
Tyrer, William, Chester, gent. Sept. 1828
Tyson, Peter, Spittle, co. Chester, farmer. Sept. 1826

VAUDREY, Hannah wife of John Vaudrey, Buglawton, gent. April 1830
Vawdrey, Henry, Hurdsfield, silk throwster. A May 1828
John, Buglawton, gent. March 1828
Venables, Mary, Chester, spinster. June 1829
Vernon, Elizabeth, Chester. Sept. 1827
Hannah, Chester, widow. Sept. 1827
Jane, Chester, spinster. A Aug. 1827
John, Twemlow, Goostrey, farmer. May 1829 (2nd grant 1845)
Vickers, James, Tilston Fearnal, Bunbury. Aug. 1830*
John, Great Budworth, surgeon & apothecary. Feb. 1827

WAGG, John, Sandbach, hatter. Oct. 1826
Wagstaff, nee Shepley, Harriet, Mottram, feme covert. A June 1827
John, Stockport, confectioner. Oct. 1830
Wagstaffe, Robert, Mottram-in-Longdendale, hatter. Sept. 1829
Wainwright, John, Allostock, yeoman. April 1829
Joseph, Werneth, Stockport, spinner. A Sept. 1828

Walker, Humphrey, Tattenhall, farmer. Oct. 1828
John, Utkinton, Tarporley, farmer. Sept. 1830
Mary, Little Sutton, widow. Jan. 1828
Samuel, Stockport innkeeper. April 1829
Sarah, Bowden, widow. Jan. 1828
Sarah Ann, Cheadle, spinster. Oct. 1827
William, Oak Farm, Sandbach, farmer. Oct. 1829
Walkley, Daniel, Lower Withington, farmer. March 1830
Walley, James, Cooksbank, Audlem, yeoman. July 1828
Rebecca, Tarporley, widow. Sept. 1829
Samuel, Brescie Green, Tiverton, farmer. Sept. 1827
Thomas, Harthill. July 1829
William, Chester, esq. A Aug. 1827
Wallworth, Esther, Sandbach, spinster. March 1829
Walthall, Rev. Peter, rector of Wistaston, clerk. Feb. 1827
Walton, John, Carrington, yeoman. July 1827*
Samuel, Barthomley, labourer. A April 1830
William, Carrington, yeoman. Nov. 1830 (2nd grant 1850)
Warburton, Alice, Wilmslow, spinster. July 1829
Ann, Nether Knutsford, widow. March 1829 (2nd grant 1845)
John, Etchells, yeoman. July 1826
Mark, Hale, labourer & bachelor. A Aug. 1829
Peter, Rush Green, Lymm. Feb. 1829
Samuel, Elton, co. Chester, yeoman. Jan. 1826
Thomas, Heatley Heath, Lymm. Feb. 1826
William, Warburton, victualler & widower. A July 1830
Ward, James, Over Alderley, last of Bolshaw Outwood, Stockport Etchells, yeoman. April 1827
Robert, Horridge End, Hope, co. Derby, yeoman. Sept. 1829
Rev. Thomas, Neston, clerk. Sept. 1827
Wareham, Richard, Smallwood, yeoman. May 1827
Warmisham, William, Altrincham, joiner. A July 1827
Warner, Susannah, Uttoxeter, Staffs, widow. June 1828
Warrington, John, Gawsworth, bread baker. May 1828
Washington, John, Buglawton, labourer. Aug. 1830*
Joseph, Upton, yeoman. Sept. 1826*
Watson, George, Ashton-upon-Mersey, wheelwright. June 1827
George, Wirswall, co. Chester, gent. July 1830*
Job, the Lea, Aldford, gent. April 1826 (1st grant 1788)
Rachel, Sale, spinster. May 1827
William, Belvidier, Wayswall, gent. July 1830*
Worthington Thomas, Chester, mariner. A June 1827
Watts, John, Parkgate, gent. A Feb. 1828
Wearing, Joseph, Brombrough, yeoman. Oct. 1827
Weaver, Charles, Christleton, wheelwright. Oct. 1829*
Christian, Dodington, widow. April 1827
Elizabeth Ann, Tarporley, spinster. July 1826*
Thomas, Handbridge, gardener. June 1829
William, Malpas, gent. April 1827
Webb, Elizabeth, Nantwich, spinster. A Nov. 1829
Webster, Alice, Thornton-in-the-Moors, widow. March 1827
Ann, Chester, formerly Tattenhall, widow. A March 1826
Isabella, Frodsham, widow. Feb. 1828

Webster, John, Little Leigh, yeoman, Sept. 1829
Joseph, Meols, yeoman. July 1828
Welch, Charles, Nantwich, timber merchant. June 1830
George, Parkgate, shopkeeper. June 1828
Welsby, William, Acton, gent. Nov. 1830
Westray, Jonathan, Stockport, grocer. A Aug. 1829
Wevar, John, Caldercott, farmer. Aug. 1828
Whaley, Samuel, Capenhurst, yeoman. Feb. 1828
Wharmby, John, Etchells, Stockport, farmer. Nov. 1829
Wharton, Elizabeth, Horton, co. Chester. A March 1830
Wheatley, Jarvis, Cheadle, officer of Excise. Dec. 1826 (2nd grant 1858)
Wheeldon, Matthew, Sutton, traveller. May 1828
Whiston, Polly, Sutton, Prestbury, spinster. A Dec. 1827
Whitaker, Robert, Disley, farmer. Feb. 1830
Whitby, Samuel, Poulton-cum-Seacombe, servant. Dec. 1828
White, Ann, Sale, widow. A Nov. 1826
John, Bickerton, farmer. July 1827
Thomas, Nantwich, innkeeper. May 1827
William, Birkenhead, master mariner. May., 1826
Whitehead, Harriet, Great Neston. Nov. 1828
John, Altrincham, gent. Sept. 1828
Robert, Neston, gent. Nov. 1828
Whitelegg, John, Handforth-cum-Bosden, weaver. July 1828
John, Ashley, co. Chester, yeoman. Dec. 1830
Samuel, Stockport, yeoman. May 1827
Sarah, Stretton, spinster. Oct. 1827
Whitfield, Thomas, Thelwall, labourer. A Nov. 1829
Whitley, William, Dutton, yeoman. A Sept. 1829 (2nd grant 1862)
Whitney, Matthew Worthington, Macclesfield, yeoman. April 1827 (2nd grant 1841)
Whittaker, Penelope, Weston, Wybunbury. Sept. 1827
Thomas, Gawsworth, baker. June 1827
Whittakers, James, Church Copenhall, farmer. Dec. 1826
Whittell, Benjamin, Chester, chemist. A Sept. 1826
Whitter, Elizabeth, Wilmslow, spinster. July 1827
Whittingham, John, Wybunbury, yeoman. April 1827
John, Batherton, miller. June 1828
Whittle, Betty, Edward St., Stockport, widow. Feb. 1830
Whitworth, Francis, Stayley, Nottram-in-Longdendale, farmer. A Oct. 1830 (2nd grant 1855)
Jacob, Hattersall, Mottram. A May 1826
Wickstead formerly Charnley, Ellen, Southwark, Surrey, mercer. A Nov. 1827
Widders, Ann, High Leigh, spinster. Nov. 1829
Wightman, Jemima, Chester, spinster. A Dec. 1826
Wild, Henry, Great Stockport Moor, stonemason. A Nov. 1830
Thomas, Bredbury, Stockport, stonemason & bricklayer. Nov. 1830
Wilde, Peter, Hyde, Stockport, weaver. Aug. 1826
Wilding, John, Sandbach, publican. July 1826
Wilkinson, Ellen, Kinderton. July 1830
Joseph, Chester, cabinet maker. Jan. 1827
Margaret, Tarvin, widow. A June 1827
Thomas, Nether Knutsford, ironmonger. Oct. 1830
Willett, John, Nantwich, aleseller. June 1828 (1st grant 1784)
Joseph, Barker St., Nantwich. June 1830
Williams, Ann, Neston, spinster. April 1828

Williams, Catherine, Chester, widow. Oct. 1827
Grace, Chester, spinster. A July 1829
Griffith, Tranmere, yeoman. Dec. 1827*
Mary, Chester, widow. March 1828
Richard, Green Walls, Dodleston, farmer. May 1829
Roger, Lower Bebington, combmaker. March 1829
Samuel, Aston, labourer. April 1829
Sarah, Chester, spinster. A Oct. 1830*
Thomas, Oulton Lowe, Over, farmer. Oct. 1826*
William, Chester, sailor. March. 1826*
William, Eaton, Eccleston. June 1829
Williamson, Catherine, Over, spinster. Dec. 1827
John, Malpas, yeoman. March 1827
John, Warmingham, yeoman. Jan. 1828
Martha, Matley, Mottram-in-Longdendale. A June 1827
Robert, Ashton-upon-Mersey, gent. A June 1827*
Samuel, Buckley, Malpas, yeoman. Dec. 1826
William, Toft, co. Chester, publican. Nov. 1830
Wilshaw, William, Prestbury, farmer. May 1827
Wilson, Francis, Stockport, gent. July 1829
Hannah, Mottram, widow. April 1827
Lydia, Latchford. A Feb. 1829
Mary, Macclesfield, spinster. July 1829
Wilton, Martha, wife of Samuel Wilton, Runcorn. April 1830
Winfield, Richard, Waverham, retailer of beer & spirituous liquors. Nov. 1828
Winkle, Thomas, Bosley, farmer. Oct. 1828
William Webster, Buglawton, shopkeeper. May 1828
Winn, William, Macclesfield, grocer & shopkeeper. Jan. 1827
Winnington, Thomas, Mottram St. Andrew, labourer. Oct. 1829
Witter, John, Little Leigh, yeoman. Aug. 1826
Woldram, Samuel, Wharton, salt boiler. June 1829
Wolstenholme, John, Great Neston, gent. Dec. 1828
Wood, Ann, Stockport, spinster. A Nov. 1826 (later grants 1881 & 1888)
Daniel, Disley, Stockport, cordwainer. A Jan. 1826*
Francis, Cheadle Bulkeley, tailor. March 1829*
Hannah, Thorncliff, Mottram. A Nov., 1830 (2nd grant 1833)
James, Norley, brickmaker. March 1830*
John, Swanlow Lane, co. Chester, farmer. March 1829
John, Stockport, gent. April 1829
Joseph, Stockport, shuttle maker. A Dec. 1828
Martha, Dean Row, Wilmslow, spinster. A June 1829
Philip, Congleton, yeoman. Sept. 1827
Richard, Etchells, labourer. A May 1830
Samuel, Green Lane, Romiley, blacksmith. A April 1826
William, Rushton, Tarporley, farmer. A Aug. 1827
William, Henbury, Prestbury, farmer. A March 1829
Woodall, Hugh, Marthall, farmer. Dec. 1827
William, Lymm, yeoman. Aug. 1829
Woodcock, Ralph, Netherton, Frodsham, yeoman. May 1827·
Woodfine, Samuel, Barnston, husbandman. Nov. 1827
Woodins, Joseph, Chester, dyer. Sept. 1827*
Woodrooffe, Mary, Harrytown, Bredbury. A July 1830
Woodward, Alice, Daresbury, widow. Aug. 1829

Woodward, George, Crowton, Waverham, yeoman. May 1830
Joseph, Daresbury, yeoman. A May 1826
Samuel, Appleton, gent. Dec. 1826
Thomas, Pickmere, Great Budworth, yeoman. April 1830*
Woodyer, Thomas, Weaverham, tailor. May 1828
Thomas, Barrow, farmer. Aug. 1828
Woolfe, Ellen, Newton, widow. July 1828
Woolley, Eleanor, Bickley, Malpas. May 1826
George, Werneth, Stockport, shopkeeper. July 1830
Peter, Chorley, yeoman. Sept. 1828
Robert, Bardsley Gate, Mottram-in-Longdendale, gent. Oct. 1829
Woolrich, Thomas, Basford, farmer. July 1827
Wooton, Sarah, Congleton, widow. May 1827*
Worrall, Lot, Helsby, husbandman. March 1830*
John, Macclesfield, out-pensioner in the Royal Chelsea Hospital. March 1826*
John, Hill Cliff, Appleton, yeoman. Sept. 1828
Worsencroft, Jonathan, Stockport, gent. A Sept. 1826*
Worthington, Elizabeth Ann, Etchells, spinster. Nov. 1826
Hugo, sergeant of Horse Artillery in the Bengal Establishment. Jan. 1829
James, Nether Knutsford, cooper. A April 1827
Jeremiah, Henbury, Prestbury, yeoman. June 1830*
Samuel, Etchells, yeoman. Sept. 1827
Samuel, Woodford, co. Chester, yeoman. A May 1830*
Wrench, Jane, Nether Knutsford, widow. Oct. 1830
Richard, Utkinton, Tarporley, butcher. May 1830*
Wright, Alice, Northenden, singlewoman. A Nov. 1830*
Elizabeth, Altrincham, widow. May 1830*
John, Mobberley, publican. A Jan. 1826
John, Sutton, co. Chester, publican. July 1826
John, Moreton, yeoman. March 1828 (1st grant 1764)
Joseph, Thelwall, yeoman. July 1829
Margaret, Sproston, widow. April 1830
Ralph, Storeton Hall, farmer. Nov. 1827
Richard, Mobberley. July 1827
Sarah, Sproston, feme covert. A March 1828
Strethell, Nether Knutsford, gent. Oct. 1827*
Thomas senior, Lostock Gralam, victualler. Dec. 1826
Thomas, Northenden, farmer. A Feb. 1830*
Thomas, Over Peover, gent. Aug. 1830
William, Chester, bookbinder. Feb. 1827 (2nd grant 1832)
William, Moston. June 1827
William, Kinderton, innkeeper. A & Tuon April 1829
Wrigley, John, Stockport, weaver. Jan. 1830*
Mary, Newton, Mottram-in-Longdendale, widow. Aug. 1828
Wych, William, Little Warford, yeoman. Nov. 1828
Wynne, Mary, Chester, widow. A Sept. 1827

YARDLEY, Elizabeth, Plumbley, spinster. A April 1827
Yarwood, Frances, Alsager, feme covert. A May 1828
Yate, Elizabeth, Chester, spinster. June 1829
Hamlet, Arley, late of Ashton-juxta-Budworth, gent. Nov. 1826 (1st grant 1725)

Yates, Sally, Longley Hall, Sutton, Macclesfield. A Dec. 1827
Yeardsley, Job, Higher Bebington, stonemason. July 1830
Youd, Thomas, Bunbury, farrier. May 1830
Youde, Thomas, Chester, yeoman. Aug. 1830
Young, John, Higher Bebington, yeoman. March 1827*
Yoxall, Moses, Sproston, farmer. Jan. 1827
    Peter, Chester, yeoman. April 1827
    Peter, Minshull Vernon, Middlewich. Nov. 1830*

WELSH WILLS

ACKERLEY, Samuel, Sealand, Flints., farmer. A Dec. 1829
Adams, Phoebe, Hanmer, Flints. A Jan. 1828*
Bennion, Thomas, Iscoyd, Flints., farmer. June 1829
Berrisford, Richard, Halghton, Flints. March 1828
Boodle, Thomas, The Cloy, Bangor, gent. April 1830 (2nd grant 1848)

CAPPER, Philip, Iscoyd, farmer. Aug. 1826
Carr, Ann, Halghton, Flints. March 1830
Cartwright, Martha, Bronington, Hanmer, widow. March 1826
Cattrall, Thomas, Maes Lewis, Overton, Flints., farmer. Aug. 1827
Covell, John, Glanclwyd, Denbs. April 1826
Craven, Richard, Bronington, farmer. April 1828

DAVENPORT, Charles, Pickhill, farmer. Nov. 1828
Davies, Ann, Overton, feme covert. Nov. 1829
  Jane, Pickhill, Bangor, widow. Aug. 1826
  Thomas, Overton, Flints., gent. A Aug. 1830
Dawson, Mary, Wrexham, widow. July 1829
Dudleston, John, Tenswood, Bronington, farmer. Feb. 1826
Dunbabin, John, Gwerchtig, Flints., land surveyor. May 1829

EACHUS, John, Halghton, Hanmer, farmer. Oct. 1827
  John, Halghton, farmer. Dec. 1829
Edge, Samuel, Overton, Flints., tailor. April 1826
Edwards, James, Tybroughton, Hanmer, farmer. Oct. 1830
  John, serjeant in the Denbigh militia. A Dec. 1826
  John, Hanmer, Flints., farmer. Feb. 1830
Egerton, William, Gresford Lodge, esq. July 1828
Ellis, Thomas, Overton, yeoman. Aug. 1828
Evison, John, Egton, Bangor, gent. A Aug. 1827

FOULKES, Rachel, Gwernygron, Flints., last of Liverpool, spinster. Nov. 1827
Francis, Ann, Bangor, innkeeper. Oct. 1829 (2nd grant 1834)

GARNER, Rodger, Ridley Wood, Holt, farmer. A Oct. 1830
Gibbans, Samuel, Bangor, Flints., wheelwright. July 1829
Gresty, William, High Barns, Iscoyd, farmer. Oct. 1826
Griffiths, Ann, Sesswick, Bangor, widow. May 1827

HARRISON, William, Hanmer, blacksmith. July 1828
Hayes, Thomas, Gatemen, Wrexham, esq. last of St. Anns, Liverpool. Sept. 1830
Hayward, James, Tybroughton, Hanmer, servant. 1826*

Hesketh, Richard, Holt, Denbs., yeoman. March 1829*
Higgins, Richard, Hanmer, victualler. Aug. 1827
Hough. William, Sealand, Hawarden, yeoman. Dec. 1827*
Hughes, John, Saltney, last of the Manor, Hawarden. Aug. 1830
Humphreys, Ann, Holywell, spinster. A Oct. 1827 (2nd grant 1836)

JACKSON, John, Hanmer, butcher. A June 1826
Jones, Catharine Ann, New Town, Montgomery, spinster. A Jan. 1827
 Edward, Bonwin Ucha, Corwen, Merioneths. Nov. 1826
 Hugh, Pickhill, Denbs., esq. A June 1829
 John, Bangor, Flints., Sept. 1827
 Mary, Versailles, France, spinster. A Sept. 1829 (endorsed Flints.)
 Thomas, Worthenbury, yeoman. A Oct. 1827
 William, Halghton, Hanmer, farmer. May 1826

KEMPSTER, John, The Horns, Bangor, farmer. Oct. 1826

LATHAM, Thomas, Connahs Quay, Flints., fisherman. Jan. 1829
Lewis, David, Bittisfield, Hanmer, canal cutter. May 1830
 Richard, Wrexham, publican. A Jan. 1827

MADDOCKS, John, Bronington, Flints., farmer. April 1828
Martin, Thomas, Overton, Flints., gent. A Jan. 1826
 Thomas, Overton, gent. A April 1829
Matthews, Thomas, Wrexham, esq. A Aug. 1827
Montford, Thomas, Worthenbury, Flints., yeoman. May 1828
Morris, Thomas, Bettisfield, Hanmer. March 1827
Mottram, Thomas, Mold, miner. A Oct. 1829*
Moyle, Thomas, Llandingsbrook, Flints. June 1827

OWENS, Ann, Bangor, Carnarvons., widow. May 1829

PARRY, James, Holt, publican. A Nov. 1827
Phillips, Eleanor, Iscoyd, Malpas, spinster. Nov. 1830*
 John, Halghton, Flints., labourer. A April 1826
 Mary, The Lane, Hanmer, widow. Oct. 1827
Pover, William, Iscoyd. May 1828
Price, Ann, Hanmer, Flints., spinster. A Nov. 1826*
 Robert, Overton, Flints., innkeeper. Aug. 1830
Pritchard, Thomas, Bangor, Flints., labourer. A July 1827

ROBERTS, Elizabeth, Carnarvon, spinster. Dec. 1826*
 John, Liverpool, last of Carnarvon, yeoman. June 1829
 Robert Jones, Llangerniew, Denbs., clerk. June 1828
Rogers, Joseph, Little Overton, Flints. Oct. 1827
Rolland, Thomas, Higher Kinnerton, Flints., farmer. Jan. 1830*
Rowland, Daniel, Iscoyd, Holt. Feb. 1830
 John, Holt, Denbs., farmer. July. 1829
 Margaret, Beaumaris, Anglesey, widow. Feb. 1830

SHAW, William, Halghton, Hanmer, farmer. A Sept. 1829
Stant, Elizabeth, Horton Ring, Bronington, spinster. July 1826
Strange, James, Knolton, Overton, Flints., farmer. June 1826

THOMAS, George, Holt, farmer. Sept. 1828*
Sarah, Wrexham, widow. Jan. 1829
Thomas, Pentre Nant, Denbs., farmer. A May 1827
Tomlinson, William, Garwyn-vawr, esq. May 1829

VAUGHAN, Richard, Halghton, Flints., farmer. A Jan. 1829
Voice, John, Shordley, Flints., May 1828

WILLIAMS, John, Pool Park, Denbs., gent. Jan. 1828
Thomas, Bronington, Hanmer, yeoman. July 1826
William, Carnarvon, esq. Dec. 1828
Williamson, Thomas, Warnatoe, Worthenbury, Flints. Oct. 1830
Woodfin, Hannah, Iscoyd, spinster. A Oct. 1827*
Woollam, Richard, Whitchurch, co. Salop, feltmaker. A June 1827 (endorsed Flints)
Wright, Edward, Manchester, last of Denbigh. May 1826

YOUD, Thomas, Kinnerton, Flints., farmer. July 1829

INDEX OF PLACES

When a name occurs more than once on the same page, the number of times is given in parentheses.

ABBEY COURT, Chester, 174
Abbey Foregate, Shrewsbury, 123
Abbot's Grange, Chester, 170
Abram, Wigan, 16, 26, 81(2), 124
Accrington, 2, 12(2), 17, 23, 33, 36, 44, 52, 75, 96, 102, 118
Accrington, New, 96
Accrington, Old, 111
Acton, 145(2), 153, 159, 164, 169, 171, 178, 180(2), 183
Acton, Weaverham, 169
Acton Grange, 144, 175, 179
Adlington, 2, 21, 56, 83, 87, 110, 147, 149, 152, 153, 165, 170, 173, 174
Affeside, Tottington, 46
Africa, 19, 43
Agden, Bowdon, 162
Agden, Malpas, 175
Aigburth, 7(2), 110
Ainsworth, 6, 16, 41, 46(2), 54, 65, 78, 94, 132, 141
Aintree, 61, 65, 88
Alcumlow, Astbury, 173
Aldbury, Herfordshire, 164
Aldcliffe, 41
Alderley, 163, 171
Alderley, Nether, 145, 147, 165, 169, 171, 175
Alderley, Over, 160, 173, 174, 182
Aldersey, 173
Aldersey, Coddington, 165
Aldersey, Prees co. Salop, 150
Alderroot, Chadderton, 120
Aldford, 182
Alexandria, 14
Alkrington, 77, 102
Allerton, 93, 117
Allerton Lodge, 109
Allostock, 146, 153, 156(2), 157, 173, 181
Almshill, Cheetham, 140
Alpraham, 155, 156, 160, 172
Alsager, 164, 185
Alston, 33, 95
Alt, Ashton-under-Lyne, 53
Alt Hill, 3, 91
Altcar, 45, 54, 81
Altham, 98
Altham Hall, 2
Altrincham, 143(2), 144, 151(2), 154(2), 156, 157(3), 158(2), 159, 162(2), 163, 168(2), 169, 170, 172(2), 174(2), 175, 179, 181, 182, 183, 185
Ambleside, 52
Ambwell, Foulridge, 95
America, 20, 22, 87, 141, 156
America North, 8, 23, 34, 45, 77
America, South, 19, 78, 79, 107
Ancoats St., Manchester, 136
Anglesey, 188
Anglezark, 25, 43
Anderton, 1, 73, 76, 78, 89, 168(2)
Antrobus, 150, 152, 171
Appleby, Westmorland, 119
Appleton, Cheshire, 143, 145, 148, 151, 156, 158, 172, 185(2)
Appleton, Widnes, 63, 104
Arbury, 137
Ardshaw Clough, 136
Ardwick, 3, 5, 6, 13(2), 17, 45, 49, 77, 99, 102, 103, 106, 112, 113, 114, 125, 130, 131, 133, 135, 136, 154
Ardwick, Higher, 106, 121
Ardwick Place, Manchester, 45, 109
Arkholme, Rossendale, 18
Arley, 185
Arley Hall, Frodsham, 167
Armfield, Mottram, 149
Armley, Yorks., 27
Ashes, Saddleworth, 14
Ashfield House, 25
Ashley, Bowdon, 154, 177(2), 183
Ashton, 33, 78, 113
Ashton-in-Makerfield, 20, 26, 39, 56, 64, 67(2), 68, 77(2), 78, 84, 87(2), 92, 104, 127
Ashton-under-Lyme, Staffs., 175
Ashton-under-Lyne, 3-140 *passim*
Ashton-upon-Mersey, 152(2), 153, 155, 157, 162, 163, 172, 175, 177, 182, 184
Ashton, Tarvin, 149
Ashworth, 23, 25, 72, 80, 99
Askham, Westmorland, 22
Asmall Lane, Scarisbrick, 56
Aspull, 2, 10, 76, 98, 107
Astbury, 151, 152, 162, 168(2) 169, 173, 174, 176, 181
Astley, 3(2), 36, 39(3), 48, 59, 68(2), 81,

96, 102, 112, 115, 119
Aston, 173, 178, 184
Aston, Budworth, 169, 177, 185
Aston, Nantwich, 167
Aston, Runcorn, 175
Aston, Wrenbury, 176
Atherton, 18, 22, 26(2), 36, 42, 43(2), 45, 60(2), 63, 66, 71, 74, 77, 83, 93, 97(2), 108, 111, 115, 116(2), 120, 137, 138, 139
Atherton's Quay, 5
Audenshaw, 3, 14, 26, 42, 43, 62, 77, 79, 119, 139
Audlem, 145, 146, 151, 159, 163, 164, 170, 171(2), 176, 182
Audley, [Staffs.], 180
Aughton, 2,3, 5, 13, 31, 55, 56, 85, 98(3), 100, 109, 128, 136(2)
Austerlands, Saddleworth, 10, 118, 126(2),
Austerson, Acton, 180

BACK LANE, Macclesfield, 171
Backford, 155, 160
Bacup, 4, 5, 7, 21, 26, 29, 31, 33, 52, 54, 58, 64, 80(2), 92, 98, 105, 106, 110, 113(2), 118, 123
Baddiley, 163
Baguley, 146, 152, 163, 164, 168, 179,
Bahia, Brazil, 19, 79
Bakewell co. Derby, 86
Balderstone, 28, 46, 56
Balladin Brook, Tottington, 56
Bamford, 11, 27, 40, 109, 110
Bangor, 187(6), 188(4)
Banister Hall, Walton-le-Dale, 118
Bank, Oldham, 101, 102
Bank End, Whalley, 55
Bank Lane, Walmersley, 55, 98
Bank Top, Ashton-under-Lyne, 19, 66, 139
Bank Top, Oldham, 93
Bank Top, Wincle, 152
Bank Quay, Warrington, 78, 112
Bankhouse, Bredbury, 176
Banks, co. Lancs., 13
Banks, Todmorden, 21
Bankside, Bury, 98
Bankside, Rossendale, 94
Barbadoes, 49, 119
Barbold [?Parbold], 39
Bardsea, 95
Bardsley Gate, 185
Bardsleys, Crompton, 73
Barker Lane, Blackburn, 56(3)
Barker St., Nantwich, 183
Barley with Wheatley Booths, 105
Barlow Fold, Bury, 49
Barnes Green, Blackley, 25
Barney Brook, Newhall, 152
Barnshaw, Sandbach, 161
Barnston, 184
Barnton, 153, 167
Barracks, Saddleworth, 99
Barrow, 150(2), 162, 167, 171, 185
Barrow, Little, 152
Barrowfields, 121
Barrowford, 5, 53, 75, 120, 131
Barrowford Booth, 30, 120
Barthomley, 146(2), 153, 156, 171, 180, 182
Barton, 51, 62, 65, 79, 119, 126, 168
Barton Close, Prestwich, 17
Barton Wood, Warrington, 124
Barton-upon-Irwell, 27, 34, 37, 43(2), 45, 48, 51, 67, 69, 88, 91, 95, 107, 126
Barwood Lee, Bury, 45
Basford, 185
Bass Land, Walmersley, 71
Bath, 5, 79, 137
Bath St., Liverpool, 26
Batherton, 183
Baxenden, Whalley 136(2)
Beardwood, Blackburn, 111
Bearshill, 92, 113
Beaumaris, Anglesey, 188
Bebington, 147, 152, 164, 173, 177
Bebington, Higher, 163, 166, 186(2)
Bebington, Lower, 145, 161, 184
Becconsall, 6
Bedford, Leigh, 2, 10(2), 14, 49, 50, 66, 80, 84, 97, 107, 117(2), 129
Bedford Row, Middlesex, 22, 111(2)
Bedford Square, Middlesex, 24
Beeston, Bunbury, 144, 174
Belfield, Rochdale, 20
Bellthorne, 61
Belvidier, Wayswall, 182
Bengal, 185
Benthouse, 119
Bentlanes, Eccles, 57
Bentley, 62
Bentley Hall, Bury, 11
Bents, Colne, 104
Berbice, S. America, 107
Berches, Ashton-under-Lyne, 137
Berks, Ashton-under-Lyne, 118
Berkshire, 96, 128
Besom Hill, Oldham, 40
Betchton, 148, 149, 164, 170, 179
Betley, Staffs., 144
Bettisfield, Hanmer, 188
Bickerstaffe, 5, 28, 30, 37, 41, 57, 69, 76, 83(2), 90, 116
Bickerton, 154, 166, 172, 183
Bickley, Malpas, 155, 169, 172(2), 185
Biddenden, Kent, 145
Bidston, 83, 159, 172
Big Rigg, Egremont, 13
Billinge, 2 9(2), 11, 23, 33, 39(3), 49, 62(3),

69, 85, 97(2), 98(2), 116, 125, 136
Billinge Chapel End, 81, 116
Billinge Higher End, 7, 62
Billington, 15, 25 41, 52, 92, 114, 137
Birch, Hopwood, 93
Birch House, Farnworth, 61
Birch of Zell, Switzerland, 31
Birchenley, Colne, 22
Birchenley Lane, 6
Birchley, Billinge, 33
Bird in Hand, Rochdale, 107
Birdholme, Chesterfield, 105
Birkacre, Chorley, 86
Birkdale, 1, 68, 84(2), 109
Birkenhead, 161, 163, 165(2), 171, 183
Birks, Ashton-under-Lyne, 124
Birmingham, 134, 174
Birtle cum Bamford, 27, 40
Birtles, 148
Birtshaw, Crompton, 26
Bispham, 74, 79
Bispham Hall, Billinge, 62
Bittisfield, Hanmer, 188
Black Clough, Crompton, 134
Black Moss, Whitley Booth, 131
Black Road, Macclesfield, 178
Blackbrook, Manchester, 15
Blackburn, 1-138 *passim*
Blackey Nook, Saddleworth, 112
Blackford Bridge, Bury, 37(2)
Blackhouse Lane, Bury, 47
Blackleach, Saddleworth, 29
Blackley, 8, 25, 36, 71(3), 72, 77, 93, 115, 125(2), 129, 133
Blackmoss, Pendle, 11
Blackrod, 7, 38, 49, 83, 85, 97, 102, 104(2) 114(2), 126
Blackwater St., Rochdale, 31
Blaguegate, Lathom, 102
Blakebey Nook, Saddleworth, 105
Blakeley, 2
Blakenhall, 148(3), 169
Blakow Hill, Barrowford Booth, 30
Blocklane, Oldham, 132
Boars Head, Bolton, 51
Boardmans, Tottington, 76
Boarshurst, Saddleworth, 16
Bold, 41(3), 42, 74, 101, 128, 136, 140
Bolee, Middleton, 100
Bollin Fee, Wilmslow, 171
Bollin Hall, Wilmslow, 171
Bollington, 143(2), 144, 148(2), 150, 153(2), 156, 167, 181
Bollington, Prestbury, 150, 166, 178
Bollington Cross, 166
Bolshaw Outwood, Stockport Etchells, 182
Bolton (Great Bolton, Bolton-le-Moors), 1(2), 9-140 *passim*
Bolton, Little, 3, 13, 17, 20(2), 23, 26(2), 30, 34, 35, 40, 43, 46, 61, 67(2), 71, 73, 98, 102, 108, 110, 111, 122, 128, 161
Bolton-by-the-Sands, 34
Bombay, 7
Bonwin Ucha, Corwen, 188
Booth Smithy, Little Budworth, 170
Boothfold, Rossendale, 4(2), 62, 80(2)
Booths Town, 116
Boothstown, Eccles, 66, 86
Bootle, 15, 70, 81, 89, 90, 101
Bootle-cum-Linacre, 101
Bootle St., Manchester, 92
Bosden, 149, 151, 156, 158, 162, 163, 166, 168, 183
Bosley, 150, 155, 159, 173, 176, 179, 180, 184
Bostock, 174(2)
Boston, 74
Boston, America, 20, 22
Botthorne, Great Marsden, 46
Bottom of Greenacres Moor, 15, 59, 125
Bottom of Lane, Rochdale, 40
Bottom of Moor, Oldham, 41
Boughton, 151, 160, 175
Boughton, Great, 143(2), 153, 155, 172, 174(2), 178
Bowden, 152, 156, 157, 159(4), 162(2), 163, 165(2), 170, 173, 175, 176, 177, 180(2), 182
Bowkhouse, Saddleworth, 101
Bowland, Little, 29, 129
Boyerfold, Stayley, 169
Boyton [?Royton], 122
Bradfield, Yorks., 108
Bradford, Yorks., 131
Bradford Mill House, 154
Bradley, 144
Bradley, Great Marsden, 54
Bradley, Lower, 99
Bradley, Malpas, 172, 177
Bradley Lane Head, 101
Bradshaw, Bolton, 38, 47, 62, 115
Bradshaw Hall, Cheadle Moseley, 163
Bradwall, 180
Bramhall, 157, 158, 163, 168, 173, 175, 178, 179, 180
Bramhall Hall, 153
Branwood, Rochdale, 51
Brazil, 19, 31, 40, 45, 79
Bredbury, 144, 158, 165, 168, 170, 176, 177, 183, 184
Bredbury Green, 180
Breightmet, 15, 18, 89, 99, 117, 125, 126
Brening Croft, Leyland, 52
Brescie Green, Tiverton, 182
Brereton, 149, 173
Brereton-cum-Smethwick, 168
Bretherton, 3, 7(2), 8, 16, 31, 40, 68, 92,

109,111
Brick Field, Rochdale, 33
Brickfield, 4
Bridge, Prestwich, 128
Bridge End, Bacup, 64
Bridge End, Rossendale, 4
Bridge End House, Davenham, 181
Bridge Mill, Rochdale, 87
Bridge Trafford, 155
Bridgemere, 161, 167, 177
Bridport St., Liverpool, 87
Briercliff, 44, 92, 116
Brimstage, 146
Brimmy Croft, Yorks., 43
Brin, Cuddington, 150
Brindle, 17, 30, 37, 54, 74, 84(2), 92, 107, 118, 133(4)
Brindley, 152, 154, 160, 175
Brinnington, 148, 163, 167, 175, 176
Brinscall, Leyland, 14, 43
Brinsup, Deane, 43
Broad Oats, New Accrington, 96
Broad Green, West Derby, 58
Broad i'th Lane, Spotland, 51
Broad Lane, Rochdale, 134
Broadbottom, Mottram, 147, 177
Broadeth Lane, 103
Broadhalgh, Rochdale, 62
Broadlane, 176
Broadmeadow, 112
Broadway, Southwark, 26
Broadway Lane, Oldham, 88
Brock Bolton, 137
Broken Cross, 153
Bromborough, 41, 146, 150, 155, 156, 168, 182
Brompton Row, Middlesex, 50
Bronington, Hanmer, 187(3), 188(2), 189
Brook, Walton-on-the-Hill, 19
Brook Bottom, 46
Brook St., Chester, 171
Brookbottom, Saddleworth, 137(2), 139, 140
Brookhead, Cheadle, 178
Brookhouse, 11(2)
Brookshaw, Bury, 71
Brookside, Oswaldtwistle, 103
Brooksmouth, Bury, 99
Broomhall, 169
Broomhill, Barrow, 167
Broomhouse, Eccles, 57
Broomhouse Lane, Eccles, 50, 66
Brotherod, Rochdale, 64
Broughton, Manchester, 3, 11, 24, 32, 33, 64(2), 74, 98(2), 124, 140
Broughton Hall, Manchester, 58
Broughton St., Salford, 25
Brow, Saddleworth, 103
Brown Edge, Lymm, 164
Brown Hill, Saddleworth, 76
Brown Lodge, Rochdale, 17
Brownbank, Butterworth, 5
Brownbirks, Whalley, 47
Brownley Green, Northenden, 176
Brownlow Hill, Liverpool, 32, 72
Brownlowe, Astbury, 174
Brownwardle, Rochdale, 119(2)
Broxton, Malpas, 143, 148, 177
Bruen Stapleford, 156, 161, 172
Burnedge, Castleton, 87
Brunswick Square, Middlesex, 168
Buckclough, Whalley, 23
Buckley, Malpas, 184
Buckley Fold, Bury, 46
Buckley Wells, Bury, 15
Budworth, 160, 170, 171, 177, 185
Budworth, Great, 147, 152, 154, 157, 162, 168, 171, 179, 181, 185
Budworth, Little, 148, 152, 154, 170(2)
Buershill, Castleton, 64
Buersille Bridge, Rochdale, 11
Buerton, 180
Buglawton, 145, 164, 167, 181(2), 182, 184
Buille Hill, Eccles, 9
Bullock Smithy, Stockport, 158
Bullshead, Whalley, 30
Bunbury, 144, 145, 154(2), 155, 156(2), 160, 161, 166(2), 170(2), 175, 181, 186
Burgh, Chorley, 23(2)
Burland, 153, 158
Burn, Crompton, 56
Burnage, 10, 21, 83, 132
Burnley, 13, 18, 29, 33, 37, 40, 44, 58, 64, 71, 76, 91, 92, 93, 96(2), 101, 102, 114, 116, 137
Burnley Wood, 131
Burscough, 1, 7, 10(2), 16, 31, 44, 68, 70, 71, 74, 84, 85(2), 88, 119, 125, 127
Burscough Bridge, 106
Burscough Hall, Chorley, 15
Burton, 171
Burton, Chorlton Row, 4
Burton, Tarvin, 176
Burtonwood, 4, 9, 43, 59, 63, 72, 121, 140
Burwardsley, 154, 170
Bury, 1-140 *passim*
Bury St. Edmunds [Suffolk], 17
Bury St., Salford, 8
Butcher Lane, Bury, 11
Butley, Prestbury, 145, 158, 173, 174, 181
Butterworth, 5, 80, 87, 88. 106, 109, 110, 121,132.
Buxton, Derbys., 36, 147
Byley-cum-Yatehouse, 149

CABBAGE HALL, 138
Cadishead, 5, 19, 31, 50, 51, 53, 57(2), 90,

103, 112, 113, 123
Cadiz, Spain, 21
Calcutta, 128
Caldercott, 183
Calder Moor, Littleborough, 73
Caldwell Brow, 103
Caldy, West Kirby, 151
Call Green, Stockport, 172
Calliands, Butterworth, 80
Camelfield Cottage, 100
Camforth Lodge, Lancaster, 67
Campobello, New York, 89
Capenhurst, 165(2), 183
Capesthorne, 147
Captain Fold, 23
Car, Rossendale, 75
Carishead [? Cadishead], 75
Carlisle, 136
Carnarvon, 188(2), 189
Carr Bank, Atherton, 66
Carr Hall, Haslingden, 52
Carr Mill, St. Helens, 43
Carrington, 89, 152(5), 158, 171, 175, 176, 182(2)
Carrion Crow, Oldham, 133
Carry Bridge, Colne, 76
Carshalton, Surrey, 109
Carter Place, Haslingden, 110
Cartmel, 25
Castle, Chester, 167
Castle Hall, Dukinfield, 77
Castle Hill, Hale, 172, 173(2)
Castle Northwich, 151, 167(2), 179
Castleshaw, Saddleworth, 72(2)
Castleton, 34, 37, 45, 62(2), 64, 79, 87, 97, 121, 137
Catch End Lane, Eccles, 45
Catches, Spotland, 72
Catley Lane Head, 30
Cavan, Ireland, 60
Chaddesley Corbett, 125
Chadderton, 4, 49, 63, 66, 77, 96, 102, 108, 111, 115, 120, 128, 139
Chadwick, 40
Chamber, Oldham, 89
Chamber Hall, Bolton, 94
Chapefield, Pilkington, 2
Chapel Field, Prestwich, 37
Chapel Hill, Rossendale, 52(2)
Chapel House, 18
Chapel House, Ashworth, 80
Chapel House, Rochdale, 46
Chapel Lane, Hoghton, 28
Chapel-en-le-Frith, Derbys., 2
Charles Town, South Carolina, 156
Charlestown, Ashton-under-Lyne, 72, 73, 87, 136
Charnock Heath, 55
Charnock Richard, 5, 107
Chatburn, 12, 17, 37, 52, 60
Chatterton Hey, Bury, 54
Cheadle, 154, 162, 174, 177(2), 178(2), 181, 182, 183
Cheadle, Staffs., 126
Cheadle Bulkeley, 144, 150, 159, 160, 164, 169, 184
Cheadle Hulme, 145
Cheadle Moseley, 150(2), 159, 163
Cheapside, London, 127
Cheetham, 11, 15, 28, 39, 40, 48, 50(2), 51(3), 52, 56, 58(2), 68, 73, 93, 101, 104(2), 105, 135, 139(2), 140(3)
Cheetham Hill, 50, 68, 130
Cheetham St., Rochdale, 128
Cheetwood, 17, 74
Chelbourne, Rochdale, 50
Chelsea Hospital, Royal, 185
Cheltenham, 100
Chesham, Bury, 49, 54, 62
Chester, 33, 90, 143-186 *passim*
Chesterfield, Derbys., 87, 105
Cheswardine, Salop, 160
Chichester, 135
Chidlow, 166
Childwall, 68, 94(3), 117, 130(2), 136
Chipping, 75, 107
Chirge, 36
Cholmondeley, 147, 154
Cholmondeley,House, Piccadilly, Middlesex, 150
Cholmondeley Park, 144
Cholmondeston, Acton, 168, 169
Chorley, 1(2), 9, 10, 15, 20, 22, 23(2), 34, 43(2), 46, 49(2), 53, 54, 56, 60, 62, 67(2), 72, 86, 89, 93, 96, 100, 113, 116, 119, 126, 129, 134, 137, 141, 145, 163, 168, 185.
Chorley Moor, 115
Chorlton, 7, 22, 48, 70, 107, 131, 172
Chorlton Row, 2, 4, 6(2), 8, 10, 13, 17, 18, 22, 23(2), 28, 30(2), 31, 32(3), 35(2), 39, 45, 46, 47, 48, 51(2), 52, 58(2), 62, 63, 68, 70, 71, 72, 73, 76, 77(2), 83, 84, 85, 86(2), 88, 89, 90, 91, 92, 96, 102, 106, 112, 116, 117, 118, 119, 121(2), 123(2), 125, 128(2), 130, 132, 134(2), 139
Chorlton-cum Hardy, 10, 22, 47, 67, 102, 124
Chowbent, 13, 26, 36, 60, 66, 69, 83, 97, 104, 109, 112, 116, 138
Chowley, 167
Christleton, 145, 171, 172, 182
Church, 16, 29, 111
Church Coppenhall, 147, 156, 167, 183
Church Hulme, 145, 150, 160
Church Lane, Castleton, 37
Church Lawton, 168
Church Minshull, 159
Church St., Middleton, 19

Church Shocklach, 180
Church Stile, Rochdale, 72, 101
Church Stretton, 78
Churchkirk, 36
Churchtown, North Meols, 112
Churchgate, Bolton, 78
Churton, Farndon, 176
Clare Castle, Ireland, 107
Clarkesfield, Prestwich, 77(2)
Clay Lane, Rochdale, 73
Clayton, 3, 117, 119, 131
Clayton Mills, Manchester, 20
Clayton-le-Dale, 55, 111, 130, 131
Clayton-ley-fold, 5
Clifton, Eccles, 36, 51, 60, 102(2), 115
Clifton, Gloucs., 91
Clitheroe, 6(3), 10, 15, 26, 32, 33, 35, 40, 55, 56, 82, 93, 114, 122
Cliviger, 80, 115, 137
Close, Rochdale, 48
Clough House, Rochdale, 21
Cloughfield, Rossendale, 94
Cloughfolds, Rossendale, 92, 94, 122
Cloy, Bangor, 187
Clubhouses, 51
Clubmoor, 66
Coal Bank, Spotland, 113
Coal Clough, Habergham Eaves, 127
Coat, Cliviger, 80
Cobhouse, Middleton, 71
Cobhouse, Walmersley, 71
Cockermouth, Cumberland, 66, 72
Cockham, 55
Cocksbank, Audlem, 182
Cockshill, Ashton-under-Lyne, 10
Cocky Lane, 139
Coddington, 150, 165, 170
Cogshall, 148
Coldhurst, Oldham, 37, 59
Coldvale Brow, Rochdale, 64
Coldwall Brow, Spotland, 23
Coldweather House, 106
Collier Hill, Oldham, 35
Collinge Croft, Oldham, 132
Collinge Fold, 27
Collyhurst, 8, 36, 73, 140
Colne, 6, 12, 16, 22, 37, 48, 52, 54, 61, 76, 79, 82, 98, 100, 104, 115, 120, 124, 131, 134(3), 139
Colne, Lower, 35
Colne Field, 15, 50
Colne Waterside, 124
Comberbach, 154(2), 160
Combermere, 152
Coney Green, Radcliffe, 93
Congleton, 143-184 *passim*
Congleton Edge, 177
Coniston, 3, 36, 57
Connahs Quay, 188
Constable Bridge, Rossendale, 15
Conway Place, Liverpool, 5
Coopershaw, Kettleshulme, 148
Coppost Edge, Prestbury, 150
Coppull, 14, 53
Copy Nook, Blackburn, 40, 131
Corby, 64
Cork, Ireland, 27, 50
Cornhill, Liverpool, 38
Corwen, 188
Cotton, 157
Court Hill, Oldham, 87
Cow Clough, Spotland, 81
Cowhill, Prestwich, 15, 49, 125
Cowlishaw, 26
Crabb Hall, 175
Crabtree Lane, West Derby, 100, 132
Crabwall, Chester, 167
Cragg, Colne, 82
Cranage, Holmes Chapel, 168
Cranberry Lodge, 17
Crawshaw Booth, Rossendale, 61, 66, 80, 100, 117
Crescent, Salford, 63
Cresdens, North Meols. 18
Crewe, 152, 153, 171(2)
Croft, Winwick, 21, 26, 57, 63, 72, 92, 94, 120
Crofts Bank, Barton-upon-Irwell, 51
Cromberry Lodge, 16
Crompton, 26, 46, 56, 59, 61, 73, 75, 80, 87(2), 88(2), 92, 120, 123, 134(2)
Crompton, High, 95
Crompton, Low, 40
Crompton Fold, 57
Cronton, 28, 104, 128
Cropper St., Manchester, 65
Crosby, 54
Crosby, Great, 21(2), 24, 32, 46, 60, 69, 117
Crosby, Little, 18, 40, 104, 129
Cross, Rossendale, 55
Cross Bank, 46, 77, 88
Cross Hall, Chorley, 43
Cross St., Chester, 180(2)
Crossens, North Meols, 129
Crosshall St., Liverpool, 77, 82
Crosthwaite, Cumberland, 109
Croston, 45, 66, 88, 99, 124
Crouch End, Middlesex, 60
Crowden Brook, Mottram in Longdendale, 168
Crowley, Great Budworth, 154, 158, 161
Crowley, Over Whitley, 146
Crown Court, Old Change, London, 88
Crowthorn, Ashton-under-Lyne, 77
Crowton, 150, 173
Crowton, Waverham, 160, 185
Croxteth Park, 99

Crumpsall, 20, 50, 59, 72, 74, 127, 139(2)
Cuerden, 36, 128
Culcheth, 7, 8, 17, 25, 34, 46(2), 58, 63, 68, 97(2), 104, 112, 113, 140
Culcheth Hall, 125, 137
Cumberland, 10, 66, 109, 114, 126
Cuppin St., Chester, 161, 167
Curzon St., Burnley, 71

DALTON, 54, 59, 72, 89, 102
Dane Bank, Congleton, 168
Dane Cottage, Astbury, 152
Darcey Lever, 3, 30
Daresbury, 146(3), 155, 184, 185
Darley Hall, 100
Darlington, co. Durham, 44
Darnhall, Whitegate, 155
Darwen, 61, 112
Darwen, Lower, 29, 33, 35, 47, 111
Darwen, Over, 20, 28, 36, 42, 74(3), 76, 79, 84, 113(2), 127, 141
Davenham, 145, 157, 160, 178, 181
Davis, Bury, 49
Davyhulme, Eccles, 32, 41, 57, 63, 76, 126, 129
Dawson Croft, Salford, 116
Day Green, Hassall, 162
Deane, 33, 43, 44, 80, 139
Deanrow, Wilmslow, 155, 160, 184
Deansgate, Bolton, 110
Deansgate, Manchester, 80, 106
Deardengate, Haslingden, 4
Debucca, Africa, 43
Delamere, 149, 155, 162, 168
Delph, Saddleworth, 13, 15, 16, 46, 72, 83, 99, 110, 112, 113, 121, 140
Demerara, 83, 91
Denbigh, 187, 189
Denfield Hall, Rostherne, 170
Denneby, Rotheram, 77
Denshaw, Saddleworth, 76(2), 101, 140
Denton, 2, 4, 27(3), 29, 47, 85, 117, 132, 140
Denton Lane, Prestwich, 4
Derby, 38(2)
Derbyshire, 2, 16, 35, 36, 58, 84, 86, 87, 93, 105, 114, 147, 149, 157, 176, 182
Desford, co. Leicester, 114
Didsbury, 12, 50, 51, 52, 119, 129, 130
Didsbury, Runcorn, 155
Diggle Edge, Saddleworth, 15
Diggles, 15
Diglee House, Yardsley-cum-Whaley, 157
Dilworth, 36
Disley, 147, 176, 178, 180, 183, 184
Ditton, 52, 117, 132
Dobcross, Saddleworth, 15, 109
Dobfield, 19
Dobroyd, 40
Dock St., Sculcoates, 55
Dodcot-cum-Wilkesley, 151
Dodcross, Saddleworth, 53
Doddington, 182
Dodford, co. Northampton, 114
Dodleston, 184
Dods Green, Newhall, 162
Dog Lane End, Dukinfield, 176
Doghill, Oldham, 19
Doghill End, Crompton, 120
Dominica, Island of, 4
Doncaster, 59
Dorsetshire, 172
Douglas, Isle of Man, 11, 41, 58, 153
Douglas Green, Pendleton, 10
Dove Bank, Little Lever, 92
Dover St., Piccadilly, Middlesex, 33
Downham, 52, 106, 128, 139
Downholland, 7(2)
Drayton, Salop, 153
Droylsden, 11, 14, 26, 39, 47, 86, 110, 114, 119, 129
Dublin, 99
Duckworth, 26
Duddon, Tarvin, 147, 154(2), 155, 175(2)
Dudley, co. Worcester, 148
Duke St., Edgehill, 81
Duke St., Liverpool, 135
Dukinfield, 77, 143, 144, 146, 151(2), 158, 160(2), 163(3), 164, 165, 166, 167, 170, 176, 177, 180
Dukinfield Lodge, 159
Dumfries, 69
Dumplington, Eccles 23, 45, 107
Dunham Massey, 143, 149, 152, 153(2), 159(2), 162(3), 165(3), 173, 174, 178
Dunham on the Hill, Thornton, 143, 175(2)
Dunnyshop, Accrington, 2
Durham, county of, 44, 98
Dutton, 156, 169, 183
Dutton, Lancs., 57, 81
Dutton Hall, 171
Duxbury, 14, 127
Dyke Green, Rochdale, 75

EAGLEY, Little Bolton, 23
East Challon, 20
East Indies, 5, 152, 153
Eastham, 181
Eastham Ferry, 178
Eaton, 149, 154
Eaton, Astbury, 168
Eaton, Eccleston, 184
Eaton, Tarporley, 145, 168, 177
Eccles, 3, 8, 9, 11, 19, 20, 23, 24, 27, 32, 36, 40(2), 41, 44, 45, 47, 48, 50, 51, 57(2), 66(2), 69, 70, 71, 74, 76, 79, 86, 88, 90, 99, 101, 108, 109, 126, 129, 136, 140
Eccleston, 8, 10, 28, 31, 33, 48, 61, 64, 65,

66, 75(2), 88, 98, 99, 120, 124(2), 127, 131(2), 139
Eccleston, Cheshire, 164
Eccleston, Prescot, 19, 43, 46, 65, 100
Eccleston Low Steads, 127
Edenfield, Bury, 37, 62, 67, 131
Edgbaston St., Birmingham, 174
Edge Hall, Malpas, 154
Edge Hill, 9, 12, 19, 32, 33, 44, 58, 67, 81, 82(2), 85, 97, 101, 106, 107, 111, 125, 129, 131, 132
Edge Lane, Oldham, 66
Edge Lane, West Derby, 35
Edgeley, Cheadle, 161, 174, 179, 181
Edgeley, Manchester, 42
Edges, 98
Edgeside, Rossendale, 54, 92
Edgeworth, 4, 37, 89, 93, 98, 110, 117, 138
Edward St., Stockport, 183
Egerton, Malpas, 155
Egremont, 13
Egton, Bangor, 187
Elibank, Stockport, 179
Ellerbeck, 60(2)
Ellesmere, 174
Ellesmere Port, 161
Elswick Lodge, 105
Elton, 126, 128, 151, 161(2), 165, 182
Enfield, Whalley, 31
Entwisle, 8, 74
Epworth St., Walton-on-the-Hill, 64
Ernshaw Barn, Rossendale, 92
Etchells, 145, 169, 170, 179, 180, 182, 184, 185(2)
Etchells, Stockport, 156, 162, 183
Euxton, 47, 67, 76, 138
Evans House, Wiswall, 94
Everton, 7, 9(2), 16, 18, 21, 23, 35, 37, 44, 48, 55, 57, 65, 66, 69, 70, 73, 79, 82, 90, 92, 94, 101, 102, 112, 125, 130, 133, 136
Extwistle, Burnley, 76

FADDILEY, 146
Failsworth, 11, 14, 26, 49(2), 52, 59, 61, 72, 93(2), 116
Fairfield, Manchester, 27, 29, 39, 53, 61, 85
Fallibroome, Prestbury, 160
Fallowfield, 10, 129
Far Bank House, Wheatley Booth, 64
Farndon, 149, 152, 165(2), 169, 176
Farnworth, 9, 30, 40, 51, 58, 61, 73, 79, 80, 91, 108, 110(2), 124, 125(2), 129, 137
Farrington, 86, 95
Farther Heights, 4
Fazakerley, 68(2)
Fearnhead, 30(2), 128
Fearns, Rossendale, 120
Fence, Pendle, 105
Fence House, Pendle, 115
Fennywood, Little Budworth, 148
Fernilee, Hope, 157
Fernlee, Saddleworth, 137
Fields, Ashton-under-Lyne, 135
Fife, Scotland, 1
Finney Cote, Tottington Lower End, 98
Fitton Hill, Ashton-under-Lyne, 10
Flash House, Butterworth, 132
Flaxmoss, 35, 110
Fleet St., Liverpool, 89
Fletcher Fold, Bury, 17
Flixton, 8, 11, 12, 27, 39, 63, 89, 108, 117, 122
Flookersbrook, 153, 180
Fold, Oldham, 51
Forest of Pendle, 47, 105, 115, 118
Forest of Rossendale, 64
Formby, 7, 14, 18, 19, 34, 72, 84, 92, 105(5), 106, 111, 126(2), 136
Fort St. George, Bombay, 7
Foulk Stapleford, Tarvin, 173
Foulreaks, Yorks, 2
Foulridge, 25, 95
Four Lane Ends, Bunbury, 145
Four Lane Ends, Tottington, 63
Fowleach, Oldham, 134
France, 64, 188
Francil, Rochdale, 23
Frandley, Seven Oaks, 161
Frankby, West Kirby, 173
Freetown, Bury, 54
Frierhill, Accrington, 36
Frodsham, 143, 144(2), 150, 152(2), 155(2), 158, 160(3), 161(4), 163, 165(2), 166, 167, 169, 171, 172, 175, 176(3), 182, 184
Fulneck, Leeds, 27
Furnace, Cheshire, 158
Further Barn, Shuttleworth, 58
Further Hill, Rossendale, 30

GALE, Rochdale, 59(2)
Gambleside, 4, 94
Gantley Lane, Billinge, 49
Garston, 22, 138
Garwyn-vawr, 189
Gate, Littleborough, 59
Gate & Pickup Bank, 10
Gate Inn, Rochdale, 59
Gatley, Stockport, 151, 166
Gatemen, Wrexham, 187
Gawsworth, 145, 148, 149, 151, 166, 175, 180(2), 182, 183
Gayton, Heswall, 147
Gedling, Notts., 95
Gee Cross, Werneth, 174, 179

Geertrindenburgh, Netherlands, 41
Gemspit, Bury, 15
Gerards, Stockport, 181
Gibhill, 43
Gigg, Bury, 134
Gilda Brook, Eccles, 69, 70
Gillibrand Hall, 44
Glanclwyd, Denbigh, 187
Glasgow, 69, 164
Glazebrook, 3, 22, 94
Gleadehill, Euxton, 76
Glodwick, Oldham, 122(3)
Glossop, Derbys., 35, 58, 84
Gloucestershire, 60, 91
Goals Mill, Prestwich, 128
Godley, Mottram, 144, 147, 167, 181(3)
Goit Hall, Stockport, 170
Golborne, Winwick, 21, 22, 23, 35, 48, 89, 115, 120, 121
Goldenhill, Staffs., 114
Goldshaw Booth, 6, 20, 93
Goldstone, Cheswardine, 160
Gooden Lane, Bury, 4
Gooden Lane, Heywood, 27, 110
Goodshaw, 4, 56, 64, 83
Goodshaw Chapel, 94
Goose Green, Pemberton, 121
Goose Lane, Macclesfield, 179
Goostrey, 22, 181
Gorsey Clough, Tottington Lower End, 92
Gorstage, Weaverham, 146
Gorton, 10, 63, 101, 104, 112, 115, 134
Gosforth, Cumberland, 10
Goss St., Chester, 164
Goyts Moss, Taxal, 173
Granada, West Indies, 55
Grane, Haslingden, 107
Grange, Oldham, 12, 25, 106
Grappenhall, 144, 147, 150, 159(3), 166, 169, 171
Grasscroft, Rochdale, 53
Gravilhole, Thornham, 122
Grays Inn, Middlesex, 50
Greasby, 144
Great James St., Bedford Row, Middlesex, 5
Green Ground, 78
Green Heys, Manchester, 117, 133
Green Hurst, 9
Green Lane, Barton-upon-Irwell, 67
Green Lane, Droylsden, 39
Green Lane, Romiley, 177, 184
Green St., Bolton, 105
Green Walls, Dodleston, 184
Greenacres, Oldham, 14(2)
Greenacres Moor, Oldham, 15(2), 27, 59(2), 122, 125, 134
Greenfield, Thelwall, 178
Greengate Hill, Middleton, 50
Greenoughs Row, Wigan, 8
Greens Brandwood, Rochdale, 4
Greens House, Cliviger, 115
Greens Mill, Rossendale, 80
Greenwich Hospital, 120, 132
Gresford Lodge, 187
Grindle St., Manchester, 67
Grosvenor St., Chorlton Row, 121
Grove House, Liverpool, 48
Guernsey, Isle of, 3
Guide, Lower Darwen, 111
Guide Lane, Ashton-under-Lyne, 113
Guilden Sutton, 154, 177
Gurnett, Prestbury, 149
Gwaynynog, co. Denbigh, 150
Gwerchtig, Flints., 187
Gwernygron, Flints., 187

HABERGHAM, Burnley, 93
Habergham Eaves, 28, 66, 76, 104, 106, 111, 127
Hacking Hall, Billington, 25
Hackinsall, 11
Hades, Rochdale, 23
Hag Side, Radcliffe, 89
Haggate, Burnley, 44, 91
Haggate, Lower, 116
Hague, Mottram, 151
Haigh, Wigan, 56, 81, 88, 117(3)
Hale, Bowdon, 149, 156, 157, 159(4), 170, 172, 173(4), 180(3), 182
Hale, Childwall, 2, 12, 19, 48, 76, 78, 97, 103, 136(2)
Hale Bottom, 121
Halebank, 76, 103
Halewood, 57, 73, 104
Halewood Green, 45
Halghton, Flints., 187(4), 188(3), 189
Halkethleaths, Scotland, 82
Hall Car, Rossendale, 4
Halliwell, Deane, 12, 33, 35, 53, 56, 89, 92, 94, 97, 101, 111
Halsall, 24, 58, 72(3), 80, 102, 104, 116, 137, 138
Halton, 147, 152, 156, 173, 181
Halton, Little, 24, 89
Hamburg, 85
Hampstead, 178
Hampsthwaite, Yorks., 103
Hampton, Malpas, 148, 172
Hampton Hall, 170
Handbridge, Chester, 150, 155, 173, 179, 180, 182
Handforth-cum-Bosden, 149, 162, 163, 166, 168, 183
Handley, 150
Hanging Lees, Rochdale, 43
Hankelow Mill, Audlem, 159
Hanmer, Flints., 187(7), 188(8), 189

Hapton, 27, 137
Hardshaw, Windle, 30(5), 44(2), 56, 59, 92, 111, 120, 125
Hargreave, Padiham, 124
Hargreave, Tarvin, 151, 154, 168(2)
Hargreave Fold, Rossendale, 30
Hargreaves, Rossendale, 35
Harpurhey, 3, 24, 106, 132(2)
Harrytown, Bredbury, 184
Hart Common, Westhoughton, 112
Hartford, 143, 154, 164, 169
Harthill, 149, 159, 182
Hartleys, Manchester, 47
Hartshead, Ashton-under-Lyne, 66, 83, 118
Harrington, Liverpool, 6, 7, 10, 11, 34, 36, 45, 55, 65, 70, 71, 75, 83, 89, 92, 130
Harrock Hall, 104
Harrop Cote, Yorks., 17
Harrop Green, Saddleworth, 137
Harropfold, Rainow, 167
Harst Brook, Ashton-under-Lyne, 77
Hartington upper Quarter, Derbys., 149
Harwood, 18, 46, 50, 54, 63, 93
Harwood, Great, 18(2), 33, 35
Harwood, Little, 131
Haslingden, 4, 5, 11, 16, 21, 24, 28, 34, 35, 47, 52(3), 55, 58(3), 62, 81(2), 89, 102, 105, 107(2), 108, 110, 114, 119, 134
Haslingden Grange, 95
Haslington, 62, 145, 156, 162
Hassall, 162
Hassall Green, Betchton, 164
Hatherton, Wybunbury, 144, 153, 180
Hattersall, Mottram, 183
Hattersley, 158, 178
Hatton, 150, 151, 160(2), 164, 168
Hatton, Wharton, 168
Hatton Heath, Saighton, 175
Hatton Heath, Waverton, 181
Haughton, Manchester, 11, 18, 22(2), 41, 45, 76, 114, 125
Haughton, Little, Worsley, 135
Haughton Grange, 85
Haulgh, Bolton, 79
Hawarden, Flints., 188(2)
Hawkins Lane, Rainow, 151
Haworth Cross, Rochdale, 87
Haworth Fold, Habergham Eaves, 116
Hax Moss, Aslingden, 47
Hay, Tintwistle, 170
Hay Head, 92
Haydock, 1(2), 31, 45, 46, 48
Hayton, 125
Haywood, Audlem, 163
Hazlehurst, Ashton-under-Lyne, 112, 122
Heady Hill, Bury 100
Heald, Bacup, 80
Heald Mill, Mobberley, 164
Healds Green, Chadderton, 63
Heap, 17, 91, 103
Heap Brow, Bury, 64
Heath Charnock, 39
Heatley Heath, Lymm, 157, 182
Heaton, 51, 75, 80
Heaton, Leek, 33
Heaton, Little, 35, 48, 58, 64(2), 67, 118
Heaton Norris, 1, 4, 9, 11, 12, 14, 17, 22, 24, 31, 38, 45, 58, 59(2), 62, 63, 64. 70, 74(2), 76, 85(2), 91, 93(2), 99(2), 111, 113, 115, 121, 124, 125, 128, 129, 139
Heaton Park, 34
Hebers, Middleton, 74, 123
Hedge End, Great Harwood, 18
Height Barn, Rossendale, 58
Heights, Accrington, 23
Heightside, Padiham, 1
Helsby, 166, 167, 185
Helton, Bury, 62
Henburn Bridge, 55
Henbury, 147, 148, 149, 157, 164, 184, 185
Henfield, Blackburn, 94
Henheads, Rossendale, 5, 95
Herculaneum Pottery, Toxteth, 131
Hereford, 79
Hermitage, Crompton, 80, 158
Hertfordshire, 164
Hesketh, 133, 140
Heskin, Eccleston, 4, 33, 54, 92(2), 119
Heswall, 143, 146, 147, 154
Heversham, Westmorland, 41
Hey Chapel, 77
Hey Head, Gambleside, 94
Hey Houses, Tottington, 19
Heyhead, Great Marsden, 83, 94
Heyhead, Little Marsden, 133
Heyrod, Ashton-under-Lyne, 77
Heyside, Royton, 57
Heywood, 27, 43, 46, 93, 103(2), 110(2), 13
Higginshaw, Royton, 50
High Field, Liverpool, 95
High Leigh, 150, 166, 169(2), 170, 177(2), 1
High St., Stockport, 163
Higham, Pendle, 47, 96, 109
Higher Barns, Iscoyd, 187
Higher Booths, 21
Higher Constabley, Rossendale, 130
Higher Hethersall, 25
Higher Lane, Pilkington, 62
Higher Lane, Prestwich, 56
Higher Shore, 122
Higher Tonsharp, 2
Higher Woodhill, Bury, 129
Highfield, 95
Highfield, Pendleton, 137
Highlands, Royton, 61(2)
Highlane, Marple, 168(2)

Highwhitaker, Padiham, 119
Hight Lane, 64
Hilbre Island, 161
Hill Cliff, Appleton, 185
Hill St., Harrington, 75
Hillgate, Stockport, 175, 177
Hillhouse, Brindle, 133
Hinderton, 152
Hindley, 8, 10, 14, 15, 34(2), 38, 58, 67, 71(2), 76, 78, 86, 97(2), 103, 120, 122
Hinds, Bury, 9
Hoarstones, Goldshaw Booth, 20
Hockenhull, 167
Hoggarth End, 6
Hoghton, 2, 13, 23, 28, 74, 123, 126, 137
Holcombe, Tottington, 63, 128, 138
Holden, Haslingden, 28, 52, 55
Holden Fold, 60, 61
Holebottom, Oldham, 21
Holehouse, Mottram, 162
Holehouse, Tottington, 16
Holme, Haslingden, 125
Holland, 46, 98
Hollant St., Spotland, 118
Hollinfare, Warrington, 140
Hollingreave, Saddleworth, 109, 110
Hollingreen, 3
Hollingwood, 53, 123
Hollingworth, 53, 111, 113, 144, 161, 166, 175, 177
Hollins, Oldham, 64, 76, 108, 127
Hollinsgreen, 97, 125
Hollinwood, 4(2), 35(2), 40, 43(2), 47, 74, 78, 118(2), 120, 121, 123, 133, 138(2), 140
Hollinworth Smithy, Prestbury, 160
Holme Field, Rossendale, 131
Holme Wood, Tarleton, 100
Holmes, Tarleton, 27, 139
Holmes Chapel, Burnley, 58, 99, 167, 173
Holt, Denbighs., 187, 188(3), 189
Holt Hill, Tranmere, 147, 170, 173, 177, 180
Holt Hill, Whalley, 67
Holt Town, Manchester, 88, 139
Holywell, 188
Homer Hill, Bury, 100
Hoo Green, Mere, 171
Hoole, Little, 53, 120, 133
Hoole, Much, 2, 4, 23, 41, 118
Hoole Bank, 148
Hooley Hill, 24, 25, 27, 140
Hoose, 146, 167, 178
Hoose Heath, Knutsford 175
Hope, Derbyshire, 157, 182
Hope Green, Adlington, 154
Hopkin Mill, 35
Hopwood, 35, 74, 87, 93, 95, 110
Hornby Lodge, Delamere, 162
Horns, Bangor, 188
Horridge, End, Hope, 182
Horsecroft, Spotland, 80
Horton, Tilston, 152, 183
Horton Ring, Bronington, 188
Horwich, 13, 17, 21, 28, 36, 46, 50, 58, 68, 69, 83, 85, 86, 94, 97, 99, 107, 133, 141
Hough, Wilmslow, 148, 163, 166, 178
Houghton, 12, 67, 83, 98, 113, 129(2), 137, 139(2)
Houghton Nook, Altham, 98
Howarth, co. Durham, 98
Howarth Cross, Rochdale, 126
Hoylake, 146
Hoyle Hey, 80
Hubby Causway, Barrowford Booth, 120
Huddersfield, 175
Hull, Yorks., 3, 123
Hulme, 6, 8, 9, 10(2), 13, 16, 18, 23, 25(2), 33, 34, 35, 42, 45, 54, 60, 62, 83(2), 92, 94(2), 95, 96, 98(2), 103, 106, 110, 121, 122, 127(2), 129, 135(2), 136
Hulton, 55
Hulton, Little, 14, 24, 43, 58, 99, 124
Hulton, Middle, 15, 31, 49, 58, 91
Hulton, Over, 14, 97, 108
Huncoat, 116
Hundersfield, 55, 117, 119
Hunsterson, Wybunbury, 180
Hunt Lane, Chadderton, 108
Huntingdonshire, 69
Huntington, 181
Hurdsfield, 96, 145, 150, 173, 175(4), 179, 181
Hurleston, 173
Hurst, Ashton-under-Lyne, 56, 76, 87, 137
Hurst Cross, Ashton-under-Lyne, 22, 123
Hurst St., Ashton-under-Lyne, 105
Hutton, 44
Huyton, 9, 37, 65, 104
Hyde, 144, 158(2), 160, 162(2), 167(2), 174, 183
Hyde Hall, 176

IDDENSHALL, St. Werburgh, 177
Ince, Cheshire, 154, 161(2), 180
Ince, Wigan, 20(2), 23, 40, 95
Ince Blundell, 111, 112, 126
Ince-in-Makerfield, 18, 20, 49, 59, 75, 79, 139
Ince Hall, Makerfield, 79
Inckfield Mill, Rochdale, 125
Ingersley, Prestbury, 177
Inghams, Leyland, 79
Inghead, 61
Ingol Lodge, 34
Ireland, 27, 50, 60, 82, 107
Irlam, 18(2)
Irwell House, Manchester, 90
Iscoyd, 187(3), 188(3), 189
Isle of Man, 26, 28, 53, 90, 98

Islington, 73
Italy, 85

JACKSON FOLD, 98
Jamaica, 24, 34, 47, 57, 60, 104
John St., Bedford Row, Middlesex, 111(2)

KEARSLEY, Deane, 12, 24, 30, 64, 68, 79, 97, 122, 126
Keckwick, Runcorn, 162
Keelendre, Ellesmere, 174
Kelsall, 148(2), 153(2), 157, 164, 177, 179
Kenches, Saddleworth, 19
Kendal, 97, 106, 125
Kensington, Middlesex, 121
Kensington, West Derby, 24, 74
Kent, 52, 145, 180
Kent St., Liverpool, 63
Kenyon, 65, 133
Kercroft Nook, 119
Kerdles, Rossendale, 117
Kermincham, 143, 150, 162
Kerridge, Prestbury, 162
Kersall, Manchester, 108
Kersall Moor; Broughton, 74
Keswick, Cumberland, 109, 114
Kettleshulme, 146, 148, 154, 159, 173
Key Wood, Bury, 73
Kidderminster, 114, 129
Kinder, Glossop, 84
Kinderton, 148, 183, 185
Kinderton Hall, 179
Kingsley, Frodsham, 154, 167, 168
Kingston, Jamaica, 57
Kinknall, Culcheth, 25
Kinnerton, 189
Kinnerton, Higher, 188
Kinswood Green, Wrenbury, 162
Kirkaldy, Fife, 1
Kirkby, 4, 5, 16, 20, 81, 106, 139
Kirkby Clough, Kettleshulme, 173
Kirkby Kendal, 106
Kirkdale, 23, 52, 85, 89, 96, 120, 133
Kirkhoms [? Kirkham], 98
Knar, Saddleworth, 137(2)
Knat Bank, Bamford, 109
Knolton, Overton, 188
Knot Lanes, Ashton-under-Lyne, 3, 17, 114
Knothill, Rochdale, 62, 80(2), 81
Knowlwood, Walsden, 120
Knowsley, 24, 38, 46, 57, 92, 124, 126
Knutsford, 122, 149(2), 157, 160, 161(2), 163, 164, 171(2), 172, 174, 175
Knutsford, Nether, 102, 143, 144, 146, 147, 150, 154, 157(5), 158, 160, 161, 168, 170, 173, 178, 182, 183, 185(3)
Knutsford, Over, 63, 179

LACH DENNIS, 157
Lady Barn, 137
Ladyhouse, Rochdale, 87(2)
Lamberhead Green, Orrell, 12
Lambran, 46
Lancashire Hill, Heaton Norris, 85
Lancaster, 5, 6, 15(4), 32, 57, 67(3), 80, 109, 125
Lane, Hanmer, 188
Lane, Stayley, 166
Lane End, Chadderton, 77
Lane End, Hopwood, 74
Lane End, Prestwich, 115
Lane Ends, Little Marsden, 54
Lane Head, Bacup, 58
Laneside, 134
Laneside, Great Mearley, 51
Laneside, Prestwich, 59, 121
Laneside, Spotland, 75, 81
Langley, Middleton, 109
Langley Hall, Middleton, 134
Langtree, Standish, 30, 73, 74, 76
Lansdown Place, Brunswick Square, Middlesex, 168
Largy, Ireland, 60
Latchford, Grappenhall, 144, 148, 150, 156(157, 159, 160, 163(2), 164, 166, 167, 168, 169(3), 171, 176, 184
Latchford Hall, Blackley, 2
Lathom, 5, 6, 7, 9, 10(2), 11, 25, 31(2), 32, 39, 41, 52, 60, 69, 73, 81, 89, 100, 101, 102(3), 107, 111, 117, 124(2), 130, 133, 134, 135, 139
Laughton, Lincs., 24
Law House, Rochdale, 75
Lea, 162
Lea, Aldford, 182
Lea Forge, 156
Lea Mill, 154
Leagram, 62
Leasgill, Westmorland, 42
Leasowe Castle, 147
Leavengreave, Rochdale, 17
Leeches, Shuttleworth, 54
Leeds, Yorks., 27, 72
Leek, Staffs., 33, 41
Lees, 19, 65, 74, 85, 121, 150
Lees, Ashton-under-Lyne, 19, 33, 86, 91
Lees, Bury, 100
Lees, Oldham, 22, 112
Leftwich, 143, 149, 150. 171, 180
Leghale, Trawden, 53
Leghorn, Italy, 85
Leicestershire, 21, 84, 114
Leigh, 4, 14, 23, 41, 46, 48, 59, 60, 66, 69, 77(2), 81, 84, 85, 97(2), 107, 140
Leigh, Little, 164, 169, 170, 183, 184
Leigh, Scotland, 19

Leighton, 150
Levenshulme, 12, 54, 71, 138
Lever, 58, 68
Lever, Great, 46
Lever, Little, 48, 80(2), 92, 102
Lever Edge, Middleton, 109
Leyland, 6, 8, 14, 22, 25, 38, 52, 53, 56, 57, 71, 79(3), 125, 129(4)
Leyland Lane, Leyland, 14
Lilford, Northants., 79
Lilley Lanes, Ashton-under-Lyne, 19
Lily Hill, Pilkington, 30
Lima Leone, Africa, 19
Limefield, Ashton-under-Lyne, 124
Limefield House, Bury, 71(2)
Limehurst, 51
Linacre, 45, 101, 103
Linacre Marsh, 69
Lincoln, 4
Lincolns Inn, Middlesex, 2, 39, 49, 155
Lincolnshire, 24
Linedred, 64
Lisbon, Portugal, 160
Liscard, 178, 179, 181
Litherland, 11, 29, 74, 97(2), 105, 113, 124, 136
Little Green, Cheetham, 139
Little Green, Middleton, 7, 118
Little Hayfield, Derbys., 114
Little Heath, Dunham Massey, 162
Little Lever Hall, 47
Little London, North Meols, 69
Little Moss, Ashton-under-Lyne, 11, 47
Little St. Johns, Chester, 156
Littleborough, 59, 73, 91
Littlecleg, Butterworth, 110
Littlemoorhend, Whalley, 31
Littlewood, Bury, 49
Littlewood Cross, Bury, 134
Liverfold Herley, Rochdale, 36
Liverpool, 1-141 *passim*, 170, 174
Livesey, 29(2), 36, 56, 126, 134
Llandegai, Carnarvons., 163
Llandingsbrook, Flints., 188
Llangerniew, Denbighs., 188
Loadhill Platting, Saddleworth, 140
Lockwoodhey, Saddleworth, 132
Lodge, Nantwich, 169
Lodge Lane, 81
Lodge Lane, Liverpool, 14
Lodge Stand, Prestwich, 123
London, 14, 29, 36, 53, 74, 87, 88, 114, 122, 127, 132, 154, 163
Longborough, Leicesters., 84
Longclough, 118
Longford, 27
Longlands, Matley, 170
Longley Hall, Macclesfield, 186
Longport, Staffs., 135
Longsight, 81, 85
Longton, 5, 18, 25, 90, 95(2), 114, 117, 118, 120, 133, 134(3)
Longworth, Bolton, 30, 122, 133
Longworth Bank, Bolton, 67
Loppington, Salop, 170
Lords Court, Oldham, 48
Lords Fields, Shocklach, 158
Lostock, 18(2), 25, 42, 50, 64, 65(2), 96, 97(2), 99, 102, 112
Lostock, Eccles, 24
Lostock Gralam, 151, 160, 164, 166, 179, 185
Lostock Hall, 116
Louisiana, 24
Lovely Hall, Blackburn, 128
Low Clough, Whalley, 62
Low Green, Hindley, 103
Low Head, Spotland, 126
Low Hill, Liverpool, 18, 45, 63(2), 87, 119
Low Hill Coffee House, Liverpool, 95
Lowcross, Tilston, 177
Lower Cleggs Wood, 38
Lower Croft, Elton, 128
Lower Eaves, Tottington, 30
Lower Hey Mill, Rochdale, 23
Lower House, West Derby, 21
Lower Lomas, 21
Lower Mill, Rochdale, 80
Lower Place, Castleton, 62
Lower Place, Rochdale, 45, 61, 110
Lower Shore, 14
Lower Swain Road., Rochdale, 21
Lower Town House, Rochdale, 91(2)
Lower Tunshill, Butterworth, 106
Lower Walton, 156
Lower White Lee, Pendle, 54
Lowerfield, Wardle, 76
Lowerhouse, Habergham Eaves, 76
Lowton, 6, 7, 12, 13, 25, 56, 76, 106, 115, 125, 139
Lowton Common, 7
Lumber St., Liverpool, 112
Lunatic Asylum, Lancaster, 32
Lupton St., Bolton, 48
Lutterworth, Leics., 21
Lydiate, 2, 68, 74, 105, 111
Lyme, 167, 173
Lyme Handley, 145
Lymm, 152(3), 156(3), 157, 164, 171, 175, 176, 182(2), 184
Lytham, 6, 99

MABFIELD, Withington, 83
Macclesfield, 143-186 *passim*
Macclesfield Forest, 151
Madeley, Staffs., 28, 145
Madras, East Indies, 5
Maes Lewis, Overton, 187
Maghull, 16, 35, 48, 57, 64, 94, 111

Maidenhead, Berks., 96
Main Grass, Mottram, 149
Maller Inglane, Goodshaw, 83
Malpas, 143, 144, 148(2), 150, 153(2), 154(2), 155(3), 156, 164, 169, 172(3), 175(3), 177, 180, 182, 184(2), 185, 188
Man, Isle of, 11, 41, 58, 153
Manchester, 1-141 *passim,* 189
Manchester Collegiate Church, 38
Manchester St., Oldham, 132
Manor, Hawarden, 188
Mansfield St., Liverpool, 69
Mantelow Gate, Saddleworth, 112
Maranhao, Brazil, 40
Marbury, 146, 152, 173
Mardyke, Rochdale, 61
Market Harborough, 113
Marl Earth, Castleton, 45
Marland, Castleton, 79
Marld Earth, Rochdale, 77
Marple, 150, 151, 153, 154, 161, 162, 169(2) 174(2), 175
Marsden, Great, 8, 46, 54, 83, 99
Marsden, Little, 54, 63, 131, 133
Marsh Green, 59
Marshouse, 149
Marston, Budworth, 147, 177(2)
Marthall, 151, 152, 184
Martholme, 25
Martins, 81
Martinscroft, 12, 15, 21
Martinscroft Green, 17
Marton, 121, 144, 166, 168, 178
Marton, Prestbury, 156
Marton, Whitegate, 149, 162
Marylebone, London, 87
Matley, Mottram, 158, 170, 184
Mawdesley, 1, 2, 28, 30, 66, 88, 134, 136, 141
May Place, West Derby, 108
Mayerscroft, 44
Meadow Croft, Bury, 86
Meadowhead, Rossendale, 54
Meadows, Birtle, 27
Meanwood, Rochdale, 121
Meanwood Brow, Rochdale, 55
Mearley, Great, 51
Medlock Vale, 65
Melling, 59, 73, 76
Mellisons, Ashton-under-Lyne, 77
Mellor, 8(2), 27, 29, 34, 52, 88, 115, 129(2)
Mellor, Derbys., 93
Meols, 183
Mere, 157, 161(2), 171
Mew, 3
Mickle Key, 113
Micklehurst, Mottram, 169, 176
Middlesex, 2, 5, 22, 24, 26, 33, 39, 50(2), 60, 84, 87, 111(2), 112, 121, 124, 148, 150, 155, 159, 168
Middleton, 3, 7(2), 11, 15, 18, 19, 20(2), 21(2), 23, 27(4), 33, 40, 49, 50, 54, 59(2), 60, 64(3), 66, 67, 71(2), 72(2), 74, 81, 86, 87, 88, 93(2), 96, 100, 101, 104, 105, 106 108, 109(3), 110, 112, 116, 118, 120, 122, 123, 124, 126(2), 128, 134(2), 137
Middleton Wood, 48
Middlewich, 31, 144, 146, 147(2), 149, 150(2 153(2), 154(3), 159, 160(3), 161, 162(4), 163(2), 164, 165, 167, 171, 179, 186
Midgeley, Wincle, 158
Mile End, Stockport, 173
Milkstone, Rochdale, 21
Mill Bottom, Prestwich, 140
Mill Bottom, Saddleworth, 109
Mill Brook, Mottram, 143, 177
Mill Hill, Little Bolton, 13, 35
Mill Hill, Livesey, 126
Mill St., Harrington, 55
Mill St., Liverpool, 33
Millend, 9
Millend, Gawsworth, 180
Millhouse, Adlington, 166
Millington, 148
Milnrow, 25, 64, 109, 120(2), 121
Milnthorpe, Heversham, 41
Minshull Vernon, 148, 150, 164, 174, 186
Mitton, 23
Mobberley, 147(2), 148, 152, 157, 168, 170, 175, 180, 185(2)
Mold, 188
Monks Coppenhall, 170
Montgomery, 188
Monton, Eccles, 51, 71
Monton Lane, 96
Moor, Daresbury, 155
Moor Gate, Rochdale, 87
Moort St., Ormskirk, 66
Moore, 164, 169(2)
Moorend, 54
Moorgate, Stayley, 160
Moorhole, Middleton, 49
Moorland, Brereton, 168
Moorlane, Bolton, 122
Moorside, Bury, 71, 119
Moorside, Flixton, 11, 27, 89
Moorside, Wardle, 72
Moreton, 153, 175, 185
Morley, 145
Mortfield, Bolton, 18
Morton, 156
Morton Wood, Salop, 176
Moss, Colne, 100
Moss Brook, Widnes, 90
Moss Brook Lodge, Widnes, 47

Moss End, Smallwood, 161, 169
Moss Gate, Crompton, 123
Moss Lane, 28
Moss Lane, North Meols, 105
Moss Lane, Prestwich, 8
Moss Side Tottington, 140
Mossgrove, 46
Mosshouse, Church Lawton, 168
Mossley, Ashton-under-Lyne, 4, 19, 52, 77, 90, 119, 139
Moston, 30, 74
Moston, Warmingham, 162, 163, 185
Mottram, 143(2), 144(2), 147(2), 149(3), 150, 151, 156, 162, 163, 166, 167, 169, 170(2), 175, 176(2), 177(3), 178, 181(2), 183, 184(2)
Mottram in Longdendale, 144, 157, 158, 161, 165, 168, 169, 170, 171, 176, 177, 180, 181(2), 183, 184, 185(2)
Mottram Moor, 159
Mottram St. Andrews, 149, 157, 169(3), 172, 184
Mouldsworth, Tarvin, 153, 164
Moulton, 152, 175
Mount Green, Rochdale, 50
Mount House, Prenton, 167
Mount Pleasant, Hampstead, 178
Mount Pleasant, Oldham, 19, 77, 85, 93
Mount Vernon, Liverpool, 86, 118
Mountains, Rochdale, 122
Muckleton, Salop, 16
Mumps, Oldham, 25, 120
Musbury, 102, 110
Musbury, Bury, 62
Musbury, Haslingden, 107
Mytham, Saddleworth, 17

NABBS, Walmersley, 67
Nabbs Horse, Tottington, 20
Nantwich, 145-183 *passim*
Nashville, United States of America, 175
Nassau, North America, 23, 34, 45
Nathan Row, Oldham, 119
Naz-end, Colne, 139
Near Nar Side Chapelry, Colne, 12
Nelson House, 61
Neston, 143, 148, 166, 170, 172(2), 178, 182, 183(2)
Neston, Great, 105, 151, 155, 183, 184
Neston, Little, 152, 161
Netherlands, 41, 98
Netherlees, Ashton-under Lyne, 111
Netherton, Frodsham, 135, 138, 167, 184
Nettledale, Peckforton, 154
New Bank, Oldham, 59
New Barns, Pendlebury, 86
New Brook House, 71
New Crane St., Chester, 158
New Delph, 16
New Gate, Shuttleworth, 47
New Hall, 43
New Hall Hey, Rossendale, 4
New House, Castleton, 43
New Inn, Crawshaw Booth, 117
New Lower House, Oldham, 87
New Orleans, Louisiana, 24
New Providence, North America, 23, 34, 45
New Richmond, Pendleton, 52
New South Wales, 64
New Town, Montegomery, 188
New Windsor, Salford, 110
New York, Ameriça, 42, 87, 89
New York, Glossop, 58
Newbarn, Rochdale, 75
Newbold, Rochdale, 62
Newburgh, Lathom, 81, 105, 107, 111
Newcastle-under-Lyne, 80, 115, 144
Newchurch, 5, 80, 98, 119
Newchurch, Rossendale, 4, 25, 29, 52, 55, 83, 131
Newellhead, Yate & Pickup Bank, 56
Newfoundland, 136
Newhall, 152, 161
Newhey, Rochdale, 30
Newmarket, Manchester, 1
Newport, Staffs., 17
Newroad, Rochdale, 30
Newry, Ireland, 82
Newton, 22, 34, 41, 45, 49, 58(2), 63(2), 71, 98(2), 100, 108, 132, 134, 152, 156, 157, 185
Newton, Frodsham, 146, 153, 169
Newton, Manchester, 13, 80, 81, 93, 100(3)
Newton, Middlwich, 147, 154, 160, 162, 164, 165, 171
Newton, Mottram, 143, 150, 163, 176, 178, 185
Newton Heath, 5, 17, 47, 68, 165
Newton-in-Makerfield, 17, 108
Newton-le-Willows, 17, 81, 102, 140
Norbury, 145, 152, 153, 154, 156, 158, 172, 178
Norbury, Stockport, 158, 178
Norley, Frodsham, 160, 170, 184
North Britain, 34, 69
North Meols, 6(2), 7(2), 18, 27, 45, 47, 60(2), 63, 64, 65, 69(2), 75, 90, 105(2), 109, 112, 129, 139, 140
North Moor, Oldham, 8
North Rode, 162, 164
Northamptonshire, 114
Northbury Booths, 167
Northen Etchells, 149, 167, 175
Northenden 145, 159, 166, 171, 172, 176, 185(2)
Northgate, Blackburn, 16
Northgate, Oldham, 122
Northumberland St., Middlesex, 87

Northwich, 146, 148(2), 149, 152, 156, 161, 166
Nottingham, 37
Nottinghamshire, 95
Nova Scotia, 77
Nuttall Farm, 8

OAK FARM, Sandbach, 182
Oak Hill, Blackburn, 52
Oakenhead Wood, Haslingden, 105
Oakfield, 94
Oakmere, Delamere, 168
Occleston, Middlewich, 144, 179
Odd Rode, Astbury, 162, 169, 173, 177
Offterton, 172
Ogden, 96, 121
Oilmill, Rochdale, 66
Olberdeston, 55
Old Beachin, 170
Old Change, London, 88
Old Lane, Chadderton, 139
Old Meadows, Rossendale, 113(2)
Old Turks, Radcliffe, 128
Oldcastle, 159
Oldenoat, Oldham, 27
Olderroot, Oldham, 93
Oldfield, Dunham Massey, 153(2), 159, 174
Oldfield Rd., Salford, 39, 89
Oldham, 2(3), 8-140 *passim*
Oldham Lane, Oldham, 77
Oldham Road, 5, 72, 138
Oldham St., Manchester, 29
Olive Mount, Wavertree, 120
Ollerseat, Glossop, 35
Ollerton, 157, 161
Openshaw, 27, 31, 82, 89, 93, 102, 110, 124, 137(2)
Orford, 34, 40, 76
Orford Lane, Warrington, 22
Orford, Rd., Manchester,137
Ormskirk, 2(2), 6, 9, 10, 13(2), 19, 29(2), 38(3), 44(2), 45, 46, 47, 48, 51, 57(2), 63, 64, 66, 67(2), 75, 77, 85(2), 88(2), 90, 92, 95, 96, 99(4), 100(2), 104, 108, 111(2), 116(2), 124, 126, 127(2), 130(2), 131(2), 133, 135, 138(2), 139
Ormston Lodge, Barton-upon-Irwell, 34
Orrell, 5, 12, 39, 43, 74, 92, 106, 117
Orton, Huntingdonshire, 69
Osbaldeston, 28
Oswaldtwistle, 61, 73, 103, 129
Oswestry, Salop, 164
Oulton Lodge, 145
Oulton Lowe, 163, 184
Oulton Park, 36
Outwood, Prestwich, 32, 48, 51, 123
Over, 143, 153, 167, 170, 176(2), 180, 184(2)
Over Lane, Over, 147
Over Poole, 168
Overchurch, 149
Overton, Flints., 187(5), 188(4)
Overton, Frodsham, 156, 176
Overton, Malpas, 175
Overton, Little, Flints., 188
Oxford, 139
Oxhey, Saddleworth, 56, 87, 112

PADDINGTON LODGE, Edge Hill, 101
Padiham, 1, 14, 119, 123, 124
Padiham Green, Hapton, 27
Paddiley, 158
Pagheight, Accrington, 102
Pall Mall, Liverpool, 127
Parade St., Rochdale, 32
Parbold, 121, 127. *See also* Barbold
Park Hall, Ashton-under-Lyne, 23
Park House, 55
Park House, Butley, 158
Park House, Crompton, 75, 88
Park House, Gawsworth, 145
Park House, Pendlebury, 28
Park Lane, Pilkington, 69
Parkfield, Middleton, 27, 124
Parkgate, 146, 170, 174, 178, 180(2), 182, 183
Parkhill, Whalley, 117
Parr, 14, 20, 43(3), 61, 86, 120, 128, 138
Parracklumb, Bacup, 113
Parsons Fold, Radcliffe, 2
Partington, 36, 149, 156, 162
Pasmons, Rochdale, 57
Pasture, Cliviger, 137
Patricroft, 8, 23, 26, 27, 107
Peasfurlong, Culcheth, 139
Peckforton, 151, 154, 156, 171
Pemberton, 5, 9, 17, 31, 39, 60, 78, 90(2), 97, 103, 121(2), 132, 137
Pendle, 11, 47, 54, 105, 115, 118, 120
Pendlebury, 9, 28, 69, 72, 86, 89, 96
Pendleton, 4, 8, 9(2), 10, 21, 24(3), 28, 33, 35, 52, 57, 59, 60, 67, 81, 84, 85(2) 88, 94, 96, 98, 99, 101, 104, 105, 106, 107, 116, 121, 125, 128, 136, 137(3)
Penisarnant, Llandegai, 163
Penketh, 12, 22, 41, 42, 60
Pennington, Leigh, 39, 41, 63(2), 77(2), 85, 100, 124, 135(2), 140
Penrith, Cumberland, 126
Pentre Nant, Denbighs., 189
Penwortham, 6, 10(2), 16, 27, 61, 80, 92, 95, 116(3)
Peover, 168
Peover, Great, 162
Peover, Little, 152, 170
Peover, Lower, 157, 158, 173, 178
Peover, Over, 152, 162, 163, 167, 180(2), 185

Peplow Hall, 25
Petham, Kent, 180
Piccadilly, 56
Piccadilly, Middlesex, 33, 150
Pickhill, Bangor, 187(2), 188
Pickmere, Budworth, 185
Pickup Bank, 10, 56, 60
Pigs Lee, Bury, 62
Pikelow, Haslingden, 5
Pilkington, 2, 8, 11, 14, 17, 30, 36, 48, 55, 62(2), 69, 70, 71, 86, 97, 113, 121, 123
Pilsworth, 21, 30, 65, 89
Pipe Hill, Staffs., 68
Pippins Bank, Bacup, 29
Platt Bridge, Ince-in-Makerfield, 75
Plattin, Castleton, 121
Platting, Rochdale, 23
Playmouth Hospital, 85
Pleasant St., Haslingden, 108
Pleasington, 37, 40, 41, 96
Pleremore, Chaddesley Corbett, 125
Plumley, Budworth, 158, 173, 179, 185
Plunge, Bury, 115
Plymouth Dock, 85
Polefield, Manchester, 47
Polly Green, 108
Polygon, Ardwick, 13, 99
Polygon, Manchester, 39
Pool, Acton, 164
Pool Hall, Muckleton, Salop., 16
Pool Park, Denbighs., 189
Poole Lane, Failsworth, 11
Port St., Manchester, 42
Portico, Prescot, 65
Portugal, 159
Portwood, 70, 148, 163(3), 164, 171, 175, 176
Pott Shrigley, 159
Potters Row, Radcliffe, 2
Pough Kepsy, New York, 42
Poulton, 30, 53, 94, 136, 149, 183
Poulton Lancelyn, 158, 165
Poulton with Fearnhead, 30(2)
Pownall Fee, Wilmslow, 169
Poynton, 164, 169
Prees, Salop, 150, 176
Preesall with Hackinsall, 11
Prenton, 167
Prescot, 1(2), 4, 9, 12(3), 16, 17, 26, 33, 43(3), 46(2), 57, 58, 65, 67, 69, 71, 73, 76(3), 95, 97, 100(2), 101, 111(2) 113, 119, 120, 124, 126, 127(3), 129, 139, 141
Prescot Hall,19
Prestbury, 146, 148(2), 149, 150(2), 156, 157, 158, 160(2), 161, 162, 166, 173(3), 174(2), 175(2), 176, 178(2), 180, 181, 183, 184(2), 185
Preston, 5, 10, 13(2), 14, 28, 29, 43, 44, 59, 60, 81, 83
Preston Brook, 158
Preston-on-the-Hill, 148, 160, 179
Prestwich, 4(2), 8, 9, 11, 15, 17, 18, 32(2), 33(2), 34, 35, 37, 39, 40(2), 41, 48, 49, 51, 56, 59, 61(2), 62, 63, 64, 66, 74, 77(2), 90, 93, 94, 97, 104, 114, 115, 116, 118, 121, 122(2), 125(3), 127, 128(3), 134, 140
Puerto Cabello, South America, 78
Pulford, 149, 167

QUARLTON, 16, 28
Quebec, 23
Queen St., Salford, 109
Quick, Saddleworth, 132
Quick Edge, Saddleworth, 19

RADCLIFFE, 2(4), 5, 10, 13, 14, 32, 50, 52, 80, 85(2), 89, 93, 128, 129, 141
Radcliffe Bridge, 9, 51, 52, 97, 115
Radcliffe Hall, 109
Radfield Head, 79
Rainford, 7(2), 13, 19, 40, 41, 45, 48, 49, 61, 63, 79, 88, 94, 107(2), 108(2), 115, 130, 131, 138
Rainhill, 1(2), 43, 86, 102, 104, 108, 127
Rainow, 143, 148(2), 151, 164, 166, 167, 169, 171, 181
Rainow Low, 181
Ramsbottom, Bury, 72, 117
Ramsgrove, Blackburn, 14, 67
Randwick, Gloucs., 60
Ravenhead, 70
Ravenshore, Tottington, 47
Rawtenstall, 27, 62
Rawtenstall Forrest, Rossendale, 4
Read, 60
Reading, Berks., 128
Realshaw, Wharton, 180
Reaseheath, 180
Reddish, 8(2), 18(2), 35, 46, 57, 70, 74, 77(2), 124, 179
Redvales, Bury, 15, 32, 40, 102
Redwalls, Bury, 118
Reeds, Rossendale, 102
Revige Four Lane Ends, Blackburn, 76
Rhodes, Middleton, 81
Rhodes House, Oldham, 8
Ribchester, 11, 101
Richmond Row, Liverpool, 113
Ridley, 158
Ridley Wood, Holt, 187
Ridgehill & Lanes, Ashton-under-Lyne, 79
Ringley, 6
Ringley Bridge, 48, 132
Ringway, 146, 173, 175
Rio de Janeiro, Brazil, 31, 45, 88

Ripon, Yorks., 44(2)
Rishton, 35, 54, 98
Risley, Winwick, 21, 104
Rivington, 1, 40, 48, 108, 112(2)
Rixton-cum-Glazebrook, 3, 51, 94
Roading Fold, 59
Roby, 7, 8, 16, 19, 22, 81, 129
Rochdale, 4-140 *passim*
Roe Cross, Mottram, 144
Roe Park, Astbury, 169
Roebuckloe, Saddleworth, 137
Romiley, 177, 179, 184
Rooden Lane, Prestwich, 13, 22, 26, 33(2)
Rosbottom, Ashton-under-Lyne, 49, 65, 77
Roscommon St., Walton-on-the-Hill, 103
Rose Hill, Bolton, 15, 30
Rossendale, 4(6), 5, 15, 18, 21, 25, 29, 30(3), 33, 35, 46, 52(3), 54(5), 55(2), 58, 61, 62, 64(3), 75, 80(4), 83(2), 92(4), 94(4), 95, 100, 102, 104, 113, 117, 120, 122, 130, 131(3)
Rostherne, 147, 158(2), 166, 170, 176
Rotherham, Yorks., 77
Rothery, Scotland, 7
Rough Hill, 16
Roughbank, Rochdale, 59
Roughlee Booth, 51
Roughley Gate, Oswaldtwistle, 129
Roundabout Barn, Upholland, 20
Roundthorn, 2, 25
Rowe Green, Eccles, 11, 27
Rowton, Christleton, 172(2)
Roxbury, Oldham, 77
Royal Hotel, Chester, 180
Royton, 23, 40, 42, 50, 57, 61(2), 68, 71, 72, 76, 81, 86(2), 111, 122(3), 123, 133
Royton Lane, 21
Rudheath, Davenham, 144, 171, 178
Rudheath Lordship, 166
Rufford, 1, 119
Rugley, 13
Rumworth, 28, 35, 44, 51, 56, 63, 99, 100, 116, 137, 139, 140
Runcorn, 11, 79, 143, 145, 149, 154, 155(2), 156, 158, 160, 162, 163, 164, 165, 166, 172, 174, 175, 178, 184
Runcorn, Higher, 171
Rush Green, Lymm, 182
Rusholme, 44, 63, 86, 96, 129, 139
Rushton, 42, 170, 184
Rushyfields, Crompton, 59
Ryehill House, Haslingden, 102
Ryley Green, 13

SABBATH CHURCH, Salford, 22
Sabden, Pendleton, 35
Saddleworth, 10, 14, 15(2), 16, 17, 19(2), 20, 22, 29, 46, 53(3), 56, 71, 72, 76(3), 79, 83, 87, 99(2), 101(3), 103, 105, 109(3), 110(3), 112(3), 113(2), 118, 121, 122, 126, 132(5), 137(6), 138, 140(4)
Saddleworth Fold, 101, 132
Sadlers, Goldshaw Booth, 93
Saighton, 144, 175
St. Ann, Liverpool, 187
St. Bartholomew Close, London, 122
St. George, Westminster, 7
St. Georges Rd., Manchester, 3
St. Helens, 18, 28, 43, 45, 54, 56, 61, 67, 70, 79, 99(2), 106, 115, 116, 127
St. John St., Chester, 165
St. Johns, Newfoundland, 137
St. Martins in the Fields, Chester, 176
St. Martins in the Fields, Westminster, 135
St. Martins Lodge, Chester, 159
St. Pauls Square, Liverpool, 130
St. Peters Port, Guernsey, 3
St. Thomas, Southwark, 26
St. Werburgh, 177
Sale, 107, 145, 151(2), 155, 168, 170, 174, 175(2), 177(2), 182, 183
Salesbury, 131
Salford, 1-140 *passim*
Salford, New Bailey Prison, 35
Salford Wood, 66
Salop, 16, 150, 153, 160, 164, 170, 176, 177
Saltney, 188
Salusbury, 152
Samlesbury, 8, 17, 117
Sandbach, 145, 147, 148, 151(4), 152, 153, 154, 156, 158(2), 160(2), 165, 169, 175, 176(2), 177, 178, 179(2), 180, 181, 182(2), 183
Sandbach Heath, 146
Sandiway, 158, 160
Sandown Hall, Wavertree, 79
Sandy Gate, Habergham Eaves, 66
Sandy Lane, Pendleton, 128
Sandy Lane,Royton, 42
Sandy Lane End, Roby, 16
Sankey, 55, 100, 138
Sankey, Great, 55, 80, 84, 108, 117, 129
Sark Hill, Blackburn, 34
Sattersford, Rainow, 181
Saughall, Great, 146
Saughall Massie, 146(2)
Scarisbrick, 7, 14, 21, 29, 36, 38(2), 52, 56(2), 57(2), 60, 65, 85, 94, 98, 132, 139
Scarrs,Little Marsden, 63
Scatcliff, Accrington, 52
Scholes, Wigan, 17, 126
School Lane, Rochdale, 17, 70, 73
Scoonhoven, Holland, 98
Scotland, 7, 19, 82

Scout, 4
Scoutfold, 47
Sculcoates, Yorks., 55
Seacombe, 149, 157, 166, 178(2), 183
Sealand, Hawarden, 187, 188
Seelfold, 72
Seller St., Chester, 180
Senterns Well, Openshaw, 31
Sephton, 32, 112, 128, 141
Sesswick, Bangor, 187
Sett, Oldham, 8
Sevenacre Brook, Blackburn, 55
Sevenoaks, Over Whitley, 160, 161
Seymour St., Liverpool, 35
Shadsworth, 55
Shaftesbury, Dorset, 172
Shakerley, 32, 73, 100, 113(2)
Shallcross, Derbys., 176
Sharples, 75, 98, 108, 117, 124
Sharston Green, Northenden, 145
Shaw, Crompton, 87(2), 134
Shaw Chapel, Crompton, 61
Shaw Edge, Crompton, 92
Shaw Heath, Stockport, 169
Shaw Lane End, Rochdale, 139
Shawclough, Rochdale, 81, 126
Shawcross, Rochdale, 46
Shawforth, Rochdale, 16, 36
Shaws, Saddleworth, 53
Shaws Brow, Liverpool, 4, 95
Sheep Hey, Prestwich, 93
Sheffield, Rochdale, 25
Sheffield, Yorks., 140
Shelderslow, 19
Shersin within Henheads, Rossendale, 95
Shetford, 51
Shevington, 7, 42, 45, 119
Shipbrook, 144
Shipgate St., Chester, 175
Shipley Hall, Ashton-under-Lyne, 81
Shcoklach, 157
Shocklach Oviatt, 159, 177
Sholver, Oldham, 19
Shone Fold, Levenshulme, 138
Shordley, Flints., 189
Shorrockford, 60
Shorrockhey, 37
Shrewsbury, 123, 158, 177
Shude Hill, Manchester, 13, 98
Shuttleworth, 47, 54, 58
Siddall Moor, 27
Siddington, Prestbury, 147, 149(2), 157(2), 166
Silver Hill, Saddleworth, 111
Silver St., Bury, 1
Simonstone, 64, 132
Simonswood, 5, 39, 57, 138(2)
Sinderland, Dunham Massey, 159(2), 172
Singleton, Prestwich, 125
Skelmersdale, 3, 47, 60, 61, 85, 104, 113, 136
Slack, Newchurch, 98
Slackcote, 17
Slate Lane, Ashton-under-Lyne, 77
Slipper Hill, Foulridge, 25
Slaone St., Middlesex, 124
Small Bridge, Rochdale, 4, 23, 55(3)
Smallshaw, Rossendale, 92
Smallwood, 161, 169, 182
Smith Fold, Bolton, 110
Smithy Hoale, Livesey, 134
Snape Hill, Outwood, 123
Snelson, 167
Sollom, 7, 39, 51
Somerford, 158, 181
Somerford Booths, 168, 173, 179
Sound, 160
South Carolina, 156
South Gate House, Middlesex, 112
South Hawes, North Meols, 6, 67, 75
Southants., 67
Southern St., Manchester, 135
Southfield, Colne, 16
Southport, 7, 19, 47, 52, 53, 58, 68, 78(2), 110
Southwark, 26, 115, 183
Southworth with Croft, 120
Spain, 21
Speakedge, Rochdale, 62
Spear Brow, Blackburn, 52
Speke, 90, 115, 118
Spen, Goldshaw Booth, 6
Spitalfields, London, 36
Spittle, 172, 181
Spotland, 4, 23, 26, 51, 57, 62, 63, 72, 75, 80(2), 81(2), 83, 86, 102, 113(3), 118(2), 126
Spotland Bridge, 55, 77, 118
Spotland Tops, 40
Spring Gardens Terrace, Middlesex, 59
Spring Mill, Oldham, 33
Spring Side, Ashton-under-Lyne, 121(3)
Spring Valley, Isle of Man, 53
Springfield Cottage, 120
Sproston, 157, 180, 185(2), 186
Sproston Hall, 179
Spurstow, Bunbury, 161, 175
Square, Todmorden, 123
Square, Walsden, 40
Stack, Spotland, 83
Stafford, 52
Staffordshire, 17, 28, 33, 41, 68, 80, 114, 126, 135, 137, 140, 144, 145
Stakehill, Middleton, 20, 110
Staley, 160, 165(3), 166, 169(2), 174, 176, 183
Staley Bank, 38
Staley Hall, 147
Staley Wood, 157, 177

Stalybridge, 19, 24, 48, 49, 56, 65, 80, 91, 93, 99, 111, 112, 113, 116, 129, 134, 139
Stand, Pilkington, 123
Stand Lane, 30, 50
Stand Lane, Pilkington, 14, 86, 97
Stand Lane, Prestwich, 39, 118
Standiford, Staffs., 68
Standish, 7, 15, 18, 30, 40, 41, 66, 69, 73, 74, 76, 83, 98, 102, 112, 140
Standlees, Ashworth, 25
Standon Hall, Newcastle-under-Lyne, 80
Stanedge, Saddleworth, 132
Stanhill, Whalley, 56
Stanney, 164
Stanneylands, 164
Stanthorne, 153, 155
Stanthorne Hill, 165
Stapeley, Wybunbury, 158, 180
Statham with Lymm, 156
Steam Mill St., Chester, 179
Steephouse, Branwood, 51
Steven St., Chester, 165, 179
Stockbrook, Chadderton, 115
Stockham, Runcorn, 156
Stockport, 143-185 *passim*
Stockport Etchells, 157, 182
Stockport Moor, 183
Stockton, 85
Stoke, 145, 146, 155(2)
Stoke-upon-Trent, Staffs., 137
Stone Hill, Walton-on-the Hill, 70
Stonefold, Rossendale, 64
Stonepitfield, Rochdale, 109
Stonyhurst, Mitton, 23
Stoops, Habergham Eaves, 28
Storeton Hall, 185
Stott Field, Royton, 72
Stourport, Worcs., 129
Strand, Middlesex, 87
Strangeways, 8, 41, 42, 80, 105, 107
Strawberry Hill, Pendleton, 4
Street End, Petham, Kent, 180
Stretford, 7, 10, 11, 16, 39(2), 50(4), 65(3), 74, 76, 86, 90, 106, 112(2), 115, 135
Stretton, 146, 170, 183
Strines, 132
Strood, Kent, 52
Stubbins Lane, Tottington Lower End, 35
Stublach, Middlewich, 147
Styall, Wilmslow, 143, 158(2), 176
Styall Green, 176
Summerseat, Bury, 55
Summerville, Manchester, 130
Sunning Hill, 22
Sunny Side, Higher Booths, 21
Sunny Side, Salford, 134
Surrey, 26, 109, 115, 183
Sutton, 3, 57, 92, 99, 104, 106, 131, 143(2), 147, 156, 169, 178(2), 183, 186
Sutton, Macclesfield, 153, 185
Sutton, Prescot, 124
Sutton, Prestbury, 148, 150, 183
Sutton, Little, 143, 173, 181, 182
Sutton Coldfield, Warwicks., 115
Swanlow, 153
Swanlow Lane, 184
Swinton, 17, 23, 47, 71, 95, 96, 104, 110, 135, 136, 139
Switzerland, 31

TABLEY, 162(2), 169
Tabley, Nether, 166, 178
Tabley, Over, 146, 147, 149, 157, 162
Tain Barn, Castleton, 137
Tame Water, Saddleworth, 53
Tan Pitts, Rishton, 54
Tarbock, 8, 40, 51, 90, 138
Tarleton, 3, 27, 28, 38, 39(2), 51, 52, 55, 64, 67, 71(2), 78, 100, 122, 124, 133, 139
Tarlscough, Ormskirk, 48, 119
Tarporley, 143, 145, 158, 163, 164, 168(2), 170, 176, 177(3), 182(3), 184, 185
Tarvin, 144(2), 148, 149, 151, 153, 154, 155, 161, 163, 168(2), 173(2), 176, 17 178, 183
Tattenhall, 155, 162, 171, 174, 182(2)
Tatton, 158
Tatton Mill, 158
Taunton, 2, 109, 110
Taxall, 173, 179
Teddington, Middlesex, 149
Tempest Hey, Liverpool, 58
Temple, Mill Bottom, Saddleworth, 109
Tenswood, Bronington, 187
Tenter House, Spotland, 118
Tetlow Fold, Manchester, 110(2)
Thames Bank, Westminster, 127
Thelwall, 154, 161, 167, 178, 183, 185
Thoresby, Yorks,, 96
Thorncliff, Mottram, 184
Thornham, 122(2), 123(2), 134
Thornley, Chipping, 107
Thorns Clough Mill, Saddleworth, 132
Thornton, 108, 143
Thornton-le-Moors, 161, 154, 182
Thorp, Royton, 122
Thorpe St., Thornham, 122
Thorpes, 46
Threapwood, 163, 164, 171
Three Lane Ends, Rochdale, 103
Three Lane Ends, Saddleworth, 113
Thurstaston, 169
Thurston Clough, Saddleworth, 19, 137
Thurstones, 15
Thwaite, Coniston, 57

Tib Lane, Manchester, 26
Tilston, 152, 156, 177
Tilston Fearnall, 145, 170, 181
Tilston Hall, 155
Timperley, 147, 149, 161, 168, 173, 176, 180
Timperley Lodge, 145
Tintwistle, 156, 170, 179
Titchfield, Southants., 67
Tithebarn St., Liverpool, 105
Titherington, Prestbury, 157, 171
Tittleshaw, Tottington, 86
Tiverton, Bunbury, 154, 170, 174, 182
Toad Lane, Rochdale, 25, 98
Tockholes, 84, 139
Todmorden, 21, 23(2), 29, 64, 81, 98, 109, 123
Todmorden Edge, 94
Toft, 145, 184
Toft, Knutsford, 122, 172
Tom Bottom, Ashton-under-Lyne, 48
Tonge, 11, 40, 49, 64, 66, 74, 83, 104, 107, 110(2), 128, 140
Tonge Bridge, Rossendale, 21
Tonge Hall, 30
Tongend, Rochdale, 59(2), 87, 110
Top of Bank, Rossendale, 54
Top of Brindley, 154
Top of Green, Chadderton, 66
Top of Heath, Bury, 17
Top of Hebers, Middleton, 109
Top of Heights, Ashton-under-Lyne, 74
Top of Lee, Bury, 4
Top of Ridge, Burnley, 29
Top o'th Hill, Butterworth, 87
Torkington, 162, 174
Torkington Hall, 174
Tothill St., Westminster, 21
Tottenham, Middlesex, 26
Totting, Bury, 41
Tottington, 19, 20, 29, 46, 47, 55, 56, 63(2), 71, 74, 76, 86, 92, 102, 107, 110, 117, 122, 127, 138, 140
Tottington Higher End, 30, 65
Tottington Lower End, Bury, 16, 35, 59, 62, 92, 95, 98, 124
Tottleworth, Rishton, 35
Touchet Hall, Middleton, 59
Town Row, West Derby, 39, 105
Townley Park, 36
Toxteth, 89
Toxteth Park, 7, 11, 16, 20, 27, 28, 32(2), 33, 37, 42, 48, 49(2), 53, 55, 60, 63, 65, 68, 71, 77, 81(2), 83, 84, 85, 88, 90, 91, 96, 99, 101, 104, 107(2), 111(2), 114, 115(2), 118, 121, 127, 130, 131, 134(2), 138, 139, 141
Trafford, 153, 167, 174
Trafford Hall, 172, 173
Tranmere, 147(2), 154, 167, 184
Tranmere, Upper, 170
Tranmere Ferry, 98
Travis Mill, 54
Trawden, 53, 115, 134, 136
Trawden, Near, 134
Trent, Colne, 37
Trichinopoly, East Indies, 152
Trubsmithy, 26
Trusty Hillock, Radcliffe, 2
Tuebrook, West Derby, 72
Tulketh, 57
Tumbo, Tonge, 140
Tunicliffe, Spotland, 4
Tunstead, Rossendale, 54
Turkey Hall, Rochdale, 110,
Turton, 11, 37, 49, 80, 93, 94(2), 106, 129
Twarl Hill, Ashton-under-Lyne, 77
Twemlow, 171, 175, 181
Tybroughton, 187(2)
Tyldesley, 18, 32, 33, 36, 43, 48, 49, 73, 96, 100, 111, 113(2), 114

ULNES WALTON, 1, 30, 87, 111, 120, 134
Ulverston, 140
Underbank, Stockport, 148, 159
Undersfield, Rochdale, 66
Underwood, Spotland, 62
Unicorn, Radcliffe, 80
United States of America, 175
Unsworth, 17, 41, 78, 100, 103, 128
Upholland, 9(2), 16, 20, 22, 25, 34, 48, 58(2), 59(2), 73, 86, 89, 115, 117(2), 137
Upper Mill, Saddleworth, 19, 20, 79, 138
Upper Newington, Liverpool, 118
Upper Pit St., Liverpool, 130
Upton, 168, 175, 182
Upton, Macclesfield, 156
Upton, Overchurch, 149
Upwood Cottage, Crumpsall, 72
Urmston, 2, 67, 68, 91, 108, 128, 132
Urnwick, Winwick, 26
Utkinston, Tarporley, 158, 164, 176, 182
Uttoxeter, Staffs., 182

VERSAILLES, France, 188
Vicars Hall, Worsley, 85
Vicars Moss, Rochdale, 81
Vineyard, Oldham, 101

WACKERSALL, 108
Walgherton, Wybunbury, 166
Walkers, Saddleworth, 122
Wall Bank, Rochdale, 108
Wallasey, 144, 147, 153, 165
Walmersley, 51, 55, 67, 71(2), 98, 124
Walsden, 40, 120
Walshaw, Bury, 33

Walshaw Lane, Bury, 125
Walton, 10, 23, 156
Walton Hall, Liverpool, 28
Walton Lane, Bolton, 85, 127
Walton Lodge, Walton-le-Dale, 22
Walton-le-Dale, 1, 7, 17, 22, 26, 28, 35, 42, 80, 84(2), 85, 101, 111, 113, 114(2), 118, 127, 128, 138
Walton-on-the-Hill, 3, 7, 19, 52, 63, 64, 70, 72, 78, 89, 96, 103, 111, 135, 138(2), 139
Warburton, 150, 180, 182
Wardle, 10, 72, 76
Wardlefold, Rochdale, 76
Wardleworth, 6, 21, 43, 116, 123, 133, 139
Wardleworth Brow, Rochdale, 62, 109, 121
Warford, Great, 145, 150, 151, 163, 164(2), 175
Warford, Little, 185
Warks Moor House, Disley, 176
Warmingham, 162, 165, 184
Warnatoe, Worthenbury, 189
Warren Lane, Accrington, 96
Warrington, 2-140 *passim*
Warwickshire, 115
Water Foot, Rossendale, 30, 46
Waterhead Mill, Oldham, 12, 15, 17
Waterhouse, Bollington, 167
Waterhouses, Ashton-under-Lyne, 73, 99
Waterloo Rd., Stockport, 153
Waterside, Oswaldtwistle, 61
Waverton, 145, 148, 181
Wavertree, 5, 6, 25, 32, 37, 50, 56, 63, 79, 86, 93, 100, 101, 120, 136
Wayoth, 61
Wayswall, 182
Wear, Rossendale, 54
Weaver, 157, 163
Weaver Bank, Minshull Vernon, 148
Weaverham, 143, 146, 153, 157, 159, 160, 166, 169, 176, 178, 184, 185(2)
Wednesbury, Staffs., 140
Weelwood, Tarvin, 144
Welch Whittle, Standish, 127
Well o'th Lane, Rochdale, 91
Well Stile, Ashton-under-Lyne, 114
Wellfield Hall, 55
Wellington, Salop, 13
Wellington St., Chester, 165
Wensleyfold, 1
Werneth, Stockport, 143, 147(2), 150, 151, 159, 162, 163, 166, 171, 174, 180, 181, 185
Wervin, 153
West Derby, 21, 24, 30, 35, 39, 41, 45(2), 50, 58(2), 63(3), 68, 72, 74(2), 77, 81, 82, 88, 94, 98(2), 99(2), 104, 105, 107, 108, 109, 117(2), 118(2), 119, 120, 130, 131(3), 132, 138
West Indies, 55
West Kirby, 145, 149, 151, 173, 174
West Riding, Yorks., 43
Westby, 29
Westhend, Lathom, 101
Westhoughton, 16, 17(2), 23, 29, 33, 39, 42, 46(2), 47, 48, 54, 55, 60(2), 71, 76, 78, 83(2), 107, 111, 112, 133(2)
Westleigh, 31, 51, 97, 104, 107, 118
Westminster, 7, 21, 84, 127, 134
Westmorland, 22, 42, 119
Weston, 153, 158, 161(3), 168
Weston, Wybunbury, 148(2), 183
Westward, North Meols, 105
Westwood, Tarvin, 144
Wettenhall, 166
Whaley cum Yeardsley, Taxall, 157
Whaley Bridge, Taxall, 179
Whalley, 18, 23, 26, 30, 31(2), 47, 55(2), 56, 59, 62, 66, 67, 117, 133, 136(2)
Whams, Saddleworth, 110
Wharton, 145, 146, 168, 169, 179, 180, 184
Wheatley Booths, 64, 105
Wheatley Lane, Pendle, 118
Wheelock, 146, 158
Wheelock House, Sandbach, 176
Wheelton, 58, 79, 121
Wheelton House, 133
Whikstown, North America, 8
Whiston, 6, 12(2), 29, 57, 69, 77, 110, 141
Whitchurch, 22, 101, 108(2), 155, 189
White Gate Bridge, Chadderton, 4
White Smithy Bar, Cheetham Hill, 50, 123
Whitechapel, Middlesex, 159
Whitecroft, Oldham, 102, 116
Whitegate, 149, 155, 162
Whitehaven, 60, 76
Whitehead, 96
Whitfield, 5(2), 8, 32, 59, 61, 87, 92, 128, 141
Whitefield House, Roby, 8
Whitley, Budworth, 171
Whitley, Higher, 146, 159(2), 160, 161
Whitley, Lower, 154, 155, 160
Whitley Booth, 131
Whittakers, Oldham, 93
Whittle-le-Woods, 10, 25, 43(2), 56, 72, 116, 121, 125, 133
Whittlestonehead Lane, 140
Whitworth, 57, 81, 121, 122, 133
Wickstead Hall, 155(2)
Widnes, 4, 37, 43, 47, 63(2), 65, 73, 90, 96, 104, 107
Wigan, 2-139 *passim*
Wigtown, North Britain, 34
Wildboar Clough, 151(2), 159(2)
Wilderspool, 147
Wilksley, 151
Willaston, 172

Willmers, 108
Wilmorleach, 53
Wilmslow, 144(2), 147, 148, 155, 156, 157, 160, 166, 169, 170, 171(2), 179(2), 181, 182, 183, 184
Wilpshire, 13, 27
Wimbolds Trafford, 157
Wincham, 147, 155, 168, 171, 172
Wincle, 151, 152, 157
Windle, 30(2), 36, 37, 44, 50, 76, 82, 93, 108, 125
Windlehurst, Marple, 151
Windley, 67
Windsor, Toxteth, 81
Windsor Place, Pendleton, 33
Windy Harbour, 37
Winewall, Colne, 48
Winstanley, 5, 12, 17, 37, 43, 53(2), 99, 104, 136
Winstanley Hall, 7
Winton, Eccles, 41, 69, 79
Winwick, 6, 16, 21(3), 25, 26, 30, 31, 35, 49, 56, 63, 72, 94, 120, 124, 129(2), 139
Winwick with Hulme, 25
Wirksworth, Derbys., 16
Wirral, 180
Wistaston, 167, 173(2), 176, 182
Wiswall, 94, 182
Withenshaw, 160
Within Trees, Walton-le-Dale, 1
Withington, 15, 24, 32, 65(2), 75, 83, 91, 99, 118, 122, 125, 131
Withington, Lower, 145, 166, 168, 178, 182
Withington, Old, 178
Withnell, Leyland, 13, 79
Witton, 6, 62, 146(2), 148, 153, 155, 157, 160, 161, 164, 165, 168(2), 172, 173, 174, 178(2), 179
Wogden Moor, Little Hulton, 58
Wolston, 120
Wood Bank, Bredbury, 168
Wood Park, Ashton-under-Lync, 99
Wood Shutes, Audley, 180
Wood St., Middleton, 96
Wood St., Salford, 26
Woodbrooke, 106
Woodend, Prestwich, 116
Woodford, 179, 185
Woodhead, Mottram, 170
Woodhouses, Ashton-under-Lyne, 52, 53, 114, 139
Woodley, Bredbury, 170
Woodley, Stockport, 159
Woodside, 155
Woolfold, Bury, 14
Woolley, Mottram, 156
Woolrend, Saddleworth, 71
Woolston with Martinscroft, 12
Woolton, Little, 7, 44, 88(2)
Woolton, Much, 1, 20, 75, 77, 89, 130, 139
Worcester, 103
Worcestershire, 129, 148
Works Moor, Disley, 178
Worleston Rookery, Nantwich, 151
Worrockhall Foot, Saddleworth, 99
Worsley, 20, 26(3), 27, 48, 53, 66, 68, 78(3), 80, 85, 93, 95, 110, 116, 120, 135
Worsthorn, 21, 122
Worston, Clitheroe, 26, 133
Worston, Whalley, 26
Worth, Prestbury, 157, 180
Worthenbury, 38, 188(2), 189
Worthington, 97
Wrenbury, 145, 150, 151, 160, 162, 176, 180
Wrenbury-cum Frith, 151, 174
Wrexham, 187(2), 188(2), 189
Wrightington, 2, 30, 36, 45, 63, 88, 95
Wrigley, 127
Wrigley Brook, Bury, 59, 73
Wybunbury, 148(2), 151, 153, 160, 161, 166, 170, 174, 180(4), 183(2)

YATE & PICKUP BANK, 56
Yate Bank, Blackburn, 36, 56
Yorkshire, 2, 3, 17, 19, 27(2), 43, 44(2), 72, 77, 96, 103, 108, 131, 140
Yorkshire St., Rochdale, 126
Yorkshire St., Wardlesworth, 43

INDEX OF OCCUPATIONS

When a name occurs more than once on the same page, the number of times is given in parentheses

ACCOUNTANT, 61, 70, 118
Agent, 13, 24, 31, 38, 42, 49, 84, 102, 116, 124, 127, 130, 158, 163
Alderman (of Chester), 147(2), 155, 169
Ale seller, 157, 183
Alehouse keeper, 65, 95, 107, 156
Alias, 41
Anchorsmith, 34, 167
Apothecary, 24, 87, 137, 143, 172, 178, 181
Appraiser, 4
Apprentice, 124
Architect, 29, 159, 181
Artillery, Horse, 185
Artillery driver, 13
Artist, 38
Asylum, lunatic, 32
Attorney, 13, 42, 64, 103, 164, 167
Attorney-at-law, 8, 49, 55, 57, 86, 95, 119
Attorney's clerk, 71, 75
Auctioneer, 11, 56, 64, 96, 98, 99, 101, 112, 116, 150, 169

BACHELOR, 1, 3, 12, 18(2), 48, 85, 100, 122, 124, 132, 133, 135, 172, 182
Badger, 43
Bailiff, 92, 124
Baker, 21, 24, 58, 60, 66, 70, 78, 82, 91, 99, 110, 121, 130, 151, 159, 165(2), 168, 183
Bandbox manufacturer, 25
Banker, 21, 38, 58, 150, 175
Barber, 82, 128
Baron: of Crewe, 152; of Lilford, 79
Baronet, 43, 152, 155
Barque: Sir W. Scott, 126
Basket maker, 128
Beer brewer, 40
Billiard room keeper, 49
Biscuit maker, 45
Blacking manufacturer, 57
Blacksmith, 5, 8, 11, 12, 19, 22, 28(2), 47(2), 55, 63(2), 66, 70, 72, 73, 76, 79, 81, 84, 88(2), 105, 112, 121, 123, 125, 127, 128, 129(2), 132, 134, 135, 136, 138, 140, 148, 151(2), 152(2), 160(2), 162, 168, 170, 171, 179, 184, 187
Bleacher, 9(2), 14, 18, 31, 35, 63, 71, 81, 106 166
Block cutter, 24
Block maker, 28, 68
Boat builder, 6, 9, 37, 41, 127
Boat owner, 118
Boatman, 9, 93, 135
Bombardier, 153
Bookbinder, 13, 118, 185
Bookkeeper, 7, 9, 12(2), 14(2), 15, 17(2), 20, 21, 22, 23(2), 24 29, 31(2), 33, 34, 40, 43(2), 53, 55, 56, 57, 61, 62, 65, 66, 67, 70, 73(2), 74, 75, 76, 79, 81, 88, 89, 90(2), 93(2), 95, 97, 98, 103(3), 109, 116, 119, 123, 139(2), 149, 159, 163
Bookseller, 44, 91, 115
Bootmaker, 43, 55
Brandy merchant, 100
Brassfounder, 2, 10, 61, 107, 128
Brazier, 20, 101, 103, 126, 151, 157
Bread baker 107, 148, 151, 182
Brewer, 20, 40, 42(2), 43, 52(2), 68, 69(2), 75, 86, 89, 100, 102, 103, 108, 133, 167
Brewer, common, 31, 32, 42
Brewer, retail, 45
Brewer's clerk, 146
Bricklayer, 6, 9, 13, 14, 29(2), 32, 34, 38, 49, 60, 90, 105, 107, 112, 116, 117, 126, 133(3), 140, 162, 163, 165(2), 177(3), 183
Brickmaker, 3, 20, 47, 137, 156, 184
Bricksetter, 112, 124, 129
Brig: Civilian, 83; Dido, 69, 86; Mary, 36, 83; Neptune, 31; Perbriet, 117; Sarah, 41
Broker, 23, 39, 79, 80, 101, 130, 132, 150, 160
Brushmaker, 113(2)
Builder, 1, 24, 29, 65, 80, 97, 123, 133, 147, 148, 151
Butcher, 1, 2, 4, 6, 7, 10, 12, 14, 15(3), 17(2), 18, 20(2), 25, 26, 28, 29, 30, 32, 38, 45(3), 52, 54(2), 57, 58, 59, 60(2), 62, 67, 68, 71, 73, 78, 79, 86, 88(2), 92, 93, 98, 99, 101, 104, 108, 109, 114, 118, 120, 121, 126, 127, 128, 130(2), 131(2), 133, 138, 144, 145(2), 147, 148, 157, 169, 174, 185, 188
Button maker, 179
Button manufacturer, 145, 170

CAB MAKER, 14
Cabinet maker, 1, 3, 7, 12, 20, 22, 34, 36, 38, 42, 47, 63, 67, 70, 84, 88, 91, 92, 97, 103, 104, 109, 120, 135, 151, 160, 176, 181, 183
Calender man, 69
Calanderer, 15, 34, 85, 134
Calico maker, 117
Calico manufacturer, 12
Calico printer, 4, 6, 11, 14(2), 16, 21, 26, 29, 74, 79, 80, 82, 86, 96, 103, 104, 107, 121, 126, 132, 141, 175
Canal cutter, 188
Captain: in the Army, 114; in the Militia, 33, 134; in the Navy, 82; of a ship, 40, 164
Captain's clerk, 66
Car keeper, 92
Carder, 44
Cardmaker, 25, 74
Carpenter, 2, 18(2), 25, 34, 38, 45, 59(2), 60, 70, 72, 82(2), 83, 85, 86, 87, 97, 113, 117, 124, 125, 144, 148, 157, 162, 168, 169, 174, 177, 178, 180(2)
Carrier, 18, 19, 50, 61, 68, 77(2), 88, 92, 99, 119, 122, 124, 132, 150, 158, 161(2), 172
Carrier, common, 58, 123, 131
Cart owner, 2, 43, 45, 58, 101, 118
Cart proprietor, 45
Carter, 43, 70, 72, 86, 97, 103, 105, 116, 118, 119, 129, 172, 178
Carver, 90, 153
Cattle dealer, 46
Chairmaker, 53, 76, 106
Chandler, 68
Chapman, 4, 6, 9, 16, 54, 56, 62, 65, 78, 81, 97, 117, 128, 146, 176
Check manufacturer, 39, 90, 167
Cheese factor, 25, 117, 134, 144, 159, 167
Cheesemonger, 117, 136
Cheesemongers, Company of, 163
Chemist, 19, 44, 107, 164, 183
Chief mate, 43
China dealer, 129
Civil engineer, 73
Clerk, 7, 8, 9(2), 15, 20, 24, 39, 46, 47, 52, 54, 56, 60, 61, 68, 72, 90, 94, 98, 99, 101(2), 103, 104, 114, 118, 121, 132, 135, 140, 147, 155, 160(2), 164(3), 167, 176, 181, 188
Clerk in the Custom House, 88
Clerk in the Customs, 35, 92, 94
Clerk [in Holy Orders], 108, 153, 156(2), 169, 170, 173, 176, 178, 181(2), 182(2)
See also Reverend
Clockmaker, 8, 44, 124, 137, 157, 161, 162, 165
Clogger, 18, 19, 22, 31, 42, 68, 115
Cloth dresser, 83, 95, 124
Clothes dealer, 40
Clothier, 4, 15(3), 17(2), 19, 49, 53, 56, 72(3), 83, 87, 93, 96, 99, 101, 103, 105, 112(2), 132(2), 137(2), 138, 160, 165, 166, 169, 174
Coach driver, 41
Coach proprietor, 28, 70, 71, 100, 120, 127, 176
Coach wheelwright, 127
Coachmaker, 32, 42, 131
Coachman, 8, 39, 44, 55, 78, 89, 90, 99, 102, 107, 116, 140, 163, 174,
Coal agent, 136, 158
Coal banksman, 121
Coal dealer, 38, 49, 50, 68, 107, 127
Coal master, 72
Coal merchant, 10, 14(2), 33, 36, 178
Coal miner, 4, 14, 64, 79, 80, 99, 119, 134, 138(2)
Coffee house, 95
Collar maker, 174
Collector of Excise, 45, 153
Collier, 14, 31, 46, 49, 72, 78, 117, 121, 158
Colour maker, 45
Combmaker, 184
Commissary General, Deputy, 137
Commission agent, 33, 83
Commission broker, 88
Confectioner, 13, 26, 36, 41, 78(2), 123, 128, 157, 165, 181
Constable, Deputy, 85
Contractor, 60, 98
Contractor for Docks, 31
Cook, 66, 91
Cooper, 5, 6, 12, 24(2), 25, 27, 28, 29, 31(2), 33, 36, 37, 38, 39, 42, 45, 56, 65, 68, 70(2), 73(2), 75, 84, 85, 90, 92, 93, 96, 101(2), 105(4), 116, 118, 121, 122, 127(2), 138(2), 141, 143, 145, 172, 185
Coppersmith, 82
Cordwainer, 8, 12, 14, 21, 33, 36, 50, 52, 59, 63, 74(2), 75, 84, 85, 92, 96, 97, 98, 99, 101, 104, 116, 119(2), 132, 134, 136, 137, 152, 153, 157, 159(2), 163, 165, 168, 172, 173, 174, 178, 179, 184
Cork cutter, 38, 100
Corn dealer, 9, 10, 16, 22, 36, 43, 48, 63, 70, 118, 145, 170, 174
Corn factor, 126, 135
Corn merchant, 14
Cotton broker, 15, 97, 99(2), 140
Cotton carder, 51, 91, 92
Cotton commission agent, 49
Cotton dealer, 45, 53, 112, 119

Cotton manufacturer, 3, 4, 10, 11, 14, 23(2), 26, 36, 44, 46, 48, 59(3), 60, 61, 71, 74(2), 77, 80(2), 85, 86, 87, 90, 99(2), 113, 115, 116, 117, 119, 120, 121, 123(2), 125, 128, 157, 159, 163(2), 166, 177
Cotton merchant, 51, 73, 77, 86, 91, 124, 128, 133
Cotton rover, 177
Cotton spinner, 2, 3, 5, 7(2), 8, 10, 17(2), 19(4), 24, 25(2), 26, 33, 35(2), 39, 40, 48, 53(2), 55, 56, 59, 68, 72, 73, 76, 77(2), 80, 82, 85, 86, 90, 91(2), 93, 94, 97, 99, 100, 103, 105, 106, 107, 109, 110, 111(2), 112, 113, 118, 120, 121, 122(3), 129, 134, 136(3), 146, 147, 148, 163(2), 164, 166, 168, 169, 171, 173, 176, 177(2)
Cotton stretcher, 53
Cotton twister, 89
Cotton warper, 126
Cotton weaver, 2, 5, 13, 25, 33, 36, 40, 45, 62(3), 66, 72, 77, 81, 87(2), 110, 122, 123, 124, 125, 134(2)
Counterpane manufacturer, 3, 79. 111
Cow doctor, 107
Cowkeeper, 37, 48, 53, 71, 96, 97, 111, 117(2), 126, 127, 136, 138, 158
Crofter, 154
Cupper, 64
Currier, 45, 50, 98, 109, 122, 138, 156, 177
Custom house officer, 120
See also under Officer
Cutler, 16, 55
Cutter, 128
Cutter: Margaret, 53

D.D., 153
Day labourer, 151
Dealer: in clothes, 111; in cotton yarns, 39; in earthenware, 91, 177; in malt, 97
Delf master, 62(2), 85
Delfman, 11, 39
Dentist, 107
Designer, 34
Dissenting minister, 72, 129, 154, 176
Distiller, 20, 88, 100
Dock gate man, 70(2)
Docks, contractor for, 31
Doctor in Divinity, 39, 153
Doctor of Laws, 155
Doctor of Medicine, 51, 78, 90, 127
Doctor of physic, 42, 44, 81, 82, 89, 122, 151
Draper, 4, 6, 16, 21(3), 24, 28, 34, 35, 42, 44, 45, 48, 57, 66, 69, 77, 79, 81, 82(2), 83, 90, 96, 106, 111, 113, 115(2), 121, 122, 123, 130, 146, 147, 161, 164(2), 166, 173
Dresser, 108
Dressmaker, 28, 58, 70, 117, 123, 126
Drug grinder, 70
Druggist, 1, 12, 19, 32, 38, 42, 73, 87, 107, 113, 117, 134, 162, 167, 168, 169, 172
Drysalter, 27, 30, 35, 122
Dyer, 23, 29, 31, 49(2), 62(2), 65, 66, 67, 74, 79, 102, 104, 110, 114, 120, 122, 127(2), 134, 139, 178, 184

EARL OF STAMFORD, 177; Wilton, 34
Earthenware dealer, 21, 99, 129
Earthenware manufacturer, 12
Egg merchant, 84
Elder, 11, 32, 47, 49, 57(2), 65, 75, 96, 110, 125, 126, 135, 144, 154, 167(2), 175, 179, 180, 181(2)
Embosser, 134
Engineer, 46, 73, 75, 118, 139, 144
Engraver, 36, 42, 59, 78, 114
Esquire, 2-189 *passim*
Excavator, 85
Excise officer, 24, 37, 113, 114
See also under Officer
Exciseman, 154
Export officer, 110, 135
Export surveyor of Excise, 55

FACTOR, 95
Farmer, 1-189 *passim*
Farmer's servant, 154
Farrier, 15, 16, 37, 124, 186
Feather dealer, 22
Feather merchant, 103
Fellow of Manchester Collegiate Church, 38
Felt maker, 11, 144, 189
Feme covert, 3, 11, 16, 25, 27, 28, 34, 37, 52, 74, 80, 83, 88(2), 90, 92, 97, 101, 104, 105, 115, 125, 131, 132, 133, 147, 171, 172, 173, 181, 185(2) 187
File cutter, 4, 27, 64, 90
Filer, 6, 96
Fish hook manufacturer, 80
Fisherman, 39, 63, 146, 188
Fishmonger, 120, 135, 140
Flagger, 158
Flannel weaver, 76
Flatman, 178
Flax dresser, 70, 106, 135
Flour dealer, 4, 8, 13, 18, 25, 34, 36, 58, 81, 85, 98, 102, 109, 118, 120, 121, 132(2), 135, 136, 167, 175
Flymaker, 12
Foundryman, 82
Fuller, 118

Fulling miller, 51, 128
Furniture broker, 72
Fustian cutter, 6, 54, 55
Fustian manufacturer, 10, 20, 77, 120, 123, 129
Fustian shearer, 31, 59(3)
Fustian weaver, 58

GAMEKEEPER, 145
Gardener, 4, 6, 13, 25, 28, 35, 47, 52, 63, 64, 65, 69, 79(2), 93, 143(2), 145, 147, 155, 158, 160, 164, 166, 167, 173(2), 177, 178, 180, 182
Gentleman, 1-189 *passim*
Gentleman's servant, 172
Gentlewoman, 10, 26, 179
Gilder, 90
Gingham manufacturer,23
Glass cutter, 99
Glass dealer, 138, 160
Glass worker, 70
Glassman, 65
Glazier, 1, 6, 9, 14, 16, 19, 21, 31, 49, 54, 56, 100, 107, 125(2), 132, 144(2), 146(3), 150, 153, 166, 172, 174, 175
Glove manufacturer, 160
Glue manufacturer, 6, 71
Gold hand maker, 9
Goldsmith, 70
Governor of the New Bailey Prison, 35
Grocer, 1, 8(3), 13, 14, 18(3), 26(2), 29(2), 34, 35, 38, 40, 44(2), 54, 64, 76, 79(2), 80, 82, 84(2), 94, 96, 98, 104, 106, 108, 109, 112, 113, 116, 121, 124, 129, 134, 136, 139, 140, 148, 151, 153(2), 155, 164, 165, 168, 176, 179, 183, 184
Groom, 49, 80, 178
Gunsmith, 5, 13, 103

H.M. FORCES, 136
H.M. Schooner Pickle, 106
H.M. Service, 13
H.M. Ship Margaret, 35
Haberdasher, 15
Hair cutter, 121
Hairdresser, 3, 78, 105, 109, 117, 119, 121, 137, 143
Hardware maker, 5
Hardware manufacturer, 77
Hat finisher, 10, 31
Hat manufacturer, 27, 41, 43(2), 74, 89, 101, 102, 109, 124, 176
Hatter, 8, 18(2), 19, 22, 27, 29, 31, 39, 57, 59, 64, 73, 85, 93, 94, 104, 109, 114, 130, 137, 139(2), 140, 150(2), 153, 158, 159, 162(2), 163, 167, 181(2
Hawker, 83, 157
Hay cutter, 112
Heald knitter, 42
Heald manufacturer, 54
Hemp dresser, 106
Hide merchant, 45
Higgler, 151, 157
Hingemaker, 56
Hoopmaker, 41
Hop dealer, 24
Horse Artillery, 185
Horse breaker, 139
Horse trainer, 146
Hosier, 37, 42, 46, 61, 86, 132, 144, 178(2)
Hospital: Greenwich, 120, 132; Plymouth, 85; Royal Chelsea, 184
Hostler, 176
House carpenter, 33
House painter, 38, 76
Housekeeper, 28
Husbandman, 2, 4, 7(4), 10(3), 15, 18, 21, 22, 26(2), 29(2), 30, 33, 35, 37, 38, 46, 48 54, 64, 72(2), 83, 86, 92, 97, 98, 102(2 116, 120, 122, 123, 129, 131, 135(2), 140, 144, 145, 160, 163(2), 168, 169, 178, 184(2)

IMPORTER of linen, 53
Infant, 44, 68, 83, 109, 121(2), 171
Innholder, 93, 102
Innkeeper, 1-188 *passim*
Insurance broker, 3
Irish linen merchant, 77
Iron liquor maker, 96
Ironfounder, 37, 70, 89, 113, 114, 124, 125, 154, 176
Ironmaster, 95
Ironmonger, 5(2), 6, 39, 43, 50, 57, 66, 71, 90, 99, 115, 119, 133, 134, 138, 149, 151, 163, 173, 178, 183
Ironmoulder, 151

JOINER, 1-182 *passim*
Joint will, 27
Journeyman ironmonger, 134

KING of the Netherlands, 41
Knight, 9

LABOURER, 1-188 *passim*
Laceman, 61
Land agent, 10
Land measurer, 144
Land surveyor, 82, 154, 187
Land waiter, 3
Landing waiter, 4, 78, 91, 108
Law stationery, 114
Lawyer, 139

Leather currier, 123
Leather cutter, 98
Letterpress printer, 28, 54, 131
Lieutenant: in Army, 26, 119; on half pay in Navy, 131; in Royal Navy, 143
Lieutenant-Colonel, 98
Linen draper, 19, 24, 38, 49, 59, 70, 75, 82(2), 108, 111, 128, 134, 166, 177, 178
Linen manufacturer, 53, 62
Linen merchant, 2, 77
Liquor merchant, 6, 38, 49, 50, 54, 87, 88, 95, 128, 175
Livery stable keeper, 4, 9, 13, 17, 46, 110
Lock tenter, 162
Lodging house keeper, 91

M.A. 180
M.D., 79, 83
Machine maker, 3, 29, 34, 35, 54, 59, 61, 64, 68, 77, 84, 96, 100, 116, 119, 128, 129, 130, 137, 138, 141
Mailcoach guard, 109
Major: in Army, 116; in service of the King of the Netherlands, 41
Maker up, 76, 134
Maker up of goods, 89
Maker up of twist, 85
Malt dealer, 97
Maltster, 101, 148, 157, 163, 164, 166, 169, 174
Manager, 10, 55
Manufacturer, 6, 9, 10, 28, 31, 33, 34(3), 46, 50, 57, 60, 62, 63, 64, 67, 78, 80, 86, 88, 94, 101, 104, 106, 107, 109, 114, 118, 124, 125, 127, 131, 137(2), 138
Manufacturing chemist, 111
Mariner, 2-138 *passim*, 141, 146, 155, 158, 165, 182
Market gardener, 94
Marquis of Cholmondeley, 150
Married woman, 153
Mason, 50, 59, 82, 131, 147, 153, 156
Master Carter, 70
Master of a ship, 67; acting, 106
Master R.N., 95
Master mariner, 2, 3, 6, 13, 18, 19, 22, 23, 32, 33, 41, 49, 51, 53, 57(2), 60, 62, 67, 68, 72, 73, 74, 82, 87, 91, 94, 101, 104, 106(2), 111, 115, 123, 126(2), 127, 130, 134, 171, 183
Master porter, 55, 122
Mathematical instrument maker, 57, 179
Mechanic, 21, 79, 93, 140, 143, 147
Mercer, 2, 16, 117, 183
Merchant, 1, 4, 7, 10-125 *passim*, 135(2), 136(2), 141, 154, 156, 159, 166, 171, 176
Merchant ship: Bolivar, 122; Clyde, 31; Cornwall 68, Huskisson, 68, 129; John & Mary, 107, Julian, 122; Kingston, 20, 104; Perneth, 22; True Blue, 66
Merchant's clerk, 21
Methodist preacher, 59
Militia; Denbigh 187; Lancashire, 33, 134
Miller, 8, 10, 45, 48, 59, 63, 64, 71, 84, 91, 96, 98, 101, 127(2), 134(2), 153, 154, 155, 158, 159(2), 164, 169, 179(2), 183
Milliner, 117
Millstone maker, 71
Millwright, 45, 69, 83, 102, 108, 116, 162
Miner, 26, 188
Miniature painter, 85
Minister: 63; dissenting, 72, 129, 154, 176; of the Gospel, 24, 55, 101, 107, 141; Roman Catholic, 65, Wesleyan, 90
Minor, 90, 148
Moulder, 15, 171
Musician, 75, 116, 165
Muslin manufacturer, 101, 133

NAIL manufacturer, 92
Nailmaker, 83, 116
Nailer, 50, 99, 136, 137
Navy, Royal, 82, 95, 131, 143
Navy agent, 97
Needle manufacturer, 80
Nurseryman, 7, 17, 64, 70
Officer; 23, 30; in the Customs, 25, 35, 82, 84, 86, 90, 125, 130; in the Excise, 25, 32, 57, 66, 74, 80, 104, 119, 155, 163, 183; superannuated, 134
Oil manufacturer, 20
Oil merchant, 55
Oilman, 131
Optician, 70
Organist, 30
Out-pensioner, 120, 132, 185
Overlooker, 3, 8
Overseer: 115; of the poor, 1

PACKER, 19, 63, 106
Painter, 7, 8, 15, 16(2), 21(2), 23, 38(2), 42, 48, 52, 59, 60, 82, 83, 85, 87, 96, 99, 107, 138, 144(2), 153(2), 177
Pansmith, 160
Papermaker, 30, 48
Parish clerk, 29, 83, 90, 101, 134, 151
Park gardener, 34
Passenger agent, 51
Patten maker, 114, 143
Pattern card maker, 92
Pattern maker, 38
Pavior, 11, 20, 46, 49, 89, 132, 153, 164
Pawnbroker, 17(2), 21, 37, 40, 46, 47, 50, 54, 59, 64, 72, 78, 80, 83, 92, 106, 135, 149, 169
Pay master, 134

Pensioner, 112, 120, 132, 184
Pickmaker, 20
Picture frame maker, 32
Pilot, 4, 63, 101(2), 123
Pin manufacturer, 137
Pipe manufacturer, 116
Pipemaker, 115
Planter, 107
Plaster manufacturer, 70
Plasterer, 10, 28, 41, 59, 65, 66, 75, 85, 116(2), 139, 165, 179
Plumber, 1, 5, 6, 9, 21, 36, 56, 100, 107, 125(2), 132, 135, 144, 146(2), 150, 166, 169(2), 172, 174
Police officer, 73, 108
Pork dealer, 112
Porter, 5, 9, 36, 39, 41, 53, 106, 107, 114, 130, 132, 140
Porter dealer, 42, 47, 49
Portrait painter, 131
Postman, 171
Postmaster, 171
Potmaker, 5
Potter, 36
Pottery, Herculaneum, 131
Preacher, 51
Print cutter, 25
Print glazier, 119
Printer, 8, 23, 49, 75, 131, 139, 154
Private (Army), 14, 47, 68, 93, 138, 152
Proctor, 153
Professor of music, 127
Provision dealer, 88, 90, 125
Provision merchant, 117
Public notary, 153
Publican, 1-188 *passim*

QUARRYMAN, 150, 166

RAG DEALER, 115
Rag merchant, 32, 90
Rector: of Harthill, 159; of Whitechapel, 159; of Wistaston, 181; of Worthenbury, 38
Regiment: 1st, 138; 91st, 47; 1st Foot, 152; 15th Foot, 14; 22nd Foot, 68; 37th Foot, 50(2); 41st Foot, 34; 49th Foot, 106; 54th Foot, 137; 63rd Foot, 116; – Foot, 152; 25th Infantry, 119; 10th Veterans, 93
Retailers of beer and spirituous liquors, 184
Retailer of wines and spitits, 169
Reverend, 148, 149, 153, 156(2), 169, 170, 173, 176, 177, 178, 180, 182. *See also* Clerk [in Holy Orders], Minister
Rigger, 81
Rock getter, 173
Roller coverer, 17
Roman Catholic minister, 65
Ropemaker, 29, 42, 44, 47, 62, 99, 103, 117, 126, 136
Roper, 48
Rule maker, 57

SADDLER, 9, 10, 15, 22, 35, 62, 90, 93, 94, 107, 126, 144, 157, 166, 168, 171, 174
Saddletree manufacturer, 112
Sail canvas manufacturer, 43
Sailcloth manufacturer, 73
Sailmaker, 18, 34, 59, 70, 105
Sailor, 34, 184
Salesman, 48, 78, 84
Salt boiler, 184
Sawmaker, 52
Sawyer, 20, 76, 80, 150
Scale beam maker, 3
Scale board maker, 78
Schoolmaster, 1, 3, 6, 11, 12, 13(2), 23, 29, 34, 44(2), 46(2), 52, 57, 63(2), 64, 67, 68, 74, 76, 83, 94, 106, 107, 108, 123(2), 126, 129, 133, 134, 149, 152, 154, 162, 174. *See also* Teacher
Schooner: Salisbury, 12, 58
Seaman, 16, 21, 42, 56, 69, 70, 73, 79, 83, 86, 87, 88, 93, 112, 114, 115, 116, 117, 127, 136, 138
Second mate, 31
Seedsman, 7, 8, 28, 70
Senior, 146, 159, 185
Sergeant, 185, 187
Sergeant major, 34
Servant, 36(4), 78, 85, 96, 98, 131, 137, 146, 147, 150, 159, 165, 174, 177, 183, 187
Servant man, 24, 101
Sexton, 30, 41, 164
Sheriff's officer, 80, 85
Ship: Alert, 66; Alexander Lindo, 134; Ardent, 41; Arowra, 73; Bolivar, 122, Bounty Hall, 89; Catharine, 67; Civilian, 83; Clyde, 31; Cornwall, 68, Dido, 69, 86; Finchett, 135; Hardy, 91; Huskisson, 68, 129; Jamaica, 70; Jame McUrey, 164; John & Mary, 107; Julian, 122; Kingston, 20, 104; Lady Combermere, 133, 135; Lively, 56; Margaret, 35, 53; Margate, 68; Mary, 36, 83; Molly, 136; Neptune, 31, 65; Perbriet, 117; Perneth, 22; Pickle, 106; Prince Regent, 28, 40; Reliance, 53; Salisbury, 12, 58; Sarah, 41; Sir W. Scott, 126; Thomas Parsons, 40; True Blue, 66; Walter Scott, 34; William Park, 44; William Rathbone, 73
Ship agent, 34
Ship broker, 51
Ship builder, 45, 102, 136

Ship carpenter, 1, 47, 58, 85, 105
Ship chandler, 19, 44
Ship cooper, 105
Ship owner, 48
Shipwright, 24(2), 33, 39, 44, 52, 60, 72, 75, 82, 91, 96, 115, 126, 138
Shoe dealer, 29, 58
Shoe manufacturer, 153
Shoemaker, 6, 20, 30(2), 31(2), 32(2), 39, 41, 47, 51, 52, 53, 54, 55, 59, 65, 67, 68, 69, 71, 75, 77, 78, 86, 87, 89, 90, 100, 104, 106, 111, 119, 120, 124, 129, 132, 133, 136, 137, 140, 149, 156, 165, 168, 169, 171, 172, 173
Shopkeeper, 1-184 *passim*
Shopman, 84
Shuttlemaker, 61, 169, 179, 184
Silk dyer, 172, 174
Silk manufacturer, 5, 140, 144, 148, 157(2), 159, 160, 162, 163(2), 171, 174
Silk merchant, 12, 172
Silk throwster, 6, 143(2), 144(2), 145, 147, 148, 150, 151, 153, 154, 157, 181
Silk trimming maker, 145
Silk twister, 159
Silk warper, 58
Silk weaver,87, 171, 175, 179
Silkman, 156, 178, 179, 181
Silversmith, 57, 89
Singlewoman, 3, 4, 12, 34, 39, 57, 69, 78, 89, 94, 118, 131, 136, 146, 166, 185
Sir, 9, 53, 152
Sizer, 131
Skinner, 24, 147, 154, 180
Skipmaker, 128
Slate dealer, 84
Slater, 12, 65, 113, 144, 147, 148
Slubber, 71
Smallware dealer, 16, 136
Smallware manufacturer, 8, 23, 36, 58, 60 62
Smallware weaver, 8, 50
Smith, 83, 102, 175
Soap boiler, 29, 89
Soapmaker, 42
Soldier, 5, 106, 137
Solicitor, 9, 20, 41, 86
Spindlemaker, 15, 115, 150
Spinner, 17, 19, 66, 126, 181
Spinster, 1-189 *passim*
Spinster [a man], 56
Spirit dealer, 24, 53, 78, 85, 89, 103, 125
Spirit merchant, 14, 22, 43, 97, 134, 135, 164
Stable keeper, 20, 69, 123
Stationer, 44, 115, 145, 165
Staymaker, 60, 95, 145
Steel manufacturer, 67
Stocking manufacturer, 125
Stone cutter, 26, 136
Stone getter, 21(2), 63, 69
Stone merchant, 143
Stone pot man, 19
Stonemason, 3, 11, 15(2), 22, 27, 29, 32, 37, 42, 52, 55, 56, 57, 58, 62, 72, 75, 83, 88, 92, 101, 111, 122, 124, 130, 131, 132(2), 136(2), 144(2), 145, 146, 164, 183(2), 186
Straw hat manufacturer, 126
Sugar baker, 127
Sugar refiner, 37
'Supposed to be of Bolton', 120
Surgeon, 1, 6, 10, 11(2), 14, 16(2), 24, 26(2), 29, 33, 40, 41, 47, 49, 51, 53, 55, 64, 72, 75, 78, 80, 89, 90, 97, 103, 104, 109, 113(2), 114, 115, 118, 121, 122(2), 125, 135, 138, 143, 146(3), 147, 150, 152, 154, 157, 161, 163, 168, 172(2), 173, 181
Surgeon dentist, 107
Surveying general of Excise, 64
Surveyor, 36, 41, 108, 113, 123, 137, 180; road, 139, 173
Surveyor of Excise, export, 55

TAILOR, 9, 10(2), 12, 24, 27, 34, 37, 43(2), 51, 57(2), 61, 62, 64, 66, 68(2), 70, 71(2), 74(3), 76, 79, 80, 81(2), 82, 84, 86, 92, 93(3), 99, 102, 107, 111, 113, 116(2), 118, 124, 126, 127, 131, 140, 144, 146, 147, 148, 150(2), 151, 152, 156, 161, 166, 167(2), 169, 173(2), 177(2), 178, 180(2), 181(2), 184, 185, 187
Tallow chandler, 4, 19, 67, 68, 107, 149, 155
Tanner, 22, 63, 103, 153, 159(2), 166, 168, 169, 177
Tavern keeper, 85
Tax collector, 44
Tea dealer, 18, 41, 82, 85, 116, 121, 153
Teacher, 27, 71, *See also* Schoolmaster
Teacher in foreign languages, 66
Teacher of music, 39
Tenant, 34
Tide surveyor, 76
Tide waiter, 37, 116, 129
Timber dealer, 138, 176
Timber merchant, 30, 32, 46, 52, 61, 69, 130(2), 140, 144, 145(2), 146, 175, 176, 179, 180, 183
Tinner, 101
Tinplate worker, 21, 50, 86, 133, 178
Tobacco manufacturer, 100
Tobacconist, 5, 15, 20, 80, 102(2)
Tollbar keeper, 166
Tollgate keeper, 124

Traveller, 35, 95, 112, 145, 183
Travelling draper, 71
Trunkmaker, 9
Tuition bond, 6, 9(2), 10, 13, 17, 20, 23, 24, 25(2), 28, 30, 31, 34, 41(2), 43, 48, 50, 55, 57, 60, 67, 68(2), 69, 79, 80, 84, 85, 88(2), 90(2), 94, 101, 102, 104, 106, 107, 114, 118, 120, 121, 123, 131, 133, 148, 158, 159, 160, 161, 167, 170, 173, 181
Turber, 32, 63, 66, 76, 96, 110, 144, 147
Turnkey, 8
Twine spinner, 70
Twist commission agent, 49
Twist dealer, 50
Twister, 153

UMBRELLA MANUFACTURER, 19, 29
Underlooker of coal mines, 141
Upholsterer, 20, 123, 130, 151, 153, 172
Uxor, 12

VELVET DRESSER, 108
Victualler, 1-143 *passim,* 149(2), 151, 157, 173, 174, 176, 182, 185, 188
Vinegar merchant, 104
Vitriol manufacturer, 20

WAITER, 42, 58
Waiter in H.M. Customs, 11
Warehouse keeper, 7
Warehouseman, 10, 12, 15, 17, 23, 24, 27, 28, 30, 32, 37, 38, 41, 43, 45, 47, 49, 51, 53, 58, 64, 67, 74, 81(2), 102, 105, 107, 114, 124, 129, 132, 136
Warper, 5, 8, 44, 102, 124
Watch case maker, 69, 73, 77, 136
Watch finisher, 106
Watch movement maker, 67
Watch spring maker, 73
Watch tool maker, 63, 73
Watch verge maker, 65
Watchmaker, 1, 19, 23(2), 24, 44, 51, 56, 66, 69, 81, 86, 98, 100, 109, 121, 124, 137(2), 138, 152, 157(2), 162, 165, 166
Waterman, 165, 170
Weaver, 1-185 *passim*
Webster, 160
Wesleyan Methodist preacher, 37
Wesleyan Minister, 90
Wharfinger, 64, 158
Wheelwright, 1, 2, 6, 16, 31, 32, 55, 57, 59, 75, 94, 107, 115, 116, 121, 122, 129(2), 130, 139(2), 141, 156(2), 157, 161, 162, 172, 173, 177, 182(2), 187
Whipmaker, 11, 54
White Cooper, 63
Whitesmith, 22, 43, 114, 166, 171, 173, 174, 179
Whitster, 2, 10, 13, 26, 74, 125, 128
Widow, 1-189 *passim*
Widower, 41, 50, 52, 60, 98, 115, 118(2), 125, 128, 136(2), 137, 141, 149(2), 152, 154, 162, 164, 177, 179, 182
Will: deposited in the office for safe custody, 178; joint (two testators), 27; missing, 144, 146, 147(2), 148(2), 153, 156, 161, 162; nuncupative, 28; original transmitted to York, 25, 37, 49, 98; two on the same sheet of paper, 63; with neither status nor residence of testator on record, 46, 127
Wine dealer, 103
Wine merchant, 51, 52, 56, 78, 164, 172
Wire worker, 13
Wood turner, 151(2)
Wool seller, 27
Woollen clothier, 30
Woollen draper, 18, 48, 56, 64, 82, 101, 130, 164
Woollen manufacturer, 16, 30, 55, 58, 61, 64, 71(2), 77, 102, 119, 122, 123(2), 126, 132, 133, 139
Woollen slubber, 132
Woollen weaver, 11, 19, 23(2), 35, 40(2), 55, 61, 62(2), 66, 75, 76, 80, 83, 92, 102, 106, 110, 113
Woolstapler, 16(2), 21, 91, 125
Worsted spinner, 15(2)

YARN DEALER, 45
Yeoman, 1-189 *passim*
Younger [junior], 135, 157, 159, 180